Arabic Script

GABRIEL MANDEL KHAN

Arabic Script

STYLES, VARIANTS, AND
CALLIGRAPHIC ADAPTATIONS

Translated from the Italian by
ROSANNA M. GIAMMANCO FRONGIA, Ph.D.

ABBEVILLE PRESS PUBLISHERS
New York • London

English Language Editon
Translator: Rosanna M. Giammanco Frongia, Ph.D.
Editor: Susan Costello
Cover Designer: Julietta Cheung
Copyeditor: Mary Christian
Production Editor: Ashley Benning
Production Director: Louise Kurtz

First published in the United States of America in
2001 by Abbeville Press, 22 Cortlandt Street, New
York, NY 10007.

Printed and bound in Spain by
Artes Gráficas Toledo, S.A.U.
D.L.TO:303-2001

First edition

10 9 8 7 6 5 4 3 2 1

Front cover: The Archangel Michael from the Ajaib
al-Makhlukat of al-Kazwini. Iraq, late fourteenth
century. Courtesy of the Freer Gallery of Art,
Smithsonian Institution, Washington, D.C. (54.52v)
Back cover: Calligraphy in the form of a lion, by an
unknown Sufi *alide*. Iran, sixteenth century

Note: The illustrations without legend are calligraphic examples excerpted from Hakkāzāde
Mustafa Hilmi Efendi, *Mizānü'l Hat* (1849).

Page 2: *thuluth jali* calligraphy by Mustafa Raqim,
1797, Topkapi Saraÿë Museum, Istanbul

All the illustrations in this book were graciously
made available by the author.

The drawings on pages 22–23 are the work of
Alessandro Nastasio.

Library of Congress Cataloging-in-Publication Data
Mandel Khan, Gabriel.
[Alfabeto arabo. English]
Arabic script: styles, variants, and calligraphic
adaptations / Gabriel Mandel Khan; translated from
the Italian by Rosanna M. Giammanco Frongia. —
1st English ed.
    p. cm.
Includes index.
ISBN 0-7892-0710-9
1. Calligraphy, Arabic. I. Title.
NK3633.A2M3613 2001
745.6' 19927—dc21
00-052588

TRANSLATOR'S NOTE
For transliteration of Arabic words and names, I fol-
lowed primarily the rules of the Middle Eastern
Studies Association of America, as published in the
International Journal of Middle Eastern Studies
(Cambridge, Mass.) and the *Chicago Manual of
Style*. I also consulted the *ALA-LC Romanization
Tables* published by the Library of Congress (1991).
For the transliteration of most proper names, I con-
sulted the "Index of Proper Names" of *The Ency-
clopaedia of Islam*, new edition, E. van Donzel,
B. Lewis, and C. Pellat, eds. (Leiden: E. J. Brill, 1978).
When in doubt, I followed the *Chicago Manual of
Style*'s recommendation to simplify. For pronuncia-
tion, I consulted J. A. Haywood and H. M. Nahmad,
A New Arabic Grammar of the Written Language
(Cambridge: Harvard University Press, 1978).

For citations from the Qur'ān I used *The Noble
Qur'ān: The First American Translation and Com-
mentary*, by T. B. Irving (al-Hajj Ta'lim 'Ali) (Brattle-
boro, Vt.: Amana Books, 1992). For citations from
Omar Khayyam, I used the translation of E. H. Whinfield in *The Sufistic Quatrains of Omar Khayyam*,
introduction by Robert Arnot (New York: M. Walter
Dunne, Aladdin Book Company, 1901) and *Quatrains from Omar Khayyam, done into English by
F. York Powell* (Oxford: Howard Wilford Bell, 1901).

Every effort has been made to reach rightful
copyright owners. The publisher will gladly correct
all omissions in future editions.

CONTENTS

ٵٵٵٵٵٵٵٵٵٵٵٵٵٵٵٵٵٵٵٵٵٵٵٵٵٵٵٵٵٵٵ
ب ٱٱٱٱٱٱٱٱٱٱٱٱٱٱٱٱٱٱٱٱٱٱ
ثثثثثث ثثثث ٔ ٔ ٔ ٔ ٔ ٔ ٔ ٔ
خ جج ثب ٔ ٔ ٔ ٔ ٔ ٔ ٔ ٔ ٔ ٔ ٔ
خخخخخخخخخخ جج جججج ذ ٔ نذنذنذ
نذ زززززز ززززززززززز ٔ زش شش
ششششششششششششششششششش ش ض ضضض
ضضض ظ ظ ظظظظظظظ ظ ظ غغغغ
غغغغ ف فففف ففف ف ق قققق
ق ق ك ككك ككك ل ككك ل للللللللللل

B6019

للل لل مم مممم ن نننن
نن ييييييييييييييييييييي ن نن
نن ةةةةةةةةة هه ةة و وووووو
ؤؤؤؤؤؤ لالالالالالالالا ي ي
ي ي ي ج لجلم لم ملي ن ء ١٢٣٤٥٦٧٨٩٠ ؟
( ) ؛؛؛ «««««««««««« »»»»»»»»
ٓ ٓ ٓ ٓ ٓ ٓ ٓ ٓ ٓ ٓ ٓ ٓ ٓ
ٓ ٓ ٓ ٓ ٓ ٓ ٓ ٓ ٓ ٓ ٓ ٓ

نسخي برتولد
Naskhi Berthold

لتراست

١ملم
15.0mm

1256

INTRODUCTION

As the Prophet's sufferings grew, he exclaimed: "Bring me writing tools, that I may set down in writing what will save you from error after me."

Al-Bukhari, *The Sayings of the Prophet* (Title 3, 39:4)

In the night between the twenty-sixth and twenty-seventh of the month of Ramadan, in the year A.D. 612 of the Gregorian calendar, the "Night of Destiny" that all Muslims hold sacred, the first verse of the Qur'ān descended upon the prophet Muhammad (sura *al-Alaq*, 96:1–5): "Read, in the name of the Lord who creates, creates man from a clot! Read, for your Lord is most generous; [it is He] who teaches by means of the pen."

Thus was exalted the divine origin of the calamus, the reed pen that still today is the proper tool for elegant Arabic script. This veneration of writing naturally extended to reading, which is the source of all knowledge and paths of ascent, both scientific and spiritual.

From this belief sprang a powerful culture of the book and a love of the written word that turned Islamic calligraphy into an elevated, noble art. Almost higher than painting, such art can only be fully appreciated if one approaches it as one does music: like music, it has its own rules of composition, rhythm, harmony, and counterpoint— elements that bring joy to the eye of the experienced beholder and to the lover of beauty and form.

From the earliest days of Islam, Arabic writing evolved from an imperfect, primitive form to compositions rich in "hands" (also called "styles" or "characters") and a wealth of tracings such as lines, spaces, types, and other graphic arrangements.

It is not our intent to retrace the history of the alphabet in this book. Undoubtedly, the concept of alphabet originated in the Fertile Crescent, the region that extends from Egypt to Mesopotamia, an area that throughout the millennia has been so profoundly and diversely religious. In all likelihood, the alphabet evolved from the collusion between sedentary tribes and the nomadic groups that periodically attacked them. For social, economic and political reasons, sedentary tribes developed a need to create pictograms, and nomadic peoples

Opposite page: A sheet displaying *naskhī* dry transfer characters.

developed phonetic values from the pictographic meanings, thus arriving at the alphabet.

The first elaborate example of an alphabet dates from the fourteenth century B.C.: it is the alphabet from Ugarit, Syria, of Sinaitic derivation (seventeenth century B.C.). In all likelihood, the Arabic alphabet—a member of the Semitic alphabet group—is the result of that evolutionary endeavor. One precursor of the Arabic alphabet was undoubtedly Aramaic, possibly also Nabataean and Egyptian demotic script. Stylistically, however, the earliest version of Arabic script— which has squarish shapes—resembles, at least superficially, the earlier form of the Syriac alphabet known as Estrangelo.

In searching for the probable origins of the Arabic alphabet, it is useful to look at Nabataean inscriptions, such as that of Umm al-Jimal (c. A.D. 250); the epitaph found at Namaran on the tomb of the pre-Islamic bard Imru' al-Qays (328); the inscription from Zabad (512); and the bilingual epitaph from Harran in Greek and Arabic (518). Another Nabataean inscription from Umm al-Jimal, dated from the sixth century, closely resembles the formal fifth-century Arabic alphabet in use among the Hira and Anbar tribes in the north of the Arabian peninsula, and introduced to Mecca by Bishr ibn 'Abd al-Malik. This was the script used by the prophet Muhammad (c. 570–632) and his

Above, left: Nabataean inscription from Umm al-Jimal, c. A.D. 250.

Above, right: Nabataean inscription from Namaran for the pre-Islamic bard Imru 'al-Qays, 328.

Below: Paleo-Arabic inscription from Zabad, 512. It begins with the *basmala*.

Bottom: Bilingual inscription from Harran, taken from a tomb. The paleo-Arabic text begins with the words *Ānā Sharḥīl* (I [am] Sharhil).

scribes, including Zayd ibn Thabit, who was to draw up one of the first complete Qur'āns at the time of the Uthman caliphate (644–656). This first type of alphabet, of north Arabian origin, is what was probably called at the time *jasm.*

But we shouldn't digress. The need to write the Qur'ān, to deliver the word of God intact and legibly, immediately brought many enhancements to the primitive *jasm* script that had been introduced to Mecca and Medina under the name of *ḥijāzī.* Local styles, which took their names from their place of origin and had no great distinctive characteristics, developed. Finally, a first, rough form of Kufic evolved, followed by the classic Kufic script that was adopted throughout the Arab world, from Spain to Iran.

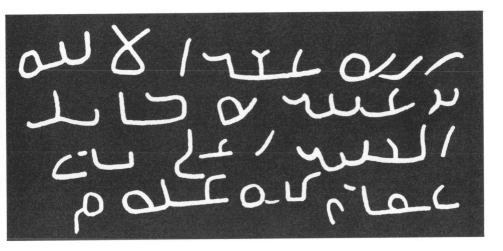

In Mecca and Medina, the rounded *mudawwar* and the triangular *muthallath* styles arose, as well as *etim*, a combination of those. These hands later gave way to *mā'il*, a slanted style, to *mashk*, an extended style, and to *naskh*, an inscriptional style. Thus, unlike the other Islamic arts that were still bent on imitating the classical forms of late antiquity, we can trace a history of Arabic calligraphy from the year 632. The earliest documents from this period may be found today in the library of the San'a mosque in Yemen.

Another paleo-Arabic inscription from Umm al-Jimal, sixth century. It begins with the words *Āllāh ghafran* (God, forgive).

From its inception, the Arabic alphabet was differentiated into two broad calligraphic currents: *muqawwar wa mudawwar*, characterized by curved and rounded styles, and *mabsūt wa mustaqīm*, having elongated and straight styles. Squarish, geometric hands such as *ma'il* and all types of Kufic lettering belong to the second current, while all cursive hands belong to the first. Early on, however, it was Kufic—

which, incidentally, originated in the city of Hira, not Kufa—that emerged as the most popular script, and the only one used to write the Qur'ān. It is remarkable to see how this script was adapted into the so-called Qarmatian or "eastern" Kufic, a beautiful, creative graphic lettering as fine as any accomplished Western abstract work of art.

As a result of the systematic revision of the Qur'ān imposed by Caliph Uthman, who died in 656, and the second systematic revision accomplished by Abd al-Malik the Umayyad (646–705), the short vowels were indicated with special marks in a process of vocalization (*tashkīl*) of the language. Accomplished primarily for religious reasons, this revision also met a real need for verbal clarity. At first, during the reign of Mu'awiya ibn Abi Sufyan (661–680), Abu al-Aswad al-Du'ali, the mythical founder of Arab grammar (d. 688), decreed that vowels should be indicated by dots of various colors. This method was

taught by the disciples of theologian Nasr ibn Ajini.

In a second phase, during the reign of Abd al-Malik ibn Marwan (685–705), diacritical marks to distinguish homographic letters were conceived by Nasr ibn 'Asim (d. 707) and Yahya ibn Ya'mur (d. 708), under the direction of Minister al-Hajjaj ibn Yusuf. One dot under the line was used for *b*, two dots above the line for *t*, and three dots above the line for *th*.

In a third phase, short vowels and other notations began to be expressed with specific marks or signs (see pages 90–91), as follows:

Letter sent by the prophet Muhammad to Mundhar ibn Saui, conqueror of al-Hasa. Baghdad, Museum of Iraqi Antiquities.

ﺑﺴﻢ ﻣﺤﻤﺪ ﻋﺒﺪﻩ ﻟﻠﻪ ﻋﺒﺪ

ﺍﻟﻠﻪ ﺍﻣﺎﻣﻮ ﺍﻣﺮ ﺍﻟﻤﻮ ﻣﺴﻠﺮ ﻓﻰ

ﺳﻨﻪ ﺍﺳﺮﻭﺳﺴﺤﺮ ﺑﻌﺰﺍ ﻟﻠﻪ ﻣﻨﻪ

fatḥa for *a*; *kasra* for *i*, and *ḍamma* for *u*; *waṣla*, a ligature mark; *tashdīd*, a mark indicating a double consonant; *sukūn*, a mark indicating the absence of a short vowel after a marked consonant, and *tanwīn*, an ending after a final short vowel, which in Arabic is the ending that takes the place of the indeterminate article. For more details, refer to the glossary at the end of this book. All these improvements were the work of Khalil ibn-Ahmad al-Farahidi (d. 786), a lexicographer from Basra, who also perfected the first cursive form called *thuluth* (also known as *thülth* or *sülüs*), from which more than seventy secondary variations developed.

Arabic, of course, like Hebrew, is written from right to left, thus a book begins on what the Western reader would consider to be the last page. Two more characteristics unique to Arabic writing are the lack of capital letters and of word division at the end of a line. In Arabic, one carries the complete word to the following line using, if needed, aesthetic extensions of the last word to fill in the preceding line.

As a rule, in the past the language also lacked punctuation marks such as exclamation points, question marks, periods, and commas. In their place, literary formulas were used, such as beginning a phrase with *wa* (the conjunction "and"), signifying that the previous phrase ended in a period. Another formula was to use the verb *qāla*

Above: An inscription placed in the Dome of the Rock mosque in Jerusalem in 692 by order of the Umayyad Abd al-Malik (646–705).

Below: Inscription of the Caliph Mu'awiya (661–680), dated 677.

ﻫﺪﺍ ﺍ ﻟﺴﺪ ﺳﺪ ﻟﻌﺒﺪ ﺍﻟﻠﻪ ﻣﻌﻮﻳﻪ

ﺍﻣﺪ ﺍﻟﻤﻮﻣﺴﺮ ﺑﻨﻴﻪ ﻋﺒﺪ ﺍﻟﻠﻪ ﺑﺮﻃﻬﺮ

ﺑﺎﺩﺭ ﺍﻟﻠﻪ ﻟﺴﻨﻪ ﺛﻤﺮ ﻭﺧﻤﺴﻴﺮﺍ

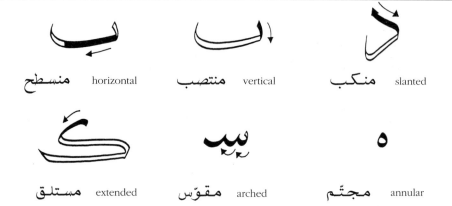

منسطح horizontal	منتصب vertical	منكب slanted
مستلق extended	مقوّس arched	مجتّم annular

(to say, to tell) in situations where we might use a colon or quotation marks.

Ali (656–661), the fourth "Righteous Caliph" and the Prophet's son-in-law, was a well-known calligrapher. During his lifetime, Arabic calligraphy developed two primary centers: the Mecca and Medina School, and the Kufa and Basra School. A third school was formed somewhat later, at Isfahan.

Thus, the history of the written language, like Islamic culture in general, retraced the parallel development of the other arts. The highly civilized populations conquered by the Arabs of the Arabian Peninsula—the Turks, the Iranians, the Afghans, the Indians, the North Africans, and the Spanish Andalusians—created all that we recognize today as being typical of Islamic civilization. For this reason, the history of Islamic calligraphy is far from linear, as it flourished in multiple and simultaneous cultural centers and experienced sudden parallel developments that coexisted for long stretches of time in the many countries that comprise the vast Islamic world.

In addition to the square, austere Kufic style, another type of writing had been in use since at least 643, especially for writing on papyrus and parchment. It was a neat, clear, easily legible, well-proportioned

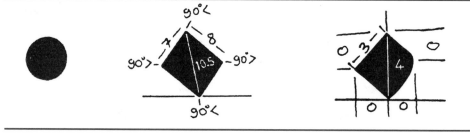

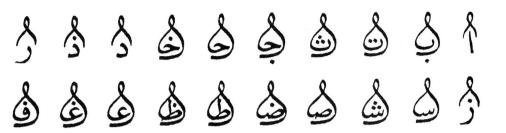

script that immediately became the favorite of koranic scribes and copyists of all kinds of theological, philosophical, and scientific treatises. Variants of this script evolved that also became popular. It became the Arabic script par excellence, and was the vehicle for disseminating knowledge to all corners of the Islamic world.

Thus, just as in the first two hundred years Islamic religion made vast inroads among the populations of Asia, Africa, and even Europe, over the centuries the use of the Arabic alphabet spread well beyond the confines of Arabic language. It replaced previous forms of writing and became the script of numerous other languages, including Turkish and all its dialects from Turkey to Chinese Turkestan, Farsi in Iran, Slavic in Bosnia, Andalusian Spanish (using the *jamia* style), Hindustani, a form of Hebrew, Berber, Swahili, Sudanese, and other lesser languages, especially in Indochina and Indonesia.

Thus, a multitude of new Islamic converts coming from diverse cultural, ethnic, and religious backgrounds brought to the Islamic language, culture, and religion a whole wealth of concepts and values that, beginning in the middle of the eighth century, were to contribute

Above: An example of the capital letters proposed in Egypt by Muhammad Mahfuz in 1930.

Below: Arabic letters with indications of the capital letters.

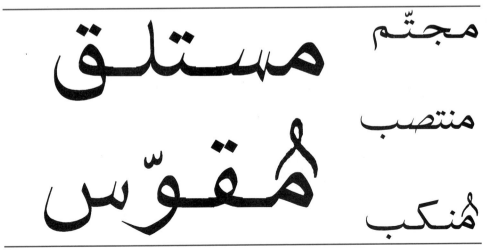

to make Islamic civilization among the richest ever, a fascinating world dense with themes, literatures, and page after page of artistic calligraphy.

Under the reign of the Umayyads (661–749) many skilled calligraphers copied large editions of the Qur'ān in Kufic script, although for bureaucratic texts, four cursive scripts became fashionable: *ṭūmār, jalīl, niṣf,* and *thuluth* (and its variant, *thuluthayn*). Khalid ibn Hajjaj, the official calligrapher of Caliph al-Walid (705–715), wrote both in *ṭūmār* and *jalīl*; furthermore, for everyday needs, the *niṣf* (one-half) script was created. Later, the calligrapher Qutba al-Mihrr (d. 771) created new stylistic variations on the four basic scripts: *āl-Jalīl āl-Kabīr* (the majestic), *āl-Ṭūmār āl-Kabīr* (the great sheet), *āl-Niṣf āl-Thaqīl* (the heavy one-half) and *āl-Thuluth āl-Kabīr* (the great one-third).

During the first reign of the Abbasids (750–1055), the calligraphers Ibn Jilani and Ishaq ibn Hamad developed twelve different hands from the earliest classical scripts, later perfected by Vizier Abu Ali Muhammad ibn Muqla (886–940). This vizier created a vibrant, lively script, the earliest form of *naskh*, while in the Maghreb the scribe Ibn Ibrahim Timimi composed one of the first treatises on calligraphy, the *Tohfat āl-Wāmiq.*

Vizier Ibn Muqla also created a proportional system of letters (*khaṭ mansūb*) by inscribing each letter within a circle and giving letters codified proportional dimensions using dot notations (*noqta*). He also set down and classified the traits of the most popular "six classical styles of writing" (*āqlām-i sitta*). These scripts are: *muḥaqqaq* (which means strongly expressed, tightly woven); *rīḥān* (the name of the basil plant); *thuluth* (one-third); *naskhī* (suppression, cancellation); *tawqī'*, a variant of *thuluth*; and *riqā'*, a smaller version of *tawqī'*. A good calligrapher was required to study, know, and write all of these styles. Thana al-Abdulat and Zaineb Shehede (known as Sitt al-Dar) are two women of this period who excelled in the art of beautiful writing.

We should mention, however, that this writing fervor that touched all of the Muslim world since the earliest days was also due to the wide diffusion of paper, which the Chinese had invented, along with printing, in the first century A.D. Introduced to Islamic countries, paper became widely used after the conquest of Samarkand by Ziyad ibn Salih in 751. Printing, however, though known and in use since the ninth century, was not as popular, as personalized handwritten books were much preferred.

Examples of *riqā'* characters.

Above: A hadith (saying) of the prophet Muhammad drawn by Fethi Karamani. Istanbul, Suleymaniye Pestev Pasha, 608.

Below: A hadith of the prophet Muhammad drawn by Usuli. Istanbul, Suleymaniye Fatih Kutuphanesi, 5429.

Besides, printing with movable types was (and still is) a laborious process (see pages 16–17, a typographer's case), and tabular engraving of a text in a cursive style was a lengthy and complex endeavor. Because the copyists (*warrāqīn*) were organized into an efficient capillary network of corporations, the difference in cost and time between copying a manuscript and printing a book was minor, so that there was little incentive to promote the craft of typography. In the tenth century, the copy shop of Abd Allah Abu Sa'id al-Mullah in Baghdad had so many copyists that it could produce in one day twelve copies of a 164-page handwritten and bound volume.

A monumental and lapidary style, Kufic continued to be the favorite script for copying the Qur'ān, while *thuluthayn* (two-thirds) was the script for notations and *niṣf* that of government chancelleries. Four principal forms of Kufic developed: *muraqqa'*, flowery and foliated; *mukhamal*, written on a floral background; *muzfar*, with plaited upward strokes; and *handasī*, with geometric lettering inspired by Chinese calligraphy and Iraqi-Iranian forms. The Qarmatian Kufic style is particularly beautiful, evocative of the values and interpretive freedoms of the best modern art. We note that the Qarmatians were open-minded Iranian dissidents who were hostile to the Arabs; in 899 they built a strong kingdom on the western bank of the Persian Gulf.

After Vizier Ibn Muqla, during the Abbasid era, two calligraphers, Ibn al-Bawwab and Yaqut al-Musta'simi, opened a celebrated art school. Abu al-Hasan ibn Hilal, known as Ibn al-Bawwab, from Baghdad (d. 1022 or 1031) created the *mansūb fā'ikh* style (elegant *mansūb*) from which the Iranian calligraphic school was derived. Among his pupils was Muhammad ibn Khazin from Dinawar, who created the *riqā'* and the *tawqīt* styles, and Khoja Abu Ali, who invented *ta'līq*, a cursive, nervous, concise style. Jamal al-Din Yaqut al-Musta'simi (1242–1298), who created the *yāqūt* style, a variant of *thuluth*, is also known for modifying the nib of the calamus by clipping it at an angle. The Turkish calligraphic school grew from the use of this nib.

In the twelfth century, besides the Ayyubid *naskhī*, other styles became popular or were perfected further. They were: *muḥaqqaq*, characterized by broad, curving, downward strokes; a wider, rhythmic, steady *thuluth*; and a classic *rīḥān*. From these, more typical, regional scripts developed, such as the Iranian *nasta'līq*, ideal for the calligraphy of poetry and covered in detail later in this book; North Africa's *maghribī*, consisting of the *qayrawānī*, *fāsī*, and *sudani* styles; Spain's Andalusian; and India's *biḥārī* style.

Thuluth jalī calligraphy by Abd Allah Sayrafi.

The *basmala* in five Kufic styles, from reliefs of the ninth, tenth, and twelfth centuries.

From their very inception, these styles became part of the classic tradition. Calligraphers studied them on *mufradāt*, which are catalogs or models that illustrated the proportions and size of each style. As mentioned, the most popular classic proportional system was that of Ibn al-Bawwad, which reported the dimensions and thickness of the letters by using squared dots (*noqta*).

1	3	4	5	6	7	8	9	10	11	12	13	14	15
16	19	20	21	22	23	24	25	26	27	28	29	30	31
32	33	36	37	38	39	40	41	42	43	44	52	54	55
56	60	62	63	64	65	66	68	69	70	71	72	73	74
76	77	78	79	80	81	82	84	85	86	88	89	90	91
'92	94	95	97	98	99	100	101	105	108	109	111	112	114
115	116	117	119	120	121	122	123	124	125	126	127	128	129
130	131	132	133	134	135	136	137	138	140	142	145	149	150
151	152	153	154	155	156	157	158	160	161	162	163	167	168
169	172	173	174	175	176	178	179	180	181	183	184	185	187
188	189	191	192	193	195	196	200	201	202	204	205	207	208
211	214	215	216	219	221	222	223	225	226	228	229	230	231
233	234	235	236	237	241	242	243	244	245	246	247	252	257
258	265	266	268	270	271	275	277	280	282	283	284	287	289
290	291	292	293	294	295	296	297	298	299	300	301	302	303

The long travail that brought Arabic writing from its origins to its full maturity and its highest calligraphic achievements in the thirteenth century had a period of arrested development when Genghis Khan's Mongols conquered a large part of the Islamic world, founding the vastest empire known to man. This interruption lasted until the Ilkhanids—the Mongol viceroys who ruled central Asia—converted to

The case of an Arab typographer with its movable type characters.

304	305	306	307	308	309	310	311	312	313	314	315	316	317
318	319	320	321	322	323	324	325	326	327	328	329	330	331
332	333	334	335	336	337	338	339	340	341	342	343	344	345
346	347	348	349	350	351	352	353	354	355	356	357	358	359
360	361	362	363	364	365	366	367	368	369	370	371	372	373
374	375	376	377	378	379	380	381	382	383	384	385	386	387
388	389	390	391	392	393	394	395	396	397	398	399	400	401
402	403	404	405	406	407	408	409	410	411	412	413	414	415
416	417	418	419	420	421	422	423	424	425	426	427	428	429
430	431	432	433	434	435	436	437	438	439	440	441	442	443
444	445	446	447	448	449	450	451	452	453	454	455	456	457
458	459	460	461	462	463	464	465	466	467	468	469	470	471
472	477	478	479	480	481	482	483	484	485	488	489	490	491
492	493	494	495	496	497	500	553	581	598	599	634		

Islam and became enlightened patrons of the arts. At the beginning of the fourteenth century one of the foremost Ilkhanid calligraphers was Abd Allah Hamadani. Together with Ahmad Surahwardi, he founded two central Asian schools, whose preeminent teachers were Mubaraqq Shah al-Qubt (d. 1311), Sayyid Haydar (d. 1325), and Mubarak Shah Suyufi (d. 1334). They were all Sufi masters (the Sufis are Islamic mystics, organized in well-ordered brotherhoods) who succeeded in combining the mystical sentiment that inspired them with feelings of art and aesthetic perfection.

In the Mediterranean basin, the Mamluks, a Turkish dynasty that ruled Egypt from 1250 to 1517, were also enlightened patrons of the calligraphic art. The founders of this dynasty had repelled the Mongol invasion to the West, effectively saving Europe. One preeminent Mamluk was Abd al-Rahman ibn al-Sayigh, who founded an important school and in 1397 composed a large, six-foot-high Qur'ān in *muḥaqqaq* script, in competition with similar Ottoman and Uzbek works.

Thus, the art of calligraphy (*khaṭṭ*) knew a long series of traditionalist masters, including the great Ahmad Qarahisari (d. 1556), Sheikh Hamdullah (1436–1520), and Hafiz Osman (1642–1698), as well as innovative masters who fall into two leading schools, the Iranian and the Turkish. With the rise of these two schools, unusual stylistic forms, rather than becoming established as new hands, were seen as being stylistic variations on the look of the classic types. Among these new hands were large, monumental formats such as *jalīl* and, especially, *thulūth jalī,* in which the Iranians Abd Allah Sayrafi, Baysonghor, Ali Rida Abbasi-i Tabrizi, and Muhammad Rida Imami-i Isfahani were especially active. Other hands were *musalsal* (strung together), which required great skill; *siyāqat* and *tarassul,* used in government documents; and *syakat,* a style adopted in Turkey by Janissaries.

Early on in Iran, a local hand was used, the *pīrāmūz* (spelled *kīrāmīz* in Arabic*),* which still survives in a few rare works. It evolved into two major schools: that of Khurasan, founded in Herat by Ja'far ibn Ali (d. c. 1456), and the southeastern school typified by Abd al-Rahim al-Khwarezmi. The most popular styles at the time were the *ta'līq,* founded by Abd al-Hajj from Astarabad, and a more elegant style, the *nasta'līq* (a variant on *naskh* and *ta'līq*), which means "like birds in flight." It was created by Mir Ali ibn Hasan from Tabriz, who adapted the cut of the calamus nib to create it. Also used, though not as extensively, was the *riyāsī,* perfected by Imad al-Din al-Husayni.

Later, among the better-known followers of Qhoja Abu Ali were Sayyid Mir Imad (d. 1615), who excelled in the *ta'līq* script, and Abd al-Mejid Taliqani, who was unsurpassed in a new form of writing, the *shikasteh*. In Iran, the *nasta'līq* became especially popular, and even a Safavid ruler, Hassan Khan Shamlu (d. 1688), excelled at calligraphy in this style.

In particular, the Iranian school generated the Indian school, which developed a typically strong, robust local *naskh* style and a *behari* style evocative of baroque rhythms. The Indian school had many excellent teachers, especially under the Moguls, the dynasty of Afghan Turks who claimed to be descended from the Mongol emperors and who ruled India from 1526 to 1857. Among this line of calligraphers we recall especially Shihab al-Din in the twelfth century, Ashraf Khan (d. 1572), and Ja'far Khan. On the other hand, the Chinese Muslims who were in direct contact with Afghanistan, Uzbekistan, and India adapted Arabic writing into a fluttering, discontinuous style called *sini*, used especially on artifacts destined for the Ottoman market.

The Turkish school had two great initial masters: Uthman ibn Ali, known as Hafiz Osman, whose teachings are still followed today, and Hamd Allah Amasi (1436–1520), a Sufi shaykh who penned important treatises and even counted the Ottoman emperor Bayazid II among his students. Calligraphy among the Turks reached such a splendid artistic level that a saying was born: "The holy Qur'ān was revealed in Mecca, recited in Egypt, and written in Istanbul."

Many schools branched out from these two teachers, each with its own great artists, so numerous that we can recall here only the most prominent. One typical Turkish hand was the *dīwānī*, developed by Ibrahim Munif, which was an official, chancery style suited for many decorative variations (see pages 118–119). Other, traditional calligraphies—for example, the *shikasteh*, *shikasteh āmīz*, and *jalī* styles—were rejuvenated. The *dīwānī jālī* variant is also known as *humāyīnī*. Over time, the *sumbulī* hand evolved from the *dīwānī* as well.

In addition to these variants, the Ottomans also devised special styles, such as the *zulf-i 'arūs* (curly); the *siyāqat*, a very functional style; the *gulzār* mode, which consists of filling the empty spaces between the letters with floral or figured motifs; the *muthannā* (or *mutannāzar*) style—also known as *aynali* or *ma'kūs* (reflected) or *khatt-i muthannā* (self-facing calligraphy)—which repeats a phrase in mirror fashion (pages 132–133); the *tuğra*, a complex, fluttering type of signature (pages 128–129); and in particular, words or phrases

Monogram letters in *sunbulī*, a non-traditional style.

arranged so as to form figured compositions, especially of animals—faces, horses, birds, or lions (pages 152–157).

Besides these scripts, we should also mention a folkloric, rather than artistic, style called *ghubār* or *ghubārī* (dust, dusty), an almost microscopic hand invented in Turkey. Using this script, all the text of the Qur'ān, consisting of 77,934 words, was written on one single ostrich eggshell by Isma'il Abd Allah, also known as Ibn al-Zamakjala (d. 1386). Qasim Ghubari (d. 1624) did the same on a sheet measuring only eighteen by twenty-two inches (45 × 55 cm), while Mehmet Shefik Bey (1819–1879) wrote the Qur'ān on ninety-nine rosary beads. Known as *ghulān*, this script is still alive today, thanks to such contemporary artists as Nasib Makarim from Lebanon and Dawud al-Husayni from Afghanistan.

Arabic script is written on an ideal horizontal line, from which various curls and peaks rise above or fall below it. These calligraphic directions are said to symbolize the union of the values of the exterior, material, visual world (*ẓāhir*) with those of the interior, intimate, spiritual realm (*bāṭin*). For this reason, the art of calligraphy flourished in particular among the Sufi brotherhoods, becoming their preferred representational form. Furthermore, it was readily adapted to the three leading tongues of the Islamic world: Arabic, the language that universalized religious and scientific thought; Iranian, the language that expressed in the highest possible form the values of art and poetry; and Turkish, the language that institutionalized earthly laws and social organizations.

Thus, there was a time in Iran for the sinuous *ta'līq*, sensitive to poetry, and in Turkey for the imperial *dīwānī* and the clerical *riqā'*. The *ta'līq* style (suspension) was a result of combining *tawqī'*, *riqā'*, and *naskh*, and in it still survives an echo of the Pehlevi and Avestan scripts. The *riqā'*, a hand that includes a simple form and a larger one (*jalī*), was given precise rules by the Turkish Mumtaz Bag, councillor to Sultan Abdulmecid I (1823–1861). Several Ottoman sultans tried their hand at the *dīwānī* style, undoubtedly the richest in movement and in unique traits. Another Turkish form is the broad *shikasteh* (also known as *shikasta ta'līq*, or broken *ta'līq*), which has a rich sense of rhythm.

Of course, both tradition and renewal, the evolving of taste and refinement through the centuries, and the changing environments all contributed to inspire ever new variants and individual expressions in the art of calligraphy. The Great Tradition is still alive and fertile today,

Above: Notes written in *ta'līq*, found in the margins of a treatise on the value of terms copied by Diya' al-Din Gumushkhanevi in 1843.

Below: Notes found in the margins of a treatise on cosmogony copied in 1812.

just as the Arabic script is still being renewed under the calami of new artists, including those in the West. Both classic and individual hands have multiplied throughout the centuries.

All these forms can be variously admired on the great expanses of mosque walls and in the almost microscopic minuteness of miniature art. Stone, metal, wood, faience, fabric, paper—every possible medium—has given a variety of themes and solutions to Arabic calligraphy from the very beginning, and the adventure continues to this day as Muslim calligraphers create new works, look for original solutions, and study modern styles. In 1930 Muhammad Mahfuz endowed Arabic with capital letters, called *ḥurūf āl-Taj*. In Istanbul every year, the cultural organization IRCICA organizes an international competition of traditional calligraphy and miniature painting; many modern artists include calligraphy in their works in highly sensitive and innovative iconographic adaptations. The work of artists such as Hassan Massoudi and his followers is proof that Arabic calligraphy is a living art capable of continuously renewing itself.

Painters also are experimenting with the versatility and potential for adaptation of Arabic writing. Among these—and this list is admittedly incomplete—we should mention Mohamed Melehi and Cherkaoui and Mustafa Rajaoui from Morocco, Yussef Saidah and Saad Kamel from Egypt, Nasser Assar from Lebanon, Ahmed Chibrine from Sudan, Hossein Zenderoudi from Iran, Majib Belkodja from Tunisia, Rachid Koraichi, Shakir Hassan, and Kamal-Boullata. Especially distinguished are the many Turkish masters, including my own teacher, Fevzi Gunuc, professor of calligraphy at the Seljuk University of Konya, and Mehmet Buyukcanga, Faruk Atabek, Filiz Kaya, Asuman Comezoglu, Bekir Pekten, and Sami Oksuz.

All this iconographic richness—heritage of all of humanity, beyond ethnic or religious boundaries—gives manifold meanings to the saying that "writing is an expression of the invisible."

The revelation of the Qur'ān began by mentioning the calamus, and the sixty-eighth sura (chapter) opens with these words: "By the pen, and whatever they record." Again, the Qur'ān tells us: "If only the trees on earth were pens and the [inky] sea were later on replenished with seven other seas, God's words would never be exhausted." (31:27) Indeed, for the Muslim, writing is intimately linked to the identity of God and the gifts he has bestowed upon his earthly creatures. The vitality of Arabic writing throughout the centuries is an accomplished testimonial of this.

Above: The frontispiece of the work *Bedāiü'l-Hattiyye mina'r—Ravdati'n-Nebeviyye*, published in Istanbul in 1993 by Islam Tarih, Sanat ve Kultur Arashtirma Merkezi (IRCICA).

Below: The logo for the exhibition *The Art of the Mamluks* organized in 1981. Washington, D.C., Smithsonian Institution.

USING THE CALAMUS

The natural implement of Arabic writing, as that of Hebrew, is the calamus (*qalam*), a pen cut from a piece of reed. The reed used is the common giant reed or ditch reed—*Arundo donax* or *Phragmites communis*—which grow along watercourses (fig. 1). Calami can also be made using the thinner stems of roses or even some types of grass. Calami have different diameters, varying from a millimeter or two to three-quarters of an inch (2 cm). The wide-nib calami can also be made from thin strips of fruitwood.

After a section approximately ten inches (24 cm) in length is cut, the cane is dropped on a hard surface; the sound it makes will tell the craftsman whether it is free of holes or cracks, thus usable for a nib.

The nib is then cut using a straight, sharp, thin razor-like blade. The cut must be made from the body of the cane toward the tip, with a slight concave curve (fig. 2). The tip is then flattened on all sides until it resembles a bird's beak; at this point, the nib is cut at a slant by

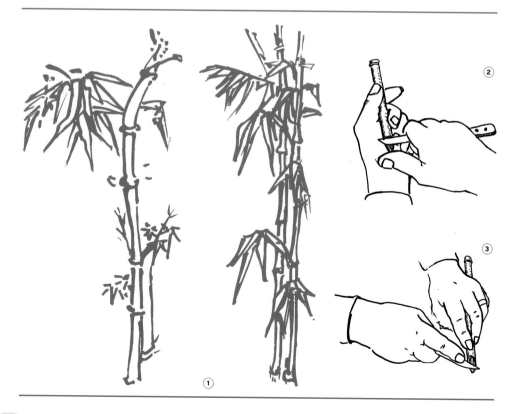

placing the cane on a special surface (fig. 3). Finally, the nib is cut vertically, in a position suitable to specific proportions (down to midway of the nib, or two-thirds, etc.); the various ways of cutting the nib make the calamus suitable for writing different calligraphic styles. We could even say that each character has its own slant (fig. 4).

The calamus is filled with silk waste, a woolen wad, or even a small sponge, so that when dipped into the inkwell it will absorb a certain amount of ink, and prevent the nib from becoming damaged if it hits the bottom of the inkwell.

The term *qalam* (plural, *āqlām*) is derived from the radical *q-l-m*, which yields a first-form verb, *qalama* (to cut, to prune). It is also the familiar name of the ninety-sixth sura of the Qur'ān (*al-Alaq*: "The Clot"), as the fourth verse says: *Ālladhī 'allama, bīl-Qalam* (He who teaches by means of the pen).

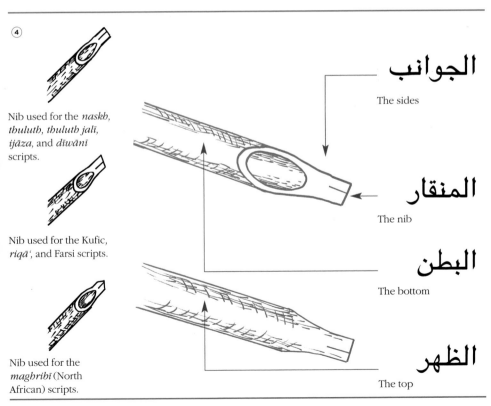

(4)

Nib used for the *naskh, thuluth, thuluth jalī, ijāza*, and *dīwānī* scripts.

Nib used for the Kufic, *riqā'*, and Farsi scripts.

Nib used for the *maghribī* (North African) scripts.

الجوانب
The sides

المنقار
The nib

البطن
The bottom

الظهر
The top

Alphabet sequence (from left to right):

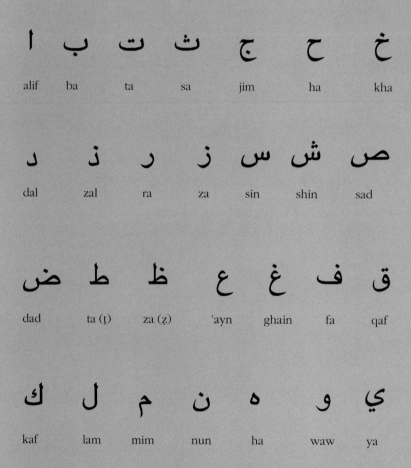

ا	ب	ت	ث	ج	ح	خ
alif	ba	ta	sa	jim	ha	kha

د	ذ	ر	ز	س	ش	ص
dal	zal	ra	za	sin	shin	sad

ض	ط	ظ	ع	غ	ف	ق
dad	ta (ṭ)	za (ẓ)	ʾayn	ghain	fa	qaf

ك	ل	م	ن	ه	و	ي
kaf	lam	mim	nun	ha	waw	ya

In North Africa the following sequence is used:
alif - ba - ta - sa - jim - ha - kha - dal - zal - ra - za - ta - kaf - lam - mim - nun - sad - dad -
ʾayn - ghain - fa - qaf - sin - shin - ha - waw - lam-alif - ya

THE LETTERS OF
THE ALPHABET

ALIF

Name: **alif**.
Transliteration: the sign '
   or **ā**.
Pronunciation: long **a**, as in
   f**ai**r (for special signs, see
   pages 90–91).

Final		Medial		Initial		Isolated	
‏ا‏	Alarz	‏ر‏	Diwani	‏ا‏	Nastaliq	‏ا‏	Isolated
‏ا‏	Al-Waleed	‏ا‏	Fairuz	‏ا‏	Omar		
‏ا‏	Al-Qahira	‏ا‏	Firdawsi n.	‏ا‏	Rabee		
‏ا‏	Al-Ruha	‏ا‏	Hadith	‏ا‏	Rouqai		
‏ا‏	Amin	‏ا‏	Hijaz	‏ا‏	Shuweifat		
‏ا‏	Annees	‏ا‏	Jarash	‏ر‏	Sidon		
‏ا‏	Baalback	‏ا‏	Jiddah	‏ا‏	Silwan		
‏ا‏	Baghdad	‏ا‏	Kufic	‏ر‏	Sirius		
‏ا‏	Beirut	‏ا‏	Najaf	‏ر‏	Suraya		
‏ا‏	Byblos	‏ا‏	Naskh	‏ا‏	Tadmur		
‏ا‏	Dimashk	‏ٯ‏	Naskh cont.	‏ا‏	Thuluth		

Characters

The first letter of the Arabic alphabet is the sign ' (*alif*); it has a guttural sound.

In the art of reciting the Qur'ān (*tajwīd*), it has the characteristics of sonority, tonicity, and softening, and the antonymies of lowering and opening.

This letter is the module of the whole calligraphic system. Calligraphers vary its length, measuring it in square points, or dots (*noqta*), as for other letters. The width of the *alif* is one point, and its length can vary from three to twelve points; for example, in the *naskhī* it has a height of five points, in *thuluth*, nine. From the length of the *alif* the diameter of a circle inside which all the other letters are written is also calculated. The characteristics of this letter are linearity (*qawam*), axiality (*mihwarī*), balance (*mu'tadilan*), and a straight stroke (*muntasiban*).

Because the shape of the *alif* resembles the numeral 1, it symbolizes the selfness of God as well as his unity. Thus, this letter takes on the archetypal value of the whole alphabet, which it begins, and is thus also identified with Adam, the father of humankind (and thus any diacritical sign affirming this letter's value is identified with Eve).

The three main positions of Islamic prayer are: standing, like the *alif*; kneeling, like the *dal*; and prostrate, like the *mim*. These three letters also make up the name Ādm (Adam). According to the mystic Ibn Ata' Allah Abbas (d. 1309), "this name is derived from *ulfa* (good company), because it unites and agrees (*ta'līf*) with the other letters." For some sects, however, the *alif* represents Satan, because like him "it does not bow" to God (*ālīf mutaakhar al-Sujūd*).

Grammatically, *alif* is an interrogative particle (*ā Zaydun fy āl-Bayti?*: Is Zayd home?).

In the *Ḥurūf* system, *'ilm āl-Ḥurūf* is the science of the secrets of the letters of the alphabet, also known as *'ilm āl-Ābjad*, or *sīmiyā'*, from the Greek σημεια (letter magic, used in mystical speculation and magical practices); *alif* represents the number one, and belongs to the element of fire.

Examples of some of the oldest versions of the letter *alif* in lapidary Kufic.

COMPOSITIONS WITH·THE *ALIF* LETTER

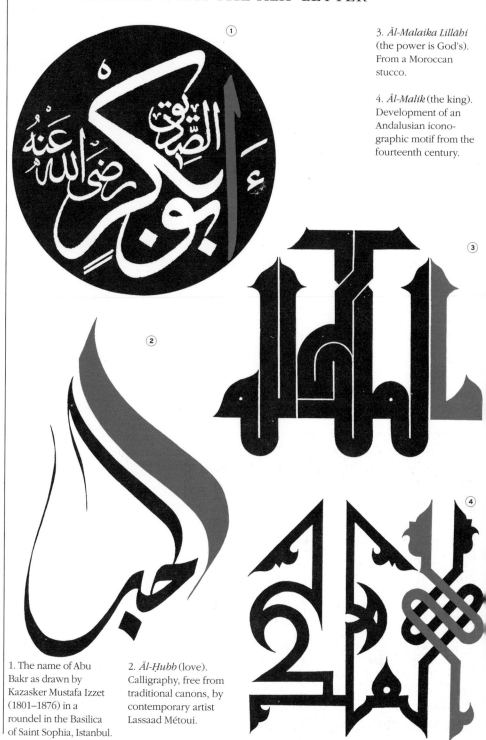

3. *Āl-Malaika Lillāhi* (the power is God's). From a Moroccan stucco.

4. *Āl-Malik* (the king). Development of an Andalusian iconographic motif from the fourteenth century.

1. The name of Abu Bakr as drawn by Kazasker Mustafa Izzet (1801–1876) in a roundel in the Basilica of Saint Sophia, Istanbul.

2. *Āl-Ḥubb* (love). Calligraphy, free from traditional canons, by contemporary artist Lassaad Métoui.

5. The *alif* of the word *Allah* in the center. It is surrounded by the "Light Verse" (Qur'ān, 24:35).

6. Kinetic effect produced by the lengthening of the letters *alif* and *lam* in Mamluk calligraphy with the name of Sultan Husayn ibn Shaban ibn Kalaun. Egypt, 1362.

7. A *basmala* drawn in *dīwānī jalī*, with aesthetic emphasis of the *alif*s and the *lam*s, by Yahya Zakariyya 'Adawi, an artist born in Bethlehem in 1962.

THE LETTERS OF THE ALPHABET

BA

Name: **ba**.
Transliteration: **b**.
Pronunciation: **b**, as in **b**ig.

	Final		Medial		Initial		Isolated
طب		طبو		بو		ب	

Characters						
ب	Alarz	ٮ	Diwani	ب	Nastaliq
ب	Al-Waleed	ب	Fairuz	ب	Omar
ب	Al-Qahira	ب	Firdawsi n.	ب	Rabee
ـب	Al-Ruha	ـل	Hadith	ب	Rouqai
ب	Amin	ب	Hijaz	ب	Shuweifat
ب	Annees	ب	Jarash	ب	Sidon
ـلب	Baalback	ب	Jiddah	ب	Silwan
ـلب	Baghdad	ب	Kufic	ٮ	Sirius
ب	Beirut	ب	Najaf	ب	Suraya
ب	Byblos	ب	Naskh	ب	Tadmur
ب	Dimashk	ب	Naskh cont.	ب	Thuluth

Ba is the second letter of the alphabet; it is labial.

In the art of reciting the Qur'ān (*tajwīd*) it has the characteristics of sonority and tonicity and the antonymies of vibration, lowering, opening, and volubility.

Just as *alif* is the first vertical letter, *ba* is the first horizontal letter and it is suitable for representing other letters such as *ta*, *tha*, and *nun*, according to the diacritical signs placed above or below the stroke. It is the initial letter par excellence, because it opens the *basmala* (*Bismi Āllāhi āl-Raḥmani āl-Raḥymi*: "In the name of God, the Mercy-giving, the Merciful"), the formula with which all the suras (chapters) of the Qur'ān, except for the ninth, begin. (We note, incidentally, that the Bible also begins with a *B*.)

The diacritical sign placed below the stroke represents, for scholars of Islamic esoteric lore, the origin, essence, and being of all things, in strict analogy with the *bindu* (.) of Tantrism and yoga. For this reason, some Muslims, though in disagreement with orthodox theology, believe that the content of all revealed Scripture is found in the Qur'ān; in turn, that the content of the Qur'ān is found all in the first sura, the Fātiḥa; that all the content of the Fātiḥa resides in the *basmala* and

the whole content of *basmala* is enclosed inside *B*'s diacritical point. This exegesis was accepted by, among others, Abdullah ibn Mas'ud (seventh century) and Abd al-Karim al-Jili (d. 1494), according to whom the *B* of *Bismi* represents the resplendent beauty of God (*Bahā'*), the *S* his greatness (*Sanā'*), and the *L* his sovereignty (*Mamlaka*).

Grammatically, b^i (a, in, next to) gives a causative meaning to some verbs and gives to verbs of motion the meaning of "carrying, bringing, taking away."

Finally, this letter is a symbol of mediation, introduction, and presentation. In the "science of the secrets of letters" (*'ilm āl-Ḥurūf*), the letter *ba* represents the number two, and belongs to the element of air.

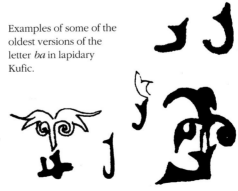

Examples of some of the oldest versions of the letter *ba* in lapidary Kufic.

THE LETTERS OF THE ALPHABET

THE LETTER *BA* IN VARIOUS *BASMALAS*

1. *Basmala* done in *thuluth jalī*, drawn by Nafiz Mahmud Oncu. Turkey, 1946.

2. *Basmala* in *thuluth jalī*, drawn by Nayzen Emin Efendi (1883–1945). Turkey.

3. *Basmala* in foliated Kufic; Anatolian Seljuk art. Caratai Museum, Konya, Turkey.

4. *Basmala* in *thuluth*, drawn by Muhammad Taher Efendi. Turkey, 1836.

5. *Basmala* in *thuluth jalī*, drawn by Mustafa Halim Ozyazici. Turkey, 1956.

6. The letter *ba* as
seen in examples by
Hakkazade Mustafa
Hilmi Efendi (d. 1852),
in the calligraphy code
Mizanu'l Hatt, 1849.

7. *Basmala* in *ta'līq,*
drawn by Mir Malik
Declami. Iran, seven-
teenth century.

8. *Basmala* in *ta'līq,*
drawn by Hasan
Celebi, 1937, in the
Suleymaniye mosque
of Istanbul.

9. A liberal interpreta-
tion of the *basmala* by
Ahmed Karahisari
(1468–1556). Istanbul,
Suleymaniye
Kutuphanesi.

THE LETTERS OF THE ALPHABET

TA

Name: **ta**.
Transliteration: **t**.
Pronunciation: **t**, as in **t**able.

Final		Medial		Initial		Isolated
طت	ط	طتو	تو	ت		ت

Characters

Final		Medial		Initial	
ت	Alarz		Diwani	ت	Nastaliq
ت	Al-Waleed	ت	Fairuz	ت	Omar
ت	Al-Qahira	ت	Firdawsi n.	ت	Rabee
ت	Al-Ruha	ت	Hadith	ت	Rouqai
ت	Amin	ت	Hijaz	ت	Shuweifat
ت	Annees	ت	Jarash	ت	Sidon
ت	Baalback	ت	Jiddah	ت	Silwan
ت	Baghdad	ت	Kufic	ت	Sirius
ت	Beirut	ت	Najaf	ت	Suraya
ت	Byblos	ت	Naskh	ت	Tadmur
ت	Dimashk	ت	Naskh cont.	ت	Thuluth

Ta is the third letter of the alphabet (the plural is *ta'at*); it is prepalatal.

In the art of reciting the Qur'ān (*tajwīd*) it has the characteristics of tonicity and softening and the antonymies of lowering, opening, and whispering.

This letter has great esoteric value, especially for Islam's mystics—the Sufis—because it is the first letter of the term *tawḥīd*, the science of professing God and his singleness (*waḥda*), and so it symbolizes monotheism, faith in the oneness of God.

It also symbolizes the state of ecstasy, the discovery of and return to God (*thawba*).

In this respect, the great Muslim mystic and Sufi martyr Hosein Mansur al-Hallaj (857–922) wrote a poem (*Muhatta'at* No. 49 with a *mim* rhyme and a *wāfir* meter), wherein he traces the word *tawḥīd* through enigmas: "Three letters without diacritical sign, two with signs and this is the whole speech. The first designates those who find it and the other serves for everyone to say 'yes.' As to the other letters, it is the mystery of the night, where it is no longer a question of traveling or stopping."

Explaining the above, we note that in Arabic the term *tawḥīd* is written with two letters, each of which has two diacritical signs, the *ta* and the *ya*, and three letters without signs: the *waw*, the *ha*, and the *dal*. Grammatically, *ta* is part of an oath, *ta-Āllāhi:* by God.

In the "science of the secrets of letters" (*'ilm āl-Ḥurūf*) this letter represents number four hundred and belongs to the element of air.

Calligraphic examples by Hakkazade Mustafa Hilmi Efendi, taken from the *Mizanü'l Hatt*.

THA

Name: **tha**.
Transliteration: **th**.
Pronunciation: emphatic **th**,
 as in **th**ink.

Final		Medial		Initial		Isolated
ث	Alarz	ٹ	Diwani	ث	Nastaliq	ث
ث	Al-Waleed	ث	Fairuz	ث	Omar	
ث	Al-Qahira	ث	Firdawsi n.	ث	Rabee	
ث	Al-Ruha	ث	Hadith	ث	Rouqai	
ث	Amin	ث	Hijaz	ث	Shuweifat	
ث	Annees	ث	Jarash	ث	Sidon	
ث	Baalback	ث	Jiddah	ث	Silwan	
ث	Baghdad	ث	Kufic	ث	Sirius	
ث	Beirut	ث	Najaf	ث	Suraya	
ث	Byblos	ث	Naskh	ث	Tadmur	
ث	Dimashk	ث	Naskh cont.	ث	Thuluth	

Tha is the fourth letter of the Arab alphabet; it is a palatal-gingival letter.

In the art of reciting the Qur'ān (*tajwīd*) it has the characteristic of softening; its antonymies are lowering, opening, atony, and whispering.

Tha is the abbreviation for *thānīt*, which means a second of a minute. Poems whose verses end with the letter *th* are called *thā'iyyt*.

This letter is a symbol of consolidation (*thubūt*). In the "science of the secrets of letters" (*'ilm āl-Ḥurūf*) it represents number five hundred and belongs to the element of water.

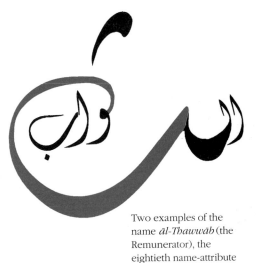

Two examples of the name *āl-Thawwāb* (the Remunerator), the eightieth name-attribute of God.

JIM

Name: **jim**.
Transliteration: **j**.
Pronunciation: **j**, as in **J**ohn.

	Final		Medial		Initial		Isolated
ڄ ط	Alarz	ج	Diwani	ج	Nastaliq		
ⴹ	Al-Waleed	ح	Fairuz	ج	Omar		
ح	Al-Qahira	ح	Firdawsi n.	ح	Rabee		
ح	Al-Ruha	ح	Hadith	ح	Rouqai		
ع	Amin	ح	Hijaz	ح	Shuweifat		
ع	Annees	ح	Jarash	ح	Sidon		
ح	Baalback	ح	Jiddah	ح	Silwan		
ح	Baghdad	ح	Kufic	ح	Sirius		
ح	Beirut	ح	Najaf	ح	Suraya		
ح	Byblos	ح	Naskh	ح	Tadmur		
ح	Dimashk	ح	Naskh cont.	ح	Thuluth		

Characters

Jim is the fifth letter of the Arab alphabet, a subpalatal letter.

In the art of reciting the Qur'ān (*tajwīd*) it has the characteristics of sonority, tonicity, and softening and the antonymies of vibration, lowering, and opening.

In dictionaries, *j* is the abbreviation for *jam'* (plural).

In the "science of the secrets of letters" (*'ilm āl-Ḥurūf*) it represents number three and belongs to the element of water.

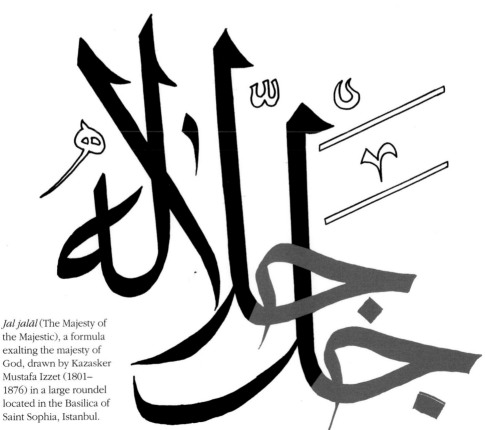

Jal jalāl (The Majesty of the Majestic), a formula exalting the majesty of God, drawn by Kazasker Mustafa Izzet (1801–1876) in a large roundel located in the Basilica of Saint Sophia, Istanbul.

THE LETTERS OF THE ALPHABET

HA

Name: **ha**.
Transliteration: **ḥ**.
Pronunciation: strongly
  aspired **h**, like the **h** in
  hotel and the Spanish **j**
  in **j**ota.

Final		Medial		Initial		Isolated
خط		طحو	حو			ح

Characters	Final		Medial		Initial	
	ح	Alarz	૯	Diwani	ح	Nastaliq
	곱	Al-Waleed	ح	Fairuz	ح	Omar
	ح	Al-Qahira	ح	Firdawsi n.	ﻪ	Rabee
	ح	Al-Ruha	ﺣ	Hadith	ع	Rouqai
	ع	Amin	ﻪ	Hijaz	ح	Shuweifat
	ع	Annees	ﺣ	Jarash	ع	Sidon
	ح	Baalback	ح	Jiddah	ح	Silwan
	ح	Baghdad	ﺣ	Kufic	ﻪ	Sirius
	ح	Beirut	ﺣ	Najaf	ﻪ	Suraya
	ح	Byblos	ح	Naskh	ٮ	Tadmur
	ح	Dimashk	ح	Naskh cont.	ح	Thuluth

Ha is the sixth letter of the Arab alphabet; it is guttural. In the Arab system of pronunciation it is an unvoiced, pharyngeal, spirant consonant (*rikhwa mahmusa* or *awsaṭ āl-Ḥalq*).

In the art of reciting the Qur'ān (*tajwīd*) it has the characteristic of softening; its antonymies are whispering, lowering, atony, and opening.

This letter has an esoteric meaning for the Sufis because it is the first letter of the verb *ḥabba* (to love): *Ĩnna Āllāh jamyl yuḥibbu āl-Jamāl* (Truly God is beautiful and loves beauty). Thus also the saying: *ḥabba man ḥabba wakariha man kariha* (He loves whomsoever he chooses to and he hates whomsoever he wishes to).

This letter symbolizes human intuition. In the "science of the secrets of letters" (*'ilm āl-Ḥurūf*) it represents number eight and belongs to the element of earth.

Below: Calligraphy by Mehmet Shefik Bey (1819–1879), in which the *ha* of Hassan (good) is repeated seven times and written as a final letter to underline its aesthetic rhythm.

KHA

Name: **kha**.
Transliteration: **kh**.
Pronunciation: guttural **ch**,
as in the Scottish lo**ch**.

Final		Medial		Initial		Isolated
طخ خ		طخو خ		خو خ		خ

Characters

Final		Medial		Initial	
خ	Alarz	خ	Diwani	خ	Nastaliq
خ	Al-Waleed	خ	Fairuz	خ	Omar
خ	Al-Qahira	خ	Firdawsi n.	خ	Rabee
خ	Al-Ruha	خ	Hadith	خ	Rouqai
خ	Amin	خ	Hijaz	خ	Shuweifat
خ	Annees	خ	Jarash	خ	Sidon
خ	Baalback	خ	Jiddah	خ	Silwan
خ	Baghdad	خ	Kufic	خ	Sirius
خ	Beirut	خ	Najaf	خ	Suraya
خ	Byblos	خ	Naskh	خ	Tadmur
خ	Dimashk	خ	Naskh cont.	خ	Thuluth

42

Kha is the seventh letter of the Arab alphabet; it is guttural. In the Arab system of pronunciation it is a fricative, post-velar, unvoiced consonant (*rikhwa mahmūsa musaʿliya* or *min ādnā āl-Ḥalq*).

In the art of reciting the Qurʾān (*tajwīd*) it has the characteristics of elevation and softening and the antonymies of whispering, atony, and opening.

In the esoteric literature of the Sufi brotherhoods it symbolizes the eternal good (*khayr dāʾim*).

In the "science of the secrets of letters" (*ʿilm āl-Ḥurūf*) it represents number six hundred and belongs to the element earth.

Below: Calligraphy by Muhammad ʿAbd al-Aziz al-Rifaʿi. Egypt, 1928.

Right: Examples of some of the oldest versions of the letter *kha* in lapidary Kufic.

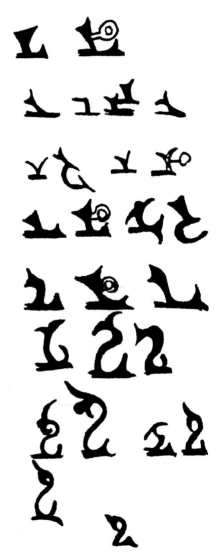

DAL

Name: **dal**.
Transliteration: **d**.
Pronunciation: **d**, as in **d**ead.

Final		Medial		Initial		Isolated
ۮ	Alarz	و	Diwani	د	Nastaliq	د
◨	Al-Waleed	د	Fairuz	د	Omar	
ۮ	Al-Qahira	ۮ	Firdawsi n.	ۮ	Rabee	
؎	Al-Ruha	ۮ	Hadith	د	Rouqai	
ۮ	Amin	ۮ	Hijaz	د	Shuweifat	
ۮ	Annees	ۮ	Jarash	و	Sidon	
ط	Baalback	ۮ	Jiddah	د	Silwan	
ۮ	Baghdad	ۮ	Kufic	و	Sirius	
د	Beirut	ۮ	Najaf	و	Suraya	
د	Byblos	د	Naskh	ۮ	Tadmur	
ۮ	Dimashk	ۮ	Naskh cont.	ۮ	Thuluth	

44

Dal is the eighth letter of the Arab alphabet; it is prepalatal.

In the art of reciting the Qur'ān (*tajwīd*) it has the characteristics of sonority, tonicity, and softening and the antonymies of vibration and lowering.

In Sufi esoteric literature and in the *Contemplations* of the Hurufi, a deviant sect, it symbolizes the equilibrium of all things created.

In the "science of the secrets of letters" (*'ilm āl-Ḥurūf*) it represents number four and belongs to the element of earth.

Because of this, and also because it is the initial letter of the verb *daāba fī āw 'alā* (to work, to labor, to be committed, to make an effort in something for someone; to work with commitment, to do something with effort; to labor unceasingly; to apply oneself, to dedicate oneself; to be constant; to become accustomed to), in the esoteric world this letter represents the earthly condition of human beings who are forced to labor in the realm of material things, but must also evolve spiritually and strive to behave in the best possible way among a multitude of challenges and temptations.

Examples of some of the oldest versions of the letter *dal* in lapidary Kufic.

DHAL

Name: **dhal**.
Transliteration: **dh**.
Pronunciation: **th**, as in **th**at
 or **th**is.

Final		Medial		Initial		Isolated
ذ	Alarz	ذ	Diwani	ذ	Nastaliq	ذ
ذ	Al-Waleed	ذ	Fairuz	ذ	Omar	ذ
ذ	Al-Qahira	ذ	Firdawsi n.	ذ	Rabee	ذ
ظ	Al-Ruha	ذ	Hadith	ذ	Rouqai	ذ
ز	Amin	ذ	Hijaz	ذ	Shuweifat	ذ
ز	Annees	ذ	Jarash	ذ	Sidon	ذ
ظ	Baalback	ذ	Jiddah	ذ	Silwan	ذ
ظ	Baghdad	ذ	Kufic	ذ	Sirius	ذ
ذ	Beirut	ذ	Najaf	ذ	Suraya	ذ
ذ	Byblos	ذ	Naskh	ذ	Tadmur	ذ
ذ	Dimashk	ذ	Naskh cont.	ذ	Thuluth	ذ

Characters

Dhal is the ninth letter of the Arab alphabet; it is gingival and vibrating.

In the art of reciting the Qur'ān (*tajwīd*) it has the characteristics of sonority and softening and the antonymies of lowering, opening, and atony.

In Sufi esoteric knowledge, it symbolizes the heart of an idea, the kernel of a thing.

In the "science of the secrets of letters" (*'ilm āl-Ḥurūf*) it represents number seven hundred and belongs to the element of fire.

Above, left: Examples of some of the oldest versions of the letter *dhal* in lapidary Kufic.

Above, right: The formula *fi dhimmat Āllāh* (under the protection of God).

Below: The title of the fifty-first sura: *āl-Dhāriyāt* (Winnowing).

THE LETTERS OF THE ALPHABET

RA

Name: **ra**.
Transliteration: **r**.
Pronunciation: rolled **r**, as in
   Ruth.

	Final		Medial		Initial		Isolated
ر	Alarz	ر	Diwani	ر	Nastaliq		
ل	Al-Waleed	ر	Fairuz	ر	Omar		
ر	Al-Qahira	ر	Firdawsi n.	ل	Rabee		
ل	Al-Ruha	ل	Hadith	ـ	Rouqai		
ر	Amin	ل	Hijaz	ر	Shuweifat		
ر	Annees	ل	Jarash	ر	Sidon		
ر	Baalback	ر	Jiddah	ر	Silwan		
ر	Baghdad	ر	Kufic	ر	Sirius		
ر	Beirut	ر	Najaf	ر	Suraya		
ر	Byblos	ر	Naskh	ر	Tadmur		
ر	Dimashk	ر	Naskh cont.	ر	Thuluth		

Ra is the tenth letter of Arab alphabet. It is vibrating, apical, alveolar, and voiced (*tafkhīm*).

In the art of reciting the Qur'ān (*tajwīd*) it has the characteristics of sonority and moderation and the antonymies of deflection, repetition, opening, lowering, and atony.

It symbolizes a part, a message, the sura. In the "science of the secrets of letters" (*'ilm āl-Ḥurūf*) it represents number two hundred and belongs to the element of earth.

Examples of some of the oldest versions of the letter *ra* in lapidary Kufic.

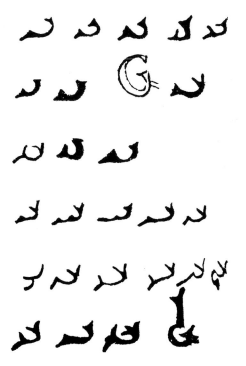

THE LETTERS OF THE ALPHABET

ZA

Name: **za**.
Transliteration: **z**.
Pronunciation: soft **z**, as in **z**ero.

ز

Final		Medial		Initial		Isolated
طز					ز	

ز	Alarz	ز	Diwani	ز	Nastaliq
ز	Al-Waleed	ز	Fairuz	ز	Omar
ز	Al-Qahira	ز	Firdawsi n.	ز	Rabee
ز	Al-Ruha	ز	Hadith	ز	Rouqai
ز	Amin	ز	Hijaz	ز	Shuweifat
ز	Annees	ز	Jarash	ز	Sidon
ز	Baalback	ز	Jiddah	ز	Silwan
ز	Baghdad	ز	Kufic	ز	Sirius
ز	Beirut	ز	Najaf	ز	Suraya
ز	Byblos	ز	Naskh	ز	Tadmur
ز	Dimashk	ز	Naskh cont.	ز	Thuluth

Za is the eleventh letter of the Arab alphabet and is lingual.

In the art of reciting the Qur'ān (*tajwīd*) it has the characteristics of sonority and softening and the antonymies of deflection, repetition, lowering, opening, and volubility.

It symbolizes achievement.

In esoteric alchemy, it represents the process of change, because it is the initial letter of the terms mercury (*zaybaq*), vitriol (*zāj*), and sulfuric acid (*zayb, zāgin*). *Zār* is also the exorcism practiced by women.

In the "science of the secrets of letters" (*'ilm āl-Ḥurūf*) it represents number seven and belongs to the element of water.

Below: The title of the forty-third sura, *āl-Zukhruf* (Luxury).

Bottom: The title of the thirty-ninth sura, *āl-Zumar* (Throngs).

SIN

Name: **sin**.
Transliteration: **s**.
Pronunciation: **s**, as in **s**ew.

Final		Medial		Initial		Isolated
طس طسو		طسو طس		سو سو		س س

Final		Medial		Isolated	
س	Alarz	ﺳ	Diwani	س	Nastaliq
ﻟﺲ	Al-Waleed	س	Fairuz	س	Omar
س	Al-Qahira	س	Firdawsi n.	س	Rabee
سر	Al-Ruha	للس	Hadith	س	Rouqai
س	Amin	س	Hijaz	س	Shuweifat
س	Annees	س	Jarash	س	Sidon
للس	Baalback	س	Jiddah	س	Silwan
سر	Baghdad	سر	Kufic	ﺳ	Sirius
س	Beirut	سر	Najaf	ﺳ	Suraya
س	Byblos	س	Naskh	س	Tadmur
س	Dimashk	س	Naskh cont.	س	Thuluth

Sin is the twelfth letter of the Arab alphabet and is lingual.

In the art of reciting the Qur'ān (*tajwīd*) it has the characteristic of softening and the antonymies of whispering, lowering, opening, and atony.

S is the abbreviation of *sū'al* (question); *salaam* (peace, greetings); *sahm* (a surface unit of measurement); and *santimitr* (centimeter). In grammar, *sa* is the abbreviated form of *saūfa*, a prefix of the imperfect tense, to which it gives the meaning of future.

It symbolizes the glory of God.

In the "science of the secrets of letters" (*'ilm āl-Ḥurūf*) it represents number sixty and belongs to the element of water, though in North Africa it is believed to belong to the element of fire.

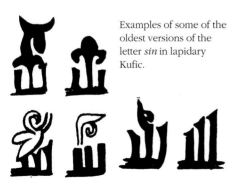

Examples of some of the oldest versions of the letter *sin* in lapidary Kufic.

SHIN

Name: **shin**.
Transliteration: **sh**.
Pronunciation: **sh**, as in
shall.

Final		Medial		Initial		Isolated
طش		طشو		شو		ش

Final		Medial		Initial	
ش	Alarz	ﺵ	Diwani	ش	Nastaliq
شا	Al-Waleed	ش	Fairuz	ش	Omar
ش	Al-Qahira	ش	Firdawsi n.	ش	Rabee
شر	Al-Ruha	لش	Hadith	ش	Rouqai
ﺵ	Amin	ش	Hijaz	ش	Shuweifat
ﺵ	Annees	ش	Jarash	ش	Sidon
لش	Baalback	ش	Jiddah	ش	Silwan
شر	Baghdad	ش	Kufic	ﺵ	Sirius
ش	Beirut	ش	Najaf	ﺵ	Suraya
ش	Byblos	ش	Naskh	ش	Tadmur
ش	Dimashk	ﺵ	Naskh cont.	ش	Thuluth

Shin is the thirteenth letter of the Arab alphabet and it is subpalatal.

In the art of reciting the Qur'ān (*tajwīd*) it has the characteristic of lowering and the antonymies of whispering, opening, diffusion, and softening.

It is the abbreviation of *shāri'a*: path, way.

In Sufi esoteric knowledge, this letter symbolizes personal destiny.

In the "science of the secrets of letters" (*'ilm āl-Ḥurūf*) it represents number three hundred and belongs to the element of fire, while in North Africa it is believed to belong to the element of earth.

Above: The letter *shin* from a *maghribī* Qur'ān in a monumental Kufic type from 1023.

THE LETTERS OF THE ALPHABET

SAD

Name: **sad**.
Transliteration: **ṣ**
Pronunciation:
emphatic **s**, with
tongue pressed
against the edge of
the upper teeth, then
withdrawn forcefully.

Characters

Final		Medial		Initial		Isolated
ص	Alarz	کی	Diwani	ص	Nastaliq	ص
ص	Al-Waleed	ص	Fairuz	ص	Omar	
ص	Al-Qahira	ص	Firdawsi n.	ص	Rabee	
ص	Al-Ruha	ص	Hadith	ص	Rouqai	
ص	Amin	ص	Hijaz	ص	Shuweifat	
ص	Annees	ص	Jarash	ص	Sidon	
ص	Baalback	ص	Jiddah	ص	Silwan	
ص	Baghdad	ص	Kufic	ص	Sirius	
ص	Beirut	ص	Najaf	ص	Suraya	
ص	Byblos	ص	Naskh	ص	Tadmur	
ص	Dimashk	ص	Naskh cont.	ص	Thuluth	

Sad is the fourteenth letter of the Arab alphabet and is lingual.

In the art of reciting the Qur'ān (*tajwīd*) it has the characteristics of sonority, elevation, occlusion, and softening and the antonymies of whistling, whispering, and atony.

It is the abbreviation of *ṣafḥat* (page) and *ṣafar*, the name of the second month in the Muslim lunar year.

It symbolizes sincerity and truth.

In Arabic, the term *ṣād* also means "copper."

In the "science of the secrets of letters" (*'ilm āl-Ḥurūf*) it represents number ninety and belongs to the element of water.

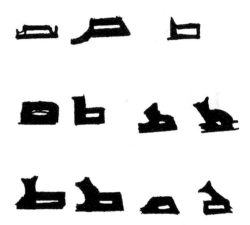

Above: Examples of some of the oldest versions of the letter *sad* in lapidary Kufic.

THE LETTERS OF THE ALPHABET

DAD

Name: **dad**.
Transliteration: **ḍ**.
Pronunciation:
emphatic **d**, similar
to that of **sad**.

	Final		Medial		Initial		Isolated
طض طض		طضو		ضو		ض	

Characters							
ض	Alarz	ض	Diwani	ض	Nastaliq		
ظا	Al-Waleed	ض	Fairuz	ض	Omar		
ض	Al-Qahira	ض	Firdawsi n.	ض	Rabee		
ضر	Al-Ruha	ض	Hadith	ض	Rouqai		
ض	Amin	ض	Hijaz	ض	Shuweifat		
ض	Annees	ض	Jarash	ض	Sidon		
ظـ	Baalback	ض	Jiddah	ض	Silwan		
ضر	Baghdad	ظ	Kufic	ض	Sirius		
ض	Beirut	ظ	Najaf	ض	Suraya		
ض	Byblos	ض	Naskh	ض	Tadmur		
ض	Dimashk	ض	Naskh cont.	ض	Thuluth		

Dad is the fifteenth letter of the Arab alphabet and is subpalatal.

In the art of reciting the Qur'ān (tajwīd), the letter *dad* has the characteristics of sonority, elevation, occlusion, and softening and the antonymies of extension and atony.

It symbolizes "to disclose."

In the "science of the secrets of letters" (*'ilm āl-Ḥurūf*) it represents number eight hundred and belongs to the element of air.

Examples of some of the oldest versions of the letter *dad* in lapidary Kufic.

THE LETTERS OF THE ALPHABET

TA

Name: **ta**.
Transliteration: **ṭ**.
Pronunciation: emphatic **t**,
articulated like **sad** and
dad.

	Final		Medial		Initial		Isolated
بط	ط	بطو	طو		ط		ط

Characters

Final		Medial		Isolated	
ط	Alarz	ط	Diwani	ط	Nastaliq
ط	Al-Waleed	ط	Fairuz	ط	Omar
ط	Al-Qahira	ط	Firdawsi n.	ط	Rabee
ط	Al-Ruha	ط	Hadith	ط	Rouqai
ط	Amin	ط	Hijaz	ط	Shuweifat
ط	Annees	ط	Jarash	ط	Sidon
ط	Baalback	ط	Jiddah	ط	Silwan
ط	Baghdad	ط	Kufic	ط	Sirius
ط	Beirut	ط	Najaf	ط	Suraya
ط	Byblos	ط	Naskh	ط	Tadmur
ط	Dimashk	ط	Naskh cont.	ط	Thuluth

Ta is the sixteenth letter of the Arab alphabet and is prepalatal.

In the art of reciting the Qur'ān (*tajwīd*) it has the characteristics of sonority, elevation, occlusion, and softening and the antonymy of vibration.

It is the abbreviation of *qyrāṭ*, a unit of measurement.

In the esoteric texts of the Sufi masters this letter, taken in isolation, symbolizes divine holiness.

In the "science of the secrets of letters" (*'ilm āl-Ḥurūf*) it represents number nine and belongs to the element of fire.

Examples of some of the oldest versions of the letter *ta* in lapidary Kufic.

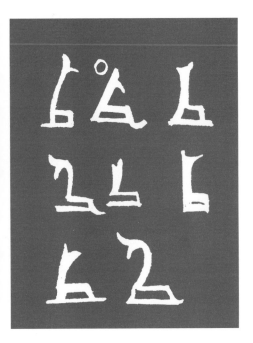

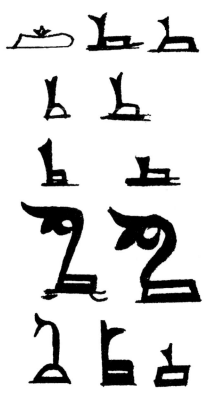

ZA

Name: **za**.
Transliteration: **ẓ**.
Pronunciation: emphatic **z**,
   articulated like **sad**, **dad**
   and **ta**.

Final		Medial		Initial	Isolated
بظ	ظ	بظو	ظو		ظ

Final		Medial		Isolated	
ظ	Alarz	ظ	Diwani	ظ	Nastaliq
ظ	Al-Waleed	ظ	Fairuz	ظ	Omar
ظ	Al-Qahira	ظ	Firdawsi n.	ظ	Rabee
ظ	Al-Ruha	ظ	Hadith	ظ	Rouqai
ظ	Amin	ظ	Hijaz	ظ	Shuweifat
ظ	Annees	ظ	Jarash	ظ	Sidon
ظ	Baalback	ظ	Jiddah	ظ	Silwan
ظ	Baghdad	ظ	Kufic	ظ	Sirius
ظ	Beirut	ظ	Najaf	ظ	Suraya
ظ	Byblos	ظ	Naskh	ظ	Tadmur
ظ	Dimashk	ظ	Naskh cont.	ظ	Thuluth

Characters

Za is the seventeenth letter of the Arab alphabet and is gingival.

In the art of reciting the Qur'ān (*tajwīd*) it has the characteristics of sonority, elevation, occlusion, and softening and the antonymy of atony.

It symbolizes the epiphany or manifestation of God.

In the "science of the secrets of letters" (*'ilm āl-Ḥurūf*) it represents number nine hundred and belongs to the element of water, though in North Africa it is considered to belong to the element of air.

Above, right: The seventy-fifth name-attribute of God, *āl-Ẓāhir* (the Visible).

'AYN

Name: **'ayn**.
Transliteration: '. A strong,
 guttural sound.

Final			Medial			Initial			Isolated
ع ط			طعو			عو ع			ع

Final		Medial		Initial	
ع	Alarz	ع	Diwani	ع	Nastaliq
E	Al-Waleed	ع	Fairuz	ع	Omar
ع	Al-Qahira	ع	Firdawsi n.	ع	Rabee
ع	Al-Ruha	ع	Hadith	ع	Rouqai
ع	Amin	ع	Hijaz	ع	Shuweifat
ع	Annees	ع	Jarash	ع	Sidon
ع	Baalback	ع	Jiddah	ع	Silwan
ع	Baghdad	ع	Kufic	ع	Sirius
ع	Beirut	ع	Najaf	ع	Suraya
ع	Byblos	ع	Naskh	ع	Tadmur
ع	Dimashk	ع	Naskh cont.	ع	Thuluth

64

'Ayn is the eighteenth letter of the Arab alphabet and it is guttural.

In the art of reciting the Qur'ān (*tajwīd*) it has the characteristics of sonority, softening, and moderation and the antonymies of lowering and opening.

It is the abbreviation for '*adād* (number).

It symbolizes the source of intellect.

In the "science of the secrets of letters" ('*ilm āl-Ḥurūf*) it represents number seventy and belongs to the element of earth.

Above: The name of '*Ali* in specular calligraphy.

Below: Examples of some of the oldest versions of the letter '*ayn* in lapidary Kufic.

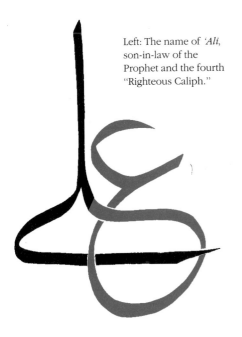

Left: The name of '*Ali*, son-in-law of the Prophet and the fourth "Righteous Caliph."

GHAIN

Name: **ghain**.
Transliteration: **gh**.
Pronunciation: a laryngeal-
  guttural **gr** similar to a
  gargling sound.

	Final		Medial		Initial		Isolated
غ	Alarz	غ	Diwani	غ	Nastaliq
غ	Al-Waleed	غ	Fairuz	غ	Omar
غ	Al-Qahira	غ	Firdawsi n.	غ	Rabee
غ	Al-Ruha	غ	Hadith	غ	Rouqai
غ	Amin	غ	Hijaz	غ	Shuweifat
غ	Annees	غ	Jarash	غ	Sidon
غ	Baalback	غ	Jiddah	غ	Silwan
غ	Baghdad	غ	Kufic	غ	Sirius
غ	Beirut	غ	Najaf	غ	Suraya
غ	Byblos	غ	Naskh	غ	Tadmur
غ	Dimashk	غ	Naskh cont.	غ	Thuluth

Characters

Ghain is the nineteenth letter of the Arab alphabet and it is guttural.

In the art of reciting the Qur'ān (*tajwīd*) it has the characteristics of sonority, elevation, and softening and the antonymies of opening and atony.

It symbolizes total mystery.

In the "science of the secrets of letters" (*'ilm āl-Ḥurūf*) it represents number one hundred and belongs to the element of earth, while in North Africa it is believed to belong to the element of water.

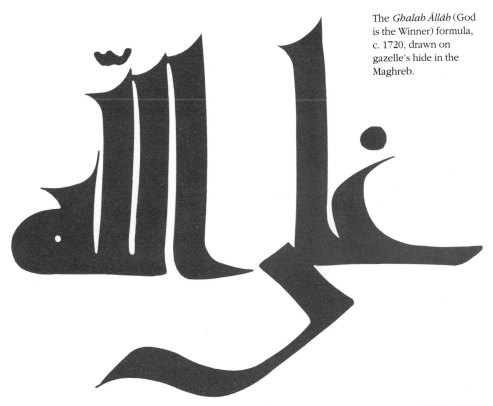

The *Ghalab Āllāh* (God is the Winner) formula, c. 1720, drawn on gazelle's hide in the Maghreb.

FA

Name: **fa**.

Transliteration: **f** (written with a dot underneath in North Africa).

Pronunciation: **f**, as in **f**ool.

	Final		Medial		Initial		Isolated
بغ	ف		بغو		فو		ف

Characters

Final		Medial		Initial	
ف	Alarz	ف	Diwani	ف	Nastaliq
فا	Al-Waleed	ف	Fairuz	ف	Omar
ف	Al-Qahira	ف	Firdawsi n.	ف	Rabee
ف	Al-Ruha	فا	Hadith	ف	Rouqai
ف	Amin	ف	Hijaz	ف	Shuweifat
ف	Annees	ف	Jarash	ف	Sidon
ف	Baalback	ف	Jiddah	ف	Silwan
ف	Baghdad	ف	Kufic	ف	Sirius
ف	Beirut	ف	Najaf	ف	Suraya
ف	Byblos	ف	Naskh	ف	Tadmur
ف	Dimashk	ف	Naskh cont.	ف	Thuluth

Fa is the twentieth letter of the Arab alphabet; it is an unvoiced, fricative, labio-dental consonant (*rikhwa shafawiyya mahmūsa*).

In the art of reciting the Qur'ān (*tajwīd*) the letter *fa* has no characteristics and its antonymies are whispering, atony, lowering, opening, and volubility.

It serves as the abbreviation for *faddān*, a unit of area measurement equal to 45,217.776 square feet (4,200.833 sq. m).

It symbolizes the tongue.

In the "science of the secrets of letters" (*'ilm āl-Ḥurūf*) it represents number eighty and belongs to the element of fire.

فاء متطرفة

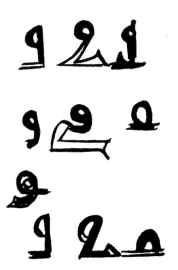

Above and left: Examples of some of the oldest versions of the letter *fa* in lapidary Kufic.

Below: The letter *fa* from a *maghribī* Qur'ān in monumental Kufic of 1023.

THE LETTERS OF THE ALPHABET

QAF

Name: **qaf**.

Transliteration: **q** (written with only one dot above in North Africa).

Pronunciation: a **k** sound from the back of the throat.

Final			Medial			Initial			Isolated
بق	ق		بقو	قو		قو	ق		ق

Final		Medial		Initial	
ق	Alarz	ح	Diwani	ق	Nastaliq
ڤ	Al-Waleed	ق	Fairuz	ق	Omar
ق	Al-Qahira	ق	Firdawsi n.	ق	Rabee
ق	Al-Ruha	ق	Hadith	ء	Rouqai
ـَ	Amin	ق	Hijaz	ق	Shuweifat
ق	Annees	ق	Jarash	ق	Sidon
ق	Baalback	ق	Jiddah	ق	Silwan
ڹ	Baghdad	ق	Kufic	ح	Sirius
ق	Beirut	ق	Najaf	ح	Suraya
ق	Byblos	ق	Naskh	ق	Tadmur
ق	Dimashk	ق	Naskh cont.	ق	Thuluth

70

Qaf is the twenty-first letter of the Arab alphabet and it is uvular.

In the art of reciting the Qur'ān (*tajwīd*) it has the characteristics of sonority, elevation, softening, and tonicity and the antonymy of opening.

It serves as the abbreviation for *daqyqat* (minute) or *daqā'iqu* (minutes). *Qaf* is also the name of a legendary mountain.

This is a special letter, since it is the title of the fiftieth sura of the Qur'ān, whose opening verse reads as follows: "Qaf. By the majestic Qur'ān!" In this respect, we note that there are twenty-nine suras that begin with abbreviations (*fawātiḥ Ḥurūf muqatta'a*), composed of either just one letter or groups of from two to five letters. A total of fourteen letters are used, or half of the Arab alphabet: *a, ḥ, r, s, ṣ, t, ', q, k, l, m, n, h, y*. Sometimes the Prophet invoked God by uttering these two phrases: "Oh ka-ḥa-ya-'ain-sād" or "Oh ḥā-mīm-'ayn-sīn-qāf." Some of these letters grouped together give the word *alrḥmn* (*al-Raḥmān*: the Merciful). Commentators have sought many explanations (twelve, according to *Tha'ālibī*, 1:3), though none are totally valid nor satisfactory. Possibly they are initials, abbreviations, clarifying expressions, unknown names or attributes of God, symbols of the Ineffable Names, or names of the Qur'ān. Or maybe they are oaths, formulas of praise, or names of the suras. Some exegetes believe that they might be the initials of the Prophet's scribes, who collected the suras. Since the Qur'ān is recited by singing it psalm-like (*tajwīd*), some see in these letters the rules of psalmody, or kind of psalmody reading key. Finally, it is said: "Every book has its mystery, and the mystery of the Qur'ān is in its initials."

In the "science of the secrets of letters" (*'ilm āl-Ḥurūf*) this letter represents number one hundred and belongs to the element of water.

The formula *Qul āmantu bi-Llāhi . . .* which begins a saying of the Prophet. Drawn in *thuluth* calligraphy in 1924 by Muhyi al-Din Nevevi. Istanbul.

THE LETTERS OF THE ALPHABET

KAF

Name: **kaf**.
Transliteration: **k**.
Pronunciation: **k**, as in
  kitten.

	Final		Medial		Initial		Isolated
ـك	Alarz	گ	Diwani	كـ	Nastaliq	كﺀ	
ـك	Al-Waleed	ك	Fairuz	كـ	Omar		
ك	Al-Qahira	ﻜ	Firdawsi n.	كـ	Rabee		
ـك	Al-Ruha	ڪ	Hadith	ك	Rouqai		
ك	Amin	ك	Hijaz	كـ	Shuweifat		
ك	Annees	ﻚ	Jarash	ك	Sidon		
ـك	Baalback	ك	Jiddah	ك	Silwan		
ـ	Baghdad	ـك	Kufic	گ	Sirius		
ك	Beirut	ـك	Najaf	كـ	Suraya		
ك	Byblos	ك	Naskh	ك	Tadmur		
ك	Dimashk	ﮎ	Naskh cont.	ك	Thuluth		

Characters

72

Kaf is the twenty-second letter of the Arabic alphabet and is uvular.

In the art of reciting the Qur'ān (*tajwīd*) it has the characteristics of softening and tonicity and the antonymies of whispering and lowering.

K is the abbreviation of *kīlūmitr* (kilometer). In Syria, Lebanon, Jordan, and Iraq, it is also the abbreviation of *kānūn āl-Āwwal* (the month of December) and of *kānūn āl-Thāniy* (January). In grammar, *ka* is a preposition indicating how, how much, inasmuch as, in the capacity of (*ka ālāwwali*: as before, as in the beginning; *ka al'ādāti*: as usual, as customary).

It symbolizes the verb of creation, *kun* (let there be . . .).

In the "science of the secrets of letters" (*'ilm āl-Ḥurūf*) it represents number twenty and belongs to the element water.

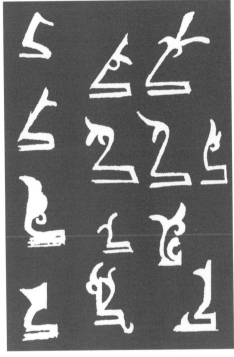

Above: Examples of some of the oldest versions of the letter *kaf* in lapidary Kufic.

Left: The letter *kaf* from a *maghribī* Qur'ān in monumental Kufic, from 1023.

LAM

Name: **lam**.
Transliteration: **l**.
Pronunciation: **l**, as in **l**ove.

	Final		Medial		Initial		Isolated
بل		بلو		لو		ل	

Final		Medial		Initial	
ل	Alarz	♂	Diwani	ل	Nastaliq
L	Al-Waleed	ل	Fairuz	ل	Omar
ل	Al-Qahira	ل	Firdawsi n.	ل	Rabee
ل	Al-Ruha	ل	Hadith	ل	Rouqai
ل	Amin	ل	Hijaz	ل	Shuweifat
ل	Annees	ل	Jarash	♂	Sidon
ل	Baalback	ل	Jiddah	ل	Silwan
ل	Baghdad	ل	Kufic	♂	Sirius
ل	Beirut	ل	Najaf	♂	Suraya
ل	Byblos	ل	Naskh	ل	Tadmur
ل	Dimashk	♂	Naskh cont.	ل	Thuluth

Characters

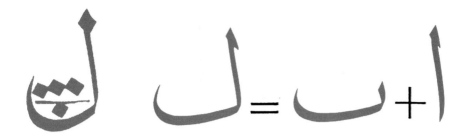

Lam is the twenty-third letter of the Arabic alphabet and is lingual.

In the art of reciting the Qur'ān (*tajwīd*) it has the characteristics of sonority and moderation and the antonymies of lowering and volubility.

L is the abbreviation of *shawwāl*, the tenth month of the Muslim lunar year.

In Arabic, *Lam* is also a person's name.

Grammatically, it is a rich particle. *La* is an adverb used as a prefix, often for the purpose of reinforcing *īnna*, to introduce the predicate, with the meaning of "certainly," "truly," "surely."

La is also the correlative conjunction of *law* and *lawlā*. It is an oath particle, with the meaning of "I swear in the name of." Placed after *ya* it signifies wonder, and its function is similar to that of the exclamation point in English, which does not exist in Arabic.

This letter is vocalized as *la* with the second- and third-person personal pronouns and *li* in the other cases, where it means "to," "for," "of." It signifies the possessive genitive, in particular the author of a text, but also: in favor of, to the benefit of, for the purpose of, on account of. After an infinitive, it introduces the direct object.

Here are some examples: "Īnna rabbiy lasaml'u āl-Du'ā'" (My Lord is so alert to anyone's appeal! Qur'ān 14:39); "law kunta taf'alu hadhā lakāna ānfa'a" (it would have been more useful if you had done such-and-such); "la'amruka" ([I swear] on your life); "yā lal'ajabi" (how wonderful!); "yā lahu'amalin ḥasanin" (what a lovely deed!).

It symbolizes perfect understanding.

In the "science of the secrets of letters" (*'ilm āl-Ḥurūf*) it represents number thirty and belongs to the element earth.

Examples of some of the oldest versions of the letter *lam* in lapidary Kufic.

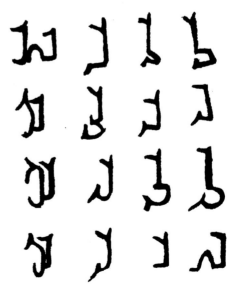

MIM

Name: **mim**.
Transliteration: **m**.
Pronunciation: **m**, as in
mask.

	Final		Medial		Initial		Isolated
بم		بمو		مو		م	
م	Alarz	ح	Diwani	ر	Nastaliq	م	
م	Al-Waleed	م	Fairuz	م	Omar		
م	Al-Qahira	م	Firdawsi n.	م	Rabee		
م	Al-Ruha	م	Hadith	ر	Rouqai		
م	Amin	م	Hijaz	م	Shuweifat		
م	Annees	م	Jarash	ح	Sidon		
م	Baalback	م	Jiddah	م	Silwan		
م	Baghdad	م	Kufic	ل	Sirius		
م	Beirut	م	Najaf	ح	Suraya		
م	Byblos	م	Naskh	م	Tadmur		
م	Dimashk	م	Naskh cont.	م	Thuluth		

Mim is the twenty-fourth letter of the Arabic alphabet and is labial.

In the art of reciting the Qur'ān (*tajwīd*) it has the characteristics of sonority and moderation and the antonymies of lowering, opening, nasalization, and volubility.

M is the abbreviation of *muḥarram*, a month in the Muslim lunar year, and of *millym*, a coin worth one thousand Egyptian lira; of *tamma* ("the end"—said of a book or a thing); of *sanat mylādyyat*, a year in the Christian age. We also find this letter in the acronym *sh.m.m.*, which stands for *maḥdwdat* (limited) *maswwlyyt* (liability), which are parts of the expressions "limited liability company" and "joint stock company."

Grammatically, *ma* has the function of *mā* after prepositions, and it means "what?" (*īlā ma*: toward where? from where? for what purpose?; *bima*: with what?; *ḥattā ma*: until where?, until when?, up to what point?; *lima*: why?, for what?).

In "the science of the secrets of letters" (*'ilm āl-Ḥurūf*) it represents number forty and belongs to the element of fire. For the Hurufi esoteric sect it symbolizes the duality power of matter—power of God.

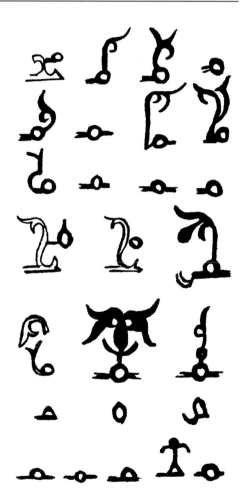

Examples of some of the oldest versions of the letter *mim* in lapidary Kufic.

NUN

Name: **nun**.
Transliteration: **n**.
Pronunciation: **n**, as in **n**ever.

Final	طن طن	Medial	طنو	Initial	نو	Isolated	ن

Nun is the twenty-fifth letter of the Arab alphabet and it is lingual.

In the art of reciting the Qur'ān *(tajwīd)* it has the characteristics of sonority and moderation and the antonymies of lowering, opening, nasalization, and volubility.

N is the abbreviation of *ramadan*, the name of the Muslim lunar month when ritual fasting is observed.

Nun also means "whale," therefore the prophet Jonah is also called *dḥu āl-Nūn* (he of the whale). Gramatically, *nun* can be used to reinforce; in that case, it is called *nūn āl-Ta'kid*; and *tanūyn* refers to nunnation, which is the indeterminate form of a noun or an adjective formed by adding a final *nun*. It corresponds to the indeterminate English articles a, an, some. Finally, a *nun* rhyme, or something having the shape of a *nun*—a crescent or half-moon—is called *nūniyya*.

In the "science of the secrets of letters" (*'ilm āl-Ḥurūf*) it represents number twenty-five and belongs to the element of air.

Examples of some of the oldest versions of the letter *nun* in lapidary Kufic.

HA

Name: **ha**.
Transliteration: **h**.
Pronunciation: an almost
silent **h**, as in **h**appy.

Final		Medial		Initial		Isolated
ه	Alarz	ه	Diwani	ه	Nastaliq	ه
▯	Al-Waleed	ه	Fairuz	ه	Omar
✗	Al-Qahira	ه	Firdawsi n.	۵	Rabee
◢	Al-Ruha	◰	Hadith	ه	Rouqai
ه	Amin	۵	Hijaz	ه	Shuweifat
ه	Annees	◳	Jarash	◔	Sidon
◢	Baalback	۵	Jiddah	ه	Silwan
◢	Baghdad	◢	Kufic	ه	Sirius
۵	Beirut	◢	Najaf	ه	Suraya
ه	Byblos	ه	Naskh	◓	Tadmur
◔	Dimashk	◶	Naskh cont.	✗	Thuluth

Ha is the twenty-sixth letter of the Arab alphabet, and is guttural.

In the Arabic system of pronunciation it is a glottal, unvoiced spirant consonant: *rikhwa mahmūsa* or *aqṣā āl-Ḥalq*.

In the art of reciting the Qur'ān (*tajwīd*) it has the characteristic of softening and the antonymies of whispering, lowering, opening, and atony.

This letter is the abbreviation of *sanat hijryyat*: the year of Hegira. It is the symbol of orientation to God.

In the "science of the secrets of letters" (*'ilm āl-Ḥurūf*) it represents number five, just as in the Syriac and Canaanite alphabets, and belongs to the element of fire.

Below: The term *Hw* (He) in specular calligraphy, the principal Sufi script.

Right: Examples of some of the oldest versions of the letter *ha* in lapidary Kufic.

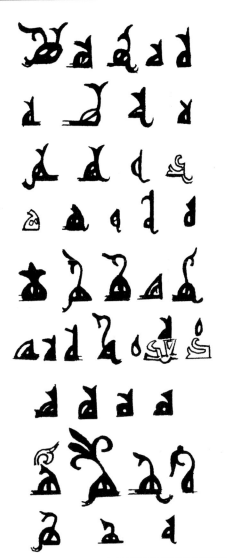

WAW

Name: **waw**.

Transliteration: **w**.

Pronunciation: long,
semi-vocalic, as in **w**hile.

Final		Medial		Initial		Isolated
و	Alarz	ﺭ	Diwani	و	Nastaliq	و
ﻟ	Al-Waleed	و	Fairuz	و	Omar	
و	Al-Qahira	و	Firdawsi n.	و	Rabee	
و	Al-Ruha	ﻭ	Hadith	و	Rouqai	
و	Amin	و	Hijaz	و	Shuweifat	
و	Annees	و	Jarash	و	Sidon	
و	Baalback	و	Jiddah	و	Silwan	
و	Baghdad	و	Kufic	و	Sirius	
و	Beirut	و	Najaf	و	Suraya	
و	Byblos	و	Naskh	و	Tadmur	
و	Dimashk	ﻭ	Naskh cont.	و	Thuluth	

Characters

82

Waw is the twenty-seventh letter of the Arab alphabet and is labial.

In the art of reciting the Qur'ān (*tajwīd*) it has the characteristics of sonority and softening and the antonymies of lowering, opening, atony, softness, and concealment.

Wa is a conjunction; it means "plus"; it is also an adversative conjunction meaning "instead" and a temporal conjunction meaning "meanwhile, while." When followed by a genitive, it introduces an oath: by, in the name of (*wa Āllāh*: by God!, in God's name!) or gives an exclamative tone to a phrase: so much!, so many!, as in *wa kāsin sharibtu* (I drank so many glasses!). Followed by an accusative, it expresses a relationship of company, contemporaneity, concomitance, as in *dhahaba wa iyyāhu* (he left together with him).

For the Sufi masters, this letter symbolizes the mystical promise of total assent to God (*wujūd mutlaq*).

In the "science of the secrets of letters" (*'ilm āl-Ḥurūf*) it represents number six and belongs to the element of air.

Below: Decoration consisting of the letter *waw* highlighted six times.

Above: Examples of some of the oldest versions of the letter *waw* in lapidary Kufic.

COMPOSITIONS CONTAINING THE LETTER *WAW*

1. Design in the shape of a boat in which the letter *waw* used in the phrase *Hū, Āllāh* (God, Himself) is highlighted. From the Mehmet Shevki Efendi (1829–1887) school in Istanbul.

2. From a drawing by Hassan Massoudi: elements of the mural decoration in the Ulu Jami'. Bursa, Turkey.

3. Boat-shaped composition by Abd al-Kader. Tunisia, twentieth century.

4. Page from a text in which the letter *waw* is emphasized by lengthening it. Calligraphy by Hassan Massoudi.

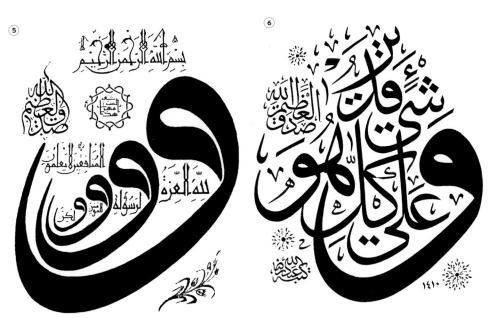

5. Excerpt from the eighth verse of the sixty-third sura with four emphasized *waws*: "*Wa* Lillāh āl-izzat *wa* liraswlihi *wa* lilmwminīn *wa* lākinna āl-Munāfiqīna lā īa'lamwn" ("Yet influence belongs to God, his messenger, and believers, even though hypocrites do not realize it"). Ulu Jami', Bursa, Turkey.

6. The phrase Ṣadaq Āllāh (The Word of God) with a verse from the Qur'ān, drawn on a wall of the Ulu Jami', Bursa, Turkey, by Mehmet Shefik Bey (1819–1879).

7. Beginning of the "Sun Verse" (ninety-first sura): The first seven verses each begin with the letter *waw*. Mural fresco from the Ulu Jami', Bursa, Turkey, built between 1379 and 1421; thanks to its numerous murals and paintings it is considered a museum of Turkish calligraphy.

YA

Name: **ya**.
Transliteration: **y**.
Pronunciation: long,
  semi-vocalic, as in **y**ell,
  br**ee**ze.

ى

Final	يو	Medial	طيو	Initial	يو	Isolated	ي

Characters

Final		Medial		Isolated / Initial	
ـي	Alarz	ئ	Diwani	ی	Nastaliq
ﯨﺎ	Al-Waleed	ي	Fairuz	ی	Omar
ي	Al-Qahira	ي	Firdawsi n.	ي	Rabee
ﴼ	Al-Ruha	ای	Hadith	ي	Rouqai
ي	Amin	ي	Hijaz	ي	Shuweifat
ي	Annees	اي	Jarash	ئ	Sidon
ﯾ	Baalback	ي	Jiddah	ي	Silwan
ـﯩ	Baghdad	ﮯ	Kufic	ئ	Sirius
ي	Beirut	ﮯ	Najaf	ئ	Suraya
ي	Byblos	ي	Naskh	ﯾ	Tadmur
ي	Dimashk	ﯾﯽ	Naskh cont.	ي	Thuluth

86

Ya is the twenty-eighth letter of the Arabic alphabet and it is subpalatal.

In the art of reciting the Qur'ān (*tajwīd*) it has the characteristics of sonority and softening and the antonymies of lowering, opening, softness, concealment, and atony.

It symbolizes God's help.

In the "science of the secrets of letters" (*'ilm āl-Ḥurūf*) it represents number ten and belongs to the element of air.

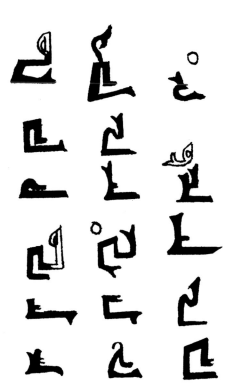

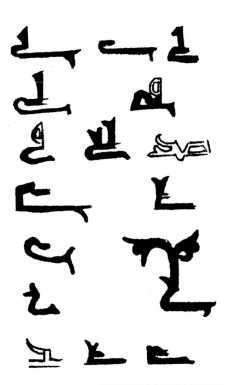

TA MARBŪṬA

Transliteration: **h** or **t**.

طة Final		Medial		Initial	ة Isolated
ة	Alarz	ة	Diwani	ة	Nastaliq
ﭐ	Al-Waleed	ة	Fairuz	ة	Omar
ﻻ	Al-Qahira	ة	Firdawsi n.	ة	Rabee
ﺔ	Al-Ruha	ﺔ	Hadith	ة	Rouqai
ة	Amin	ة	Hijaz	ة	Shuweifat
ة	Annees	ﺔ	Jarash	ة	Sidon
ﺔ	Baalback	ة	Jiddah	ة	Silwan
ﺪ	Baghdad	ﺪ	Kufic	ة	Sirius
ة	Beirut	ﺪ	Najaf	ة	Suraya
ة	Byblos	ة	Naskh	ﺔ	Tadmur
ة	Dimashk	ة	Naskh cont.	ﻻ	Thuluth

Characters

Ta marbūṭa is a tied *ta*, since it is like a *ta* but with crossed endings. It is used only as a suffix. It is transliterated as *a* when the word has no desinence, *at* when the word is followed by a desinence.

This letter is really a grammatical tool, a ligature that often defines the feminine gender, and is pronounced only when a word is tied to the following word. For example: *madinat* is pronounced *madinah* (the *t* is silent); *madinat āl-Nabi* is read *madinat-ānnabi*.

Below: The phrase *Yūladu āl-Nāsu āḥrāran sawāsiyatan* (All men are born free and equal), which ends with a *ta marbūṭa*.

Right: The term *ṣalāt* (prayer) with the *ta marbūṭa* ending, from a book of *Wirde* (sacred invocations) from Morocco.

SHORT VOWELS AND DIACRITICAL MARKS

 ḍamma: A miniature *waw* above the consonant; it signifies a short *u* vowel, as in "b**u**ll."

 fatḥa: A slanted stroke, similar to an acute accent, above the consonant; it signifies a short *a* vowel such as the *a* in "French**ma**n" or the *u* in "b**u**n."

 kasra: A slanted stroke, similar to an acute accent, below the consonant; it signifies a short *i* vowel, such as the *i* in "b**i**d."

 tanwīn (nunnation): Doubling of *ḍamma*, *fatḥa* and *kasra* (short *a*, *i*, and *u* vowels) at the end of a word; it gives the pronunciation of "un," "an," and "in," indicating the indeterminate article respectively in the nominative, accusative, and indirect cases.

 tashdīd (reinforcement, also called *shadda*): A mark signifying the doubling of a consonant; it is a small initial *s* placed above the consonant. The term is derived from the verb *ishtadda* (to be strong, robust, intense; to grow more emphatic or intense).

 sukūn (silence; also called *jazm*: truncation): A small circle placed above the consonant; it signifies the absence of a short vowel.

hamza (*al-Qaṭ'i* when disjunctive; *al-Waṣli* when conjunctive): A sort of small initial *'ayn* (') placed above the consonant. Some grammarians treat it as a consonant and thus place it at the beginning of the alphabet, where the *alif* normally is. When accompanied by a short vowel (*ḍamma, fatḥa,* or *kasra*) it is read, respectively, as *ū, ā, ī*. When it occurs at the beginning of a word—only above the *alif*—it indicates a glottal stop, a sound immediately blocked by the glottis. When it occurs in the middle of a word (with a purely orthographic support from an underlying *alif, wau,* or *ya* without the two diacritical marks, read as *ā*), it signifies a net pause after the preceding syllable, or a suspension of the voice. When it occurs at the end of a word, it is written directly on the line without an underlying consonant, and is pronounced *a'*.

madda (lengthening, also called *alif madda*): When two initial *alifs* follow each other, or when a final *alif* is followed by a *hamza*, only one is written, with the *madda* sign on top; it is a tiny horizontal *alif*, not unlike the Spanish tilde (˜). It signifies a long *ā*.

waṣla (ligature, also called *alif waṣla*): A sign that ties the pronunciation of the last short vowel declension of the preceding word to the first syllable of the following word that has this initial sign (the *alif* is silent).

maqsūra (restricted, also called *alif maqsūra*): The letter *ya* without the two diacritical marks, placed at the end of a word; it is read *ā*. It is equivalent to an *alif madda*.

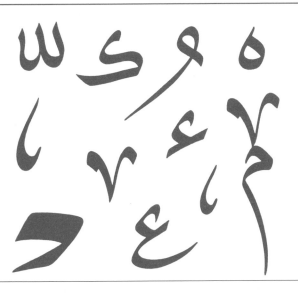

Orthographic, vocalic, and ornamental additional symbols of the Arabic alphabet, taken from the large roundels drawn by Kazasker Mustafa Izzet (1801–1876). Basilica of Saint Sophia, Istanbul.

LAM-ALIF

Name: **lam-alif**.
Transliteration: **la**.
Pronunciation: **lah**.

Final		Medial		Initial		Isolated
ﻼ	Alarz	ﻼ	Diwani	ﻻ	Nastaliq	ﻻ
ﻼ	Al-Waleed	ﻼ	Fairuz	ﻻ	Omar	
ﻼ	Al-Qahira	ﻼ	Firdawsi n.	ﻻ	Rabee	
ﻼ	Al-Ruha	ﻼ	Hadith	ﻻ	Rouqai	
ﻼ	Amin	ﻼ	Hijaz	ﻻ	Shuweifat	
ﻼ	Annees	ﻼ	Jarash	ﻻ	Sidon	
ﻼ	Baalback	ﻼ	Jiddah	ﻻ	Silwan	
ﻼ	Baghdad	ﻼ	Kufic	ﻻ	Sirius	
ﻼ	Beirut	ﻼ	Najaf	ﻻ	Suraya	
ﻼ	Byblos	ﻼ	Naskh	ﻻ	Tadmur	
ﻼ	Dimashk	ﻼ	Naskh cont.	ﻻ	Thuluth	

Characters

The *lam-alif* is not part of the traditional alphabet sequence, but it is included because of a hadith (that is, a saying of the prophet Muhammad), though that authenticity is not very credible according to the preeminent collector of such sayings, the Turkish Bukhari. Abd-al-Rahman ibn al-Saygh (1441) reported the saying as follows: "Abu Dharr al-Ghifari asked the Prophet: 'How many letters are there?' The Prophet replied: 'Twenty-nine.' His companion wondered, then counted them all one by one and triumphantly exclaimed, 'There are twenty-eight.' But the Prophet retorted: 'No, there are twenty-nine, there is also the *lam-alif.*'"

Left: Examples of some of the oldest versions of the letter *lam-alif* in lapidary Kufic.

Bottom: The formula *wa lā ghalib illā Āllāh* (power belongs to God alone), drawn by Muhammad 'Abd al-Qadir (Abd al-Kader), Tunisia, twentieth century.

VARIANTS OF THE *LAM-ALIF* LETTER

1. The *shahāda* (**Lā** *Īlāha illā Āllāh, Muḥammad rasūl Āllāh*), from a 1588 relief in the Jami' Masjid of Bukhara, Uzbekistan.

2. Various examples of the *lam-alif* collected by Hassan Massoudi.

3, 4. Examples of the *lam-alif* from a Qur'ān drawn in Kufic in the Middle Ages.

THE SUPPLEMENTAL
LETTERS

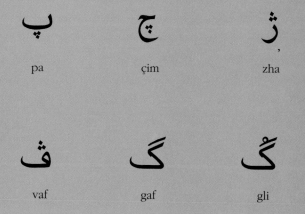

پ
pa

چ
çim

ژ
zha

ڤ
vaf

گ
gaf

گ
gli

These six letters are used only in non-Arabic languages that use the Arab alphabet.

The letters *c* and hard *g* in the Turkish phrase *Çiok güsel* (Very pretty!).

PA

Name: **pa**.
Transliteration: **p**.
Pronunciation: **p**, as in **P**eter.

Final			Medial			Initial		Isolated	
طپ	طپ		طپو	طپو		پ		پ	
	Alarz	ٮ		Diwani		پ	Nastaliq		
	Al-Waleed	ـپـ		Fairuz			Omar		
	Al-Qahira	ـپـ		Firdawsi n.			Rabee		
	Al-Ruha			Hadith			Rouqai		
	Amin			Hijaz		پ	Shuweifat		
	Annees			Jarash			Sidon		
	Baalback			Jiddah		پ	Silwan		
	Baghdad	ـپـ		Kufic			Sirius		
پ	Beirut			Najaf			Suraya		
	Byblos	ـپـ		Naskh			Tadmur		
پ	Dimashk			Naskh cont.			Thuluth		

ای دیدہ بخانهٔ خماری

کگفتم ندهی رزیلگان اخباری

کگفتا میخور که همچو ما بسیاری

رفتند وکسی باز نیامد باری

To the wine-house I saw the sage repair,
Bearing a wine-cup, and a mat for prayer;
I said, "O Shaikh, what does this conduct mean?"
Said he, "Go drink! The world is naught but air."

(Quatrain No. 80, from *The Sufistic Quatrains of Omar Khayyam,* translated by E. H. Whinfield, p. 161.)

Above: Quatrain beginning with the letter *pa,* by Persian mathematician and poet Omar Khayyam (1048–1131).

Left: The letter *p* in the word *Pamir.* From a sign in the Shahar Shata market in Kabul, Afghanistan, twentieth century.

THE SUPPLEMENTAL LETTERS

ÇIM

Name: **çim**.
Transliteration: **ç**.
Pronunciation: **ch**, as in
  China.

Final		Medial		Initial		Isolated	
	Alarz	ڬ	Diwani	ڄ	Nastaliq	ڄ	
	Al-Waleed	ڄ	Fairuz		Omar		
	Al-Qahira		Firdawsi n.		Rabee		
	Al-Ruha		Hadith		Rouqai		
	Amin		Hijaz	ڄ	Shuweifat		
	Annees		Jarash		Sidon		
	Baalback		Jiddah	ڄ	Silwan		
	Baghdad	ڄ	Kufic		Sirius		
ڄ	Beirut		Najaf		Suraya		
	Byblos	ڄ	Naskh		Tadmur		
ڄ	Dimashk		Naskh cont.		Thuluth		

Characters

چون نامه حرم ناسم بحندند پیپ ...

Top: One verse and two quatrains by Omar Khayyam that begin with the letter *çim*.

چو ها میگزرد عمر چه شیرین وچه تلخ

چون جام بلب آمد چماجوز وچه بلخ

می نوش که بعد از من وتو ماه بسی

از سلخ بغره آید از غره بسلخ

When life is spent, what's Balkh or Nishapore?
What sweet or bitter, when the cup runs o'er?
Come drink! Full many a moon will wax and wane
In times to come, when we are here no more.

(Quatrain No. 134, p. 174)

چو ها چرخ وفلک هیچ بکام تو نگشت

خواهی تو فلک هفت شمر خواهی هشت

جرگز غم دوز مرا گرد نگشت

روزیکه نیامد است وروزیکه گذشت

My life lasts but a day or two, and fast
Sweeps by, like torrent stream or desert blast,
Howbeit, of two days I take no heed:
The day to come, and that already past.

(Quatrain No. 26, p. 147)

(From *The Sufistic Quatrains of Omar Khayyam,* translated by E. H. Whinfield.)

ZHA

Name: **zha**.
Transliteration: **zh**.
Pronunciation: **zh**.

	Final		Medial		Initial		Isolated
	Alarz	ﺮ	Diwani	ﺛ	Nastaliq		Nastaliq
	Al-Waleed	ﺚ	Fairuz		Omar		Omar
	Al-Qahira	ﺚ	Firdawsi n.		Rabee		Rabee
	Al-Ruha		Hadith		Rouqai		Rouqai
	Amin		Hijaz	ﺛ	Shuweifat		Shuweifat
	Annees		Jarash		Sidon		Sidon
	Baalback		Jiddah	ﺛ	Silwan		Silwan
	Baghdad	ﺚ	Kufic		Sirius		Sirius
ﺮ	Beirut		Najaf		Suraya		Suraya
	Byblos	ﺚ	Naskh		Tadmur		Tadmur
ﺮ	Dimashk		Naskh cont.		Thuluth		Thuluth

Above: The letter *zha*, the beginning of *Zhaytun*, a man's name. From the frontispiece of a volume of poetry published in Hyderabad in 1968.

Left: One of the extremely rare words in the Urdu language that begin with the letter *zha*: *ẓhāla* (hail),

VAF

Name: **vaf**.
Transliteration: **v**.
Pronunciation: **v**, as in **v**ase.

Final		Medial		Initial		Isolated
	Alarz	ڤ	Diwani	ڤ	Nastaliq	ڤ
	Al-Waleed	ڥ	Fairuz		Omar	
	Al-Qahira	ڨ	Firdawsi n.		Rabee	
	Al-Ruha		Hadith		Rouqai	
	Amin		Hijaz	ڤ	Shuweifat	
	Annees		Jarash		Sidon	
	Baalback		Jiddah	ڤ	Silwan	
	Baghdad	ڨ	Kufic		Sirius	
ڤ	Beirut		Najaf		Suraya	
	Byblos	ڤ	Naskh		Tadmur	
ڤ	Dimashk		Naskh cont.		Thuluth	

Top: The name of the Indian city Vārānāsī (Benares).

Above: The letter *v*, the beginning of the last name Varimtov, a famous ceramist from Khiva, Uzbekistan, twentieth century.

Left: The word *Varamīn*, which in the writings of the great Persian Sufi teacher Shihab al-Din Yahya Sohravardi (1155–1191) demonstrates the illusions brought about by an active imagination (*barzakh*).

THE SUPPLEMENTAL LETTERS

GAF

Name: **gaf**.
Transliteration: **g**.
Pronunciation: hard **g**, as in
goat.

	Final		Medial		Initial		Isolated
	Alarz	گ	Diwani	گ	Nastaliq		Omar
	Al-Waleed	گ	Fairuz				Rabee
	Al-Qahira	گ	Firdawsi n.				Rouqai
	Al-Ruha		Hadith	گ	Shuweifat		Sidon
	Amin		Hijaz			گ	Silwan
	Annees		Jarash				Sirius
	Baalback		Jiddah				Suraya
	Baghdad	گ	Kufic				Tadmur
گ	Beirut		Najaf				Thuluth
	Byblos	گ	Naskh				
گ	Dimashk		Naskh cont.				

104

گر

مى نخورى طعنہ مزن مستانرا

گر توبہ دھد توبہ کنم یزدانرا

تو فخر باک کنئ کہ من مى نخورم

صد کار کنئ کہ مى خلاصئ آنرا

Blame not the drunkards, you who wine eschew,
Had I but grace, I would abstain like you,
And mark me, vaunting zealot, you commit
A hundredfold worse sins than drunkards do.

(Quatrain No. 11, from *The Sufistic Quatrains of Omar Khayyam*,
translated by E. H. Whinfield, p. 143.)

گه

گشتہ نهان رُو بکسى ننمائ

گه در صُور کون ومکان پیدائ

این جلوه گرى بجویشتن بنمائ

خود عین عیان خودى وبینائ

Now Thou art hidden, unseen of all that be;
Now Thou art fully display'd that all may see:
Being, as Thou art, the Player and the Play,
And playing for Thine own pleasure, carelessly.

(Quatrain No. 15, from *Quatrains from Omar Khayyam*, translated
by F. York Powell.)

Two quatrains by Omar
Khayyam beginning
with the letter *gaf*.

THE SUPPLEMENTAL LETTERS

Name: **none**.
Transliteration: **none**.
Pronunciation: **li**, as in
  mil**li**on.

	Isolated		Initial		Medial		Final
	ڭ	ﮒ	ﮒ	ﮔ	گﻮ	بﮔﻮ	ﺑﮓ

Characters

Isolated		Initial		Medial		Final	
Nastaliq	ﮒ			Diwani	ﮓ	Alarz	
Omar				Fairuz	ﮒ	Al-Waleed	
Rabee				Firdawsi n.	ﮔ	Al-Qahira	
Rouqai				Hadith		Al-Ruha	
Shuweifat	ﮓ			Hijaz		Amin	
Sidon				Jarash		Annees	
Silwan	ﮓ			Jiddah		Baalback	
Sirius				Kufic	ﮒ	Baghdad	
Suraya				Najaf		Beirut	ﮒ
Tadmur				Naskh	ﮒ	Byblos	
Thuluth				Naskh cont.		Dimashk	ﮓ

Left: The letters *g* (hard) and *v*, as seen in the name of the Azerbaijani musician Fakraddin Gafarov. From a concert program. Baku, Azerbaijan, twentieth century.

A few letters in the non-traditional "peacock" style (*taūs*).
Left: The letter *gli.*
Clockwise from below right: The letters *a, b, l, n.*

Right: The letter *gli,* drawn by Nasrettin Herati in the non-traditional "shaky" style (*ra'ashat*).

يولد الناس أحرارا سواسية

يولد الناس أحرارا سواسية

يولد الناس أحرارا سواسية

يولد الناس أحرارا سواسية

يولد الناس أحرارا سواسية

يولد الناس أحرارا سواسية

يولد الناس أحرارا سواسية

يولد الناس أحرارا سواسية

يولد الناس أحرارا سواسية

يولد الناس أحرارا سواسية

يولد الناس أحرارا سواسية

The first phrase of the Human Rights Charter ("All men are born free and equal"), drawn by Hassan Massoudi (Paris, twentieth century) in eleven different styles. From top to bottom: Classic Kufic, Qarmatian Kufic, modern Kufic, *maghribī, thuluth, naskhī, dīwānī,* Farsi, *dīwānī jalī, ijāza, ruqa.*

STYLES, VARIANTS, AND CALLIGRAPHIC ADAPTATIONS

EXAMPLES OF CLASSIC SEVENTH- TO NINTH-CENTURY KUFIC STYLE

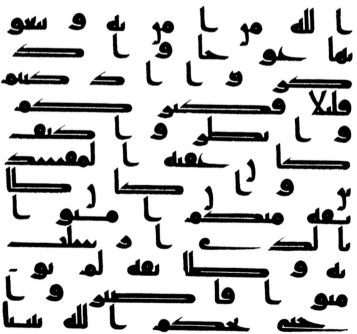

1. Excerpt from the Qur'ān commissioned by Caliph Uthman (d. 656). Istanbul, Topkapi Sarayë Museum.

2. Excerpt from a Qur'ān from the period of Caliph Uthman (d. 656). St. Petersburg, National Library.

3. Excerpt taken from an eighth-century Qur'ān. St. Petersburg, Library of Oriental Studies, 322.

4. Excerpt from a ninth-century Qur'ān, written in Iran or Iraq. Tehran, Bastan Museum, 4289.

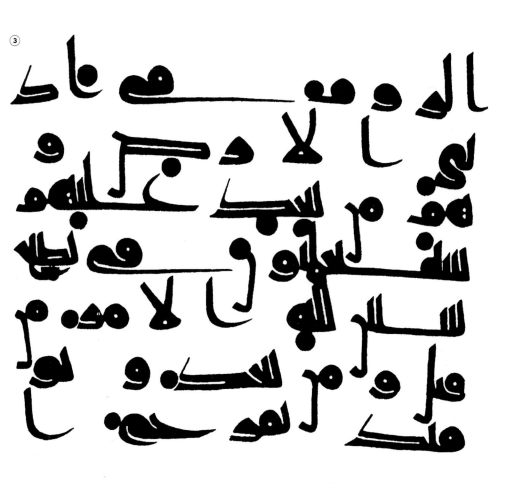

EXAMPLES OF QARMATIAN KUFIC

(1)

1. Excerpt from a Qur'ān composed by Ali al-Warraq between 1019 and 1020, probably in Kairouan, Tunisia. This Qur'ān is associated with the name of *Mushaf al-Ḥāḍinah*. Kairouan, Tunisia, Ibrahim ibn al-Aghlab Museum.

2. A phrase written in *nissabāri* Kufic.

3. Page from an eleventh-century Qur'ān, written in either Iran or Iraq. Geneva, H. H. Sadruddin Agha Khan Collection.

(2)

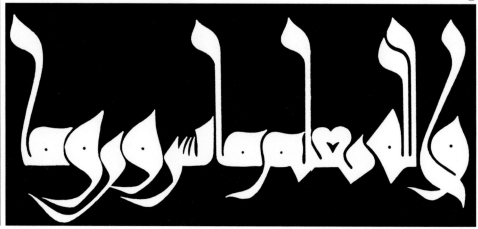

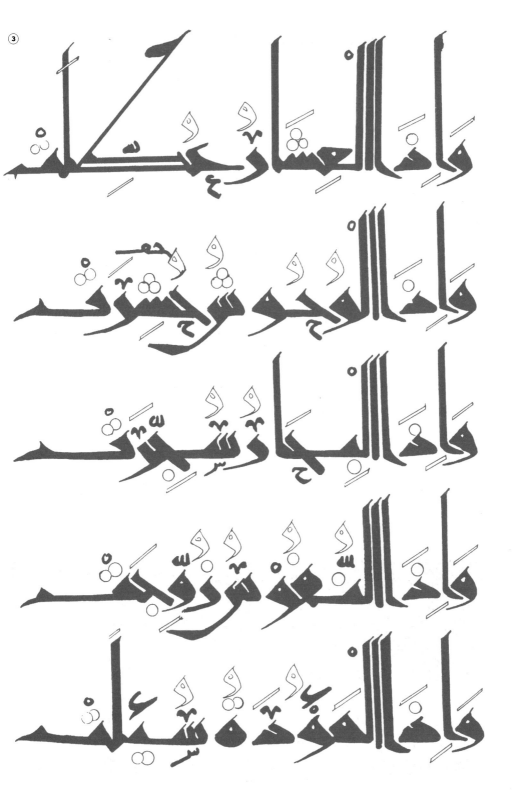

EXAMPLES OF FOLIATED AND PLAITED KUFIC

1. *Basmala* drawn in foliated Kufic. Córdoba, Spain, Grand Mosque.

2. *Basmala* in foliated Kufic. Granada, Spain, Alhambra.

3. A relief of 1107, from the Qasma Kazi mosque of Zanzibar, Africa.

4. *Basmala* in plaited Kufic.

5. *Basmala* in plaited Kufic.

6. *Basmala* in plaited Kufic by Izzet Necmeddin, 1946.

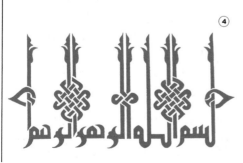

(7)

7. Plaited and flowered
Kufic, fifteenth century.
Hetimandel Palace,
Tar-o Sār, Afghanistan.

8. Plaited and flowered
Kufic, eighteenth
century. Afghanistan.

(8)

STYLES, VARIANTS, AND CALLIGRAPHIC ADAPTATIONS

1. Colophon from the book *Scrittura, espressione dell'Invisibile* (Scripture, Expression of the Invisible) by Gabriele Mandel. Milan, 1980.

Opposite: Four pages of wood-engraving.
2, 3. Surat *āl-Fātiḥa*.
4. Surat *āl-Kawthar*.
5. Surat *āl-'Aṣr*.

②

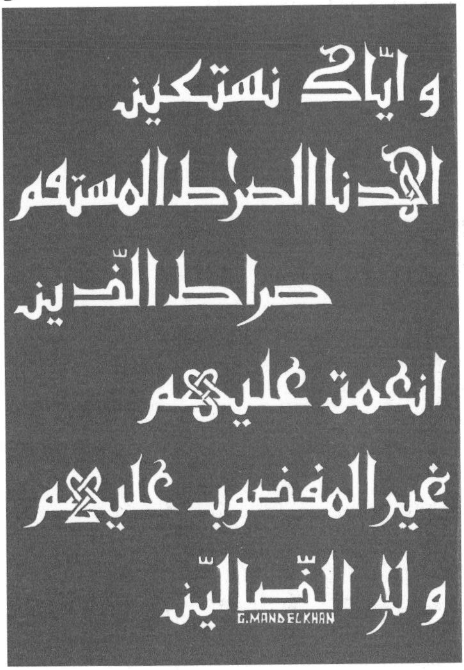

و اياك نستعين
اهدنا الصراط المستقيم
صراط الذين
انعمت عليهم
غير المغضوب عليهم
ولا الضالين
G. MANDELKHAN

③

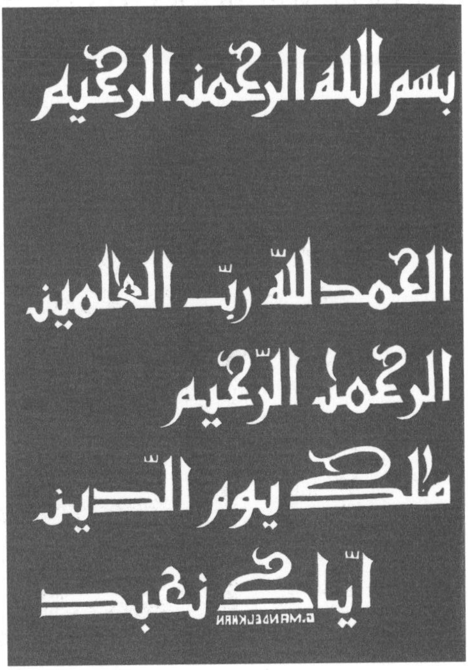

بسم الله الرحمن الرحيم
الحمد لله رب العالمين
الرحمن الرحيم
ملك يوم الدين
اياك نعبد
G. MANDELKHAN

④

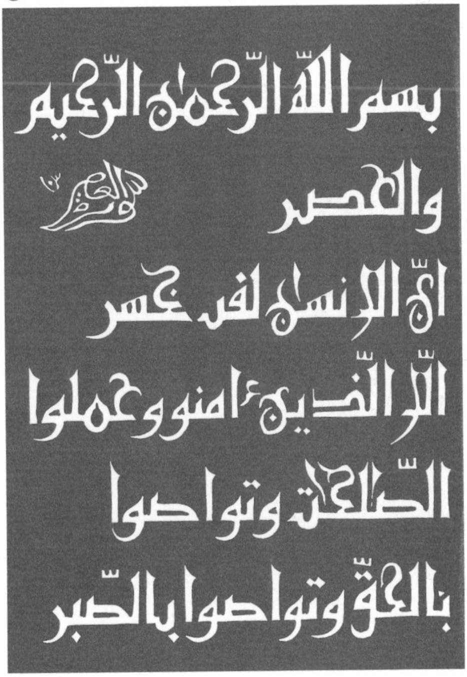

بسم الله الرحمن الرحيم
والعصر
ان الانسان لفي خسر
الا الذين آمنوا وعملوا
الصالحات وتواصوا
بالحق وتواصوا بالصبر

⑤

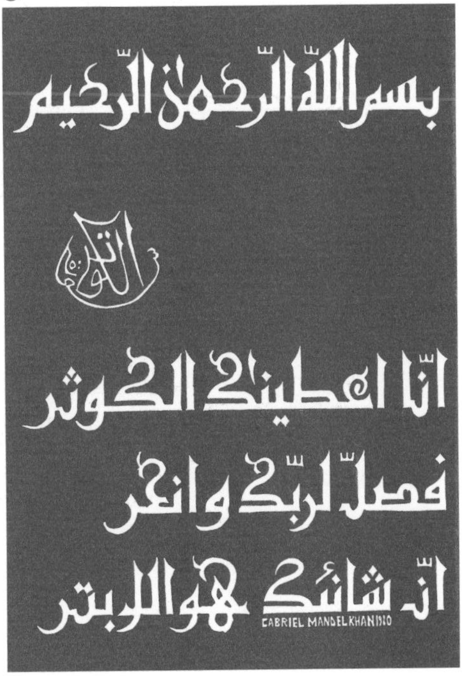

بسم الله الرحمن الرحيم
انا اعطيناك الكوثر
فصل لربك وانحر
ان شانئك هو الابتر
GABRIEL MANDEL KHANINO

SOME ASPECTS OF THE DĪWĀNĪ STYLE

1. Boat-shaped composition in *dīwānī jalī*, by Mulla 'Ali. Istanbul, 1826.

2. A title from *Kirk Hadīs Tercümen* by Usuli. Istanbul, Suleymaniye Fatih Kutuphanesi, 5427.

3. Boat-shaped composition by Mehmet Izzet al-Karkuki (Turkish, 1841–1904).

4. A page in *dīwānī jalī*.
Istanbul, Suleymaniye
Fatih Kutuphanesi.

5. A page from a
calligraphic essay from
the *Code* by Mehmet
Evki Efendi (Turkish,
1804–1887).

④

⑤

COMPOSITIONS IN THE DĪWĀNĪ JALĪ STYLE

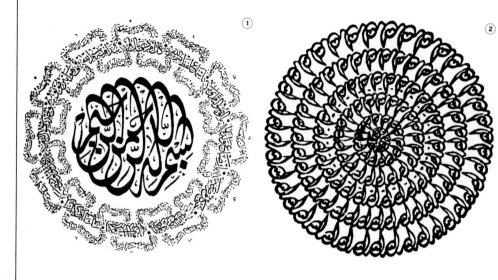

1. Composition by Abd al-Kader. The center is in *dīwānī jalī*, and the border in *thuluth* and *naskhī*. Tunisia, twentieth century.

2. Composition by Umar Yusuf al-Najjar, 1961. Jerusalem.

3. Composition by Abd al-Kader. Tunisia, twentieth century.

4. The *shahāda* by Mohamed Aziza. Tunisia, twentieth century.

5. Logo of the Sufi Jerrahi-Halveti brotherhood: *Ḥānqāh ḥaḍrat Sulṭān Muḥammad Nūr āl-Dīn āl-Jerraḥi āl-Khalwātī*. Istanbul, c. 1720.

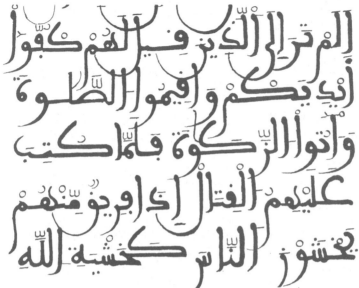

1. Detail from an Andalusian Qur'ān. Córdoba, fourteenth century.

2. Two pages from a Maghreb (North African) Qur'ān, written in Kano. Nigeria.

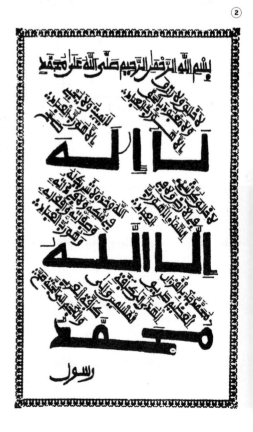

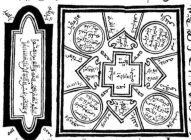

3. Page taken from a *maghribī*-style Qur'ān drawn by al-Qandusi.

4. Page from *Kitāb āl-Fawā'id āl-Ājīdā*, a book on magic by Ahmad al-Daraibi (d. 1738), in a Moroccan facsimile.

5. The name Muhammad drawn by al-Qandusi in the volume *Dalīl āl-Khayrāt* (Guide to the Celestial Gifts), 1850.

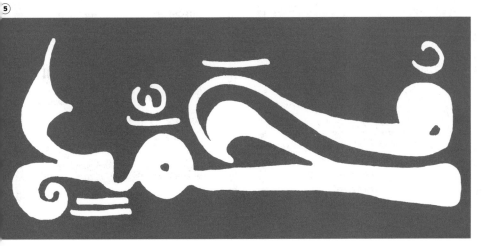

ARABIC CALLIGRAPHY IN INDIA

1. Page drawn in Indian Farsi style.

2. *Zulf-i 'arūs* calligraphy, c. 1820, India.

3. The last sura of a Pakistani Qur'ān printed in Karachi, 1976.

4. Makhrafat Qur'ān, 1842, Delhi.

INTERLACINGS IN GULZAR STYLE

1. The phrase *āl-Ḥamdu, āl-Walī, āl-Ḥamdu* (God's attributes). *Musalsal* script done in *thuluth* characters using the *gulzar* style. Drawn by Ahmed Karahisari, 1547, Istanbul.

2. *Basmala* in *thuluth jalī* drawn by Ahmed Karahisari (1468–1556). Istanbul, Islamic and Turkish Museum.

3. *Basmala* from a Qur'ān, Afghanistan, eighteenth century.

1. Central decoration of a plate done in *cloisonné* enamel from the twelfth or thirteenth century. Commissioned for an Ottoman Sultan in China. Istanbul, Topkapi Sarayë Museum.

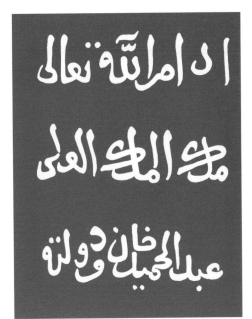

2. The second part of the *shahāda*, enamel on bronze, from the back of a vase. Istanbul, Topkapi Sarayë Museum.

3. Enamel on bronze decoration on a vase given by the Chinese Emperor Qianlong (1736–1796) to the Ottoman Sultan Selim III (1761–1808). Istanbul, Topkapi Sarayë Museum.

4. *Basmala* in *sīnī* characters.

5. A page from a Qur'ān written in Arabic and Chinese, 1892. Canton, China.

EXAMPLES OF OTTOMAN TUĞRA COMPOSITIONS

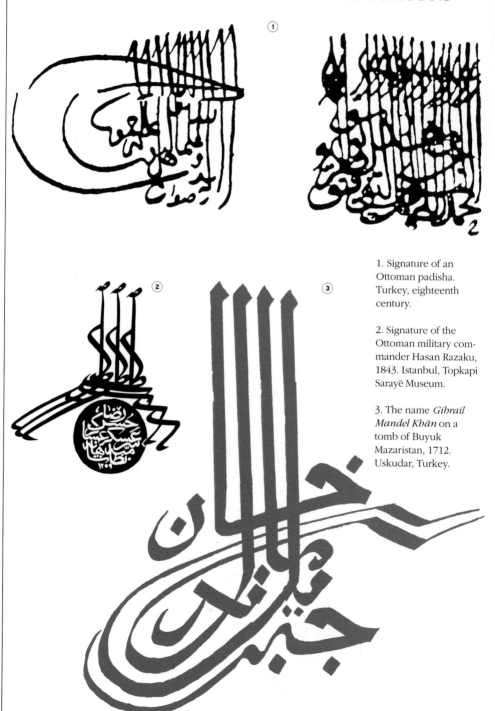

1. Signature of an Ottoman padisha. Turkey, eighteenth century.

2. Signature of the Ottoman military commander Hasan Razaku, 1843. Istanbul, Topkapi Sarayë Museum.

3. The name *Gibrail Mandel Khān* on a tomb of Buyuk Mazaristan, 1712. Uskudar, Turkey.

4

4. The phrase "I take shelter in God" drawn in *tuğra* form by Mustafa Rakim (d. 1767). Istanbul, Sabanci Hat Kollesiyonu.

5. The signature of Sultan Mahmūd Khān, drawn by Mustafa Rakim. Istanbul, Topkapi Sarayë Museum.

6. *Basmala* drawn in *tuğra* form by Hamad al-Madi.

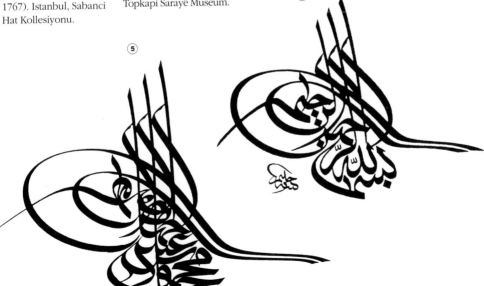

5

6

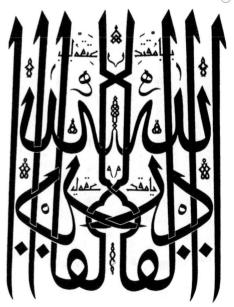

1–7. Decorations from the Ulu Jami' mosque of Bursa, Turkey, in specular style (*muthannā*). Bursa was the first capital of the Ottoman Empire. The Ulu Jami' was built between the years 1379 and 1421. Beginning in the eighteenth century, its walls were adorned by beautiful calligraphy, in paintings as well as frescoes, by masters such as Sadullah Efendi (1766–1843); Shevket Vahdeti (1833–1871); Mehmet Shefik Bey (1819–1879); Abdulfettah Efendi (1814–1896); Mehmet Nazif Bey (1846–1913); Aziz Efendi Rufai (1871–1934); and Refet Efendi (1873–1949).

⑤

⑥

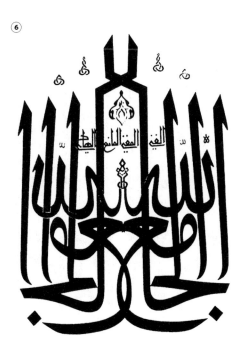

⑦

MUTANNĀZAR COMPOSITIONS

1. Specular calligraphy done in *ta'līq* style by the Turkish master Mehmet Shefik Bey (1819–1879).

2. *Mashāllāh* drawn by Emin Barin (1913–1996) of Bolu, Turkey. The calligraphic decorations in the Ataturk Mausoleum of Ankara, Turkey, and in the Grand Mosque of Karachi, Pakistan, are also his work.

3. *Basmala* in *thuluth* style by Muhammad Amin Sanat, 1920.

4. Specular calligraphy by the Turkish master Mehmet Shefik Bey (1819–1879).

5. A *müsenna* composition, also called an *aynali*, from 1896. Drawn by Abdulfettah Efendi (1814–1896).

6. The phrase *Lā ilaha illā Hū, Rabby āl-ālamīn* (No other God but him, the Lord of the worlds), drawn by Mehmet Shefik Bey (1819–1879).

7. The phrase *Ālḥamdu Lillāhi* (Glory to God), drawn in *thuluth* style by al-Muallef in 1978.

STYLES, VARIANTS, AND CALLIGRAPHIC ADAPTATIONS

133

ARABIC SCRIPT IN SORCERY

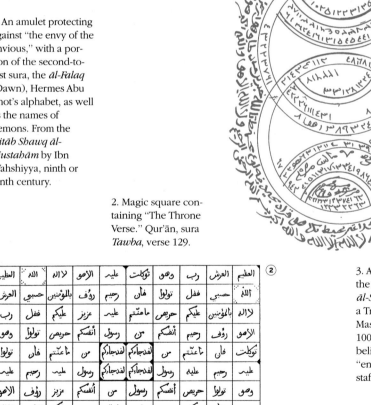

1. An amulet protecting against "the envy of the envious," with a portion of the second-to-last sura, the *āl-Falaq* (Dawn), Hermes Abu Thot's alphabet, as well as the names of demons. From the *Kitāb Shawq āl-Mustahām* by Ibn Wahshiyya, ninth or tenth century.

2. Magic square containing "The Throne Verse." Qur'ān, sura *Tawba*, verse 129.

3. Amulet suggested in the *Ghāyat āl-Ḥakīm fī āl-Siḥr* (The Purpose of a Treatise on Magic) by Maslama al-Majriti (d. 1007), which the author believed had been "engraved on Moses' staff."

4. Talisman with verses fifty-one and fifty-two of the *āl-Qalam* sura (The Pen). India, eighteenth century. Riyadh, Rifa'at Shaikh al-Ard Collection.

5. The *āl-Durr āl-Munazzam* (string of pearls) amulet, described in the *Kitāb Shams āl-Ma'ārif* by Abu al'Abbas al-Buni (d. 1225).

6. An al-Buni talisman with the tetrad of magic names and the names of the kings of jinns.

7. Talisman in the form of a magic square, still in use today in North Africa as a counter spell. It is used to fight impotence and to favor mating.

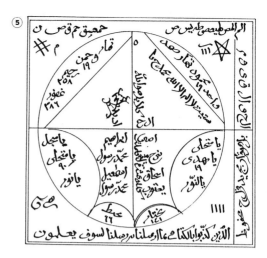

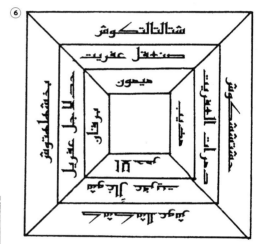

EXAMPLES FROM SCIENTIFIC TREATISES

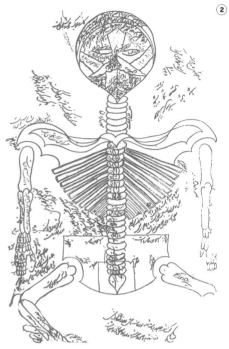

1. Page from a "Cosmogony" drawn in Iraq. Baghdad, Qahtane al-Madfa'i Library.

2. Table from the *Canon*—a fourteen-volume treatise by the Turkish Ibn Sina, better known in the West as Avicenna (c. 980–1037). London, Wellcome Institute for the History of Medicine.

3. Quadrature of the star Sirius, from a sketch by Nur al-Din al-Bitruji of Córdoba, known in the West as Alpetragius (d. 1204).

4. Astrological chart drawn in *zūlf āl-Ārus* (the style known as "the bride's curls"). Tunisia, eighteenth century.

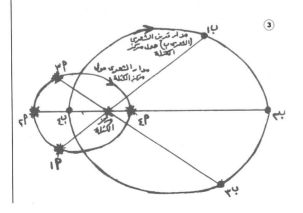

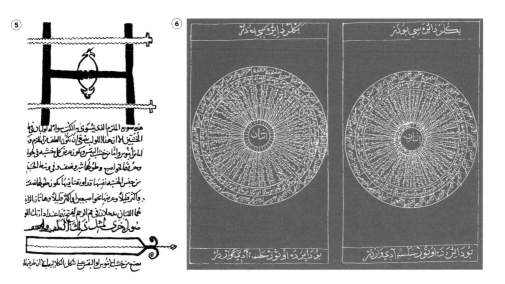

5. A page from *āl-Taṣrīf liman ʿajaz ʿan āl-Taʿalif* (Manual of Surgery) by Abu al-Qasim al-Zahrawi (d. c. 1013; known in Europe as Abulcasis). London, Ms. Hunt, f. 85r.

6. Two pages from the "Treatise on the psychiatry of spirits" by Sultan Mughi al-Din. Turkey, eighteenth century.

7. A page from the "Treatise on the brightest stars for use in constructing mechanical clocks" by Taqi al-Din (1565).

8. A table taken from the "Treatise for the identification of psychological truths" by the Sufi physician Abu Abdallah al-Jazuli (d. c. 1470).

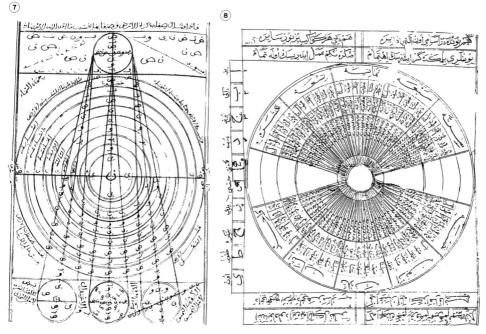

① كِتاب

إِصطِلاحات الصّوفيّة

تصنيف

كمال الدّين ابى الغنائم عبـد الرّزاق
ن جمال الدّين الكـاشى السّمرقندى
متوفى ٧٣٠ هجنة

1, 2. Frontispiece and two pages of the *Kitāb ālī-Istilāḥat āl-Ṣūfiya* (Sufi Terminology) by the Sufi master Kamal al-Din al-Qashani of Samarkand, Uzbekistan. It gives the esoteric and mystical values of the letters of the Arabic alphabet.

3. Four pages from the "Code of Calligraphy" by Abu Ali Muhammad ibn Muqla (d. 940) taken from the 1663 facsimile composed by Muhammad al-Shafa'i. Cairo, National Library.

②

باب الالف (٢)

من هدانا في ظلمة استار الجلال ۞ الى
نور الجمال ۞ محمد المصطفى و على آله
و صحبه خير صحب و آل ۞ و بعد ۞ فانى
لما فرغت من تسويد شرح كتاب منازل
السائرين وكان الكلام فيه وفيّ شرح نصوص
الحكم وتاويلات القرآن الحكيم مبنياً على
اصطلاحات الصوفية ولم يتعارف اكثر اهل
العلوم المنقولة والمعقولة ولم يشتهر بينهم
ذلك سألوني ان اشرحها لهم وقد اشرت
في ذلك الشرح الى ان الاصول المذكورة
فى الكتاب من مقامات القوم يتفرع الى
الف مقام ولوّحت الى كيفية تفريعها وما
بينت كيفية تقاريبها بتنويها ولم افصل
فروعها ودرجاتها ولم اصرح بصنوفها و تعريفها
صدّيت للاسعاف بسؤالهم وزدت على
ذلك ترويحا لقبولهم بيان ما أجيب من

الحمد لله الذى نجّانا من مباحث العلوم
الرسمية بالمن والانفصال ۞ وافضنا بروح
المعاينة من مكابدة النقل والاستدلال ۞
وانقذنا مما لا طائل تحته من كثرة القيل
والقال ۞ وعصمنا من المناظرة والمعارضة
والخلاف والجدال ۞ فانها مثار الشبه ومظان
الريب والشك والضلال والاضلال ۞
فسبحان من كشف من بصائرنا حجب
الاغيار والاشكال والإشكال ۞ والصلوة على

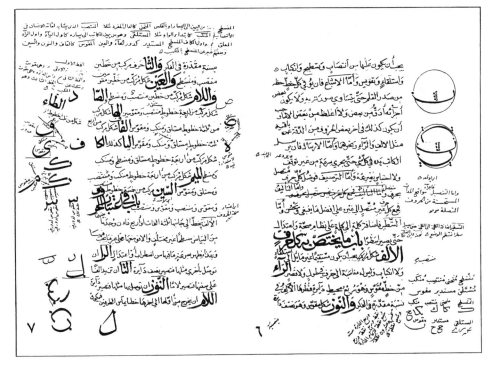

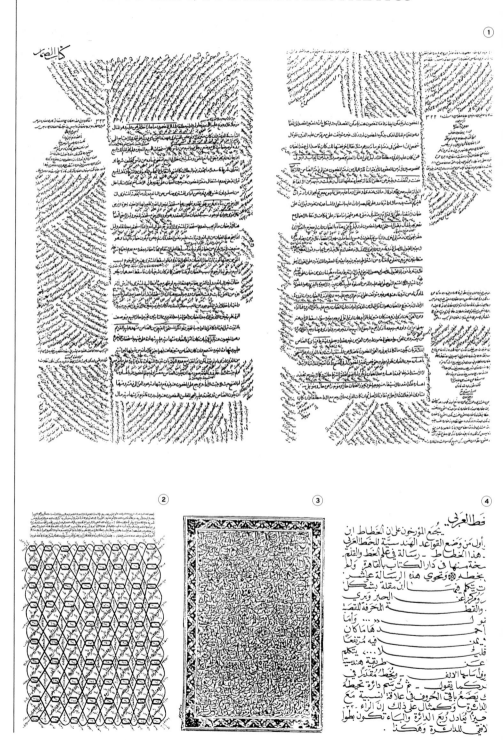

1. Arab grammar written by Muhammad Tabizi in 1872: the text is in the center with notes and glosses in the margins. Marrakesh, Morocco, B. Wardi Library.

2. Introductory page from a Qur'ān drawn in Kano, Nigeria.

3. Page written in Andalusian script. Madrid, Escorial Museum.

4. Page containing text drawn by Hassan Massoudi, twentieth century.

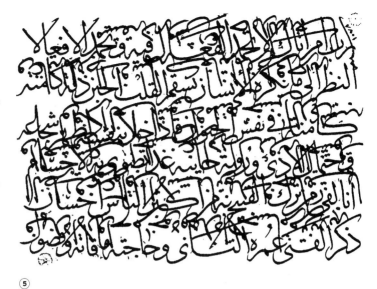

⑤

5. Calligraphic exercise of a text that can be read with double meanings, written in *thuluth* style by Mahmut Celaleddin Dagistani (d. 1829), Turkey.

6. Calligraphic exercise of a text that can be read with double meanings written in *thuluth* style by Sheikh Hamdullah (1436–1520), Turkey.

⑥

COMPOSITIONS AROUND A CENTRAL AXIS

1. "The Light Verse"
(Qur'ān, 24:35), six-
teenth century, from the
central cupola of Saint
Sophia, Istanbul.

2. Central axis composi-
tion, in different characters, with emphasis on
the letter *sin*, by Abd al-
Kader, Tunisia, twenti-
eth century.

3. Decoration of the
cupola of the Selemiye
mosque of Istanbul,
drawn in *thuluth* by
Hasan al-Tuzi.

4. Decorative composi-
tion, drawn in *thuluth*
at the end of the six-
teenth century, from the
Sokollu Mehmet Pasha
mosque in Istanbul.

STYLES, VARIANTS, AND CALLIGRAPHIC ADAPTATIONS

TILE COMPOSITIONS FOR MURAL DECORATIONS

1. Mural from the Grand Mosque of Isfahan, Iran. It reads: *Muḥammad rasūl Āllāh, āl-Ṣādiq āl-Āmīn.*

2. Mural from the Shahid Mathara *madrasa* of Tehran, Iran: *Īā Muḥammad.*

3. Mural from the Grand Mosque of Isfahan, Iran: *Bir zadū mubīrān ʿamal sanjīdad.*

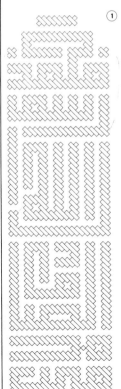

4. The *shahāda*, a mural from the Aliqula aqa mosque of Isfahan, Iran.

5. Mural from the Grand Mosque of Izd, Iran: *Ālqūt Īllāh*.

6. Mural from the Kasah Gran madrasa of Isfahan, Iran: *Āllāhu Ākbar*.

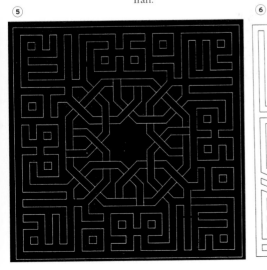

STYLES, VARIANTS, AND CALLIGRAPHIC ADAPTATIONS

1. Koranic sura no. 112: *āl-Īkhlāṣ* (Pure Faith), drawn by Ahmed Karahisari (Turkish, 1468–1556).

2. *Shahāda* done in a geometric composition often used in mural decorations.

3. The phrase *Ālhamdu Lillāhi* (Glory to God) in a geometric composition.

4. Mural composition found in the Sultan Muayiad mosque of Cairo, containing the koranic verse 2:255: *Āllāh, lā īlāha illā hw . . .* (God, no other God but Him . . .).

5. Compositon in geometric Kufic: *Āllāh-Hū* (God-Him).

6. Composition with the names: *Āllāh, Muḥammad, Ābu Bakr, Umar, Uthmān, Alī, Talḥa, Zūbair, Saad, Said, Abd Allāh, Abd āl-Raḥmān.* Drawn by Ahmed Karahisari (Turkish, 1468–1556)

for the Ahmed mosque of Istanbul, and replicated in the al-Bardini mosque of Cairo.

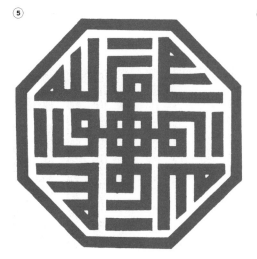

COMPOSITIONS IN THE SHAPE OF *SIKKÉ*

1. The phrase *Yā ḥazzeti Mevlāna* (O, our saintly Master), drawn by the Sufi *mevlevi* Mehmed Nazif Bey (1846–1913). Konya, Turkey, Museum of the Mevleviyya.

2. Calligraphy by Fevzi Gunuc, student of Huseyn Kurtlu, known as the Imam. Konya, Turkey, Seljuk University.

3. The two names of God: *Ḥayyu, Qayyūm* (the Living, the Subsisting), drawn in 1773 by the Sufi *qadiri* Haji Amin Siri.

4. The phrase *Yā Hū* (O, Him), drawn in 1908 by Necmeddin Okyay (1883–1976).

5. The artist's own name, drawn by the Sufi *jerrahi-halveti* Jibrail Mandel Khan, 1984.

6. The phrase *Yā hasirat Mevlāna Muḥammad Jalāl āl-Dīn Rūmī* (O, our sweet Master Muhammad Jalāl āl-Din Rumi), drawn by Mehmet Emin Efendi, 1923.

STYLES, VARIANTS, AND CALLIGRAPHIC ADAPTATIONS

COMPOSITIONS IN THE SHAPES OF DIFFERENT OBJECTS

1. *One night, under the crescent moon . . .* Composition by Hamed the Egyptian, Cairo, twentieth century.

2. Amphora decorated with the invocation *Yā Fattāḥ, yā Karīm* (O Conqueror, O Generous One). Calligraphy by Basur Ibraya, Iraq, twentieth century.

3. Amphora decorated with specular calligraphy (*muthannā*), by Mazhar Shevket, Istanbul, twentieth century.

4. Amphora with two specular *waw* letters done in *gulzār* style, Turkey, eighteenth century.

5. Amphora decorated by Muhammad Izzat al-Karkuki (Istanbul, 1904–1986).

6. Amphora containing the phrase *Wa Hū, ʿAlī, kul shaya qadīr*, drawn by Basur Ibraya.

ZOOMORPHIC COMPOSITIONS

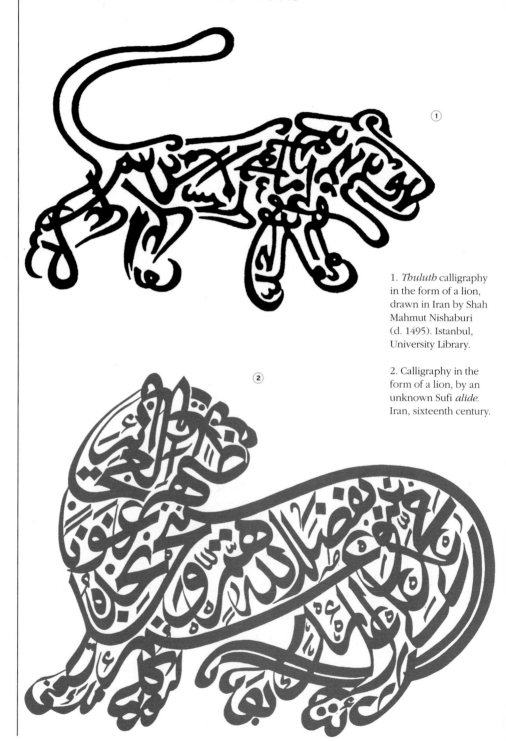

1. *Thuluth* calligraphy in the form of a lion, drawn in Iran by Shah Mahmut Nishaburi (d. 1495). Istanbul, University Library.

2. Calligraphy in the form of a lion, by an unknown Sufi *alide*. Iran, sixteenth century.

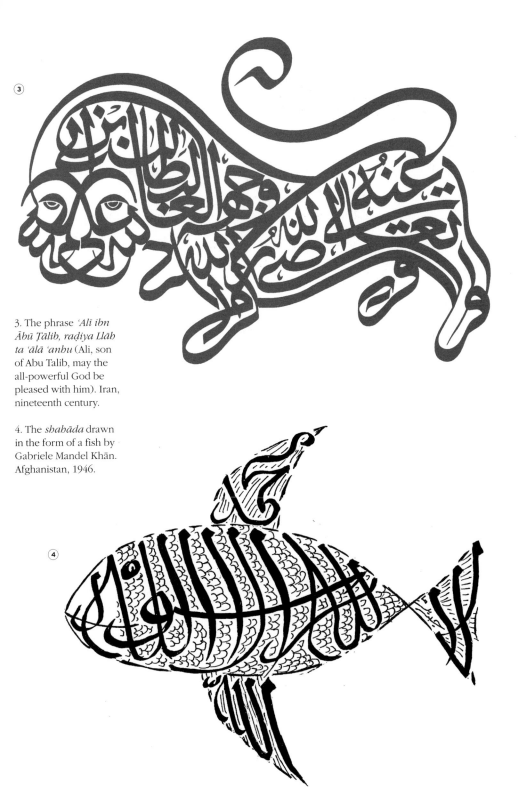

3. The phrase *'Alī ibn Ābū Ṭālib, raḍiya Llāh ta 'ālā 'anhu* (Ali, son of Abu Talib, may the all-powerful God be pleased with him). Iran, nineteenth century.

4. The *shahāda* drawn in the form of a fish by Gabriele Mandel Khān. Afghanistan, 1946.

STYLES, VARIANTS, AND CALLIGRAPHIC ADAPTATIONS

COMPOSITIONS IN THE SHAPES OF BIRDS

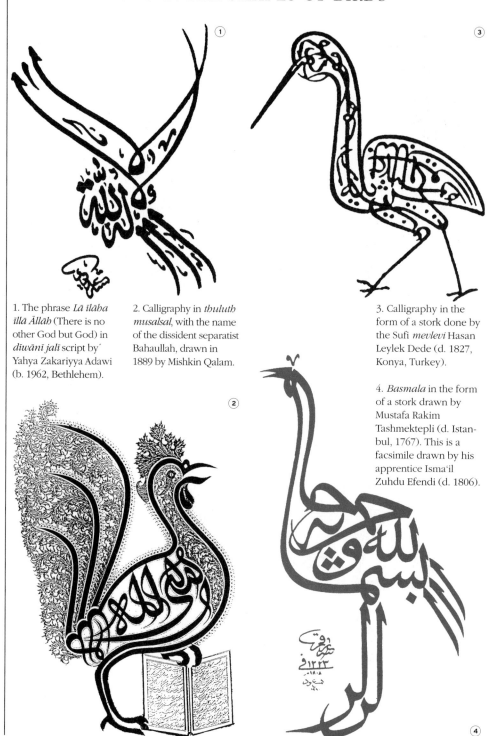

1. The phrase *Lā ilāha illā Āllāh* (There is no other God but God) in *dīwānī jalī* script by´ Yahya Zakariyya Adawi (b. 1962, Bethlehem).

2. Calligraphy in *thuluth musalsal*, with the name of the dissident separatist Bahaullah, drawn in 1889 by Mishkin Qalam.

3. Calligraphy in the form of a stork done by the Sufi *mevlevi* Hasan Leylek Dede (d. 1827, Konya, Turkey).

4. *Basmala* in the form of a stork drawn by Mustafa Rakim Tashmektepli (d. Istanbul, 1767). This is a facsimile drawn by his apprentice Isma'il Zuhdu Efendi (d. 1806).

5. *Thuluth* calligraphy in the form of a bird, Turkey, twentieth century.

6. Shiite prayer in the form of a hawk, drawn in *thuluth* style by Muhammad Fathiyab, Iran, nineteenth century.

7. Talisman with the *basmala*, drawn in the form of a bird on faience. Iznil, Turkey, 1760.

STYLES, VARIANTS, AND CALLIGRAPHIC ADAPTATIONS

ZOOMORPHIC AND ANTHROPOMORPHIC COMPOSITIONS

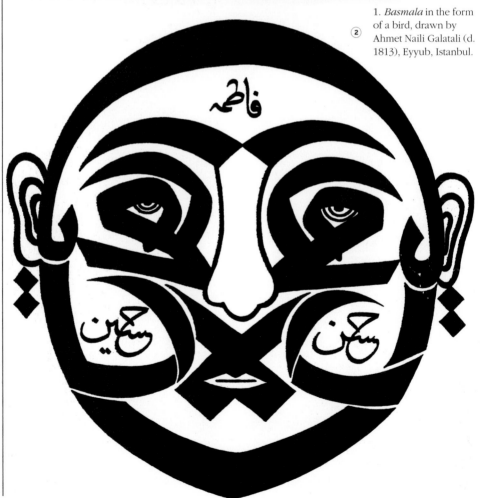

1. *Basmala* in the form of a bird, drawn by Ahmet Naili Galatali (d. 1813), Eyyub, Istanbul.

2. Composition containing the names *Muḥammad, ʿAlī, Ḥassan, Ḥusaīn, Fāṭima*, Iran, nineteenth century. Tehran, *Dergah* of the Nimatallah.

3. Amulet protecting against "transgression of the interdict" with the names *Ḥasan, Muḥammad, Alī, Āllāh*. Drawn in the form of a human face by Mirza Zahde Isfahani. Iran, 1816.

4. Shiite prayer in *naskhī* style drawn in the shape of a horse by Sayyid Husain Ali. Iran, 1848.

COMPOSITIONS IN THE SHAPES OF PLANTS AND FRUITS

1. *Basmala* in a pear-shaped composition, drawn by Abdel Aziz al-Rifaʻi, 1924.

2. *Basmala* in the shape of a tree, drawn by Gabriele Mandel. Kabul, Afghanistan, 1946.

3. The Tree of Life.
Calligraphy by Izzet
Efendi, Turkey, 1912.

4. A pear-shaped
composition drawn
by Mehmet Shefik
Bey (1819–1879).
Istanbul, Sabanci Hat
Kollesiyonu.

5. *Dīwānī* calligraphy in
the form of a pear with
the phrase: *Alḥamdu
Lillāhi, Rabbi āl'ālamīn*
(Glory to God, Lord of
the Worlds), by Nasib
Makarim. Lebanon.

ARCHITECTURAL COMPOSITIONS

1, 2. The *shahāda* in
geometric Kufic, Turkey,
nineteenth century.

3. The *shahāda* in geometric Kufic, Turkey, nineteenth century.

4. The phrase *Wa Hū, 'ala kul shaya qadīr*, drawn in *thuluth* script, Turkey, nineteenth century.

5. The *basmala* in geometric Kufic, Turkey, nineteenth century.

STYLES, VARIANTS, AND CALLIGRAPHIC ADAPTATIONS

EXAMPLES OF CALLIGRAPHY ON FAIENCE PLATES

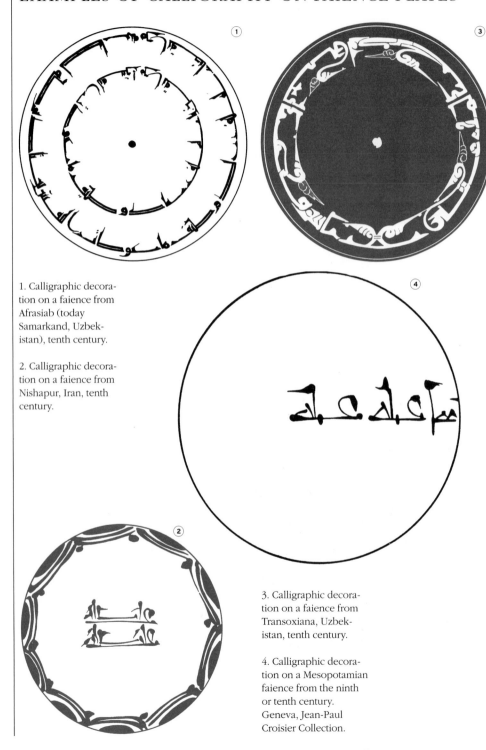

1. Calligraphic decoration on a faience from Afrasiab (today Samarkand, Uzbekistan), tenth century.

2. Calligraphic decoration on a faience from Nishapur, Iran, tenth century.

3. Calligraphic decoration on a faience from Transoxiana, Uzbekistan, tenth century.

4. Calligraphic decoration on a Mesopotamian faience from the ninth or tenth century. Geneva, Jean-Paul Croisier Collection.

5. Calligraphic decoration from an Andalusian faience, eighth century. The motif is taken from a mural found in the Alhambra of Granada, Spain.

6. Contemporary calligraphic decoration in a traditional motif, drawn on faience by Gabriele Mandel. Museum of Art, São Paulo, Brazil.

STYLES, VARIANTS, AND CALLIGRAPHIC ADAPTATIONS

CALLIGRAPHY AND OPENWORK METALS

1. Openwork iron design for use in the gold-leaf printing of a leather case, created by special order of Shah Sulayman I in 1693. We can read in *thuluth* characters: *Na'am: Innahu min Sulaymān wa innahu Bismi Llāhi āl-Raḥmani āl-Raḥimi* (Yes, he comes from Solomon, and in truth here he is: in the name of God, the Mercy-giving, the Merciful).

2. The names *Āllāh, Muḥammad, Alī* done in openwork metal embroidery on an Ottoman banner decoration, Turkey, seventeenth century. Istanbul, Topkapi Sarayë Museum.

3. Openwork iron decoration of the quiver of Ottoman Sultan Ahmed III (1673–1736). Designed by Hafiz Osman (1642–1698). Istanbul, Topkapi Sarayë Museum.

4. Openwork design on gold foil by Necmeddin Okyay (1883–1976), done by Mehmet Koseoglu, Konya, Turkey.

5. Openwork decoration on gold foil done by Oglu Rahim, representing a *sikké* (the hat worn by the Sufi *mevlevi*) placed on a throne. It contains the name of Jalal al-Din Rumi. The original sixteenth-century design is in the Mevleviyya Museum of Konya, Turkey.

STYLES, VARIANTS, AND CALLIGRAPHIC ADAPTATIONS

LEARNING HOW TO WRITE

1. A page from the book of exercises *Her Hakki mahfuz dur*, published by the Hayrat Vakfi Neshriyati. Istanbul, 1983.

2. A page from the book of calligraphy exercises *Khudāmūz khūshnūysā* by Ismail Qujani. Iran, Capdaham, 1955.

3. A page from the famous treatise *Mizānü al-Hatt* (A Measure of Calligraphy) by Hakkak-zade Mustafa Hilmi Efendi (Istanbul, 1763–1852), great-uncle of the author of this book and professor of calligraphy at the Validesultan Nakshidil School.

4. A page of *thuluth* calligraphy, by Muhammad Sijelmassi and Abdelkebir Khatibi.

⑤

الجمهورية العربية المتحدة

وزارة التربية والتعليم

الخط العربي

الكراسة الثانية

اسم التلميذ   المدرسة   السنة الدراسية

أنشأها وكتبها بتكليف من وزارة التربية والتعليم فنخبة من الأساتذة:

سيد إبراهيم   محمد علي المكاوي   عبد القادر عاشور   عبد الحميد حسن

ملتزم الطبع والنشر دار المعارف بمصر

5, 6. Frontispiece and page from the *ālkhatt ā'arabiyya* calligraphy notebook by Muhammad al-Makawi, et al.

⑥

٣٣

بركة كريم زكى ركع كاتب انكال شكل شكلك يكلف عليكم

إلى جانبك لقومك يحبوك   أكرم صغارهم كما تكرم كبارهم يكرموك ويرفعوك

ك

لك

كا

شكر

STYLES, VARIANTS, AND CALLIGRAPHIC ADAPTATIONS

167

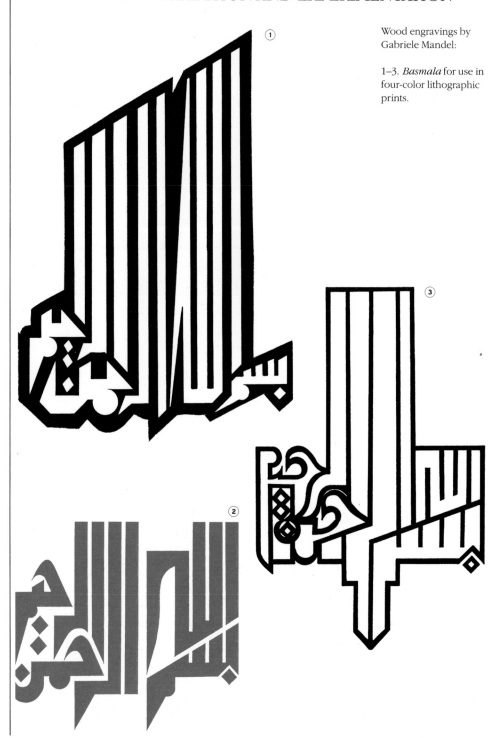

Wood engravings by
Gabriele Mandel:

1–3. *Basmala* for use in
four-color lithographic
prints.

4. Turkish proverb: "Patience is the key to serenity."

5. Emblem of the Islamic Cultural Center and Mosque of Milan.

6. Title of the book *Arabic Homilies on the Nativity*, edited by the Bishop of Jerusalem and published by Pier Francesco Fumagalli for the 2000 Jubilee. Calligraphy and decoration are done in the classic Kufic tradition.

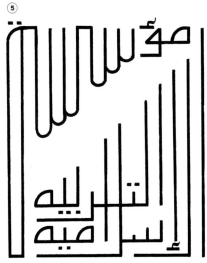

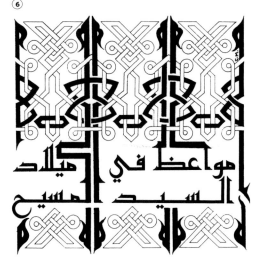

STYLES, VARIANTS, AND CALLIGRAPHIC ADAPTATIONS

CONTEMPORARY CALLIGRAPHY

4. Calligraphy consisting of the repeated word *āl-Ḥurriyya* (Liberty). Work of Hassan Massoudi, b. Nejef, Iraq.

5. Modern calligraphy containing the phrase *Lā īlāha īllā Āllāh* (There is no other God but God). Calligraphy by Emin Barin (1913–1996), Bolu, Turkey.

1. Modern calligraphy by Muhammad Meleti, Morocco.

2. Modern calligraphy by Muhammad Meleti, Morocco.

3. Modern calligraphy (the word *Āllāh* repeated ten times) by Emin Barin (1913–1996), Bolu, Turkey.

6. Modern calligraphy (the word *Āllāh* repeated eight times) by Emin Barin (1913–1996), Bolu, Turkey.

②

③

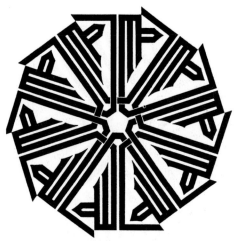

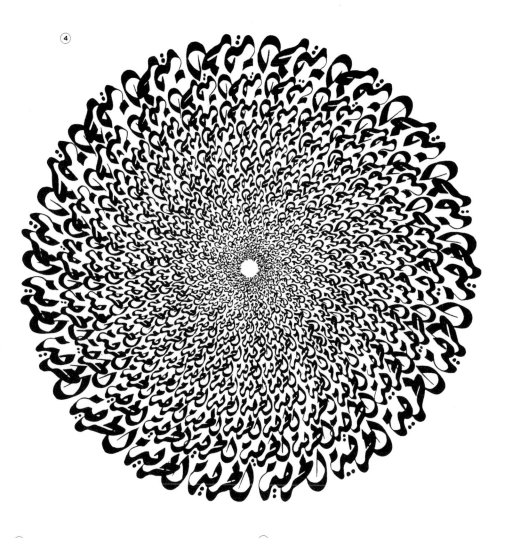

STYLES, VARIANTS, AND CALLIGRAPHIC ADAPTATIONS

1. The name *Āllāh* in an openwork design in wood by Halil Acikgoz. Konya, Turkey, twentieth century.

2. Emblem of the city of Ilgin, Turkey. From a modern relief sculpted by Mehmet Buyukcanga, Konya, Turkey. The design is laid out so it can be read in Latin characters, but it still represents the correct Arabic spelling of the name.

3. The name *Āllāh* repeated four times in a calligraphy by Emin Barin (1913–1996) of Bolu, Turkey.

4. Wood-engraved frontispiece of the short story "Oasis of Roses" by Gabriele Mandel, published in Kabul, Afghanistan, in 1946.

5. "French-Arab" calligraphic anagram designed by Khalil Abu Arafa in 1957 in Jerusalem for an edition of the celebrated *Sons et lumières* festival of Paris.

(2)

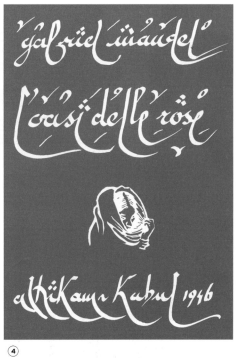

(4)

(3)

(5)

STYLES, VARIANTS, AND CALLIGRAPHIC ADAPTATIONS

173

NARRATION THROUGH IMAGES

(1)

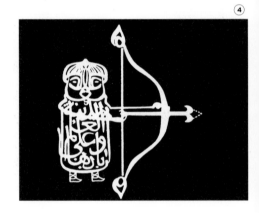

(2)

A Sufi short story.

1, 2, 3. He who is enamored (of God), passion symbolized by a lion, and the bow of spiritual strength.

4, 5, 6. The lover of God grasps the bow, stretches it, and throws an arrow against the lion-passion.

7, 8, 9. The lion bends down, avoiding the arrow, which strikes the eye of the beloved (God).

(4)

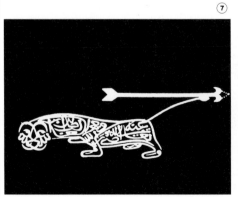

(7)

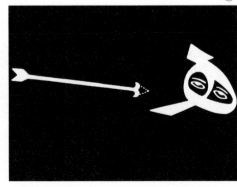

(8)

3

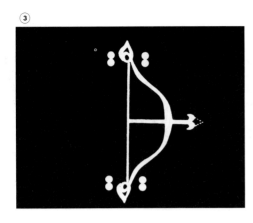

5

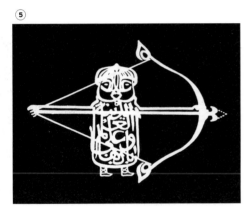

6

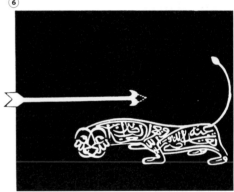

9

Calligraphic images
from a Turkish film in
which the mystical love
story is narrated through
figured drawings by
Amentii Gemisi.

GLOSSARY

ābjad: The system of equivalence among the letters of the Arab alphabet and numbers. Because each letter corresponds to a number, and vice versa, names also yield significant numbers, and these numbers, in turn, yield other terms on which the art of esoteric interpretation is based. *See also* **'ilm āl-Ḥurūf.**

āqlām-i sitta: A term meaning "the six classic styles." They are: **muḥaqqaq, rīḥān, thuluth, naskhī, tawqī'**, and **riqā'**. A good calligrapher was expected to study, recognize, and write all of them.

āl-Āsma' āl-Ḥusna: The loveliest Names (of God). They are the ninety-nine name-attributes of God quoted in the Qur'ān that calligraphers often draw individually or in different combinations.

antonymy: *See* **recitation of the Qur'ān.**

basmala: The formula *Bismi Āllāhi āl-Raḥmani āl-Raḥymi* (In the name of God, the Mercy-giving, the Merciful) with which all of the Qur'ān's suras begin (except for the ninth), as well as each act of a pious Muslim.

budūḥ: An artificial talismanic name, usually inscribed within a magic square (*jadwal*). To some authors this word means "fat," referring to a woman; for others it is the name of a spirit (*jinn*) or an ancient magician-king; actually, it has no meaning at all in Arabic.

characteristics of the alphabet letters: *See* **recitation of the Qur'ān.**

Fertile Crescent (or Fertile Half-Moon): The geographic area extending from Egypt to Mesopotamia. Starting with the Romantic period, the Europeans gave it this name because this strip of tillable land running along the African coast with the sea to the north and the desert to the south is shaped like a moon sickle.

ḍamma: A diacritical mark, similar to a lower-case *waw*, placed above a letter; it indicates the short *u* vowel.

dīwānī: A strongly balanced, slanted cursive style, written from top to bottom and right to left; it is a combination of **thuluth, naskhī,** and **rīḥān.** It was probably created by the fifteenth-century Turkish calligrapher Ibrahim Munif; its preeminent exponent was the seventeenth-century calligrapher Shahla Pasha. The style takes its name from the Turkish term *Divan-i humayun,* which means Council of Ministers.

fatḥa: A diacritical mark consisting of an oblique hyphen placed above the letter; it indicates a short *a* vowel.

fawātiḥ ḥurūf muqatta'a: Letters found at the beginning of the twenty-nine suras of the Qur'ān. They are fourteen in all, half of the Arab alphabet: a, ḥ, r, s, ṣ, t, ', q, k, l, m, n, h, y. They are used in amulets and talismans.

ghubār or **ghubārī:** A term meaning "dust" or "dusty." Any kind of microscopic writing, especially using **naskh.**

hamza (*āl-Qaṭ'i* when disjunctive; *āl-Waṣli* when conjunctive): A diacritical mark consisting of a sort of small initial *'ayn* placed above the letter. Some grammarians consider it a consonant and position it in place of *alif* in the alphabetical sequence. It may be accompanied by short vowels (**ḍamma, fatḥa,** and **kasra**) and then it is read respectively *ū, ā, ī*. When this letter is at the beginning of a word and above the *alif*, it represents a sound immediately blocked by the movement of the glottis (the glottal stop); when it occurs in the middle of a word, supported orthographically by an *alif* or a *waw*— or even a *ya* without the two dots and pronounced *ā*—it signifies a clear detachment from the preceding syllable, or a pause in the voice. When it occurs

at the end of a word, it is written without the supporting letter and therefore on the line, and it reads *a'*.

ḥarf (plural, *ḥurūf*): A letter of the alphabet (*see* **ḥurūf āl-Hijā'**).

hat: *See* **khaṭṭ.**

ḥurūf āl-Hijā': Letters of the alphabet; singular, *ḥarf.* The Islamic science that includes the subdivision of words into single letters, the study of their articulation, and the type of sound or pronunciation with the relative points of the phonetic system (*makhārji*). Thus, distinctions are made between the guttural (or laryngeal) letters *āl-Ḥalqiyya*; the prepalatal letters *āl-Niṭ'iyya*; the lingual letters *āl-dhawlaqiyya*; and the labial letters *āl-Shajiriyya.* According to the rules of articulation the letters are separated into "striking" or voiced (*majihūra*) and "stifled" or unvoiced (*mahmūsa*); velar (*muṭbaqa*) or "open" and non-velar (*munfatiḥa*); raised (*musta'liya*) and lowered (*munkhafida*). According to the degree of openness, they are separated into occlusive (*shadida*), constrictive (*rikhwa*), and intermediate (*bayniyya*).

Ḥurūf, 'ilm āl: *See* **'ilm āl-Ḥurūf.**

ijāza: *See* **riqā'.**

'ilm āl-Ḥurūf: In Islam, the science of letters is a branch of *Jafr*, a philosophical term indicating a vision of the world on a supernatural, cosmic scale. From this, the word came to indicate the science of prophesying, or more generally, the science of foretelling and predicting the future by applying various techniques such as numerology and letter decoding. With time, a literary form of *Jafr* was born, apocalyptic and oracular at the same time, that based itself on the letters of the alphabet and in turn created the Cabala in the Jewish world. Handled by magicians, at first *Jafr* was only used to study onomatomancy proper (that is, the science of divination by interpreting the sound and pronunciation of words), but because of the esoteric meanings found in the apocalyptic texts, it later became a true, independent *sīmīya'* (σημεια in white magic). Each of the twenty-eight letters of the Arabic alphabet was assigned a numerical value that, instead of following the regular alphabetic order (**ḥurūf āl-Hijā'**), followed an order that was probably derived or adapted from similar Canaanite practices applied to the first eighteen letters of the alphabet (*ā, b, j, d,* etc.). For the last ten letters, the numerical value is chiefly Arabic (in the section relating to each letter we also give its numerical value). This system was also called **Ābjad,** from the first letters arranged in this manner.

jalī (**jalīl**): A term indicating any large writing style, especially the **thuluth.**

kasra: A diacritical mark consisting of an oblique stroke below the letter; it indicates the short *i* vowel.

khaṭṭ (in Turkish, *hat*): A term indicating both writing and calligraphy.

kīrāmīz (in antiquity, *pīrāmūz*): The first hand of Muslim Iran, of which no example has survived except for the facsimile of a page created by Badri Atabay in 1972.

Kufic (or Cufic): This term derives from Kufa, an Iraqi city founded in the year 638. Kufic writing styles were created not only in that area, but also in the region of Hijaz, for example, in Mecca and Medina. The term refers to a set of hands, usually angular and imposing, that are the first classical examples of Arabic writing. At first, Kufic did not have diacritical signs. According to Ibn al-Nadim, a tenth-century scholar, this script is derived from *āl-Hīrī,* one of the four types of pre-Islamic scripts. These are: *āl-Hīrī,* meaning from the city of Hira; *āl-Ānbārī* (from the city of Anbar); *āl-Makkī* (from the city of

Mecca); and *āl-Madanī* (from the city of Medina). Until the ninth century, it was the most widely used hand for writing the Qur'ān; later, it lost its first place to the strong and fast imposition of cursive styles. Among the many forms of Kufic, especially those with foliate or plaited decorations, we note *āl-Kūfī āl-Muraqqa'*. A very elegant, aesthetically well-composed type is Qarmatian Kufic, also called Eastern Kufic.

madda: A term meaning "extension," also known as *alif madda*. When two beginning *alifs* are written one next to the other, or when a final *alif* is followed by a **hamza,** only one *alif* is written; a sign, the *madda* (a tiny *alif* written horizontally) is placed above it. It signifies an extension of the vowel *a*.

maghribī: An elaborate style from North Africa and Muslim Spain, derived from **Kufic** but more rounded. Some letters, such as *fa* and *qaf*, have their diacritical marks below instead of above.

maqsūra: A term meaning "restricted," also known as *alif maqsūra*; it is the letter *ya* without the two diacritical dots, placed at the end of a word and pronounced *ā*. It is equivalent to an *alif madda*.

muhaqqaq: A term meaning "strong expression," or "tight"; a style with a narrow right angle in many letters. Its use began in the early fifteenth century; starting at the end of the seventeenth century, it was gradually replaced by the **thuluth** style.

musalsal: A term meaning "joined together"; used to express highly skilled calligraphy in which all the letters—preferably in the **thuluth** hand—are connected together with unusual, elegant rhythmic inventions.

muthannā: Also known as *mutannāzar*, or *mūsenna*; a term meaning "self-facing." It is not so much a hand as a type of mirror, or specular, writing, when a sentence written from right to left is repeated identically from left to right. Developed by Turkish calligraphers, it was used especially with **thuluth** and Kufic hands.

naskh: A term meaning "suppression, cancellation"; an italic, or cursive, hand that originated in the earliest centuries of Arabic writing, and was already well structured by the eleventh century. It was the preferred hand in the Timurid age and again beginning in the eighteenth century, when it was revised by the Iranian Ahmad Nayrizi, who made it closer to the **nasta'līq.**

nasta'līq *(naskh-i ta'līq)*: A hand derived from combining the **naskh** and **ta'līq** hands, possibly the work of Mir Ali Tabrizi (d. 1446). Soon two currents developed: in Khurasan, by Mirza Ja'far-i Tabrizi and Azhar-i Tabrizi in the fifteenth century, and in Iran, by Abd al-Rahman-i Khwarazmi, though the latter soon disappeared. The preeminent calligrapher of the Khurasan hand was Mir Imad-i Hasani-yi Sayfi (d. 1616).

nunnation: *See* **tanwīn.**

recitation of the Qur'ān: The various rules for reciting the Qur'ān form a true discipline (*tajwīd*) based on correct psalmody (*tartīl*) of the various letters, both consonants (*sāmita*) and vowels (*musawwita*), with rhythms, accents, and pauses that take into account characteristics such as sonority, elevation, occlusion, softening, tonicity, moderation, whistling, vibration, softness, deflection, repetition, diffusion, extension, concealment, nasalization, and antonymies such as whispering, lowering, opening, volubility, atony. For each letter of the alphabet, we have given its intrinsic value according to the recitation of the Qur'ān.

rīḥān (or *rīḥanī, rayḥān, rayḥānī*): A word for the herb basil; a reduced version of **muhaqqaq**, when used in the **naskh** format. It was replaced in the seventeenth century by *naskh*.

riqā' (in Turkish, *ijāza* or *khatt-i ijāza*): A reduced version of **tawqī'.**

sauāqiṭ āl-Fātiḥa: The seven letters of the Arab alphabet (*f, j, sh, th, z, kh, ẓ*) that are not included in the text of the first Qur'ān sura (*āl-Fātiḥa*) and are considered important in the preparation of talismans.

shahāda (or *tashahhud*, a testimonial of faith): The formula "[āshhadu anna] lā ilāh illa Āllāh, [āshhadu anna] Muḥammad rasūl Āllāh": "[I witness that] there is no other God but God, [I witness that] Muhammad is God's prophet."

shikasta ta'līq: From *shikasta*, meaning "fractional": an Iranian variant of **ta'līq** but written more rapidly, developed in the fourteenth century by Khwaja Taj Salmani-i Isfahani (d. 1491). Difficult to read, it lost ground in favor of **nasta'līq** at the beginning of the sixteenth century.

shikasta nasta'līq (*khatt-i shikasta*): A type of **nasta'līq** with influences from **shikasta ta'līq,** which originated in Iran under Safavid rule at the beginning of the eighteenth century. It was used especially for correspondence, and became widespread in Ottoman Turkey for official correspondence, but not much else.

siyāqat (*siyāq*): A writing that was already in use under the Omayyads for accounting registers and everyday bureaucratic records, and still used today.

sukūn: A term meaning "quiet," also known as *jazm* (truncated); a small circle on top of the letter meaning the absence of a brief vowel.

taḥrīrī: A term meaning "epistular"; a simplified form of **shikasta nasta'līq** used for everyday correspondence.

ta'līq: A term meaning "suspension"; probably a combination of **tawqī', riqā',** and **naskhī.** It is attributed to Khwaja Abu al-Al (tenth century) or Hassan ibn Husayn ibn Ali Farisi Katib (tenth century), who were probably inspired by the sinuous shapes of the Pehlevi and Avestic alphabets. Beginning in the eleventh century, it was especially used for official bureaucratic documents. It was already fully developed by the thirteenth century, though it became fashionable only a century later, especially thanks to Ahmad ibn Ahmas-i Shirazi. It began to decline at the end of the same century, being replaced by a more calligraphic version, the **shikasta ta'līq.**

tanwīn: Nunnation; it is the doubling of **ḍamma, fatḥa,** and **kasra** (the short vowels *u, a,* and *i*) at the end of a word (twice *u*, or a special sign; twice *a*, twice *i*). As a result, these vowels are read respectively *un, an,* and *in*, and indicate the indeterminate article respectively for the nominative, accusative, and indirect cases.

tarassul: A term meaning "correspondence"; the scribes of the Council of Ministers gave this name to a simplified form of **shikasta ta'līq.**

tashdīd: Reinforcement, also known as *shaddah*: a mark that signifies a double consonant, marked as a small initial *sin* above the letter. The term is derived from the verb *ishtadda* (to be strong, robust, intense, to intensify, to be accented).

tawqī': A variant of **thuluth** with more compressed and rounded letters. In this hand, the letters *ā, d, dh, r, z, zh, l,* and *w* are connected to the following letter by a thin, sinuous upward stroke. It is used especially in colophons.

thuluth: A term meaning "one-third," because the third part of each letter is slanted; in Turkish, *sülüs*. This hand is still used today, especially in book titles. Specialists in this hand were Baysonghor (d. 1433), Asad Allah-i Kirmani (d. 1486), Abd al-Baqi-i Tabrizi (sixteenth century), Kamal al-Din Hafiz Harawi (d. 1566), Ali Quli-i Shirazi (sixteenth century), and Ali Ridha Abbasi (seventeenth century).

waṣla: A term meaning "connection," also known as *alif wasla*. A diacritical mark linking the pronunciation of the last short vowel declination of the previous word to the first syllable of the following word; the corresponding *alif* is mute.

INDEX

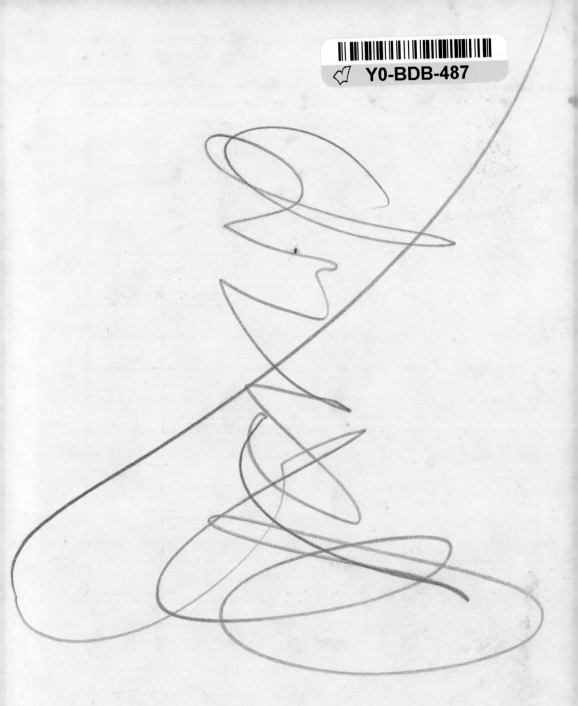

LANGUAGE FOR DAILY USE
NEW HARBRACE EDITION

NEW HARBRACE EDITION

MILDRED A. DAWSON · MARIAN ZOLLINGER

NEW YORK – CHICAGO – SAN FRANCISCO – ATLANTA – DALLAS

LEVEL BROWN

LANGUAGE FOR DAILY USE

M. ARDELL ELWELL · ERIC W. JOHNSON

HARCOURT BRACE JOVANOVICH, INC.

ACKNOWLEDGMENTS For permission to reprint copyrighted material, grateful acknowledgment is made to the following sources:

Atheneum Publishers: Illustration from *Shadow of a Bull* © 1964 by Maia Wojciechowska.

Atlantic–Little, Brown and Company: From *The Incredible Journey* by Sheila Burnford, copyright © 1961 by Sheila Burnford.

The Dial Press, Inc.: From *Canalboat to Freedom* by Thomas Fall, copyright © 1966 by Thomas Fall.

Dodd, Mead & Company, Inc.: "I Meant to Do My Work Today" from *The Lonely Dancer* by Richard Le-Gallienne, copyright 1913, 1941 by Richard LeGallienne.

Doubleday & Company, Inc.: From *Paul Bunyan and His Great Blue Ox* by Wallace Wadsworth, copyright 1926 by Doubleday & Company, Inc.; renewed 1953 by Laura C. Wadsworth.

Doubleday & Company, Inc., A. P. Watt & Son, and Mrs. George Bambridge: From "If" by Rudyard Kipling, © 1910 by Rudyard Kipling; renewed 1938 by Caroline Kipling.

E. P. Dutton & Co., Inc.: From "Quiet" in *Lad: A Dog* by Albert Payson Terhune.

Harcourt Brace Jovanovich, Inc.: "Primer Lesson" from *Slabs of the Sunburnt West* by Carl Sandburg, copyright 1922 by Harcourt Brace Jovanovich, Inc.; renewed 1950 by Carl Sandburg.

Harper & Row, Publishers, Incorporated: From *Charlotte's Web* by E. B. White. From *Tinkerbelle* by Robert Manry. From *The Wheel on the School* by Meindert DeJong, copyright 1954 by Meindert DeJong.

Holt, Rinehart and Winston, Inc.: "The Runaway" from *You Come Too* by Robert Frost, copyright 1923 by Holt, Rinehart and Winston, Inc.; renewed 1951 by Robert Frost. From *The Saturdays* by Elizabeth Enright. From "Loveliest of trees, the cherry now" from "A Shropshire Lad"—Authorized Edition—in *The Collected Poems of A. E. Housman*, copyright 1939, 1940, © 1959 by Holt, Rinehart and Winston, Inc.; copyright © 1967 by Robert E. Symons.

Little, Brown and Company: From "We never know how High" and "There is no frigate like a Book" from *The Complete Poems of Emily Dickinson.*

The Macmillan Company: From "Swift Things Are Beautiful" in *Away Goes Sally* by Elizabeth Coatsworth, copyright 1934 by The Macmillan Company; renewed 1962 by Elizabeth Coatsworth Beston.

Virgil Markham: From "How the Great Guest Came" in *The Shoes of Happiness* by Edwin Markham. From "Outwitted" by Edwin Markham.

Meredith Press: From a letter by Henry Van Dyke in *A Book of Letters*, compiled by Stella Stewart Center and Lillian Margaret Saul.

Marion Plew Ruckel: From "The Pirate Don Durk of Dowdee" by Mildred Plew Meigs in *Child Life* Magazine, copyright 1923 by Rand McNally & Company.

Scott, Foresman and Company: Entries and pronunciation key from *Thorndike-Barnhart Beginning Dictionary*, © 1962 by Scott, Foresman and Company, Chicago.

Louis Untermeyer: "Three Things," adapted from the Persian by Louis Untermeyer, from *The Golden Treasury of Poetry*, compiled by Louis Untermeyer, copyright © 1959 by Golden Press, Inc.

The Viking Press, Inc.: From *The Cheerful Heart* by Elizabeth Janet Gray, copyright © 1959 by Elizabeth Janet Gray.

Illustrated by John Buscema, Charles Fellows, Lorraine Fox, Leslie Goldstein, Joe Krush, Norman Kenyon, Symeon Shimin.

Recommendations and reviews of the titles in the feature "A Book to Read" were supplied by Jane Ann Flynn, State University College, Fredonia, New York.

Printed in the United States of America

ISBN 0-15-317275-4

CONTENTS

vii

Review Handbook

CHAPTER 1

Listening and Speaking

Millions of people all over the world sat spellbound before their radio and television sets, listening intently to words drifting down the radio waves from two American astronauts orbiting the earth 120 miles up.

The astronauts also were listening intently as their directors spoke to them from ground stations around the globe.

CAPSULE COMMUNICATOR, HAWAII: All systems on the ground look good . . .

FLIGHT DIRECTOR, HOUSTON: You're having him get out?

CC: Roger, Flight, we're GO.

FLIGHT DIRECTOR: Tell him we're ready to have him get out when he is.

CC TO GEMINI: We just had word from Houston we're ready to have you get out whenever you're ready. Give us a mark when you egress the spacecraft . . .

And so the vitally important exchange of directions and comments continued throughout the flight.

As the space walk came to an end, this conversation took place:

FIRST ASTRONAUT (inside spacecraft) TO THE CAPSULE COMMUNICATOR: This is Jim. Got any message for us?

CAPSULE COMMUNICATOR: Gemini 4. Get back in.

SECOND ASTRONAUT (outside spacecraft): OK, I'm on top of it right now.

FIRST ASTRONAUT: OK, come on in . . .

SECOND ASTRONAUT: All right . . . I'll open the door and come through there.

If it seems at first far-fetched to compare an astronaut, listening to his ground communicators, with you, listening to a teacher or parent, remember that listening skill is not acquired overnight, or even in a week or a month. You have to practice this skill' for a long time. The astronauts began early. Furthermore, exactly the same skill is required by the man floating 120 miles up in space, as by you, sitting at your desk in a classroom down on the earth.

Remember, too, that all that science has done to transmit man's thoughts and messages can be valuable only if those thoughts and messages have value. If they are unclear, or inaccurate, or misleading, the telephone and radio can do nothing to prevent them from being ineffective and even dangerous. What makes the scientific advances in communication so exciting and full of promise are, first, the fact that man can learn to communicate with language and, second, the hope that his knowledge and understanding will guide him to communicate clearly, completely, and courteously.

The inventions of science can never do more than language itself does for the betterment of mankind. The marvels of machinery can transmit the voice, but this has little meaning unless the one who is speaking has something of worth to express and expresses it well.

To Discuss

1. Does your mind wander sometimes when you are listening? Under what circumstances? Why does this happen?

2. Is it easier for you to listen when you are alone or when you are in a group? Why? Is it easier for you to listen when you know you will be questioned on what you hear?

3. Do you think there is any difference between *hearing* and *listening*? If so, what is the difference? Name some noises you *hear*. Name some things to which you *listen*.

4. Do the inventions of science in the field of communication, such as radio, make the proper use of language more, or less, important? Explain your answer.

2

Conversational Skills

A frequent need for skill in both listening and speaking occurs in conversation. Everyone would like to be able to keep people interested, to have fun talking with others, or, in more serious moments, to exchange information and ideas.

Read the passage below and decide what keeps the conversation lively.

"Hi, Fran. What do you have in that box?"

"A kitten, Emily. We can't keep her and the parakeet too. I'm taking her to the Jordan boys. Come on with me."

The Jordan boys were on their porch. "Here's pussy," said Fran. "Be good to her. I hate to give her away. She's so little she doesn't even have a name."

"We'll treat her with due respect, Fran. Let's see if she likes us," said Jim, taking her out of the box. "We've been thinking of names, but we haven't found the right one. Just listen to her purr! That's a big purr for a little puss."

"Call her Purr-Puss," said Don with sudden inspiration. "Then we'll have a 'purpose' in our lives."

"Oh, Don, what a pun!" Emily laughed. "But it's not a very good name. How about Samantha? We called our goldfish that."

"Name a cat after a goldfish! Never!" said Don. "But we'll come up with something. By the way, did you hear the program last night on animals in Africa? Dr. Roland told about visiting the Kruger Reserve where animals run at large and people stay in cages."

"People in *cages*?" asked Emily.

"Well, not exactly," Don admitted, "but people stay in their cars if they want to be safe. Dr. Roland will talk and show pictures this afternoon. We're going. Why don't you come, too?"

"Thanks. If we don't have an orchestra rehearsal, I'll come. It sounds interesting."

To Discuss

1. The following list suggests some of the signs of a good conversation. Point out examples of each in the model on page 3.

Everyone in the group listening and talking
A friendly attitude
Statements of interesting facts or opinions
Questions inviting further remarks
Explanations as needed to make points clear

2. Have you ever tried to have a conversation with someone who was not a good listener? What marks a good listener in conversation?

3. Why might a talkative person need to remind himself to draw others into the conversation?

4. If exchange of ideas brings out a difference of opinions, how can such differences be stated without hurting someone's feelings?

5. How can the tone of voice show whether the speaker means to be friendly or unfriendly? Demonstrate by reading one of the remarks in the model in contrasting tones.

6. Are there topics that should be avoided to prevent hurting feelings? Try to list some examples.

7. When or where should conversation be avoided? When should it be toned down?

8. Should persons who are naturally quiet try to talk a lot? Why or why not?

How to Hold Interesting Conversations

Think of topics that will interest others.
Do your share in the conversation.
Avoid remarks that might hurt someone's feelings.
Ask questions that encourage others to take part.
Be courteous in expressing any disagreement.
Listen to others without interrupting.

4

► **Practice: Holding Conversations**

If you are asked to start a practice conversation, try to be relaxed and informal, as you would in a real situation. Follow the guides on page 4. Here are a few ideas for topics:

An improvement needed in our school
An embarrassing experience
A television program of special interest
An athletic event
A funny incident
Favorite recordings
Books
What our city needs most
A current event
A class project

TO MEMORIZE

Primer Lesson

Look out how you use proud words.
When you let proud words go, it is not easy
    to call them back.
They wear long boots, hard boots; they walk
    off proud; they can't hear you calling—
Look out how you use proud words.

CARL SANDBURG

Carl Sandburg was one of America's most beloved writers. He is known especially for his biography of Abraham Lincoln and for his poems about the prairies, the small towns, the great cities, and the common folk of America.

In the poem above, he gives some sound advice. What is a primer? Why did he call this poem a primer lesson? Read the poem and talk about what it means. In what way could you apply its meaning to something you have discussed regarding the marks of a good conversation?

5

Giving Directions

A stranger stopped Bob on the street and asked him how to walk to the railroad station.

In his mind, Bob put himself in the position of the stranger. "I must tell him all the things he will need to know," Bob thought. "I will be careful to put the directions in the right order and not leave anything out. I will mention landmarks to help him." Here are the directions Bob gave:

Walk south on this street three blocks (pointing south).

Turn right on Wilson Street. This is the street where the old streetcar tracks are.

Go two blocks west on Wilson Street. You will come to a monument of a soldier on horseback in a small park on the left side of the street. The railroad station is on the south side of the park.

To Discuss

1. Were Bob's directions clear?
2. Do you think the directions were in the right order?
3. What landmarks did Bob mention to help the stranger?
4. Draw a map showing the route from the place where Bob was to the railroad station. Compare your map with the maps drawn by others. Did everyone show the same route? Were the directions clear?

5. If you were telling how to build a fence or load a camera, for example, would you tell what to do first, second, and so on? How could you use pictures or diagrams? How could you use demonstrations?

6. What are the characteristics of good directions? Through class discussion, prepare a set of suggestions to follow in giving directions.

▶ Practice: Giving Directions

1. Choose one of the following topics for practice in giving directions. Follow the class suggestions in **6** above.

> How to play a certain game
> How to fly a kite
> How to get from school to another place or locality
> How to drive a nail
> How to make an article of your choice
> How to set the table

2. While each speaker is giving directions, listen carefully. After he has finished, discuss them. Were they clear?

Composition: Giving Directions in Writing

A. Imagine that you are the writer of a newspaper column. Your topic for today is "How to Be Friendly." At the top of a page, list four or more things for people who wish to be friendly to try. When you have completed the list, on the same page write a paragraph including your recommendations. Try to write it so that it will make lonely people wish to follow your advice.

B. Write a humorous paragraph on one of the subjects listed below. Include at least four steps in your directions to accomplish the goal you are writing about.

> How to change your parents' minds
> How to make your sister or brother angry
> How to train your pet to do a trick

Listening for Information

Radio and television stations frequently broadcast excellent information programs, featuring speakers who are authorities on their subjects. If you can learn to listen to and remember what you hear on such programs, you will add to your knowledge, become a better student, and be a more interesting person.

To Discuss

1. In listening to radio, your ears alone bring you the message. In television, your eyes help, too. But neither eyes nor ears will be enough unless your mind is at attention. You must know what the speaker is saying. Do you know what the word *concentrate* means? How can concentrating help you to listen well?

2. As you listen, you should think how the speech can be important or interesting to you. Then you will know what you want to remember. For what purpose might you need only a speaker's main points? If you plan to retell what he is saying, might you want to remember some of the details? Which ones?

How to Listen and Remember Information

Sit where you can hear and see.
Find out what the speaker's purpose is.
Decide what parts of his speech meet your needs or interests.
Place in your "memory box" mental pictures of points to remember.
Review them, in order, to fix them in your mind.

▶ **Practice: Listening to a Program for Information**

On the facing page are pictures a speaker on television used when telling about ways in which mankind has kept records in writing. Look at the illustrations while your teacher reads you the story the speaker told. Afterward, close your book and discuss what you heard.

ILLUSTRATION 1: Here is my cat.
Her name is Patches.

Voici ma chatte.   (Vwä-see mä shät.)
Elle s'appelle Patches.   (El sä-pel Pät-ches.)

ILLUSTRATION 2: 太空人回来了

ILLUSTRATION 3: HEREISMYCAT
APSIEMANREH
TCHES

ILLUSTRATION 4: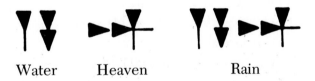

ILLUSTRATION 5:

Water   Heaven   Rain

ILLUSTRATION 6: Early Greek:

Late Greek:

Latin:

9

Some Facts About Writing Systems

In Illustration 1 the letters match the sounds of the words.

Not all people write their language with an alphabet. Chinese and Japanese, for example, use drawn lines, or characters, and each character stands for a word, as you see in Illustration 2. Unlike our system, in which letters are repeated whenever the sound is repeated, the strokes in a Japanese character differ from one word to another even when the spoken words sound the same.

Most languages that use an alphabet follow the same order we use in writing, from left to right. In the earliest Greek records, however, some scribes wrote from left to right on one line, right to left on the next, and so on, without separation of words or any punctuation. This alternating direction was called *boustrophedon*, meaning "as the ox plows." With that plan, our sentences would look like those in Illustration 3.

Before the alphabet was developed, at least two other ancient civilizations kept written records. Along the Nile, Egyptians made papyrus from reeds that grew at the river's edge and used it for rapid writing. Their sacred records, carved in stone, were written in *hieroglyphics*. Look at Illustration 4.

In Mesopotamia, between the Tigris and Euphrates rivers, people used tablets of wet clay, which they marked with a stylus. The wedge-shaped marks are called *cuneiform*, as in Illustration 5.

The alphabet was developed at least three thousand years ago, probably by Phoenicians who lived along the eastern coast of the Mediterranean Sea. The Greeks learned about it as they traded with Phoenician merchant sailors. With some changes to fit the sounds of their language, they found they could use the alphabet for writing Greek. Later, the Romans borrowed the letters from the Greeks, this time making changes to fit *their* language, Latin. See Illustration 6.

Now, most Europeans and Americans make use of the Roman, or Latin, alphabet. The alphabet of twenty-six letters provides a different sign for each sound in a word.

Listening to Directions

The main trick in listening to directions is to pay close attention. When directions are long, it is a good plan to make notes. For school assignments, the notes should contain page numbers, topics, and other details. Often, of course, it is unnecessary or inconvenient to make notes. In any case, you must use your mind as well as your ears as you listen to directions. The proof of your skill will be your ability to follow the directions you hear.

One plan to help you remember is to think of a few key words. For example, suppose your mother says, "While you are at the library, ask if we may reserve a copy of the new biography of Henry James. On the way home, please stop at Mrs. Duggan's to pick up a note she has for me." You have two things to remember, so keep in mind these key words in this order: Henry James, Mrs. Duggan.

Another way to make directions "stick" is to picture in your mind each step as it is given to you. For example:

What you hear	*What you picture*
"Turn right at a large, white farmhouse."	Try to imagine what it looks like.
"When you pass a small pond, take the next road left."	Make a mental snapshot. Can you see this picture?

To Discuss

1. When are notes needed to help you recall directions?
2. What have you found useful in helping you to remember directions?

► Practice: Listening to Directions

As your teacher reads some directions, you can test your ability to listen and follow them. The test will not be graded, but you will learn a good deal about your own listening skills. Clear your desk of books and have paper and pencil at hand.

Taking Part in Discussions

In conversation, people talk together without planning beforehand what topics to discuss. In a discussion, talk is intended to solve problems or reach conclusions about one or more selected topics. Even though discussions differ from conversations, many of the suggestions under "How to Hold Interesting Conversations," on page 4, are helpful guides for taking part in a discussion. Reread the guides and think about them as you study the model discussion below. As you read the model, notice which speakers keep to the topic and help the class make decisions.

Problem: *How Can We Learn of Good Books to Read?*

RUSS: Let's appoint a committee every month to prepare a list of books.

KAY: That's a good suggestion, but how will the committee know which books to put on the list?

RUSS: From us. Anyone who reads a good book could give the title and author to the committee.

MARTHA: Sometimes there are book reviews in magazines. They would help the committee choose books.

JEFF: Book reviews in magazines are for adults.

ROBIN: That is what I thought, Jeff, but yesterday Martha and I were in the library looking through some magazines. We found some reviews of books which may be interesting. Mother said that sometimes there are reviews of books for boys and girls in newspapers, too.

KIP: Speaking of the library—wouldn't that be the best place to learn of good books?

SID: There are some books right here in our classroom. Couldn't we have our own library? Maybe we could borrow books from school or public libraries and build up a good collection.

KAY: Maybe we could bring magazines from home, too.

KIP: Aren't we getting off the track? A classroom library is a fine idea, but we'll need another discussion to plan

12

that. Getting back to the book list, I'd like to know what the books are about.

DORIS: I was thinking about that, too. My mother keeps a card file of recipes. We could keep a card file of short book reviews. When someone reads a good book, he could write the author's name and the title on the card and also tell a little bit about the story.

MRS. O'NEIL: Are there any more suggestions? Well then, will someone summarize the suggestions that have been made? I'll write them on the board.

To Discuss

1. In the model discussion, find and read aloud examples of the following:

1. Suggestions and opinions that keep the discussion moving toward some solution
2. Suggestions that are not strictly on the topic
3. A question that helps to keep the discussion moving
4. A way of returning to the topic of discussion without hurting a classmate's feelings
5. An opinion that is not based on fact
6. A disagreement supported by facts

2. Did the group make headway in the discussion? How would you summarize the suggestions? Why is a summary a good way to end a discussion?

3. With your classmates, prepare a list of suggestions which you will follow when taking part in discussions.

▶ Practice: Holding Discussions

The class may reach decisions through discussion about one or more of the topics below. If you take part in a discussion, follow the suggestions you have prepared.

What classroom committees will we need this year?
What plans should we make for a class trip?
How can we set up a classroom library?

Using Your Voice Effectively

Have you noticed that in conversation some people are more easily understood than others? Clear speech depends on three things: *volume, rate,* and *articulation.*

To Discuss

1. What happens when you turn the *volume* up on the television set? What is another word for volume?

2. What is a *rate of speed*? What is a *rate of speaking*? Is your own rate of speaking too fast? too slow? Ask a friend.

3. Your *articulation* has to do with the distinctness of sounds you make. Give examples of poor articulation.

► **Practice: Good Habits of Speech**

1. The sounds spelled by the italicized letters in the words below are sometimes left out altogether—perhaps because of rapid speech or carelessness. Read each word aloud correctly.

fis*ts*	*l*ibrary	fif*th*	wid*th*	wha*t*
kep*t*	*e*leven	in*t*erest	fin*d*	wi*th*

2. Study the names below. What sounds should you say for the italicized letters? Read the names aloud correctly.

*R*obe*r*t	Em*i*ly	Jame*s*	Do*r*othy
Wil*l*iam	Mil*dr*ed	Louis*e*	Jac*qu*eline

3. Read aloud the words and word groups below. Say the italicized parts of the words carefully and distinctly.

le*ng*th	·poe*t*ry	pic*t*ure	wan*t to*
work*ing*	heigh*t*	proba*b*ly	leave *th*em
a*l*ready	regu*l*ar	go*ing to*	di*d you*

Going Ahead ♦ ♦ ♦ ♦

Listen to conversations for a few days as you hear them on the bus, in school corridors, and in other public places. Check them against the guides on page 4. Report to the class.

14

Alpha
Greek letter

Sounds and Spelling

Beginning with <u>A</u>

Alpha (a) is the name of the first letter in the Greek alphabet. *Beta* (b) is the second. Knowing this, can you guess the origin of the English word *alphabet*?

The Romans of old, knowing how useful an alphabet would be, borrowed the idea. They changed the letters somewhat to fit the sounds of their own language, Latin. Later, when the English used the Roman alphabet, they also made some changes. They allowed some letters to stand for more than one sound. This was especially true of vowels, and still is.

The letter *a*, for example, usually represents not only the vowel sounds in *fat* and *fate* but also in *far* and *fare*.

To spell correctly, you must know, however, that the sounds of *a* are sometimes represented by other letters. Study the list below and name the letters and letter combinations that spell each sound:

> *a* as in *fat*: lad, have, plaid
> *ā* as in *fate*: game, gaily, gay, great, reign, weigh, they
> *ä* as in *far*: cart, calm, father
> *ã* as in *fare*: pair, pear, pare, their, there, they're

Vowel pronunciations differ slightly in different localities.

Spelling Checkup

1. Dictionaries differ a little in marking sounds. Find the symbols used in yours to show the sounds of *a* given above.

2. How many words with the sound of *a* as in *fate* can you spell by filling these blanks: <u>?</u>ay, <u>?</u>a<u>?</u>e, <u>?</u>ai<u>?</u>?

3. Think of words not listed above that use the following letters to spell one of the *a* sounds: **eigh, ea, ei.**

15

Round-Table Discussions

As a result of the discussion which you read on pages 12–13, the class decided to appoint a committee of five. One day the committee decided to hold a round-table discussion of a book that many members of the class had read.

In a round-table discussion, four or five people familiar with a topic discuss it before an audience. In this discussion, the committee members were the experts and the class was the audience. The book chosen was *Big Tiger and Christian*, by Fritz Muhlenweg. It is the story of two boys who journey unexpectedly into inner Asia, where they learn a great deal about the Mongol tribes and also about themselves.

Here are some decisions the committee members made in planning their discussion:

1. They decided that the purpose of the discussion would be to point out what makes *Big Tiger and Christian* a good book.
2. They decided to answer these questions:
    a. Where did the boys start their journey? Where did they go?
    b. What was the country like?
    c. What kind of people did they meet? What did they find out about the Mongol tribes?
    d. How did the boys show that they were good travelers among strangers?
    e. What were some interesting parts of the story?
    f. Does the story have any weak points? For example, was some information left out that you wanted? Were all the descriptions clear? Did the author seem prejudiced in any way?
3. They decided to have a map to follow the boys' journey.
4. They chose a discussion leader to introduce the topic, keep the discussion moving, and give a summary.
5. They decided to invite class members to ask questions and make comments.

16

To Discuss

1. Why is it important for the group to agree on the purpose of the discussion?

2. Why is it important for the discussion group to agree on the questions to be answered?

3. How would a map help this discussion? Can you think of other things the group could show or do to add interest to the discussion?

4. What background information should the leader supply?

5. Why is a summary helpful?

6. Can you offer some helpful suggestions to follow in planning round-table discussions?

► **Practice: Holding Round-Table Discussions**

Sometime during the coming weeks, plan and take part in a round-table discussion of a book or several books. Follow the suggestions you have prepared.

Using Words Correctly: <u>let</u> and <u>leave</u>

Two verbs which are often used incorrectly are *let* and *leave*.

The verb *let* means "to allow." The verb *leave* means "to go away from" or "to go away." It is incorrect to use *leave* when you mean "allow."

Listen to these verbs as you read aloud the following sentences:

Let

1. Please *let* me go to Carol's house.
2. Dad *let* us use his tire pump.
3. Bill has *lct* us ride his horse.

Leave

1. *Leave* the party early.
2. He *left* the house before noon.
3. Has he *left* the house yet?

Use **let** when you mean "to allow."
Use a form of the verb **leave** when you mean "to go away from" or "to go away."

▶ **Practice: Using <u>let</u> and <u>leave</u>**

1. Read aloud each sentence, choosing the correct word in parentheses:

1. (Let, Leave) us look at your scrapbook, Uncle Harold.
2. (Let, Leave) me carry your package.
3. The policeman would not (let, leave) us cross the street.
4. We will (let, leave) the dog home.
5. Who has (let, left) this book on the desk?

2. Write two sentences, using *let* and *has let* correctly.

3. Write three sentences, using the verbs *leave*, *left*, and *has left* correctly.

18

Unnecessary Words

Use words that help to make your meaning clear. However, avoid unnecessary words.

Read the questions below:

1. Where was he?
2. Do you know where she is staying?

Notice that the meaning of each question is perfectly clear. It is unnecessary to end either question with the word *at*.

Now think of the meaning of *off* in each sentence below:

1. Bill got *off* his horse.
2. Carol stepped *off* the curb.

Notice that the meaning of each sentence is clear. It is unnecessary to add *of* to *off*.

► Practice: Using Words Correctly

Read aloud each sentence below, selecting the correct expression in parentheses:

1. Do you know where Jane (is, is at)?
2. I have forgotten where the old mill (is at, is).
3. Jack fell (off, off of) his bicycle.
4. Stay (off of, off) the porch.

How Our Language Grew · · ● ●

One thing to keep in mind about our language is that it is continually changing. Words such as *radio, television,* and *movies* are common, everyday words now. One hundred years ago they did not exist.

In this time of jet planes and space vehicles, new words are coming into our language at a faster rate than ever. *Astronaut* is one of these words. It comes from the Greek *astro*, which means "pertaining to the stars," and the Greek word *nautilos*, which means "sailor."

There are other words in our language that come from either *astro* or *nautilos*. See if you can think of some.

19

These tests will show you how well you remember what you have studied in this chapter. If you make a mistake in a test, take the Practice on page 21 with the same Roman numeral as this one.

Test I. Discussions

Write these sentences, selecting the word or group of words in parentheses that states the idea you prefer:

1. A discussion should (avoid, encourage) an expression of differing opinions.
2. In a discussion, a speaker should be prepared to support his opinion with (facts, more opinions).
3. In a discussion, speakers should stick to (questions agreed upon in advance, questions that will not cause arguments).
4. A good way to end a discussion is to (summarize the main points, give background information).

Test II. let and leave

Write these sentences, using the correct word in parentheses:

1. Will Mother (leave, let) the dog sleep in my room?
2. Why did you (leave, let) the book there?
3. Please (leave, let) me help you.
4. They have (let, left) us their maps, some logs, and a few cans of beans.

Test III. Good Usage

Write these sentences, using the correct words:

1. I don't know where my lunch (is, is at).
2. The man got (off, off of) his motorcycle.
3. Tell me where that town (is, is at).
4. Mary took the flowers (off, off of) the table.
5. Here is a picture of the hotel in New Orleans where we (stayed, stayed at).

Practice I.   Discussions

1. Review the lessons on pages 12–13 and 16–17.

2. Copy these two lists on the left and right sides of your paper.   Draw lines between matching groups of words.

A round-table discussion	at the end of the discussion
A summary is helpful	discourteous
Disagreements should be	keep the discussion moving
Nobody should be	should not be expressed
A question should	is held before an audience
Opinions and guesses	supported by facts

Practice II.   <u>let</u> and <u>leave</u>

1. Review the lesson on page 18.

2. Write each sentence, using *let* or *leave*, whichever is correct:

1. Please (leave, let) me hunt for him.
2. We cannot (let, leave) Tim go to your house.
3. You should (leave, let) your watch home.
4. Did Janet (leave, let) you use her skates?
5. (Let, Leave) the dog come in.

3. Write two sentences, using *let* correctly.

4. Write two sentences, using *leave* and *left* correctly.

Practice III.   Good Usage

1. Review the lesson page 19.

2. Write these sentences, using the correct words from those in parentheses:

1. I know where David (is hiding, is hiding at).
2. The car ran (off, off of) the road.
3. Where is the movie (playing, playing at)?
4. Andy jumped (off, off of) the pier.
5. Where are the rare books (kept, kept at)?

CHAPTER 2

Writing Good Sentences

You have been writing sentences for many years now. Can you tell what a sentence is? One way in which we can describe something is to tell what it does and what it looks like. Here are some of the things we can say about written sentences:

1. A sentence has a subject and a verb.
2. A sentence begins with a capital letter and ends with a period, a question mark, or an exclamation point.
3. A sentence is a group of words that makes sense by itself.

Four Kinds of Sentences

Can you name the four kinds of sentences? Find a sentence below which illustrates each kind:

1. Venus is a planet.
2. Can people live on Venus?
3. Look for information about planets.
4. How hot it is on Venus!

If you had difficulty naming the four kinds of sentences, review the following facts:

A **statement** is a sentence that tells something. It ends with a period. A statement is also called a **declarative sentence.**

A **question** is a sentence that asks something. It ends with a question mark. A question is also called an **interrogative sentence.**

A **command** or **request** is a sentence that gives an order. It ends with a period. A command or request is also called an **imperative sentence.**

An **exclamation** is a sentence that expresses surprise or strong feeling. (The exclamation may be in the form of a statement, a question, or a command, but it ends with an exclamation point instead of a period or question mark.) An exclamation is also called an **exclamatory sentence.**

Statement: Cape Kennedy is in Florida.
Question: Where is Cape Kennedy?
Command or *Request:* Look it up on a map.
Exclamation: You can't find it!
  Don't you see it even now!
  Look here!
  How slow you are!

► **Practice: Working with Sentences**

1. Read the following groups of words and tell which ones are not sentences. Those that are sentences will do one of these things: make a statement, ask a question, or give a command.

1. Where is the camping site
2. Tell us a story
3. Because Albert waited so long
4. Why did Paul wait
5. The test pilot became an astronaut
6. When Jean reported to the committee

2. Copy the groups of words above that are sentences. Punctuate them correctly.

3. Write a statement, a question, and a command or request. Be sure you begin and end each sentence correctly.

4. Study the following exclamations. Be ready to tell whether each exclamation is expressed in the form of a statement, a question, or a command. Then read the sentences aloud, letting your voice show that they are exclamations.

1. Go away!
2. You didn't tell her!
3. I won't do it!
4. What a show!

24

Read aloud each sentence, choosing the correct word or words in parentheses:

1. There weren't (any, no) foxes in this area.
2. Hasn't he (no, any) matches?
3. Wasn't there (any, no) snow in Maine?
4. Joan is (a, an) hour late.
5. Haven't you (no, any) string?
6. It was (a, an) angel cake with (a, an) icing on top.

If you made a mistake in any sentence, correct it. Turn to pages 353–54 for review and more practice.

The Two Parts of a Sentence

Read the following sentence:

A big dog barked at us.

The sentence names something: *A big dog.* It tells something the dog did: *barked at us.* A sentence has two parts:

1. **A subject** that names what the sentence is about.
2. **A predicate** that tells about the subject.

Study the sentences below. Which words in each sentence name what the sentence is about? Which words tell something about the subject?

1. The kindergarten children visited our room.
2. Each member of the class told a story.

In sentence 1, *The kindergarten children* is the subject; *visited our room* is the predicate. In sentence 2, *Each member of the class* is the subject; *told a story* is the predicate.

Now study the subjects and predicates in these sentences:

SUBJECT	PREDICATE
1. Our club	publishes a weekly newsletter.
2. Six club members	supply most of the news items.
3. Some of us	proofread the copy.

25

■ The **subject** of a sentence is the part that names what the sentence is about.

■ The **predicate** of a sentence is the part that tells something about the subject.

▶ **Practice: Subjects and Predicates**

1. Prepare to read orally the subject and predicate of each of the sentences below. Read them in this way: The subject of the first sentence is ___?___; the predicate is ___?___.

1. The old woman | sold baskets in the market place.
2. She | made them from roots and grasses.
3. Tourists from the city | liked them.
4. Several persons in our group | bought more than one.
5. Baskets like hers | are not expensive.
6. A basket maker | gathers her materials carefully.

2. Write the subjects and predicates of the following sentences under the proper headings:

> *Example:*   SUBJECT   PREDICATE
>
> The seagulls   swooped over the vessel.

1. The early settlers had great strength and endurance.
2. Their first winters in America were very difficult.
3. They built their homes from the trees in the forests.
4. Wild game provided some of the food.
5. The Indians taught the settlers many things.

3. The groups of words below are only parts of sentences. Make a sentence of each group by supplying either a subject or a predicate, as directed. Capitalize and punctuate the sentences correctly.

1. pupils in our school   (*Add a predicate.*)
2. were looking for crumbs to eat   (*Add a subject.*)
3. is my favorite author   (*Add a subject.*)
4. cut down the largest tree   (*Add a subject.*)
5. the first act in the program   (*Add a predicate.*)

Check Test 2: Capitalization and Punctuation

Take this test to see how well you remember the uses of capital letters and punctuation marks.

1. Write these sentences, using capital letters correctly:

1. The city of chicago is in cook county, illinois.
2. Many americans were born in europe.
3. The metropolitan museum of art is located on fifth avenue in new york.
4. We will visit grandmother and grandfather.
5. Are you planning a program for fire prevention week?

2. Write these greetings for friendly letters:

dear aunt mary   my dear richard   dear mrs white

3. Write correctly this greeting for a business letter:

dear dr williams

4. Write the following outline, using capital letters and punctuation marks correctly:

uses of copper
I   electrical appliances
II   utensils

For review and more practice, turn to pages 347–49 and page 351.

Check Test 3: Punctuation

Take this test to see how much you remember about the punctuation of sentences.

Write these sentences, punctuating them correctly:

1. Mary Bill and Sue were talking.
2. I paid only ten cents for this new book Mary said.
3. What a bargain that was Bill exclaimed.
4. Did you buy it at Mr Green's bookstore on Waverly Avenue Sue asked.

For review and more practice, turn to pages 350–52.

What Predicates Tell About the Subject

So far you have learned that the predicate of a sentence is the part that tells something about the subject. Now study the predicates in the following sentences. See what they tell about the subjects.

1. In this sentence, the predicate tells what the subject is doing:

The boys | are carrying an old rusty wheel home.

2. In this sentence, the predicate tells what the subject was:

Joe | was my partner.

3. In this sentence, the predicate describes the subject:

The decorations | are beautiful.

4. In this sentence, the predicate tells what happened to the subject:

The pail | was knocked over by the cow.

▶ **Practice: Telling About the Subject**

1. Write two sentences in which the predicate tells what the subject is, was, or will be doing. Sentence 1 above will help you.

2. Write two sentences in which the predicate tells what the subject is, was, or will be. See sentence 2 above.

3. Write two sentences in which the predicate describes the subject. See sentence 3 above.

4. Write two sentences in which the predicate tells what is, was, or will be happening to the subject. See sentence 4.

The Simple Subject

The subjects you have been studying are called **complete subjects.** Examine the sentences below. All the words at the left of the vertical lines belong to the complete subjects.

1. My best friend | bought a chemistry set.
2. The fear of an explosion | worries his mother.
3. I | want a chemistry set of my own.

In each complete subject above, there is a key word which is the main part of the subject. It is called the **simple subject.**

The simple subjects in the sentences above are *friend, fear,* and *I.*

The other words in a subject change or limit the meaning of the simple subject. For example, the words *My best* limit the meaning of the word *friend* to a particular friend. The words *The, of an explosion* limit the meaning of *fear,* which can mean any fear, to a particular kind of fear. Words or groups of words that limit or change the meaning of a word are called **modifiers.**

The word *I* in sentence 3 above is both the complete subject and the simple subject because it is the only word in the subject.

■ The **subject** of a sentence is the part that names what the sentence is about.

■ The **simple subject** is the main part of the subject.

■ The **complete subject** is the simple subject plus any modifiers.

29

► **Practice: Subjects of Sentences**

1. Copy the complete subject in each of the sentences below. Then draw a line under the simple subject.

    1. The Indians depended upon trees.
    2. A club was one of their weapons.
    3. Wood fires kept them warm.
    4. Their spears were made of wood.
    5. The fruits of the trees furnished them food.
    6. The bark of the birch furnished fibers.

2. In the sentences below, look first for the complete subject. Then find the simple subject and write it in a column headed "Simple Subjects." Place the other words of the subject under the heading "Modifiers."

Example: That robin on the grass fell from its nest.

SIMPLE SUBJECTS	MODIFIERS
robin	That, on the grass

    1. The man on the street bought a newspaper downtown.
    2. The newsboy at the corner stand sold all his papers.
    3. Important news of the day is on the front page.
    4. My favorite parts of the paper are the comics and sports pages.

Composition: Sentence and Paragraph Development

A. The sentences in Practice 1 above are correct, but if read as a paragraph would be dull. Develop interesting sentences by replacing the blanks in the sentences below with groups of words. Write them in a paragraph to read in class.

    1. The Indians in ___?___ depended upon trees for ___?___.
    2. When ___?___, a wooden club was one of their weapons.
    3. Whenever ___?___, wood fires kept them warm.
    4. The women of ___?___ wove baskets from ___?___ fibers.

B. Study the picture on the facing page. Then write a descriptive paragraph or two. Choose an interest-catching title.

30

The Verb in the Predicate

The predicates you have been studying are called **complete predicates.** Look again at the example sentences on page 29. All the words at the right of the vertical line in each sentence belong to the complete predicate.

The key word (or words) in the predicate of a sentence is the **verb.** Another name for the verb in the predicate is the **simple predicate.** In this book the term *verb* is used rather than the longer expression "simple predicate."

The verbs in the sentences on page 29 are *bought, worries,* and *want.* The other words in the complete predicate complete the verbs. Sometimes words in a complete predicate modify the verb.

■ The **predicate** of a sentence is the part that tells something about the subject.

■ The **verb** is the main part of the predicate of a sentence.

■ The **complete predicate** is the verb and any words that modify or complete the verb.

▶ **Practice: Finding the Parts of a Sentence**

1. Copy the following sentences. Draw a line between the complete subject and the complete predicate. Be prepared to read your answers aloud in class.

1. The castle stands in that dark forest.
2. A high wall surrounds the castle.
3. The wide moat around it discourages unwelcome visitors.
4. A famous nobleman still lives there.
5. Many tourists stay in the village nearby.

2. Now look for the verb in each sentence above. Draw two lines under each verb. Then find the simple subject in each sentence. Draw one line under each simple subject. Be prepared to read your answers aloud in class.

Check Test 4: Correct Verb Forms

1. Write each sentence, using the correct form of the verb in parentheses:

1. The wind has (blew, blown) snow on the porch.
2. Has John (drew, drawn) the cartoon for the school paper yet?
3. They (came, come) to the banquet yesterday.
4. Had the referee (blew, blown) his whistle before the touchdown was scored?
5. Your friends have (came, come) for you.

2. Write each sentence, using the correct form:

1. Jack (don't, doesn't) live far from school.
2. (Don't, Doesn't) he want to read his book?
3. It (don't, doesn't) appeal to him.
4. These plants (doesn't, don't) bloom.
5. This plant (doesn't, don't) have enough light.
6. (Don't, Doesn't) she sing well?

For review and more practice, turn to page 355.

TO MEMORIZE

We never know how high we are
Till we are called to rise;
And, then, if we are true to plan,
Our statures touch the skies.

EMILY DICKINSON

Emily Dickinson spent her life in Amherst, Massachusetts, living quietly, and for some years, alone. On the surface, her life seems uneventful. Her poems, though, tell another story. When we read them, we understand that she looked upon life as a great adventure, and that she discovered much of its beauty and meaning.

The stanza above is from one of her poems, "We Never Know How High." Talk about what it means.

Sentence Patterns: Word Order

Look at the sample of Japanese writing below:

太郎さんは私の本を読みました。

Written in our alphabet, the sentence looks like this:

Taro-san watakushi no hon o yomimashita.
(Mr. Taro) (my) (book) (is reading)

Examine the translation underneath the Japanese sentence. Is the order of the words different from that in an English sentence? How would we express this thought in English?

In English, we arrange words in a specific order, depending upon our meaning. To express the thought, "Sam chased the rabbit," we would not place words in a hit-or-miss order, like this:

Rabbit the Sam chased.

Nor would you express this thought in this way:

The rabbit chased Sam.

The first group of words makes no sense at all. The second group of words is a good English sentence, but it does not express the meaning intended. The order of words in an English sentence is very important to sense and to meaning.

● Unscramble the following word groups to make each one a sentence that is correct and makes sense:

1. a keeps diary Marianne sister my
2. her daily about she experiences writes
3. in stood the and sheep goats field
4. geese overhead fly beautiful saw we
5. white swam the two lake gracefully across swans muddy
6. artist was an picture a painting farmhouse the of

34

Check Test 5: Forms of Verbs

Write each sentence, using the correct form of the verb in parentheses:

1. (grow)   Charles has __?__ two inches this year.
2. (take)   Had Donna __?__ her cat to the veterinarian?
3. (fly)   Our neighbors have __?__ from Chicago.
4. (throw)   At the end of the game, Ted __?__ his cap into the air.
5. (known)   Haven't they __?__ Barbara for many years?
6. (take)   After my brother had __?__ his driver's test, he __?__ us for a ride.
7. (fly)   My canary __?__ out of the open window.
8. (know)   I __?__ he would come.
9. (grow)   Our neighbor's tree __?__ to a height of seven feet.
10. (throw)   Dad has __?__ those old papers away.

If you made a mistake, turn to page 359 for review and more practice.

The Order of Subject and Predicate

In most sentences, the subject comes before the predicate. Because the order of subject first and predicate next is the usual order, it is called the **natural order.**

Sometimes, to get variety in sentences or to emphasize something in a sentence, the natural order of subject first and predicate next is reversed. Then the subject follows the predicate. Such sentences as these are said to be in **inverted order.** Look at these example sentences:

NATURAL ORDER: A flickering light flashed across the bay.
       A frog leaped across the path.
       The scout crept into the woods.

INVERTED ORDER: Across the bay flashed a flickering light.
       Across the path leaped a frog.
       Into the woods crept the scout.

Do you understand now what *inverted order* means?

The Simple Subject and Verb

When you are looking for the simple subject and the verb in a sentence, always look for the verb first. It is easier to find the verb than to find the subject. Then form a question by saying the words *who* or *what* before saying the verb. Your answer will be the subject. This plan works well with any sentence, whether its subject and predicate are in natural or inverted order. For example, follow the plan to find the simple subject and verb in this example sentence:

Over the hill came the rider.

ASK: What is the verb?
ANSWER: *came*
ASK: *Who* or *what* came?
ANSWER: *rider* (simple subject)

Simple subject — *rider*; verb — *came.*

► **Practice: The Order of Subject and Predicate**

1. Find the simple subject and the verb in each of the following sentences. Two sentences follow the natural order.

1. On the stage stood my brother.
2. Beside the path appeared a large footprint.
3. Into the hallway ran the stranger.
4. In the basket were the lost tickets.
5. Suddenly the cavalry appeared over the hill.
6. Through the forest rang the sound of the ax.
7. Down crashed the mighty oak.
8. A log cabin stood in each clearing.

2. Rewrite the following statements, changing the order of subject and predicate:

1. The six hundred rode into the valley of death.
2. The bugles sounded far off across the hills.
3. The springtime comes after the stormy winter.
4. King Richard galloped into the banquet hall.

The Order of Words in Questions

In some questions, the simple subject and verb are in natural order—simple subject first, verb next.

> Who knocked on the door?
> Who hit the home run?
> What is the matter?

The simple subjects and verbs in questions like those above are easy to find. Can you name them?

Now look at the arrangement of the simple subject and verb in these questions:

1. Where are you going?
2. Did the salesman leave?
3. Where is my brother?

What is the verb in sentence 1? What is the simple subject in sentence 1? To find the answers, did you follow the two steps which you studied on page 36? Examine the steps again with sentence 1.

ASK: What is the verb?
ANSWER: *are going*
ASK: *Who* or *what* are going?
ANSWER: *you*

> Simple subject—*you*; verb—*are going*.

Notice that the verb in the sentence contains two words. The simple subject in a question often comes between two parts of a verb. Now follow the same steps with sentences 2 and 3.

To find the subjects and verbs of some questions, you may first need to rewrite the questions. Here is how you can do this. Put the subject and verb in natural order, starting the question as you would a statement. For example:

> *Sentence 1.* You are going where?
> *Sentence 2.* The salesman did leave?
> *Sentence 3.* My brother is where?

38

► **Practice: Finding the Simple Subject and Verb**

Copy the following questions on your paper. Draw two lines under the verb in each sentence. Draw one line under the simple subject. If it will help you, rewrite some of the questions. The numeral in parentheses after each sentence tells whether the verb is one word or two words.

1. Why did you return so soon? (2)
2. Who sent the letter? (1)
3. When is the next flight? (1)
4. Have you seen the new movie? (2)
5. How much hamburger shall I buy? (2)
6. What is happening to Bill? (2)
7. Where is the fisherman in the yellow slicker? (1)
8. How did the losers show good sportsmanship after the game? (2)
9. Were you entering the Tivoli Theater on Broadway last night about 8:30? (2)
10. Has the committee ordered the ice cream? (2)

Review Practice: Correct Words

Write each sentence below, choosing the correct word or words in parentheses:

1. Who (let, left) the light on last night?
2. I don't know where the carnival (is at, is).
3. Please (let, leave) us go now.
4. The car ran (off, off of) the road.
5. Where is your brother (working, working at) during the summer vacation?
6. The hard-driven ball bounced (off, off of) the wall in left field.
7. I hope the teacher will (let, leave) us have a holiday next week.
8. Where is John (going, going to)?
9. I saw Richard fall (off, off of) his bicycle.
10. Why did you (let, leave) the boys go?

Reading Aloud

Read the following lines silently and note the rhythmical phrasing of the sentences. Prepare to read the passage aloud in such a way that others will enjoy listening to you.

The huckleberry thickets had grown all summer in dense green carpets beneath the oaks. Now they were like rust-tinged clouds floating on the ground around distant bends. Acorns peppered the earth everywhere and chipmunks gathered them with urgent purpose. The spots began to disappear from fawns, and the blunt ends of the velvet-covered racks of bucks began to sharpen and take their final shapes.

From *Canalboat to Freedom* by THOMAS FALL

To Discuss

1. Whenever you plan to read a selection aloud, it is best to read it first silently. Do you know why? Can you state the reason in a sentence that begins this way?

Prepare for oral reading by reading the selection silently to make sure that . . .

2. Look back to page 14, in Chapter 1 of this book, and read the section "To Discuss." Then add after the statement you gave for part 1, above, a second statement for each of the following qualities: volume, rate of speaking, articulation.

► **Practice: Pronouncing Letter Sounds**

Make up sentences in which you use the words listed below. Read your sentences aloud to the class. Watch the letters in heavy black type.

recognize   government   singer   once

Going Ahead ♦ ♦ ♦ ♦

Find especially well-written passages in a book that you are reading and prepare to share them orally with your class. Be ready to name the book and author from which you read.

The Subject in Commands and Requests

A sentence that gives a command or makes a request often begins with the verb. Sometimes the word *please* comes first.

>(you) Call for me soon.
>(you) Turn left at the corner, sir.
>(you) Please wait a minute, Jack.

Usually in sentences of command or request, the subject is not stated. It is understood to be *you*. This is also true when the sentence includes a person's name first, before making the request.

>Jack, (you) wait a minute.
>Mother, (you) please wake me early.
>Joan, (you) call for me at eight.

Sometimes the subject of a command or request *is* expressed, as in this example:

>*You* go ahead.

■ The subject of a command or request is understood to be **you.**

Look again at the example sentences above. Notice that five of them contain commas. The name of the person to whom we are talking directly in a sentence is always set off from the rest of the sentence with a comma. If the name appears in the middle of a sentence, two commas are needed, as in the examples below:

>Call me, Jack, as soon as possible.
>Please, Ruth, try to be on time.

Use a comma, or commas, in a sentence to set off the name of the person addressed.

► **Practice: Finding the Simple Subject and Verb**

Find and tell the simple subject and verb of each sentence below. If the subject is understood but not expressed, include that in your explanation.

1. Please return the books on the table to the library.
2. What are you saying?
3. Who mowed the lawn?
4. John, repair the leak in the tire.
5. Trim the hedge, Henry.

Composition: Questions and Answers

A. Study the picture below. Then write an imaginary answer to one of these questions. Pretend you are the old sailor.

1. How did you get the ship model in the bottle?
2. What kind of speed and distance did such a ship make?
3. What was your most exciting adventure at sea?

B. Describe the harbor and the group of people as if you were standing close by. Tell what you see, hear, and smell.

How Our Language Grew · · ● ●

Do you wonder where we got the words *verb, noun, predicate, subject?* The answer is this: they all came from the Latin language.

Verb originally meant "word." And the verb usually is the most vigorous and noticeable word in a sentence, as you have seen.

Noun came from a Latin word for "name."

Predicate meant "to proclaim or preach." In a sentence, the predicate is the part that proclaims or expresses something about the subject.

Subject meant "placed under." In a sentence, the subject is the part that is placed under discussion or consideration by the predicate.

Omega
Greek letter

Sounds and Spelling

"From A to Izzard"

You have probably heard people use the phrase "From A to Z," meaning from beginning to end. Some persons use the quaint expression, "From A to Izzard." *Izzard* comes from an old French name for *z*.

In spelling, you may often wish that our alphabet matched the sounds of our language perfectly, one letter only for each sound. Then spelling would be easier. But that is not the case. For example, we have three different letters for the sound of *z*. Can you tell which letters they are?

The first is obviously *z*. You find it used at the beginning, in the middle, or at the end of words, as in *zero, lazy,* and *quiz*.

The second is *s*, which may represent the sound of *z* in the middle or at the end of words, as in *dismal* and *does*. Often when an *s* or *es* is added to a word, the *s* spells the sound of *z*, as in *rubs, boxes, changes*.

A few words begin with the letter *x*, sounded as *z*. The name of a Persian ruler who lived during the fifth century B.C. was Xerxes (zerk′sez). Can you pronounce it? How do you pronounce *xylophone*?

Spelling Checkup

1. List in three columns words spelled with *z* at the beginning, in the middle, and at the end. Try for five in each column.

2. Spell these words. Fill the blanks with *s*'s or *z*'s:

gri_?_ly   disgui_?_e   citi_?_en   exerci_?_e   pri_?_e
mi_?_er   pu_?_le   reali_?_e   suppo_?_e   surpri_?_e

3. List words like *buzz* or *whiz* that use *z* to imitate a sound.

44

Writing Sentences Correctly

Capital letters and end punctuation marks are important signals in writing sentences. They are used to make the beginnings and ends of our sentences.

Avoiding Sentence Fragments

When you write a sentence, keep all of its parts together. Do not punctuate a part of a sentence as if it were complete. A sentence part punctuated as a complete sentence is called a *sentence fragment*. Which group of words after numeral 1 below is a sentence fragment?

1. You will have to lock the door. When you leave.
2. Finding the key under the mat. Jennie let herself in.

When you leave is a sentence fragment, incomplete by itself. It is incorrectly punctuated as a sentence. You can avoid the sentence fragment in numeral 1 by keeping the parts together in this way:

You will have to lock the door when you leave.

Which group of words after numeral 2 is a sentence fragment? Rewrite the word groups to avoid the fragment.

Remember: Avoid writing sentence fragments as if they were sentences. Keep the parts of a sentence together.

► Practice: Building Sentences

1. After each numeral below, there is one complete sentence and one sentence fragment. Tell which word group, *a* or *b*, is a sentence fragment. Then read the two word groups aloud as one sentence. Write the sentences correctly on the board.

1. (*a*) We saw a bank of clouds. (*b*) Drifting slowly by.
2. (*a*) See that wonderful view. (*b*) Of Crater Lake.
3. (*a*) In the last mile of the climb. (*b*) Don noticed the broken arrow.

45

2. Some of the following word groups are sentences and some are sentence fragments. Decide which ones are fragments. Then copy the fragments on your paper, adding words of your own to make them complete.

1. The dog was standing next to his kennel.
2. A white polar bear.
3. Sitting on a floating piece of ice.
4. We bought a copy of the famous painting.
5. The red squirrel at the base of the oak tree.
6. In that large volume on the first shelf.
7. The costume was made of paper bags.
8. In the first inning.
9. On television last night.
10. The stadium was full of out-of-towners.
11. We made nut fudge the other evening.
12. Caught in a trap.

Avoiding Run-ons

Another common error in writing is to run sentences together, forgetting to use capital letters and end punctuation marks. Sometimes the wrong mark is used at the end of a sentence. Read the following passage:

My father has taught Lisa and me to ice-skate we now belong to the school skating team, our team will compete with yours next Saturday.

Where are capital letters and periods needed in the passage above? How many sentences are there in the passage? Write the sentences correctly on the board.

Did you make these changes: (1) place a period after *ice-skate*, (2) begin *we* with a capital letter, (3) change the comma to a period after the first *team* in line 2, and (4) begin *our* with a capital letter?

Remember: Separate two or more sentences from each other with capital letters and punctuation marks. Reading your sentences aloud will serve to check them.

► **Practice: Correcting Run-ons**

Write the following paragraph correctly, using capital letters and correcting end punctuation:

Pedro followed the canyon wall, he watched the sheep from a distance, his dog, Old Faithful, was on the job one old sheep wandered away from the flock, what good sense the old dog used, he just quietly nosed her back.

Going Ahead ▶ ▶ ▶ ▶

Use the subjects and predicates listed below in sentences. Add words and word groups to each part of the sentence to increase interest for the reader. Avoid fragments and run-ons.

Example: SUBJECT   PREDICATE

The boy   plodded on.

Hungry and tired, the boy plodded on, anxious to get his sheep home before nightfall.

SUBJECT	PREDICATE
1. The dog	tended the sheep.
2. Moon	shone.
3. The wind	was cold.

Sentence Patterns: Word Order

Words strung together without any particular order are meaningless. The following seven words, for example, are thrown together without any thought for the way we group words in English: *brother David for his is little looking.*

1. looking his is for David little brother
2. little is his David looking brother for
3. for looking brother little is David his
4. brother his looking is for David little

Do any of the four arrangements of words above make sense? We can rearrange these same words in many ways:

1. Little David is looking for his brother.
2. David is looking for his little brother.
3. His brother is looking for little David.
4. His little brother is looking for David.
5. Is David looking for his little brother?
6. Is little David looking for his brother?

The six word groups above are sentences; they all have meaning. Notice, however, that the different arrangements of the same words convey different meanings. You must group words together in a certain order, then, not only *to make sense* but also *to say exactly what you want to say.* Notice, for example, how the meanings of the sentences just above change with the difference in the order of the same words.

● See how many good English sentences you can make from each of the word groups listed below. Working with one word group at a time, simply rearrange the words to make sense and to convey different meanings, as we did in the lesson above. You should be able to form several sentences for each word group.

1. frightened small my the dog child
2. two asked some the strangers policemen questions
3. man the looking strange is the at gorilla

The Boundary Riders

by Joan Phipson
illustrated by Margaret Horder
Harcourt, Brace & World, Inc.

When the Thompson children, Jane and Bobby, and their 15-year-old cousin, Vincent, rode off to inspect the boundary fences of the family ranch in southern Australia, they expected to be away only a week. They did better than that, and when the fences were all inspected, they still had three days of their week left. They decided to find the way to a distant waterfall they had glimpsed along the way. They started out from camp on foot with their lunches and a box of matches. Caught by a thick mist in rough and unfamiliar territory, they could not find their way back to camp.

They soon encountered danger and terror, and suffered days of hunger. Their adventure called for courage and resourcefulness.

How the three children worked their way out of this dangerous predicament brings this thrilling story to its climax.

If you make a mistake on any test, turn to pages 52–53 and take the Practice having the same Roman numeral as the test.

Test I.   Sentences

Some of the word groups below are sentences; the others are fragments.   Copy the ones which are sentences and punctuate them correctly.

1. Can you point to the North Star
2. Walking in the woods
3. That light is a signal
4. The trout in this stream
5. Brush your teeth twice a day
6. The Big Dipper
7. What a temper he has
8. Have you ridden in a cable car

Test II.   Subject and Predicate

Copy each sentence below.   Draw a vertical line between the complete subject and the complete predicate.

1. The mountain lion is a big cat.
2. The animal weighs about 150 pounds.
3. Three other names for the mountain lion are cougar, panther, and puma.
4. This fierce animal stalks through the underbrush.
5. The big cat leaps with crushing force upon its prey.

Test III.   Finding Simple Subjects and Verbs

Write each sentence.   Underline the simple subject with one line and the verb with two lines.

1. Two hungry hawks circled the barnyard.
2. Who invented the washing machine?
3. Up and down the hall paced Coach Harris.
4. The gray horse near the gate won two prizes last year at the fair.

5. Tiny sand crabs crawled all over the beach.
6. Where is the meeting?
7. Was the rocket launched successfully?
8. Three gigantic white statues stood in the garden of the king's palace.
9. From the room came a wild scream.
10. The lighthouse in the distance warned us of the danger ahead.

Test IV.   Inverted Order

Rewrite each sentence below so that the subject and predicate are in inverted order:

1. An echo came from the valley.
2. Mary dashed into the phone booth.
3. The river boat swept around the great bend.
4. The roaring, smoking rocket went up and out of sight.

Test V.   Writing Sentences Correctly

Rewrite correctly the following sentences:

1. We saw the boys, they were playing ball on the diamond at the park.
2. I can aim better than that. With my eyes shut.
3. Our long wait was finally rewarded we got an autograph.
4. Dick's tire needs air didn't he check the pressure at the gas station?
5. The room is too warm, open the door, John.
6. In the dark the cat was invisible, I could not see her at all.
7. I was looking for the light switch, suddenly something touched me, my heart gave a great leap.
8. You can guess the cause it was nothing but old Frisky she was welcoming me home.
9. Where were you the teacher gave a test Tuesday.
10. Knock twice on the door, that will be our signal.

Practice I. Sentences

1. Review pages 23–24.

2. Read these word groups. Decide which ones are complete sentences. Copy the sentences and punctuate them.

    1. The crows are scolding the fox
    2. What smart birds crows are
    3. Do sunflowers always gaze at the sun
    4. The return of the robin
    5. Speak softly, boys
    6. From the window of the train

3. Write three sentences: a statement, a question, and an exclamation.

4. Write three commands or requests. In two of them, use the name of a person to whom you are talking.

Practice II. Subject and Predicate

1. Review pages 25–26.

2. Copy each sentence below. Draw a vertical line between the complete subject and the complete predicate.

    1. The bobcat is smaller than the cougar.
    2. It weighs about twenty pounds.
    3. The bobcat is about the size of a small dog.
    4. This little wildcat frightens many people.

Practice III. Finding Simple Subjects and Verbs

1. Read again the lessons on pages 29 and 32. Review the plan for finding the simple subject and verb on page 36.

2. Correct any errors that you made in Test III.

3. Write each sentence. Underline the simple subject with one line and the verb with two lines.

    1. Who went to the picnic?
    2. A hint of sadness lay underneath his gaiety.
    3. The fragrance of flowers stole from the garden.

4. Over the rooftops flew the toy airplane.
5. We ran across the road and into the alley.
6. Many pieces of furniture rotted beneath the blackened ruins.
7. Where do the ducks go for the winter?
8. The hulk of a battered steamer sits at the bottom of the sea.

Practice IV.   Inverted Order

1. Review page 36.

2. Rewrite each sentence below, inverting the order of the subject and predicate:

1. The aroma of roast beef came from the open window.
2. A shout of joy rolled across the playing field.
3. A rainbow appeared beyond the hill.
4. The sailor dived into the dark, rolling sea.

Practice V.   Writing Sentences Correctly

1. Review pages 45–46.

2. If you made any errors in Test V, correct them.

3. Rewrite correctly the following sentences:

1. Everyone heard the announcement. About next Friday's parade.
2. We are planning a party will you come?
3. These three pencils are Robert's, they have his name on them.
4. The bus stops here, my house is one block north of the bus stop.
5. In the parade our class will have a marching drill, the junior high school will have a band.

CHAPTER 3

Good Study Habits

If someone advertised a new way to study and promised that if followed you would get better grades with fewer hours of work, you might be tempted to invest. Actually, there are ways to study that will help to do just that. So our advertisement might have said, "First, we will tell you what those ways are. The next step is to make them your own."

Organizing for Study

It is important to get off to a good start. In studying, you must get yourself and your work organized. Test yourself with these check questions about organizing for study:

1. *Assignment*:   Do you understand exactly what you are to do?

2. *Supplies*:   Do you have at hand all books and supplies that you need?

3. *Working conditions*:   Do you work in a well-lighted, quiet place?

4. *Timing*:   Do you check your beginning time and set a completion time for yourself?

Do you start your homework at a regular time every day?

5. *Concentration*:   Do you avoid interruptions after you start work?   Do you keep your mind focused on your work?

To Discuss

Talk over the check questions above. Discuss their importance in organizing for study.

Look at the illustration on the facing page. How many points can you count that suggest good study habits?

55

Keeping Good Records

Do you keep your school records in a notebook? Your notebook can serve several purposes, such as taking notes on assignments, keeping book lists, and making a record of new words and their meanings. Many students find it helpful to organize their notebooks in sections: one for assignments and others for other types of information.

Taking Notes on Assignments

As an example of the kind of notes you might keep, read the following summary of an assignment. Notice that these notes tell *what* to do, *where* to go for information, *how* to get the information, and *when* the assignment is to be finished.

> Mon., Nov. 12. English
> Report on history of Thanksgiving
> Day. Find references in library.
> Look up history in card catalog.
> Use encyclopedia. Look through poetry
> books in room for Thanksgiving
> poem to use for report. Report due
> Fri., Nov. 16.

To Discuss

1. Notice that the notes above answer *W* and *H* questions: *What, Where, How, When.* Tell what information is given on each of these topics:

1. What to do
2. Where to go for information
3. How to get the information
4. When the assignment is due

2. Why do you think the notes are dated?

56

3. What words are abbreviated in the notes? How does each abbreviation begin? What punctuation mark follows each abbreviation?

4. Are the notes neatly and clearly written?

Read the following guides for taking notes on assignments. Write the list in your notebook at the beginning of the section for assignments.

How to Take Notes on Assignments

Write the date of the assignment and the subject on the first line.

Record the details of assignments accurately.

Use *W* and *H* questions to see that the information is complete.

Write the date the assignment is due.

Write neatly and legibly.

Write abbreviations correctly.

Review Practice: Writing Abbreviations

When you take notes or make lists, you may use abbreviations. Review some of the abbreviations you learned in earlier grades by completing the following exercises:

1. Write the correct abbreviations for names of days.

2. Write the abbreviations for the names of nine months.

3. Write the abbreviations for the italicized words below:

1. The city of Washington, *District of Columbia.*
2. Albany, *New York*
3. Mulberry *Street*
4. Bryant *Avenue*
5. Harrison *Boulevard*
6. Mill *Road*
7. Chicago, *Illinois*
8. *Doctor* H. M. Avery

Listing Books to Read

As you hear about books, write the titles and the authors' names in your notebook. You may want to add a note telling why you want to read each book. Tell whether the book is fiction or, if nonfiction, whether it is a biography, science, history, hobby book, or some other kind. Here is an example:

> *Books to Read*
>
> <u>*Insects and Plants*</u>, *by Elizabeth K. Cooper. Nonfiction, science. Tells about partnerships between insects and plants. Tells how to raise silkworms.*

Keeping a Reading Record

Soon after you have finished a book, make a record to help you remember. See the model below.

> *My Reading Record*
>
> <u>*Insects and Plants*</u>, *by Elizabeth K. Cooper. 142 pages and appendix. Science. Finished Nov. 12. Takes up bees and bee flowers, moths and the yucca, silkworms and the mulberry tree. Tells how to raise silkworms. Rating * * **
>
> <u>*The Saturdays*</u>, *by Elizabeth Enright. 175 pages. Fiction. Finished Sept. 30. Four children without a mother find out how to enjoy their Saturdays in New York. Rating * * **

To Discuss

1. What facts are included in the sample entries? Give a reason for including each kind of information.

2. How do you know whether the books in the record are *fiction* or *nonfiction*? How did the student classify the *nonfiction*?

3. What rating system did the writer use? What is the first book in the record about? How can you tell?

4. Read words from each entry that explain the contents of the book.

5. Which words are abbreviated? Are the abbreviations written correctly?

▶ **Practice: Listing Books and Keeping Reading Records**

Start keeping book lists and reading records in your notebook. Under "Books to Read" find and list a book from your classroom book shelves or the library that will give you more information on a topic you have been studying. Under "My Reading Record" list a good book you have recently read.

Check Test 6: Forms of is and are

The sentences below require different forms of *is* and *are*. Write each sentence, choosing the correct word in parentheses.

1. Joan and Margaret (isn't, aren't) cousins.
2. Our neighbors (was, were) in Alaska last summer.
3. (Is, Are) corn and wheat the main crops?
4. You (wasn't, weren't) at the party.
5. (Wasn't, Weren't) Ed and Don in the library?
6. The string beans and the mashed potatoes (is, are) overcooked today.
7. (Wasn't, Weren't) you at the game yesterday?
8. We (was, were) on our way to a meeting.
9. (Isn't, Aren't) the tulips beautiful?
10. Tim and you (is, are) the first arrivals.

Turn to page 360 to review any form you missed.

Keeping a Word List

As you read and study, you will find many words that are new to you or are used in unfamiliar ways. Such words should be kept in your notebook as a way of enlarging your vocabulary. A large vocabulary is itself one of the most useful of all study helps.

The word list should be accurate in spelling and meaning. Study the model below. Notice the information included.

> *Thurs., Dec. 14. Soc. studies book, pages 35–40, function, the particular purpose for which a thing exists. The function of the Congress is to make the laws.*
>
> *reign (pronounced rain), rule. The Revolution took place during the reign of King George III.*

To Discuss

1. Tell why it is helpful to know the date, subject, name of book, and pages from which the new words were selected.

2. Read from the model an example of a definition. Does the sample sentence add anything to the definition?

3. Why is it helpful to underline the words?

4. Where would you go to find meanings of words?

Composition: Study Habits

A. Head your page "Study Habits." Write *Part I*, and under it list the study habits suggested so far in this chapter. Add others that you think might increase your ability in school. Under *Part II*, name the things that make your studying difficult.

B. Write a composition, serious or humorous, describing your difficulties in studying and how you have tried to overcome them.

Studying Parts of Words

You can build your vocabulary and improve your spelling by observing how some words are put together. For example, study the parts of this word:

re place able

1. Notice that *replaceable* has been formed by adding syllables to one root word. Spell the root word. Use it correctly in a sentence.

2. What syllable has been placed at the beginning of the root word? Spell it. How does it change the meaning of the root word? Use the word *replace* correctly in a sentence of your own.

3. What syllable has been added at the end of the root word? How does it change the root word? Use the word *replaceable* correctly in a sentence.

■ A **prefix** is one or more syllables placed before a root word to change its meaning. Know some

■ A **suffix** is one or more syllables added to the ending of a word.

Study the words in each group below. Find the root word. What does it mean? Notice how prefixes and suffixes are used to build new words. What do the new words mean?

1. real	2. firm	3. claim	4. color
unreal	confirm	proclaim	discolor
really	firmness	reclaimed	colorless

To Discuss

1. Check in the dictionary the meaning of any unfamiliar word. Be prepared to use each word in a sentence of your own.

2. Notice the spelling of *really*. The last letter of the root word and the first letter of the suffix are the same. This makes a double consonant. Can you think of other words like this?

Practice: Building Words

See how many words you can build by adding prefixes and suffixes to these words:

clean	count	cover	collect
govern	form	press	part
frost	plant	appear	satisfy

How Our Language Grew •••

Super: The prefix *super* accounts for a large number of additions to the English vocabulary. In combination with words or word parts, it has created new words with new meanings. If there is a large dictionary to which you can refer, you might count to see how many words begin with that prefix.

When used as a prefix, *super* means "above" or "over," "higher in position," "greater than others," or "more than normal." Below are some words or word parts that may be combined with *super* to form new words. With the information given here, can you make a list of ten such words and tell what they mean?

The parts of words with which the prefix may combine are indicated below by a hyphen. Check in the dictionary for meanings if you are not sure.

WORDS OR WORD PARTS	MEANINGS
abundant	plentiful
-ficial	from a Latin word meaning "face" or "surface"
-fluity	from a Latin word meaning "flow"
highway	a main road
human	a person
intend	plan or purpose
natural	according to nature
-sonic	from a Latin word meaning "sound"
-stition	from a Latin word meaning "stand"
-vise	from a Latin word meaning "see"

62

Adding Suffixes

You have learned that when prefixes and suffixes are added to some words, the spelling of the root word does not change.

Notice how the spelling of each word below changes when a suffix beginning with a vowel is added to it.

shine	shining	slope	sloping
safe	safer	spoke	spoken

Most words that end in silent **e** drop the **e** when endings that begin with vowels are added to them.

Notice the spelling of the words given below. Note that the *e* is retained when a suffix beginning with a vowel is added. Pronounce the words and notice the soft *c* and soft *g*. If the *e* were not retained, what kind of sound might the *g* or *c* be given?

courage   courageous   peace   peaceable

If a **g** or **c** comes before a final **e,** the **e** is retained when a suffix beginning with **a** or **o** is added. If a suffix beginning with **e** is added, as in encourag**ed,** the final **e** is dropped.

Study the spelling of the words. What happens when a suffix beginning with a consonant is added to a word that ends in silent *e?*

spite   spiteful   sedate   sedately

Words that end in **e** keep the **e** when endings that begin with consonants are added to them.

Exceptions to this rule are *true* and *due*.

true   truly   due   duly

► **Practice: Adding Suffixes**

Use a suffix to build new words from each of the following words:

disbelieve	actual	pass	gain
conserve	hope	free	broke

Spell the words correctly, following the rules you have learned.

Spelling ie or ei

Study the spelling of each of the words below. In which words does the *i* come before *e*? the *e* before *i*?

chief　　friend　　receive　　believe　　neighbor

In the spelling of most words, **i** comes before **e** except after **c** or when the sound of the letters is that of **a** as in **weigh.**

There are some exceptions to the above rule. Two examples are *foreign* and *height*.

► **Practice: Spelling ie or ei**

List all the words you can think of that are spelled according to the rule of *i before e*, as stated above. Make another list of exceptions to the rule.

► **Practice: Spelling**

One word in each pair below is misspelled. Choose the correct word and write a sentence, using the word correctly.

wisht	fierce	sofen	dissimilar
wished	feirce	soften	disimilar
reign	fortunately	hopeful	feild
riegn	fortunatly	hopful	field

64

Sounds and Spelling

Facts About <u>E</u>, <u>I</u>, and <u>Y</u>

Look in the pronunciation key of your dictionary to see how the sounds of *e* and *i* are marked. Find *e* as in *bet, beet,* and *Bert.* Some dictionaries list *ur* instead of *er* for the vowel sound in *Bert.* Find *i* as in *bit* and *bite.* When *y* is used as a vowel, it usually spells one of these two sounds.

Name the letters that spell the sounds listed below:

> *e* as in *bet*:   ten, said, says, friend, many, health, leopard
> *ē* as in *beet*:   seem, scheme, scream, routine, be, key, ski, believe, deceive, people
> *ė* as in *Bert*:   jerk, shirk, work, hurt, myrtle

Name the letters that spell the following sounds:

> *i* as in *bit*:   will, system, give, sieve, guild, been, pretty, busy, women
> *ī* as in *bite*:   like, by, buy, die, dye, type, I, aye, eye, aisle, bright, height, choir

Spelling Checkup

1. From the words listed above, find how many different sounds of *i* or *e* are spelled with the letter *y*, either alone or combined with another vowel. Can you think of other words that use *y* for these sounds?

2. Look at the last three letters of *friend*; the first four letters of *health*; the first three of *says*. Can you tell a way to remember how these words are spelled?

3. Are there other words listed above for which you can plan a way to remember the spelling?

4. Think of other words with the sound of *e* in *beet* that use these spelling patterns: _?_ea_?_, _?_ie_?_e, _?_ei_?_e.

65

Review Practice: Homonyms

Words such as *rain* and *reign*, that sound alike but differ in spelling and meaning, are called **homonyms.**

The two sets of homonyms most frequently confused are *to, two, too* and *there, their, they're.* In earlier grades you studied these homonyms. Complete the following exercises to review them.

1. Write these sentences correctly, using *to, two,* or *too* in place of each blank:

1. He came __?__ the party, __?__.
2. I had __?__ pieces of candy left.
3. Give those __?__ books __?__ Jeffrey, please.
4. Bob will enjoy reading them, __?__.
5. Have you eaten __?__ much ice cream?

2. Write these sentences correctly, using *they're, there,* or *their* in place of each blank:

1. When will the girls finish __?__ lessons?
2. __?__ doing them now at __?__ homes.
3. I was __?__ when they got __?__ books.
4. __?__ coming down the street now.
5. Mr. Carter put the papers __?__.

Going Ahead ▶ ▶ ▶ ▶

Draw a "Pair Tree," naming the second pear to complete the labels in the picture below. Add other pears (pairs) to make a good crop. A large copy of your tree, as a wall chart, might be helpful to the class.

Note: Label one of each pair as follows: *no, seen, won, main, flour, rode, whole, steel, plane, grown.*

Using the Dictionary

The dictionary is one of the most valuable of all study tools. As you know, it gives you the meaning of a word, its spelling, and its pronunciation. It also provides other information.

Studying an Entry from a Dictionary Page

Here is an entry from a dictionary page. Study it carefully.

> **ro tate** (rō′tāt), **1.** move around a center or axis; turn in a circle; revolve. Wheels, tops, and the earth rotate. **2.** change in a regular order; cause to take turns: *to rotate crops in a field, to rotate men in office.* **ro tat ed, ro tat ing.**

From *Thorndike-Barnhart Beginning Dictionary*
Copyright © 1962 by Scott, Foresman and Company, Chicago.

1. *Spelling*: Notice the spelling of *rotate*. Look at the forms of *rotate* given at the end of the entry. What happens to the final silent *e* when *–ed* or *–ing* is added to *rotate*?

2. *Pronunciation*: The pronunciation is shown within parentheses after the spelling. Notice the aids to pronunciation.

1. *Syllables*: The word is divided into parts, according to the number of vowel sounds it has. How many vowel sounds are there in *rotate*? how many syllables?

2. *Accent mark*: Find the mark after the first syllable of the entry word *rotate*. This mark shows which syllable should be given greater stress in speaking.

3. *Respelling*: The respelling within the parentheses tells you how the word should be pronounced. The accent mark is shown, and the syllables are respelled in the way that best helps you pronounce them; for instance, the second syllable of *rotate* is respelled tāt. What does the diacritical mark over the *a* in tāt tell you?

3. *Meaning*: How many definitions are given for *rotate*? In addition to the definition, what other aid does the dictionary give you in understanding the meanings of *rotate*?

67

Finding Entries in the Dictionary

The first and most important aid in finding the word you want is the alphabetical order of words.

Using Alphabetical Order

How good are you at using alphabetical order?

1. Tell rapidly which letter comes before *r;* after *u;* before *h.*
2. What two letters come before *m?* after *i?*
3. What are the two middle letters of the alphabet?
4. Which letters are in the last quarter? the second?

► **Practice: Alphabetizing**

1. Write these words in alphabetical order:

nervous, divide, length, years, heavy, several, cough, pleasure

2. Alphabetize:

    1. bureau, bottle, baggage, blouse, breathe
    2. inquire, ivory, icicle, iron, imagine
    3. sparkle, sincere, scythe, strict, scandal
    4. team, tender, teacher, there, theme

Using Guide Words

The guide words printed in heavy black type at the top of each dictionary page show the first and last words on the page. If you are looking for *whistle*, would it come in alphabetical order on the page where the guide words are *whip* and *white?*

► **Practice: Using Guide Words**

In each group below, write the words that would be entries on the page where these guide words are found.

1. **exceed exclusive** except examine excite excuse
2. **juice justice** junior junket justify juggle

Studying a Dictionary Page

Study the part of a dictionary page shown below to answer these questions:

1. What are the guide words for the page?
2. Find an entry which consists of two words.
3. How does the spelling of *quarterstaff* change when it becomes plural?
4. Find a word that has two accent marks. The accent mark in blacker type is the *primary* accent. It marks the syllable that should be said with more stress. The lighter one is the *secondary* accent.
5. Find a word that has two different spellings. Which spelling comes first? Which would you use?
6. How many different meanings are given for *quick*? How is *queue* pronounced?

---

quarterstaff   511   **quill**

quar ter staff (kwôr′tər staf′), old weapon consisting of a stout pole 6 to 8 feet long, tipped with iron. **quar ter staves** (kwôr′tər stāvz′).

quar tet or **quar tette** (kwôr tet′), 1. group of four singers or players. 2. piece of music for four voices or instruments. 3. any group of four.

quartz (kwôrts), a very hard kind of rock. Common quartz is colorless and transparent, but amethyst, jasper, and many other colored stones are also quartz.

qua ver (kwā′vər), 1. shake; tremble: *The old man's voice quavered.* 2. sing or say in trembling tones. 3. a trembling of the voice.

quay (kē), solid landing place for ships, often built of stone.

Quay

queen (kwēn), 1. wife of a king. 2. woman ruler. 3. woman who is very beautiful or important: *the queen of society, the queen of the May.* 4. act like a queen. 5. female bee that lays eggs.

question mark, mark (?) put after a question in writing or printing.

queue (kū), 1. braid of hair hanging down the back. 2. line of people, automobiles, etc.

quick (kwik), 1. fast and sudden; swift: *The cat made a quick jump. Many weeds have a quick growth.* 2. coming soon; prompt: *a quick reply.* 3. not patient; hasty: *a quick temper.* 4. lively; ready; active: *a quick wit, a quick ear.* 5. quickly. 6. the tender, sensitive flesh under a fingernail or toenail: *The child bit his nails down to the quick.* 7. the tender, sensitive part of one's feelings: *The boy's pride was cut to the quick by the words of blame.* 8. living persons: *the quick and the dead.*

quick en (kwik′ən), 1. move more quickly; hasten: *Quicken your pace.* 2. stir up; make alive: *He quickened the hot ashes into flames. Reading adventure stories quickened his imagination.* 3. become more active or alive: *His pulse quickened.*

quick ly (kwik′li), with haste; very soon.

Selecting the Right Definition

In your studying, you may find that you need the dictionary definition of a word in order to get the author's meaning. The word you look up may have several meanings, numbered separately in the dictionary.

Do not hastily reach for the first definition and stop there. Try out the definition in the sentence and paragraph where you found the word. If it fits, fine. If not, look further. Always check the meaning by the context, or setting, in which the word is used. Look at these examples:

He was hurt to the *quick.*
We stood in a *queue* to get tickets.

Which of the numbered definitions on page 69 fits each sentence? If you grabbed the first definition you found, the results in these sentences would be nonsense. If you chose the right definitions, you can use them in place of the underlined words. Try it.

To Discuss

1. Why should you read through all the definitions of a word when using the dictionary?

2. What is meant by *context* in the sentence: Check the dictionary definition to see that it fits the context.

► **Practice: Selecting the Right Definition**

Look in your dictionary for the right definition of the words in italics to fit the context in the sentences below. Tell the meaning and substitute the definitions for the words.

1. We expect extremely cold winters here; they are part of the *cycle.*
2. We must send our request through proper *channels* at City Hall.
3. Only a *kink,* developed throughout life, led the old man to save every inch of string he could find.
4. These *novel* styles in sandals are comfortable.

Finding Pronunciations in the Dictionary

One of the chief uses of a dictionary is for learning how to pronounce words correctly. All dictionaries give this help, though they differ somewhat in the way they give it.

Using the Pronounciation Key

Different dictionaries use different systems to show the pronunciation of a word. Usually the system is explained in the front pages of the dictionary. In addition, there may also be a short key to pronunciation at the bottom of every other page. If you do not understand the system, refer to the pronunciation key.

Here is a key to the pronunciation of vowel sounds in the dictionary from which the sample page is taken. It will tell you how to say the words on the sample page.

hat, āge, cãre, fär; let, bē, tėrm; it, īce; hot, ōpen, ôrder;
oil, out; cup, pút, rüle, ūse; takən

▶ **Practice: Using a Key to Pronunciation**

1. In the dictionary from which the sample page was taken, short vowel sounds are unmarked. Long vowel sounds are marked this way: *ā, ē, ī, ō, ū.*

Here are the words from the pronunciation key that tell you how to say the short and the long vowel sounds. Say the words and listen for the *long* and *short* vowel sounds.

hat	let	it	hot	cup
āge	bē	īce	ōpen	ūse

Think of and be prepared to say other words that have the vowel sounds you hear in the words above.

2. A special sign is used to stand for the soft vowel sound in unaccented syllables. The sign is ə. It is called a **schwa.**

In the key on page 71, find the word that tells you how to say the sound of ə.

Say these words and listen for the unaccented vowel sound of the schwa:

a way (ə wā′)   lev el (lev′əl)   pen cil (pen′səl)
les son (les′ən)   lic o rice (lik′ə ris)   fo cus (fō′kəs)

3. Say each of the words in the pronunciation key on page 71. Listen to the different vowel sounds.

4. Pronounce every word on the sample dictionary page on page 69. Use the key on page 71 to help you.

Using the Hyphen Correctly

You may need to divide a word at the end of a line. If so, consult your dictionary to find out how it should be broken.

Divide it correctly between syllables. Then put a hyphen after the first part of the word to show where the break comes.

To Discuss

Look up the words below in your dictionary. Be prepared to answer the questions that follow on page 73.

quote   prize   report   estimate   muscle

1. Which words cannot be divided? Give a reason.
2. Which words can be divided only in one place? Write them on the board, using a hyphen to divide them correctly.

► **Practice: Dividing Words**

Divide the words below correctly between syllables. Use hyphens to show where they can be divided.

potato	sentence	hesitate	arrange
resistance	heavenly	student	departmental
review	undertake	injurious	practice

Discovering Word Meanings

It is always best to look in the dictionary for the meaning of an unfamiliar word. Sometimes this is not immediately possible. Even when it is, it may be a challenge to try first to discover the meaning without the help of the dictionary.

Getting the Meaning from the Setting

Read this sentence:

Bob was proud of his stamp collection, which made him a real philatelist.

You might guess from its use in the sentence that the word *philatelist* means "stamp collector."

Now read this sentence:

The king did not have *authoritarian* power.

What word that you know is similar to *authoritarian*? If you recognize the word *authority*, you will guess the meaning of *authoritarian*.

How to Discover the Meaning of a Word

Notice how the word fits into the thought of the sentence in which it occurs.

See if the word reminds you of one you already know.

73

► **Practice: Studying the Context of a Word**

Read the following selection. Use the guides on page 73 to help you guess the meanings of the italicized words.

In the courtyard, some of King Arthur's *celebrated* knights were about to depart on a *pilgrimage* that would take them on many *diverse* paths. Dressed in shining *mail*, with *visors* open, they *bade* their friends farewell. In their hands they *bore* their *lances* upright, while their shields with knightly *crests* hung at their sides. Finally, their farewells made, the knights turned their *mounts* abruptly and rode swiftly into the dawn. They had set out on the great *quest*.

Refer to the above selection to answer these questions:

1. Does *celebrated* remind you of a word whose meaning you already know? What is it?

2. What clues tell you that a *pilgrimage* and a *quest* are some kind of journey?

3. Does the word *diverse* remind you of another word? What is it?

4. Does the word *shining* give you a clue to the meaning of the word *mail*?

5. Look at the word *visors*. Can you think of other words that begin with *vi*? If you know the meaning of *vision* or *visible*, can you guess the meaning of *visors*?

6. What clues can you find to help you guess the meanings of the other italicized words in the paragraph?

7. Most words have more than one meaning. The dictionary may give several meanings for a word. However, the *setting*, or *context*, in which you find it will tell you which definition applies. Which of the following meanings applies to the word *mount* as used in the selection above?

    1. mountain
    2. get up on
    3. horse for riding

► **Practice: Word Meanings**

1. Use the dictionary to check the meanings of the italicized words in the selection on page 74.

2. How many definitions are given for these words: *mail, crest, quest?* Find a definition that explains their meaning in the selection.

3. What word do you need to look up in order to find a definition for *bore* as it is used in the selection about King Arthur's knights?

4. Study the *context* of the italicized word in each sentence below. Have someone read the different meanings of the word given in the dictionary. Decide which one applies to the word as it is used in the sentence. Which word changes its pronunciation?

   1. Watch the *turn* of the wheel.
      He took his *turn* at bat.
   2. He climbed a *flight* of stairs.
      The birds in *flight* formed a perfect V.
   3. I had *just* three pennies left.
      The prisoner had a *just* trial.
   4. The doctor took out John's *appendix.*
      The information can be found in the *appendix.*
   5. Our *project* is to rake the leaves.
      Will the pole *project* from the trunk of the car?
      Bill lives in a housing *project.*
      He will *project* the filmstrip on the wall.

5. In your dictionaries, find as many meanings for each word below as the number after it indicates. Write a sentence to show each meaning. Underline the word in the sentence.

      employ (2)   game (3)   match (3)
      frame (2)   grain (2)   operation (2)

6. Be prepared to read your sentences aloud. Listen carefully as your classmates read their sentences. See if you can guess the meaning of the words from their context.

TO MEMORIZE

Be not niggardly of what costs thee nothing, as courtesy, counsel, and countenance.

BENJAMIN FRANKLIN

This advice comes from *Poor Richard's Almanack*. Use your dictionary to see whether you agree with all of it. Try expressing the same idea exactly, but use your own words. Can you do it in one sentence?

Review Practice: Sentences

1. Decide which of the following groups of words form sentences, and then write each sentence correctly:

1. what a marksman you are
2. will he be able to play tomorrow
3. not a sound was heard
4. one day soon, John
5. please open the window
6. how he made that mistake

2. To each group of words in exercise 1 that is not a sentence, add words to build a sentence. Write the sentence correctly.

3. Write three different kinds of sentences about something you saw or did today: a statement, a question, and an exclamation. Then write a command. Be prepared to read your sentences aloud with the proper expression.

4. Write the paragraph below, using capital letters and punctuation marks correctly:

the discovery of fire improved man's way of life fire brought warmth to his cave it frightened away wild beasts early man soon began to cook his food he also learned to preserve food by smoking it he used fire to bake pots and forge tools fire was one of the greatest discoveries of mankind

76

TRYOUT TIME

If you make a mistake on any tests, take the Practice on page 78 with the same Roman numeral as the test.

Test I.   Prefixes and Suffixes

1. Make two words from each of the following by adding a prefix or a suffix. Try to use different prefixes and suffixes.

play	out	regular
build	coat	appoint
charge	hand	cast

2. Write each word below correctly, adding a suffix that begins with a vowel:

hope   love   peace   care

3. Write each of the above words correctly, adding a suffix that begins with a consonant.

Test II.   Finding Entries in a Dictionary

The guide words on a dictionary page are **honest–hooky**. Write the words from the list below that you would find on it.

honey	honorable
hoodlum	hoodwink
homing	honorary
hone	homeward
hoot	hope

Test III.   Finding Word Meanings

Read the following sentences. Try to discover the meaning of each italicized word from its context in the sentence. Write the meanings after the numerals 1–4.

1. He had the *crafty* look of a fox.
2. She met the hardships with *fortitude*.
3. Are the refreshments *adequate* for twenty guests?
4. The day may be clear, but I am *dubious* about it.

Practice I. Prefixes and Suffixes

1. Reread the lesson on pages 61–64 carefully. Correct any mistakes that you made on Test I.

2. Copy these sentences. Add a prefix or suffix to the incomplete word to form the word you need.

1. The ball bounded and _?_bounded across the court.
2. It was our _?_fortune to have no snow for skiing.
3. Kitty is the picture of content_?_.
4. His refus_?_ to play surprised us.
5. She spoke _?_respect_?_ to her teacher.

Practice II. Finding Entries in a Dictionary

1. Review the lesson on pages 68–69. Correct any mistakes you made on Test II.

2. The guide words on a dictionary page are **lever–lie**. Write the words from the list below that you would find on the page.

levy	license
lest	lettuce
let	lick
liable	level
library	life
lexicon	liberty

Practice III. Find Word Meanings

1. Review page 73 carefully. Correct any mistakes that you made on Test III.

2. Copy these words on your paper. Beside each, write a word that it reminds you of and that would help you know its meaning.

secondary	differ	severity
picturesque	numerical	tempestuous
cylindrical	frequency	longevity

CHAPTER 4

Learning About Nouns

The words in our language have been divided traditionally into groups called the parts of speech. One of the most often used parts of speech is the noun. You may remember that the word *noun* comes from a Latin word meaning *name.* One way of explaining how nouns work in sentences is to call them "name words." In this chapter you will find other ways to help you recognize nouns easily.

■ A noun is a word that names.

The Noun

The number of nouns in our language is very large. Many things can be named by more than one noun, so that the speaker or writer has a choice. For example, instead of *trees,* you might list *pine, cedar, hemlock,* and *fir.* If you list *man* as the noun to name a person, try now to think of other nouns you might have used for the same person. In class, pool your words to make one list on the board. How many nouns can you list?

All the nouns you have supplied above probably name persons and objects that you can see or touch. Nouns can name more, however. They can name a feeling, like *fear;* or a time, like *winter;* or a condition or state of being, like *prosperity;* or a thought or belief, like *faith.* Additional examples are listed below:

happiness	nation	week	secrecy
ambition	autumn	justice	hunger

79

▶ **Practice: Choosing Words That Name**

1. Look about the room. Mention some nouns that name things you can see or touch.

2. Mention some nouns that name what you cannot see or touch.

3. Complete these sentences with nouns. Be prepared to tell whether each noun names a person, a place, an animal, or a thing.

1. We had __?__ for dessert.
2. Is __?__ your teacher?
3. One quality I look for in a friend is __?__.
4. The __?__ lives in a large cage at the zoo.
5. Someday I should like to travel in __?__.

Check Test 7: Forms of Verbs

The sentences below require forms of verbs you have studied in earlier grades. Write each sentence, using the correct form of the verb in parentheses.

1. (write)   Who __?__ the story about the fox?
2. (give)   Dick __?__ me a pen for my birthday.
3. (eat)   Jay __?__ a peach after he had __?__ lunch.
4. (begin)   Has the concert __?__?
5. (give)   Bill and Tom have __?__ the dog a bath.

If you made a mistake on the test, turn to page 354 for review and further practice.

How Our Language Grew • • ● ●

In the past, new words were added to our language by explorers, colonists, and immigrants. More recently, travel and commerce with foreign lands have promoted an interchange of articles, customs, and ideas. When something new from another country becomes familiar to us, we tend to use the foreign noun or a noun with a slight variation in spelling or meaning.

These nouns came into English from Spanish-speaking people: *canoe, chili, mosquito, patio, rodeo.*

80

Gamma
Greek letter

Sounds and Spelling

How the Romans Changed Their Minds About <u>G</u>

The Greek alphabet did not follow the order that we use in our alphabet. After *alpha* and *beta* came *gamma* (g). When the Romans borrowed from the Greek alphabet, they left out *g* because, in their Latin language, *c* seemed to represent almost the same sound as *g*. Listen to the first sound in each of these words: *coat* and *goat*. Without *g*, the Roman alphabet began with *a b c*.

As time passes, the pronunciation of some words changes a little. The time came when the Romans found a need for both *c* and *g* after all. Then they formed the letter *G* to look like *C* with a bar at the opening, and they placed *G* in the alphabet as the seventh letter.

The letter *g* stands for two sounds in English: the hard *g*, as in *get*, and the soft *g*, as in *gem*. Study these words spelled with soft *g: danger, midget, ginger, gypsy*. One of three vowels always follows a soft *g: e, i,* or *y.* These vowels, however, may also follow a hard *g*, as in *anger, gift, shaggy*. In many words a silent *u* between *g* and *e, i,* or *y* keeps the *g* hard, as in *guest, guide,* and *guy*.

Spelling Checkup

1. Study the spelling and pronunciation of these words:

rang	sing	gorgeous	angle	dungeon
range	singe	George	angel	dungarees

2. Think of other words that insert a *u* between *g* and *e, i,* or *y* to keep the sound of *g* hard.

Three Noun Signals

Look at the italicized nouns in the following sentences:

1. The *tree* is a *juniper.*
2. An *article* in the *book* tells about the *Australians.*
3. A fine *concert* will be given in the new *hall.*

Notice that each of the nouns above is introduced by *a, an,* or *the.* You have known these three words as *articles* or *adjectives.* In this book, we shall call them **noun signals,** because they signal the approach of a noun. In fact, *a, an,* and *the* never appear in a sentence unless they are followed by a noun.

Name each noun and its signal in sentence 1 above. Do the same for sentence 2. In the first two sentences the noun signals come immediately before the noun, but a noun and its signal do not always come side by side in a sentence. In sentence 3 the noun *concert* has a modifier which comes between the noun signal and the noun. So also does the noun *hall.* Read each noun and its signal in sentence 3.

Nouns do not always need noun signals. Many times nouns are not preceded by *a, an,* or *the.* For example, study the italicized nouns in this sentence:

> *Mr. Street* always practices *honesty* and *fairness* in *business.*

However, whenever you do see *a, an,* or *the* in a sentence, you may be sure that a noun follows.

■ *A, an* and *the* frequently appear before nouns; they are called **noun signals.**

► **Practice: Noun Signals**

1. Tell which of the eight words listed below can be used as nouns. You can do this by testing with the noun signals in 1, 2, and 3 below. If the word fits with one or more of the signals, it can be used as a noun.

    1. A ___?___
    2. An ___?___
    3. The ___?___

honor	played	forgot	speech
horses	trucks	regretted	picture

2. List the nouns and the noun signals in each of the following sentences:

    1. The cabbage is in the kitchen.
    2. We will make a good salad for the luncheon.
    3. Have you a ripe tomato in the refrigerator?
    4. Please run to the store for a cucumber.
    5. Get a jar of sliced pickles, too.
    6. Put the sandwiches on a large plate.

TO MEMORIZE

They shall beat their swords into ploughshares, and their spears into pruning-hooks; nation shall not lift up sword against nation, neither shall they learn war any more.

OLD TESTAMENT

These verses from the Bible tell of the wish for peace. The men who wrote these lines so many years ago looked forward to the time when weapons of war would not be used any more and there would be no need for men to be trained as soldiers. What are "ploughshares" and "pruning-hooks"?

The verses appear on a cornerstone at the United Nations Building. Why are they appropriate there?

83

1. Write each sentence. Draw a line between the complete subject and the complete predicate.

1. The geyser erupts every hour.
2. The excited young man dropped his camera near the hot spring.
3. The steep canyon rose high above the river.
4. I see my reflection in the clear pond.
5. Our guide is a college student.
6. Bill's stamp collection is getting very large.

2. Name the simple subject and verb in each of the above sentences.

3. Study the following sentences. In each sentence the subject and predicate are in inverted order. Name the simple subject and the verb in each sentence.

1. On the table stood a bowl of roses.
2. Beneath the bench sat a timid squirrel.
3. Around my head buzzed a swarm of bees.
4. Across the blue sky floated some fleecy clouds.
5. From the laboratory of Louis Pasteur came great discoveries.
6. Across the plains sped the herd of gazelles.

4. Rewrite each of the sentences in Exercise 3, putting the subject and predicate in natural order.

Composition: Writing Nouns

A. Write sentences using each of the following words as a noun. Signal each with *a, an,* or *the.*

    play   act   crowd   order   insult   people

B. Write a paragraph about a stormy day. Use nouns that name loud noises, like howl, bang. Use verbs that describe the motion or action of noisy things. How many can you use in a sensible, interesting paragraph?

84

Sentence Patterns: Nouns and Verbs

Study the following symbols for the two parts of speech you have studied so far—*nouns* and *verbs*:

N = Noun
V = Action verb

When we combine these symbols in the same order in which nouns and verbs usually appear in sentences, we can see the basic patterns of sentences. Using these patterns as a guide, we can build sentences of our own.

The sentences below follow two of the most common patterns of English sentences:

Sentence Pattern 1: **N V**	Dogs bark.
	Lucy won.
	Bells ring.
Sentence Pattern 2: **N V N**	Politicians love speeches.
	Marta picked apples.
	Boys like sports.

When we add the noun signals *a, an,* and *the* to these two sentence patterns, we can build sentences similar to these:

The **N V**	The dogs bark.
A **N V**	A firecracker exploded.
A **N V** the **N**	A carpenter built the house.
N V an **N**	Marta picked an apple.

● Now try building sentences of your own with the following symbols. For each group of symbols, build two sentences that make sense. Do not use the same words over and over.

1. **N V**	6. A **N V** the **N**
2. **N V** an **N**	7. The **N V N**
3. **N V N**	8. A **N V**
4. The **N V**	9. The **N V** a **N**
5. A **N V N**	10. An **N V** the **N**

Common and Proper Nouns

Look at the first drawing above. What do you see? If you say "a building," your response will be correct. If you say "The Empire State Building," that, too, will be correct. Similarly, you may say that the second drawing shows a house or that it shows the *White House.*

The words *building* and *house* are nouns which name any building or any house. They are called **common nouns.** The nouns *Empire State Building* and *White House* name a particular building and a particular house. They are called **proper nouns.** Proper nouns always begin with capital letters.

What is a common noun that names what you see in the third drawing above? Now name the proper noun.

Compare the common nouns and the proper nouns listed below:

COMMON NOUNS	PROPER NOUNS
continent	Africa
country	Canada
state	Delaware
government body	Senate
document	Constitution of the United States
organization	Boy Scouts of America
building	Rosedale Public Library

A proper noun sometimes includes more than one word. In the list above you will find examples. Name them. Notice that each important word in a group of words begins with a capital letter.

If you need review on capitalizing proper nouns, turn to pages 347–48. Study the rules and examples for capital letters.

■ A noun that names a particular person, place, or thing is a **proper noun.** Any other noun is called a **common noun.**

Begin a proper noun with a capital letter. If a proper noun has more than one word, begin each important word in the group with a capital letter.

► **Practice: Writing Common and Proper Nouns**

1. For each common noun below, give a proper noun. Be prepared to write it correctly on the board.

author	language	city
river	book	month
state	ocean	street
continent	country	school

2. For each proper noun below, give a common noun:

Halloween	Library of Congress
Mt. Hood	George Washington
America	Audubon Society
Massachusetts	World War II

3. Write the following sentences, using capital letters correctly:

1. The declaration of independence is a famous american document.
2. Although a committee of statesmen made suggestions, thomas jefferson did the actual writing.
3. The continental congress, meeting in philadelphia, adopted the document in 1776.
4. The old liberty bell in independence hall in philadelphia was rung.

Singular and Plural Nouns

The singular form of a noun names one item or unit; the plural form names more than one. Most nouns add *s* or *es* to indicate a change to the plural form. This change in form is noticeable in both speech and writing.

Read aloud the words listed below. Listen to the plural sounds. You should hear three different sounds added to the singular form: *s, z,* and *ez.*

chair, chairs	wish, wishes	table, tables
lamp, lamps	lake, lakes	rose, roses
lady, ladies	crutch, crutches	clock, clocks

Now examine the written forms of the plurals above. Notice that each plural has an *s* or *es* ending. This plural ending is a special characteristic that can help you to identify words that are nouns.

Three Rules for Forming Plurals

Nouns form their plurals in different ways.

1. Most nouns form their plurals by adding *s* to the singular form, as:

desk   desks   dance   dances

2. Nouns that end in *s, sh,* soft *ch,* and *x* form their plurals by adding *es,* as:

match	matches	marsh	marshes
grass	grasses	box	boxes

3. Nouns ending in *y* following a consonant change *y* to *i* and add *es* to form the plural, as:

party   parties   city   cities

Nouns ending in *y* following a vowel add *s* to form the plural, as:

monkey   monkeys   tray   trays

88

Irregular Ways to Write Plural Nouns

1. Some nouns ending in *o* add *s* to form the plural, as:

    solo   solos   Eskimo   Eskimos   piano   pianos

    Some add *es,* as:

    tomato   tomatoes   potato   potatoes   hero   heroes

2. Some nouns ending in *f* or *fe* change *f* to *v* and add *es:*

    leaf   leaves   knife   knives

    Some simply add the *s:*

    chief   chiefs   roof   roofs   safe   safes

3. Some nouns form their plurals with irregular endings:

    ox   oxen   child   children

4. Some nouns change vowels within the word:

    woman   women   tooth   teeth

5. Some nouns do not change form for plurals:

    deer   deer   sheep   sheep

Using Your Dictionary

When plurals are not formed in the usual way, you must use the dictionary and try to remember the spelling. If the plural is formed by adding *s* or *es,* the dictionary shows only the singular form. If the plural is formed in any other way, the dictionary includes the plural as well as the singular spelling.

► **Practice: Writing the Plural Forms of Nouns**

Write the plural form of each noun below. If you are in doubt, consult the dictionary.

1. goose	4. half	7. gas	10. radio
2. house	5. tornado	8. zoo	11. dish
3. second	6. belief	9. self	12. dairy

89

Sentence Patterns:
Review of Two Patterns

Review these symbols:

N = Noun   **V** = Action verb

Sentence Pattern 1 contains a *noun* and *verb*. Sentence Pattern 2 contains three basic parts; a *noun*, an *action verb*, and a *noun*—in that order.

Sentence Pattern 1:   **N V**   Trees sway.
                                     The clouds darkened.
Sentence Pattern 2:   **N V N**   Ron repairs clocks.
                                     A friend fixed the engine.

The noun signals *a, an,* and *the* do not change the basic pattern of a sentence.

● Starting with numeral 1 and continuing in order, build five sentences following the symbols listed below. Choose your nouns and verbs from the lists beneath the symbols. Do not use a word more than once.

1. The **N V**   4. The **N V** a **N**
2. A **N V** the **N**   5. The **N V** the **N**
3. A **N V**

rooster	joke	machine	sonata
cargo	crowed	farmer	tractor
told	fireman	played	bought
car	washed	pianist	lifted

● On your paper, write the headings *Nouns* and *Verbs*. Write each of the words above under the proper heading.

One word in the group can be used as a noun or a verb. It should be written under both headings.

● Now add modifying words or word groups to your five sentences to make them more interesting.

Example: A machine lifted the cargo.
            A giant machine easily lifted the heavy cargo.

The Possessive Form of Nouns

One of the convenient short cuts provided in our language is the possessive form of nouns—the form that shows ownership. Study the nouns in italics. Where is the apostrophe?

SINGULAR POSSESSIVE	PLURAL POSSESSIVE
the *horse's* saddle	the *horses'* saddles
the *fox's* den	the *foxes'* den

How to Form Possessive Nouns

1. Singular nouns show possession with an apostrophe and *s:*

   the *boy's* books   the *country's* flag

2. Plural nouns ending in *s* show possession with an apostrophe only:

   the *boys'* books   the *countries'* flags

3. Plural nouns not ending in *s* show possession with an apostrophe and *s:*

   the *women's* hats   the *oxen's* yoke

Nouns are the only kind of word in our language that indicate possession, as shown above.

▶ **Practice: Possessive Nouns**

1. Write the singular and plural possessive of each of the nouns below. Add a noun signal and a word to name what is possessed. *Example:* ox—an ox's burden   the oxen's burden

boy   group   child   pupil   fox
monkey   lady   hero   chief   elf

2. Write the possessive forms of the nouns in parentheses:

1. The colonists objected to (King George) rule.
2. The (colonists) leaders urged the colonies to unite.
3. The minute men resisted the British (soldiers) raids.
4. They searched the (citizens) houses for smuggled goods.

How to Recognize a Noun

In this chapter you have noted several things about nouns that should help you to recognize them. To check whether a certain word is used as a noun in a sentence, ask the test questions listed below. Do not expect all test questions to apply to every noun.

1. Does the word name a person, a thing, or a place?

2. Does the word have a noun signal? Would one make sense?

3. Does the word mean more than one with an *s* or *es* ending; if not, can it be made plural that way?

4. Does the word show possession with an apostrophe or an apostrophe and *s*?

 **Practice: Recognizing Nouns**

Select the nouns in the following sentences and test them orally with the questions listed above:

1. Weird sounds issued from the cave in the forest.
2. The captain heard the sailors' shout from the ship.
3. The train climbed over the hills, ran beside a roaring river and through a long spiral tunnel.

Composition: Description

A. Select a noun that names an object in your room. Use from three to five sentences to describe it, but do not give away the name. Let the class guess.

B. Choose at least four of the following nouns and modifiers and weave them into a descriptive paragraph:

a lonely child	a fierce wind	a whispered warning
a dark night	an ugly witch	a glad surprise

Going Ahead ♦ ♦ ♦ ♦

You may be appointed for a week to read compositions of classmates who wish help before their papers are graded.

Make no corrections yourself. Explain needed changes so well that pupils can correct their own errors.

Miracles on Maple Hill

by Virginia Sorensen
illustrated by Beth and Joe Krush
Harcourt, Brace & World, Inc.

Marly was counting on miracles the day the family left the city to open the farmhouse on Maple Hill. Ever since her father had been a prisoner-of-war, he had been grouchy and jumpy. There had been bickering and uneasiness in the family, but Marly hoped that living on Maple Hill would change this. Then, even as they arrived, the first miracle of the new year was taking place. The sap was rising in the maple tree. It was maple syrup time!

Maple Hill provided many other miracles that year—the discovery of the hermit and the exciting rescue of the little foxes, for example. However, the best miracle was what happened inside Marly, Joe, Mother, and Father.

TRYOUT TIME

If you make a mistake on any of the tests, take the Practice on page 95 with the same Roman numeral as the test.

Test I. Common and Proper Nouns

Write these two headings on your paper: *Common* and *Proper*. Put each of the nouns listed below in its proper column. Use capital letters correctly.

state	roosevelt school	continent	city
building	mt. everest	australia	mountain
chicago	florida	wood county	street
june	sunday	swedish	river

Test II. Singular and Plural Nouns

Write these sentences, changing each singular noun in parentheses to plural:

1. (Tractor) help the (farmer) in their work.
2. Children must not play with (box) of (match).
3. Most (boy) and (girl) like (party).
4. At the show some (monkey) played (piano).
5. The hungry (sheep) were eating the (leaf).
6. Most (Eskimo) carry hunting (knife).
7. The (man) planted the (potato).

Test III. How Nouns Show Possession

Change these expressions to show possession with an apostrophe:

>the song of the cardinal
>the nests of the squirrels
>the coat of my brother
>the work of Grace
>the games of children
>the den of the foxes
>the wool of the sheep

↙ IF YOU NEED MORE PRACTICE ↙

Practice I.   Common and Proper Nouns

1. Make sure you know why you made the errors in your test.

2. Review the lesson on pages 86–87.

3. Write these sentences, beginning each proper noun with a capital letter:

1. The name of our school is westwood school.
2. The highest building in the world is the empire state building.
3. The city of chicago is on one of the great lakes.
4. I speak french.
5. We traveled through europe, stopping at paris, london, and rome.
6. That ship will go through the panama canal.

Practice II.   Singular and Plural Nouns

1. Look at the errors you made in the test. Find the rules on pages 88–89 and read carefully those that you forgot.

2. Write the plurals for these nouns:

goose	daisy
leaf	roof
hero	potato
gun	dish
man	cargo

Practice III.   How Nouns Show Possession

1. Study again the rules and examples on page 91.

2. Write these sentences.   Use possessive nouns.

1. Have you read (Mr. Turner) book?
2. In the tropics (man) enemy is disease.
3. The (cowboy) hat fell under the (bronco) feet.
4. The (women) club is having a fair.
5. The (countries) borders have been changed.

CHAPTER 5

Gathering and Organizing Information

Finding information and organizing it in good order is so important a part of education that you will be doing it all through junior high school, high school, and college. If you enter business or a profession, you will find this skill either required of you or a great convenience in your work.

A Research Project

Suppose that you are studying the topic "My Community's Water Supply." Before you begin to look for the information you will need, think through the problem. Decide two things: what you need to find out, and where to get the information.

Deciding What You Need to Find Out

It is wise to decide in advance what principal questions you will wish to find answers for. Read the following questions. Would they be appropriate to your project?

1. What is the source of our water supply?
2. Do we have plenty of water? Is there a danger of a water shortage?
3. What are the special problems in supplying our water?
4. How is the water brought to our homes?
5. What are some ways in which water is purified? Which of these ways is used in our community?
6. Who pays the cost of supplying our water?
7. Is our water tested for impurities? If so, how?
8. How is the amount of water a family uses measured?
9. Are families billed for the water they use?

Finding Sources of Information

After you have decided what questions need answering, think where you could find the information necessary to answer them. Which of the following resources could you use to find information about your community's water supply? Remember that you will need general information about community water supplies as a background for studying your own community's water resources.

1. *Your home:* Could you find books or other materials about water resources at home? Could you observe some things about your community's water supply in your own home?

2. *Your classroom:* Could you find books, pictures, or other materials on the topic there?

3. *The library:* Are there encyclopedias, reference books, newspapers, magazines, illustrations, and pamphlets containing information on the topic? How can you find out?

4. *Government agencies, or other organizations:* In your community or state, are there organizations that may have pamphlets, maps, or pictures that will help?

5. *Experts:* Are there experts on the topic who live in your community?

To Discuss

1. Can you think of any other sources of information about your community's water supply?

2. Read the questions below and decide where you might find answers to them. Be ready to make your suggestions in class.

1. What is the history of baseball?
2. What kind of space suit does an astronaut wear?
3. What are some typical American dishes?
4. What is the sixth grade like in England?
5. What are the main causes of automobile accidents?
6. How many records were sold in the United States in the last year?

▶ **Practice: Planning a Study**

Suppose that you are studying the following topic: "Ways of Lighting American Homes Then and Now."

1. List questions that will need to be answered as you make your study. Be prepared to read them in class. Discuss the questions with your classmates and make a class list.

2. Make a list of sources that might give you the information you need. Then make a class list of sources.

Review Practice: Word Study

1. Study these sentences. Notice particularly the differences in spelling and meaning of the homonyms. If you cannot figure out the meaning of a homonym from its context, look it up in the dictionary. Prepare to write the sentences from dictation.

1. The *capital* of California is Sacramento.
2. The legislature is in session at the *Capitol*.
3. Who is the *principal* of your school?
4. He explained a *principle* of flight.
5. Nan gave me *stationery* for my birthday.
6. Here is a *stationary* model of the engine.

2. Close your books and write the sentences above as your teacher dictates them.

Interviewing an Expert

Among the best sources of information are experts on the subject who may live in your own community. One way to obtain the information is to meet with an expert and ask your questions. This kind of meeting is an *interview*.

Preparing for the Interview

Joan wanted information on her town's water supply for a report. She wrote a letter arranging an interview with Mr. Randolph, the engineer at the town waterworks. Then she listed the questions she wanted to ask Mr. Randolph.

To ask good questions in an interview, you must know something about the subject. Read for general background on the subject. Then think of points the expert might explain or additional information he might have. List your questions in a sensible order, and mark the most important ones so that you will be sure to ask them.

To Discuss

Read these questions that Joan prepared for her interview with the waterworks engineer. Decide which are the most important questions and tell why you think so.

1. Does our water come from a lake, a river, or wells?
2. How is our water stored?
3. How long would our supply last without rainfall? Is there any danger that we will run out of water?
4. Does our water need to be treated in some way? If so, how is this done?
5. How much does it cost a year to supply water for our town? How is this cost met?
6. How many miles of pipes are used to get the water to the users?
7. Are there other facts you think our class should know about our water supply?

Taking Notes During the Interview

During the interview, listen carefully. If you do not understand an explanation, ask politely for further information.

Take brief notes during the interview. Jot down the main points and important figures or details that you may forget. Use abbreviations. However, be sure that they are abbreviations that you will understand later. After the interview, review your notes and fill in some of the details.

The way to develop confidence and skill as an interviewer is to practice. Follow the guides below in preparing for and conducting interviews.

How to Prepare for and Conduct an Interview

Make arrangements for the interview by telephone or letter.

Read for a general background on the topic.

Prepare your questions before the interview.

During the interview, listen carefully.

Take brief notes of the main points and any facts or figures you may forget.

After the interview, complete your notes.

► **Practice: Interviewing**

1. Choose a topic on which you or a classmate could speak as something of an expert after some preparation. Here are some suggested topics:

> A visit to a famous place (your choice)
> How to play a game (your choice)
> Experiences as a gardener
> How to plan a camping trip
> A hobby (your choice)

2. After you have selected a topic, choose a partner. Decide the roles each of you will play in making arrangements for the interview and during the interview. Be prepared to act your roles before the class.

3. Follow the guides for interviewing on page 101.

Composition: Writing a News Story

A. Listen carefully to the class interviews suggested above. Then select one of them as the subject of a news story. Write it as if you were a reporter for the *Morning News*. Tell who gave the interview, what the main points were, what details were surprising or new to the class, and why the report was of importance.

B. Write a news story in not more than three full paragraphs, telling as much as you can about some event or person in your community. The school newspaper may publish it or your room may wish to issue a class newspaper to include a story from each pupil.

Using Words Correctly: Correct Verb Forms

You have learned that a verb can express the time of an action. Review the forms of these verbs, which you have studied in earlier grades:

PRESENT	PAST	PAST WITH HELPER
break	broke	(have, has, or had) broken
choose	chose	(have, has, or had) chosen
drink	drank	(have, has, or had) drunk
ring	rang	(have, has, or had) rung
sing	sang	(have, has, or had) sung

Do not use a helping verb with **broke, chose, drank, rang,** and **sang.**

Use a helping verb with **broken, chosen, drunk, rung,** and **sung.**

1. Read each sentence aloud, using the correct form of the verb in parentheses.

1. Sam has (broke, broken) his watch.
2. Mary had (chose, chosen) the perfect gift for her brother.
3. Who (drank, drunk) the fruit punch?
4. The telephone (rang, rung) in the middle of the night.
5. Haven't you (sang, sung) any solos?

2. Write each sentence, using the correct form of the verb.

1. (break) Yesterday, Richard __?__ the record for the high jump.
2. (choose) We __?__ the same topic for our reports.
3. (drink) One of the girls __?__ some salt water.
4. (ring) The bell has __?__.
5. (sing) Last week our chorus __?__ two songs on the Thanksgiving program.
6. (break) The vibration had __?__ the dishes.

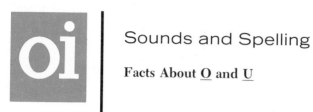

Sounds and Spelling

Facts About <u>O</u> and <u>U</u>

Find the marks your dictionary uses to show the sounds of *o* and *u*. Then name the letters or letter combinations used in spelling *o* sounds:

    o as in *cot*:   hot, John
    ō as in *coat*: float, tone, toe, blow, oh, owe, so, sew
    ô as in *core*: fore, fort, court, off, saw, salt, fault

What letters or letter combinations spell these *u* sounds?

    u as in *cut*:   sun, ton, done, flood, young, wonderland,
                        once, won
    ū as in *cute*: cube, you, ewe, few, feud, view, beauty
    u̇ as in *full*:   pull, good, could
    ü as in *fruit*: rule, school, do, two, true, move, grew

Say these words and listen to the vowel sounds: *out, oil*. Can you hear the vowel sound changing while you say the word? A speech sound that changes from one vowel to another is called a *diphthong* (dif′ thong). The two vowel sounds in *out* are *o* as in *stop* and *u* as in *pull*. The two vowel sounds in *oil* are *o* as in *go* and *i* as in *hit*.

Compare the diphthongs in *how* and *out*.

Spelling Checkup

1. Think of other words that have the sound of *o* as in *off* that follow these spelling patterns: ?_or_?, ?_our, ?_aw

2. Think of words that have an *o* sound as in *coat* with spellings like these: ?_oa_?, ?_o_?e, ?_ow.

3. Show the mark used for the *u* sound in each word below. List more words with the same *u* sound but with other letters.

      fool   should   blood   butte

Using an Encyclopedia

Interviewing an expert is an excellent way to get information on a subject. But experts are usually not available in person. Then you may turn for information to articles written by *thousands* of experts, brought together in an encyclopedia or set of encyclopedias.

What an Encyclopedia Contains

Some encyclopedias cover a very wide range of subjects and contain information on almost any topic of importance that you can think of. Others specialize in certain subjects, such as biography or science. Some encyclopedias are prepared especially for young students. They are easy to read and contain helpful pictures and study aids.

Even the best encyclopedia cannot give complete information about all subjects because of lack of space. Most of them, therefore, list at the end of many articles the names of books, magazines, or government pamphlets on the subject, or refer to other articles in the encyclopedia itself.

The important facts about many topics, such as "Radar" or "Nuclear Fission," change greatly from year to year as new discoveries or advances are made. For this reason, be sure the encyclopedia you are using is up-to-date. Look for the date of publication by finding the *copyright* notice, which gives the date of the encyclopedia. This is usually printed on the *copyright page*, which follows the *title page* at the front of each volume of the set.

To Discuss

Read each of these topics. Decide whether basic facts about the topic are likely to change greatly from year to year.

>Space Travel
>Vitamin C
>The Wombat
>The First Balloon Flight
>The Ten Most Popular Television Programs

1. Which topics suggest information that is not likely to change from year to year?

2. For which topics would you need to refer to an encyclopedia with a very recent publication date?

3. Which topic would you not find in an encyclopedia?

Finding Information in an Encyclopedia

An encyclopedia has several aids to help you locate the information you want. Here are five such aids:

1. The topics are arranged in *alphabetical order.* The guide letter and volume number are stamped on the back of each book.
2. There is an *index.* Because there may be information on a topic in several articles of an encyclopedia, turn to the index to be sure of obtaining the information you may need. The index is usually in a separate volume.
3. Each major article is divided into subtopics. *Subheadings* tell you what these subtopics are.
4. At the top of the page, there may be *guide topics.* Use them as you use guide words on a dictionary page.
5. At the end of an article, there may be *cross references* to other articles containing information on the subject. For example, the final paragraph of an article on the Aztecs might be followed by this cross reference:

>*See also* Archeology; Indian Tribes, North American, and Mexico.

To Discuss

Under what topic in an encyclopedia would you look for information on each of the following subjects? Would you need to look in more than one place? If so, why?

1. Peaceful Uses of Atomic Energy
2. Alaska under the Russians
3. Head-hunters in the Upper Amazon
4. Mining Anthracite Coal in Pennsylvania
5. The Use of Radar in World War II

▶ **Practice: Using an Encyclopedia**

1. What is the name of the encyclopedia you are using?
2. Find the index. Is there an index volume? Look up "Aztec" in the index. Read the references.
3. Turn to the article on your state. How is the general topic narrowed to the most important facts? Read the sub-headings.
4. Does the top of the page include two guide topics? If so, what does the first guide topic tell you? the second? Are the guides printed in heavy type?

How Our Language Grew • • ● ●

Orient — Occident: The word *Orient* comes from a Latin expression that meant "where the sun rises." The word *Occident* meant "where the sun sets." These words now refer to the East and the West.

To the Romans long ago the land east of the Mediterranean was the Orient. We still speak of Eastern Asia by that name and refer to the inhabitants of the Far East as Orientals.

The verb *to orient* and the noun *orientation* come from the same source. When something is set to face east or adjusted squarely with the points of the compass, it is said to be *oriented.* The term also applies to people when they are adjusted to the situation in which they find themselves. Many high schools and colleges have orientation programs for freshmen.

Using the Library

Libraries full of books of all kinds, which may be borrowed without charge, are common in many parts of our country. Perhaps you have not only a public library but a school library to serve you. Those libraries contain information on all kinds of subjects. You have only to know how to find it.

Nonfiction Books

Nonfiction books are grouped according to subject. Each nonfiction book is given a number, known as the book's *call number*. Each group of 100 numbers is assigned to books on the same general subject—for example: 100–199, Philosophy; 200–299, Religion; 300–399, Social Sciences. To locate a nonfiction book, you must get its call number from a card in the *card catalog*.

The cards in the catalog are arranged alphabetically in drawers. Each drawer is labeled with letters, such as *Aa–Am* or *Ga–Gl*. By looking at the letter label, you can tell which cards are in the drawer.

There are usually three cards in the catalog for every nonfiction book in the library: an *author* card, a *title* card, and a *subject* card. The author card is filed under the author's last name. The title card and the subject card are filed according to the first important word in the title or subject. All three cards carry the book's call number, so that you can find the number if you know the author, title, or subject.

If you are gathering information for a report, you will be looking for books on your subject. Look for a *subject* card.

Suppose, for example, that you need information on water conservation. In the *Wa* drawer of the card catalog, you may find cards for several books on that subject.

The subject is printed in capital letters on the top line of the card, as shown below. Study the subject card and notice the information it gives. The *J* at the beginning of the call number stands for *Juvenile*.

```
          WATER

 J551.4               Smith, Frances C.

   The first book of water, by F. C. Smith.

 Pictures by Mildred Waltrip.  Watts, New York,

 1959.  69 p., illus., maps.
```

To Discuss

1. What is the subject of the book?
2. Who is the author of the book? What is the title?
3. Who illustrated the book?
4. What is the name of the publisher of the book? Where was it published and when? Think of a reason for giving the publisher, and the place and date of publication. Why is this helpful information?
5. What other information is given? How is it helpful?
6. What is the call number of the book?

► **Practice: Using the Library**

Plan a visit to your school or public library. While you are there, find the answers to the questions below.

1. Where is the big dictionary located?

2. Is there more than one set of encyclopedias? If so, what are their names? Where are they located? What are the copyright dates?

3. Where is the card catalog?

4. Where are the following publications located: biographies, books on science, poetry books, fiction, magazines, picture files?

5. Which books can you take out of the library? Which books must you read there? Can you take magazines and picture files out of the library? How?

6. How can you get a library card?

Going Ahead ▸ ▸ ▸ ▸

Choose a subject with which you have already had some experience or done some reading. Take the first steps toward becoming an expert. Learn all you can through interviews, books, and further experiences of your own. For this assignment, do your reading in nonfiction books rather than encyclopedia articles, since the books will develop the topic in greater detail.

Keep a diary dating your entries and recording the information or ideas you gain and the source of your information.

Preparing a Bibliography

As you use books to find information on a topic, make a list of the books from which your information comes. Such a list is called a **bibliography.**

Giving Information on Sources

A bibliography gives the name of the author and the title of each selection listed. For example:

> Bauer, Helen. *Water: Riches or Ruin*
> Hogner, Dorothy Childs. *Water over the Dam*
> Riedman, Sarah Regal. *Water for People*

A complete bibliography may also give other information about the book: the place of publication, publisher, year of publication, and a brief description of contents or other material. Here is a more complete entry for Helen Bauer's book:

> Bauer, Helen. *Water: Riches or Ruin.* Garden City: Doubleday, 1959. Mountain reservoirs and water supply. Illustrations and maps.

To Discuss

1. Notice that books in a bibliography are listed in alphabetical order. How are they alphabetized?

2. How is the author's name written? What punctuation mark follows the author's last name? the author's full name?

3. How can you tell what the title of the book is in a handwritten or typewritten bibliography?

4. Agree with your classmates on suggestions to follow in preparing a bibliography.

▶ **Practice: Writing a Bibliography**

List these books correctly for a bibliography:

1. the earth for sam, by w maxwell reed
2. soil, water, and man, by muriel deusing
3. sun, earth, and man, by george p and eunice s bischof

111

Taking Notes

It is necessary to take notes on what you have been reading if you wish to remember and use what you learned. Study the notes which follow:

Undersea Cable
Compton's Pictured Encyc. Vol. 3, pp. 5-7

Characteristics of undersea cable
Copper core for transmission of electric current. Core surrounded by layers of insulating materials
Cable lasts from 30-40 years

Laying the cable
Especially equipped cable-laying ship follows charted path
Guiding device feeds out cable

Check the model against the guides below. Be prepared to show that the student followed them.

How to Take Notes

Write the topic at the top.
Give the title of the book, the author, and the page.
Use abbreviations that are easy to interpret.
Group facts under major headings.
Record facts accurately.

► **Practice: Taking Notes**

Take notes on a topic of your choice from two or more sources of information. Follow the suggestions above.

TO MEMORIZE

So nigh is grandeur to our dust,
So near is God to man,
When Duty whispers low, "Thou must,"
The youth replies, "I can."

RALPH WALDO EMERSON

Emerson was one of America's great philosophers. These lines are quoted from a longer poem. Tell their meaning in your own words.

Review Practice: Nouns

1. Write these sentences correctly, capitalizing the proper nouns. Underline all the common and proper nouns.

1. The capital of the united states is washington, d. c.
2. The city is on the potomac river.
3. The capitol is located at the head of pennsylvania avenue.
4. The home of the President is called the white house.
5. The lincoln memorial and the jefferson memorial are points of interest.
6. The declaration of independence is housed in the national archives building.
7. The smithsonian institution houses the spirit of st. louis, in which charles lindbergh flew across the atlantic ocean alone.
8. Not far from our nation's capital is mount vernon, the home of george washington.

2. Write the plural form of each of the following nouns:

city	bush	scarf	piano
hero	deer	potato	party
alley	goose	dwarf	calf

3. Write sentences using the possessive for these nouns:

ponies	chief	Ohio	men	Mr. March
writer	nurse	nurses	thief	thieves

113

Making an Outline

Your bibliography may contain several titles and you may have written notes from several sources — an interview, an encyclopedia, books, articles, and pamphlets. The next step is to organize your information so that it can be used to make a clear-cut, interesting report on the subject.

Using Correct Outline Form

The first step in preparing an outline is to organize your notes by topics. Decide which topics in your notes are main ideas, and which subtopics that help to explain the main ideas. Then decide on the order in which you will discuss the main topics, and finally the order in which you will present the subtopics under each main topic.

Study the form of the outline on the next page. Be prepared to answer the questions that follow.

To Discuss

1. What is the title of the outline? Which words in the title are capitalized?
2. Read the main topics. Is the wording similar?
3. How are the main topics numbered? the subtopics?
4. Are the subtopics worded in a similar way?
5. How many subtopics are divided into further details? How is each level of subtopics marked?
6. Choose examples to show that the guides below were followed.

How to Write an Outline

Mark the main topics with Roman numerals.
Mark the subtopics with capital letters.
Mark any further details with Arabic numerals.
Capitalize the letters that mark the subtopics.
Place periods after numerals or letters of topics.
Capitalize the first word of each topic.

How Rocks Become Soil
I. Action of weather
   A. How winds erode rocks
      1. Sand blown against rocks
      2. Boulders loosened
   B. How extreme heat and cold affect rocks
II. Action of water
   A. How rain wears away rock
   B. How streams and waves erode rock
III. Action of plants and trees
   A. How seeds split rocks
   B. How roots break cracks open

► **Practice: Writing an Outline**

1. Rewrite the following part of an outline in the correct form. Use capital letters and punctuation marks correctly in the outline.

the values of a part-time job
  developing different skills
    getting along with others
    making business arrangements
    doing common tasks
      keeping records and accounts
      gardening
      baby-sitting
  earning money
    becoming more independent
    learning to spend wisely
    learning to save

Conservation of Our Forests

I. Importance of forests
   A. In preventing soil erosion
   B. In conserving of water
   C. In protecting wildlife
   D.

2. In the list below, major topics and subtopics are mixed up. Copy these topics, writing them in correct outline form:

> Tennis
> Swimming
> Boating
> Table games
> Quiet recreation indoors
> Checkers
> Golf
> Active outdoor recreation
> Model making
> Hiking
> Stamp collecting

Composition:
A Science or Social Studies Paper

A. In class, list half a dozen topics related to work in science or social studies which you have recently studied. Prepare an outline for the one you know. Have two levels of subtopics.

B. Write the paper you have outlined. Start a new paragraph for each point listed with a Roman numeral. The A and B parts may both be included in the paragraph, but if the explanations or examples are too long for one paragraph, start a new paragraph for the next lettered part.

TRYOUT TIME

If you make a mistake on any test, take the Practice on page 118 with the same Roman numeral as the test.

Test I. Correct Verb Forms

Write each of the following sentences, choosing the correct form of the verb in parentheses:

1. Somebody has (drunk, drank) all the orange juice.
2. I had (chose, chosen) Ted for my team.
3. We (rang, rung) the bells at midnight.
4. Ted was sorry he had (broke, broken) the jar.
5. The glee club (sung, sang) in the town hall.

Test II. Writing a Bibliography

List the following books in alphabetical order by the authors' last names. Write them, using the correct form for a bibliography.

1. the first book of boys' cooking, by jerrold beim
2. a spy in old philadelphia, by anne emery
3. meeting in the mountains, by john b prescott
4. blue canyon horse, by ann nolan clark

Test III. Outlining

Copy the following outline and use correct punctuation and capitalization:

the moon

I facts about features we can observe
   a moonlight
      1 source of light
      2 phases of moon
   b tides
      1 relation to moon
      2 frequency
   c eclipses

Practice I. Correct Verb Forms

1. Read the lesson on page 103 and review the verbs on the same page.

2. Write the sentences below, using the correct form of these verbs: *choose, sing, break, ring, drink.* Do not use the same verb twice.

1. The baby has __?__ all her milk.
2. Yesterday we __?__ the song I liked best.
3. The racers have __?__ the speed records.
4. We __?__ the doorbell several times.
5. Jane has __?__ the prettiest costume.

Practice II. Writing a Bibliography

1. Review the lesson on page 111.

2. List the following books in alphabetical order by the authors' last names. Use the correct form for a bibliography.

1. the erie canal, by samuel hopkins adams
2. the big wave, by pearl s buck
3. joshua slocum, sailor, by beth day
4. birthdays of freedom, by genevieve foster
5. cruising to danger, by priscilla hagon
6. life and times of frederick douglass, by frederick douglass.

Practice III. Outlining

1. Reread the lesson on pages 114–15.

2. Use the following jumbled items to make an outline. Supply a title and list items correctly by indenting and using numerals and letters.

railway, transportation, by land, by air, ship, barge, freight truck, by water, helicopter, airplane

CHAPTER 6

Learning About Verbs

The groups of words below are not sentences. By adding one word, you can make each group a sentence. Try it.

1. Gary __?__ a dollar.
2. The farmers __?__ their crops.
3. The dog __?__ my slipper.

Take turns reading your sentences aloud. Did you notice that all the words you have chosen are verbs?

Every sentence must contain a verb. It is the verb that brings life to the sentence, as it did in the sentences above.

■ A verb is a word that shows action or being.

Recognizing Verbs

A verb, as you know, is the key word in the predicate of a sentence. One way to tell whether a word can be used as a verb in a sentence is to use the word with *I, you,* or *he* as the subject. If the combination of the two words makes a sentence, the word is a verb. To illustrate this, let us test these two words: *baseball* and *lose.*

I baseball.	I lose.
You baseball.	You lose.
He baseballs.	He loses.

Can *baseball* be used as a verb? Can *lose* be used as a verb?

■ If a word can be used with *I, you,* or *he* to make a sentence, it is a verb.

119

► **Practice: Recognizing Verbs**

1. Test each of the following words in the way shown on page 119. Make a list of the words that can be used as verbs.

lion	applaud	owl	howl	tell
write	window	giggle	trip	discover

2. Three of the words you listed as verbs can also be used as nouns. Try each word with the noun signal *the* or *a*. Which three words can be used as nouns? Write a sentence for each, using the word as subject of the sentence.

3. Write three sentences, using the same words as verbs.

Verbs of Action

A verb of action often expresses action that can be seen or heard, as in these sentences:

Jason *mows* the lawn regularly.
We *played* tennis all afternoon.

Name the subject of each sentence; then the verb; then the complete predicate. With action verbs, these predicates tell what the subjects *do* or *did*. Other verbs of action like them are *swim, walk, call, hit, carry*.

A verb of action can also express action of the *mind*, which cannot be seen or heard. Such verbs as *think, know, doubt,* and *wonder* express action of the mind.

Verbs of Being

Some verbs express *being* rather than action. The most common are forms of the verb *be*: *am, is, are, was, were*. Other examples include *seem* and *become*.

Verbs of being are found in predicates that tell what or where the subject *is* or *was* or what the subject *is* or *was like*.

Name the subject, verb, and complete predicate in the following sentences. What does each predicate tell about its subject?

These boys are good friends.   Mary was happy.
The girls became friends too.   She seemed busy.

► **Practice: Two Kinds of Verbs**

Read aloud the verb in each sentence below. Tell whether it is a verb of action or a verb of being.

1. Jim delivers newspapers every morning.
2. We stitched the potato sacks together.
3. I am Linda's brother.
4. The waves dashed against the cliffs.
5. Bill whistled at his work.
6. The books were on the library table.

Composition: Choosing Verbs Carefully

A. Well-chosen verbs make interesting sentences. Write the paragraph below, choosing the verbs in parentheses that would give the reader the more lively and interesting picture:

Three fire engines (went, tore) past our house. A neighbor (called, shouted), "The roof's on fire!" Children (ran, raced) down the street to see it. Several boys on bikes (rode, sped) by. Firemen were already (showering, drowning) the flames with water. Before they left, they (took away, tore out) all the blackened shingles. Amazingly, they (did, completed) their job in half an hour.

B. Study the picture below and write a paragraph giving the reader your impression of what happened.

Sentence Patterns: A Third Pattern

Study the following symbols. You have already worked with two of them.

N = Noun **V** = Action Verb

Vᵇᵉ = Verb of being (when it is part of a predicate that tells what the subject *is* or *was*)

Now that you have studied verbs of being, you can use the new symbol **V**ᵇᵉ to show a third sentence pattern:

Pattern 3: **N V**ᵇᵉ **N**

$$\text{N} \quad \text{V}^{be} \quad \text{N}$$
The students are helpers.

$$\text{N} \quad \text{V}^{be} \quad \text{N}$$
Florence is a nurse.

Here are the sentence parts which make up each of the three patterns you have studied so far:

Pattern 1: **N V** (Noun — Verb)

$$\text{N} \quad \text{V}$$
Hyenas laugh.

Pattern 2: **N V N** (Noun — Action verb — Noun)

$$\text{N} \quad \text{V} \quad \text{N}$$
The sailor scrubbed the deck.

Pattern 3: **N V**ᵇᵉ **N** (Noun — Verb of being — Noun)

$$\text{N} \quad \text{V}^{be} \quad \text{N}$$
The bird is an oriole.

Notice that in Pattern 2 the two **N**'s stand for different things: *sailor* and *deck*. In Pattern 3, the two **N**'s refer to the same thing: *bird* and *oriole*.

● Try building sentences of your own, using the following combinations of symbols as guides. Write sensible sentences and vary your sentence ideas.

1. **N V**
2. The **N V**
3. **N V** a **N**
4. **A N V N**

5. **N V**ᵇᵉ the **N**
6. **A N V** the **N**
7. The **N V N**
8. **N V** the **N**

9. The **N V**ᵇᵉ a **N**
10. The **N V**ᵇᵉ an **N**
11. **A N V**ᵇᵉ the **N**
12. **A N V** a **N**

Helping Verbs

Examine the three sentences below carefully:

1. Harry *earned* six dollars.
2. He *is working* on Saturdays.
3. He *has been earning* six dollars each Saturday.

How many words does the verb in each sentence contain? When a verb contains more than one word, the last word is called the **main verb.** The others are called **helping verbs.** What is the main verb in sentence 2? in sentence 3? What are the helping verbs?

Name each main verb listed below. Then name the helpers.

are spoken	have frozen	shall hear
is hoping	has sung	should have run
was done	had broken	may have been chosen

Words That Separate Parts of a Verb

When the main verb and its helpers are used next to each other in a sentence, it is easy to find the entire verb:

The pond *has been frozen* all winter.

Sometimes, though, the main verb and its helpers are separated by other words in the sentence. This can happen when we make a statement or ask a question.

The word *not* and words that tell *when* and *how* may come between the verb parts: We *shall* not *rehearse* our play again.

In a question, the subject often comes between verb parts: Where *have* you *been staying*?

▶ **Practice: Words That Separate Verb Parts**

Read aloud the sentences below. Name the verb in each. Then name the words that separate the verb parts.

1. I *did* not *hear* you.
2. *Can* you *hear* me?
3. She *has been* quietly *planning* her exit.
4. That rule *should* always *be* followed.

The Helping Verbs: <u>have</u>, <u>be</u>, and <u>do</u>

Look at these lists of the forms of the helping verbs *have,* *be,* and *do*:

have	be		do
have	be	are	do
has	am	was	does
had	is	were	did

In the list of verbs and their helpers on page 123, you saw the different forms of the verbs *have* and *be* used as helping verbs. These and the three forms of *do* can be used either as helping verbs or main verbs.

AS MAIN VERBS	AS HELPING VERBS
1. I *am* fond of all pets.	1. I *am reading* about dogs.
2. My dog *is* a Dalmatian.	2. He *is seen* all over town.
3. The twins *have* measles.	3. They *have recovered* now.
4. Bill *did* a dance routine.	4. He *did dance* well.

► **Practice: Main Verbs and Helping Verbs**

1. Read aloud each sentence below and name the verbs. Be sure to include the main verb and its helper or helpers.

1. You can always count on Jack.
2. We might never have found this picnic spot.
3. Have you seen Jerry lately?
4. Have you ever heard the hoot of an owl?

2. In each sentence below, tell whether the verb in italics is used as a helping verb or as a main verb.

1. John *can* swim three hundred yards now.
2. *Did* you leave your skates at the rink?
3. The huge plane *had* been ripped to pieces.
4. I *have* that stamp in my collection.

3. Write two sentences for each of the verbs listed below. In one sentence, use the verb as a main verb. In the second sentence, use the verb as a helping verb.

am	is	have	does	was

Sentence Patterns: Helping Verbs

Now that you have studied *helping verbs,* you can add a new verb symbol to your growing list.

N = Noun   V^{be} = Verb of being
V = Action verb   V^h = Helping verb

Review the three sentence patterns listed below. Notice that the **V** or **V**^{be} in each basic pattern can stand for more than one word. The predicate includes a verb and one or more helping verbs. For example, the symbols **V**^h **V** are represented by the **V** symbol in the basic pattern.

Pattern 1: **N V**

$$\text{N} \quad \text{V}^h \quad \text{V}$$
Lions can roar.

Pattern 2: **N V N**

$$\text{N} \quad \text{V}^h \quad \text{V} \quad \text{N}$$
Janet will cook spaghetti.

Pattern 3: **N V**^{be} **N**

$$\text{N} \quad \text{V}^h \quad \text{V}^h \quad \text{V}^{be} \quad \text{N}$$
Frank could have been president.

● Study the combinations of symbols listed below. Match each one with the sentence that follows the pattern.

1. **N V**^h **V N**   a. Snow has fallen.
2. **N V**^h **V**^h **V N**   b. Peter will deliver groceries.
3. **N V**^h **V**   c. Joe can be coach.
4. **N V**^h **V**^{be} **N**   d. George should have been chairman.
5. **N V**^h **V**^h **V**^{be} **N**   e. Ruth may have seen Brownie.
6. **N V**^{be} **N**   f. Bobbie has been crying.
7. **N V N**   g. Mr. Seelie was president.
8. **N V**^h **V**^h **V**   h. Babies need attention.

● Following the order of the symbols below, build sensible sentences of your own. Vary your sentence ideas. Identify the pattern of each sentence by numeral.

1. **N V**^h **V**   5. The **N V**^h **V**^h **V** a **N**
2. The **N V** a **N**   6. A **N V**^h **V**^{be} the **N**
3. A **N V**^h **V** the **N**   7. **N V**^h **V**^h **V**^{be} the **N**
4. **N V**^h **V**^h **V**   8. The **N V**^{be} a **N**

Verbs in Contractions

Sometimes verbs are combined with the word *not* to make contractions such as those italicized below:

aren't	= are not	*hasn't*	= has not
isn't	= is not	*didn't*	= did not
haven't	= have not	*doesn't*	= does not

A verb can also be combined with the words *I, he, it, we,* and *you* in some sentences, as follows:

I'm	= I am	*we're*	= we are
he's	= he is	*I've*	= I have
it's	= it is	*you'll*	= you will

Notice the apostrophe in each contraction above. An apostrophe is used in a contraction to show that a letter or letters have been omitted.

Do not let contractions confuse you when you are looking for the verb in a sentence. Remember that *n't* is never a part of the verb. The word *I, he, it, we,* or *you* is never a part of the verb. Look for the verb in each of these sentences:

1. I've heard that speaker before.
2. You'll be hearing from me soon.
3. Bill didn't arrive in time.
4. I'm waiting for Carol.

The verb in sentence 1 is *have heard.* In sentence 2, the verb is *will be hearing.* What is the verb in sentence 3? in sentence 4?

► **Practice: Finding Verbs in Contractions**

1. Name the verb in each of these contractions:

you'll	I'm	isn't	we're
didn't	aren't	you're	I've
he's	it's	haven't	hasn't
couldn't	they'll	hadn't	don't

2. Make contractions by combining each of the following verbs with the word *not*. Remember to use an apostrophe.

could is   had do
have was did are

3. Name the verb in each of the following sentences:

1. We're on our way to the band concert.
2. Band members haven't tuned their instruments yet.
3. Don't you play the flute?
4. Isn't that your brother in that old jalopy?

TO MEMORIZE

If you can talk with crowds and keep your virtue,
 Or walk with Kings — nor lose the common touch,
If neither foes nor loving friends can hurt you,
 If all men count with you, but none too much;
If you can fill the unforgiving minute
 With sixty seconds' worth of distance run,
Yours is the Earth and everything that's in it,
 And — which is more — you'll be a Man, my son!

RUDYARD KIPLING

Rudyard Kipling was a British writer. Many of his stories and poems about India brought him fame. The lines above are from the poem "If." Discuss the lines.

Review Practice:
Punctuation and Capitalization

Proofread the paragraph below to find the necessary corrections. Then rewrite the paragraph.

Have you read *The Black Stallion's Filly* it is an exciting story about a horse named Black Minx. She was Black Stallion's colt, Henry Dailey bought the colt. To train her for racing. The training was difficult. Because she was so stubborn. Finally Black Minx ran in a great race. The book is by Walter Farley.

How Verbs Show Time

Verbs have certain changes of form by which they express time. These forms are called **tenses.** The three most common tenses are PRESENT, PAST, and FUTURE.

PRESENT: I *hear* music.   PAST: I *heard* music.
FUTURE: I *shall hear* music.

In the first statement above, the verb *hear* is said to be in the *present tense.* The present tense may also be written *hears,* as in "Tom hears the music."

In the second statement, the verb *heard* expresses what happened in past time. It is therefore called past tense. The change in written form consists in adding a *d.*

In the third sentence, *hear* has a helping verb, which shows that something will happen in the future. The verb *shall hear* is said to be in the *future tense.* The helping verb *will* also shows future time when it is used with a main verb, as in "Tom will hear the music."

Most verbs form their past tense by adding **ed** or **d.**
Most verbs form a future tense by the use of **shall** or **will** as helping verbs.

► Practice: The Tenses of Verbs

1. Tell whether each verb listed below is in the present tense, past tense, or future tense:

dances	shall arrive	walks	will travel
learned	will move	listen	turned

2. Use each of the following verbs in three sentences, showing the present tense, the past tense, and the future tense:

pack   burn   admire

Principal Parts of Verbs

There are three important forms of a verb. They are called the **principal parts of verbs.** Look at the three principal parts of the verbs listed below:

PRESENT	PAST	PAST PARTICIPLE
help, helps	helped	(have, has, or had) helped
cover, covers	covered	(have, has, or had) covered

Notice in the list above that the present tense of a verb includes a form with an **s** ending and a form without the **s** ending. Of the two, the form used in a sentence depends on the subject of the sentence and whether the subject is singular or plural. Study these examples:

I help.　　　　　　　　We help.
You help.　　　　　　　They help.
He (she *or* it) helps.　　My brothers help.

Look at the list again and note the two ways that a verb can show past time. In the past tense form, the ending *d* or *ed* is added to the present tense of the verb, as in *helped* and *covered.* In the past participle form, the helping verb *have, has,* or *had* is used, as in *have helped* and *has covered.*

Verbs that form their past tense with *d* or *ed* are called **regular verbs.** Most verbs are regular verbs.

► Practice: Using the Present and Past Tenses

1. Write an original sentence using each of the following subjects and verbs. Keep the verb in the present tense, but change the ending if necessary to fit the subject.

SUBJECTS	VERBS
1. They	laugh
2. My friends	interest
3. We	try
4. You	see
5. It	fall

129

2. Complete the following sentences with two forms of a verb that show past time. The verbs you are to use are in parentheses.

1. (sprinkle) Dick __?__ the lawn this morning.
   Dick __?__ __?__ the lawn every day.
2. (help) The proctors __?__ to keep order.
   The proctors __?__ __?__ to keep order.
3. (talk) The zookeeper __?__ quietly to the lions.
   He __?__ __?__ to them since they were cubs.
4. (play) We __?__ anagrams last night.
   We __?__ __?__ anagrams since we were small.

Irregular Verbs

Some verbs in our language do not add *d* or *ed* to form their past tense. These are called **irregular verbs.** The only way to learn these verbs is to memorize their principal parts and to practice using them. Each part has its own spelling. Use the dictionary when in doubt.

Study the three forms of the verbs listed below:

PRESENT	PAST	PAST PARTICIPLE
freeze	froze	(have, has, or had) frozen
ride	rode	(have, has, or had) ridden
speak	spoke	(have, has, or had) spoken
steal	stole	(have, has, or had) stolen

The second and third principal parts of the verbs *freeze, ride, speak,* and *steal* are used correctly in the sentences below.

Mother *froze* the chicken. The river *had frozen.*
I *rode* my bike. The cowboys *have ridden* the steer.

He *spoke* of his trip. Our mayor *has spoken* to our class.

We *stole* a ride. *Has* someone *stolen* your pen?

130

The second principal part of a verb (the past tense) does not use a helping verb. Do not combine a helping verb with **froze, rode, spoke, stole.**

The third principal part of a verb (the past participle) always requires a helping verb. Use helping verbs with **frozen, ridden, spoken,** and **stolen.**

▶ **Practice: Using the Correct Verb Form**

1. Read each sentence aloud, using the correct form of the verb in parentheses.

1. (freeze) We nearly __?__ in that icy wind last night.
2. (ride) Who has __?__ on a camel?
3. (speak) He had __?__ on the subject many times.
4. (steal) The old pirate __?__ that treasure.
5. (freeze) Our water pipes have __?__ this morning.
6. (ride) The knight __?__ into the courtyard.

2. Write each sentence, using the correct form of the verb in parentheses.

1. (ride) They had __?__ on mules to the bottom of the canyon.
2. (speak) A few minutes ago, I __?__ to Mrs. Johnson.
3. (steal) Have they __?__ our idea?
4. (ride) The Indians __?__ across the prairie.
5. (freeze) The peas in our garden have __?__.
6. (steal) Burglars __?__ Aunt Elaine's jewelry.

Review Practice: Irregular Verbs

1. Write sentences using the past tense of each verb below:

break	choose	ring	leave
drink	run	do	sing

2. Write sentences using the past participles of these verbs:

write	begin	bring	drink
go	break	sing	do

131

Using Words Correctly: <u>lie</u> and <u>lay</u>

Study the three forms of the verbs below:

PRESENT	PAST	PAST PARTICIPLE
lie, lies	lay	(have, has, or had) lain
lay, lays	laid	(have, has, or had) laid

To avoid confusion, learn to match the form with the meaning of each verb. The following sentences illustrate correct usage:

To lie — to rest or recline

1. The tiger *lies* in the cage.   (present)
2. He *lay* there for a long time.   (past)
3. He *has lain* there since dinner.   (past participle)

To lay (something) — to put or place something

1. Please *lay* the tray on the counter.   (present)
2. He *laid* his books on my desk.   (past)
3. I *had laid* mine on the shelf.   (past participle)

► Practice: Using <u>lie</u> and <u>lay</u>

1. Read aloud each sentence, using the form of the verb *lie* given in parentheses:

1. After swimming, we always __?__ on the beach. (present)
2. The tree __?__ directly in our path.   (past)
3. We had __?__ in bed until ten.   (past participle)
4. If you are tired, __?__ down.   (present)
5. The dog __?__ in front of the fireplace.   (past)

2. Read the following sentences using the form of *lay* given in parentheses:

1. __?__ those cards on the table.   (present)
2. The man __?__ the rug on the floor.   (past)
3. They have __?__ the package here.   (past participle)
4. Who has __?__ the clarinet on the chair?   (past participle)

132

*Phoenician
letter*

Sounds and Spelling

The Strange Case of the Letter **H**

The letter *h* was used as a consonant by the Phoenicians in their early system of writing. When the Greeks borrowed the symbol, they called it *eta* and used it as a long *e* sound. Later, the Romans put the same symbol to use as a consonant again, and that is what it is in our alphabet.

Perhaps because the sound is no more than a puff of breath, the *h* at the beginning of a word is easily added or dropped unexpectedly. Some Americans say, "Hit's a-goin' fer to rain!" meaning "It's going to rain." A quotation in a British dialect says:

> It's not the 'eavy 'aulin' that 'urts the 'orses' 'oofs,
> It's the 'ammer, 'ammer, 'ammer on the 'ard 'ighway.

Some words do not sound the initial *h*, as in *honest*.

Spelling Checkup

1. Can you spell all the words listed below correctly?

honorable	honorary	heiress
hourly	honesty	herbs

2. A large number of words with interesting sounds begin with *h*. With a teammate, choose one or more of those listed below for careful study. Each team should prepare a conversational dialogue to entertain and teach the class the meaning of the words and how to use them.

harum-scarum	hobgoblin	hoodwink	humdrum
helter-skelter	hocus-pocus	hubbub	hurdy-gurdy
higgledy-piggledy	hodgepodge	hullabaloo	hurly-burly
hippopotamus	hoodoo	humbug	huzza

133

Choice of Verbs in Composition

To bring life and action to a page of writing, the author composes his sentences with care. His selection of verbs, especially, can add vividness to a piece of writing.

The sentences that follow are from *The Wheel on the School*, by Meindert DeJong. Read them and notice the author's choice of words.

Lina slept alone in the attic, directly under the roof tiles. A sweep of wind slashing under the tiles lifted some of the heavy tiles and tossed them like paper. They crashed back down on the roof, smashed, and went slithering down the steep roof to shatter into a thousand pieces on the cobblestone street. The attic beams groaned. A moaning, wolfish howl of wind ran down the chimney and through the trembling house.

To Discuss

1. Name the vivid verbs and descriptive words in the sentences you have just read.

2. To how many of the five senses does the author's description appeal? Explain your answer. Which one receives most attention?

3. Look at the sketch below. Name five vivid verbs that describe the action.

Composition: Selecting Vivid Verbs

A. Make sentences by adding a predicate to each of the subjects below. Choose the verbs carefully to give the reader a vivid impression.

1. A jet plane . . .
2. The lion in the cage . . .
3. Out on the playground the sixth-grade boys (girls) . . .
4. In the stillness of the forest, a gray squirrel . . .

B. Study the picture at the top of this page. Then write a paragraph describing the situation shown. Make your paragraph vivid by choosing words carefully. Include verbs that will appeal to a reader's sense of hearing, smell, and taste.

Review Practice: Irregular Verbs

Prepare to give orally two sentences for each verb below. With one sentence, use the past tense; with the other, the past participle and a helping verb.

take	snow	blow	give	draw
throw	leave	grow	write	eat

Review Practice: Sentences

Write each sentence below. Underline the simple subject with one line and the verb with two lines.

1. Many countries encouraged voyages of discovery.
2. Two of them gained an early lead.
3. Spain sponsored the expeditions of Columbus.
4. The discoveries of Columbus helped Spain in the expansion of her empire.
5. The voyages of the explorers opened new trade routes.

How Our Language Grew • • • ●

Duke: The word *duke* means "a nobleman of high rank." The source of this word is found in Latin, in which a noun, *dux*, meant "leader," and a verb *ducere*, meant "to lead."

Today in our language we find *duce*, *duct*, and *duction* combined with a number of different prefixes. Do you know the meanings of these words: *induct*, *induce*, *aqueduct*, *deduct*? Remembering the meaning of the original Latin words, see what words in our language you can name and define with the following prefixes:

PREFIX	MEANING
intro	within, as "within the circle"
in	in or into
re	back
ab	away
pro	forth
via	a way

Shadow of a Bull

by Maia Wojciechowska
illustrated by Alvin Smith
Atheneum Publishers

It was one thing to have had a father famed as the greatest of bullfighters, but quite another to be expected to repeat the glory of his father's life.

Because Manolo looked so much like his father, everyone expected him to follow in the footsteps of their hero. Men who had almost worshiped his father for his skill and courage undertook to train Manolo. They took him to see his first bullfight at the age of nine, and thereafter prepared him steadily for the day when, at twelve, he would be ready to step into the ring to face the bull that was already chosen for him.

From the first, Manolo felt that his life was in the hands of others. His own wishes seemed to make no difference. What others expected him to be determined his fate, and the fact that he wanted to live another kind of life seemed to be of no importance at all. He was destined to carry on the reputation of his father in the bull ring.

Courage was always his watchword. In the end, Manolo proved his courage in more ways than one; and perhaps the greatest proof of courage came when he made an important decision for himself.

If you make a mistake on any test, take the Practice on pages 140–41 with the same Roman numeral as the test.

Test I. Recognizing Verbs

Copy the verb in each of the following sentences. Be sure to include the main verb and its helper or helpers. If a verb is part of a contraction, write the verb.

    1. The pond is always frozen over in January.
    2. Can we build a fire on the shore?
    3. Will your father skate with us?
    4. I've seen that movie twice.
    5. Have you heard the good news?
    6. I'm not going to the carnival Saturday.
    7. Dot doesn't practice her music every day.
    8. She'll play in the recital.

Test II. Verbs of Action or Being

Copy the verb in each of the following sentences. Next to each one, write *action* if the verb expresses action, and write *being* if the verb tells what or where the subject *is* or *is like*.

    1. The pitcher threw the ball to first base.
    2. Molly sang alto in the girls' choir.
    3. Black Beauty was a wonderful horse.
    4. These apples seem better than yours.
    5. Last year I read the book *Black Beauty*.
    6. That charm bracelet is mine.
    7. We heard the honk of wild ducks.
    8. The patient becomes stronger each day.

Test III. Verbs in Contractions

Write contractions by combining these pairs of words:

does not	could not	it is	they are
he will	I am	you are	has not

Test IV. Principal Parts of Verbs

Complete the following sentences with two forms of the verb — the past in the first sentence and the past participle in the second:

(perform) 1. The juggler __?__ last night.
          2. He __?__ __?__ every night this week.

(toss) 1. The cook __?__ the pizza above his head.
       2. He __?__ __?__ it too high this time!

(wait) 1. I __?__ at the bus station an hour.
       2. Sometimes I __?__ __?__ longer than that.

(walk) 1. The tired boys __?__ into the yard.
       2. They __?__ __?__ five miles.

(ask) 1. Sue __?__ the teacher a question.
      2. She __?__ __?__ that question before.

Test V. Irregular Verbs

1. For each verb listed below, write a sentence using the past participle form of the verb:

    ride   speak   freeze   steal

2. Write each sentence below, using the correct form of the verb in parentheses:

1. (take) They have __?__ the flag down.
2. (throw) Bill __?__ the disk ten feet.
3. (eat) Have you __?__ your dinner yet?
4. (do) Who __?__ that mural?
5. (ring) The old sexton has __?__ the church bell for many years.
6. (lie) You should __?__ down and rest.
7. (lay) I thought I had __?__ my coat on the couch.
8. (lie) The kittens have __?__ in the dog's basket all morning.
9. (drink) Who __?__ all the chocolate milk this morning?
10. (go) Cynthia has __?__ to the swimming pool.

Practice I.   Recognizing Verbs

1. Review the lessons on pages 119–20.

2. Copy the verbs in these sentences:

1. I must rake the leaves today.
2. They are always blowing around the house.
3. Did Dad bring home boxes for the leaves?
4. The city truck doesn't collect until tomorrow.
5. Will you help me?
6. We'll finish before lunch.

3. Underline the main verb in your list of verbs for number **2** above.

Practice II.   Verbs of Action or Being

1. Review the lesson on pages 120–21.

2. Write these two headings on your paper: *Action Verbs* and *Verbs of Being*.   Write the verb in each of the following sentences under the proper heading:

1. Frisky chased the cows into the barn.
2. I sharpen my pencils every day.
3. The days are shorter now.
4. We ate all the brownies at lunch.
5. Mother baked them this morning.
6. My cookies became too brown.
7. Autumn seems the best time of year.
8. Were there any nuts on the ground?

Practice III.   Verbs in Contractions

1. Review the lessons on pages 126–27.

2. Write the correct forms on which you made a mistake.

3. Make contractions from these words:

I am	have not	we have
you are	he is	would not
we will	did not	they are

140

Practice IV.   Principal Parts of Verbs

1. Study the lesson on pages 129–30.

2. Write the correct forms you missed on the test.

3. Write these sentences.   Use the form of the verb called for in parentheses.

    1. (mend, *past*)   We __?__ the tennis net.

    2. (work, *past part.*)   Mother __?__ __?__ in the garden all morning.

    3. (hear, *present*)   I __?__ a noise in the street.

    4. (warn, *past part.*)   The weather bureau __?__ __?__ us of the storm.

Practice V.   Irregular Verbs

1. Study the lesson on pages 130–31.

2. Rewrite the sentences on which you made mistakes in the test.

3. Write this paragraph.   Use the correct form of the verbs.

    The squirrels have (steal) __?__ the food from the bird feeder.   Now the birds have (go) __?__ away.   We have (do) __?__ all we could to keep them around.   The suet we tied on a tree had (freeze) __?__, but the squirrels have (eat) __?__ it, too.   They do not need to (lie, lay) __?__ away food so long as they can steal it.

4. Write the correct form of the verb in parentheses.

    1. (ride)   Have you ever __?__ on the ponies at the amusement park?

    2. (speak)   Michael has __?__ to the librarian about our next visit.

    3. (lie)   The toys have __?__ under the porch all week.

    4. (lay)   __?__ your umbrellas in the bathtub.

    5. (lie)   He always __?__ in the sun too long.

    6. (eat)   Have you __?__ your lunch?

    7. (drink)   I __?__ all the orangeade.

    8. (go)   They have __?__ to the library.

CHAPTER 7

Written and Oral Reports

In preparing and giving a report, you will use many of the ideas and skills you have already learned. These include finding information, taking notes, and making an outline. You will also need to plan carefully so that the report is the right length, interesting, and well written or well and clearly spoken if it is an oral report.

Choosing a Good Topic

Most of your reports will be on assigned subjects. Sometimes, however, you may be asked to choose your own topic. Here are three factors to consider in choosing a topic for an informational report.

Can you find some information on the topic? If there is little information available, the topic is not a good one. Try putting your topic in the form of a question. If the question can be answered very briefly, it is not a good one. If the answer depends mainly on opinion, the topic is not a good one for an informational report.

Choose a topic of interest to you and to others. A problem, such as *soil conservation*, which concerns our citizens today, is a good example. Every good citizen wants to help solve such a problem, and to do his part, he must have information. There are many similar problems which are important for citizens to understand. Think of some of the current events in your community or in the fields of science and industry.

Choose a topic that is limited enough so that you can cover it in an interesting way. You can only scratch the surface of

142

a topic such as *electricity* in one report. However, you can think of a part of that subject which would make an interesting report. Here are some examples. See if you can add to the list.

The story of the electric light
The uses of electric trains
Sources of electric power
How electricity has changed the kitchen
Preventing accidents caused by electricity
Conductors of electricity
The inventions of Thomas A. Edison

To Discuss

Each of the topics below is too broad for one report. Choose a part of the topic which you think would make an interesting report. See how many topics you and your classmates can suggest.

Sports	Space travel
How to garden	Conservation
Radio	Safety
Helicopters	The Audubon Society
Sanitation	Physical fitness

As topics are suggested, have someone write them on the board. See if you can narrow some of the topics still further.

▶ Practice: Selecting a Topic for a Report

1. List five topics which you believe would make interesting informational reports. For ideas, consider your current interests, studies, reading, televiewing, discussions, conversations, or recent events.

If the first topic that comes to mind seems too broad for one report, think of a part of it that you could cover in an interesting way.

2. Read your topics to the class. Ask your classmates to judge whether your topics are limited enough for a report.

Making Your Report Interesting and Clear

A good report should have an interesting beginning, a well-organized body, and a clean-cut conclusion. The title, too, is important in making a successful report.

Planning the Title and Introduction

Choose a title that tells as briefly as possible what your subject is. Then begin your report in a way that interests others and shows the importance of your subject.

This is the way Kathryn introduced her topic. Notice how she kept her listeners in mind.

Our Town's Watershed

You may think watersheds are buildings of some kind. I did before I began reading about them. I learned that a watershed is land, a little like a huge sloping roof. The streams on one side of the highest land flow in different directions from those on the other side. I am going to tell you about the land that feeds our reservoir. You will learn how it absorbs and releases moisture and how it supplies water for our town.

To Discuss

1. Is the title of Kathryn's report brief and to the point?

2. How did Kathryn capture your *interest* in her topic?

3. Which term did she explain? Did this help make her subject clear?

4. Did she show the importance of her topic?

5. Is her introduction brief and to the point?

▶ **Practice: Deciding How to Introduce a Topic**

On the basis of the discussion above, prepare a list of suggestions for introducing a topic.

Developing a Topic from an Outline

An artist often makes a sketch of a subject, which he uses as a guide in completing his painting. You have learned to make an outline of a topic. Your outline can serve the same purpose as an artist's sketch. It contains the big ideas, and you can use it as a guide in developing the main body of your report.

Read this part of the outline which Kathryn prepared for her report on her town's watershed.

Our Town's Watershed

  I. Why a watershed is important
    A. What it is
    B. What it controls
      1. Direction of flow
      2. Rate of flow
 II. Where our watershed is
    A. Size
      1. About 160 square miles
      2. About 8 miles wide by 20 miles deep
    B. Extent
      1. Starting in Bristol Hills
      2. Including Harper Creek and tributaries
      3. Draining into Headley Reservoir

You have read Kathryn's first paragraph, in which she developed the first main topic in her outline. Now read how she developed the second main topic.

You have all visited Headley Reservoir and so you know where our water supply is stored. The water in that reservoir comes from rainfall over a large area—160 square miles of farms, hills, and forests. This area is about eight miles wide at its widest place and twenty miles deep.

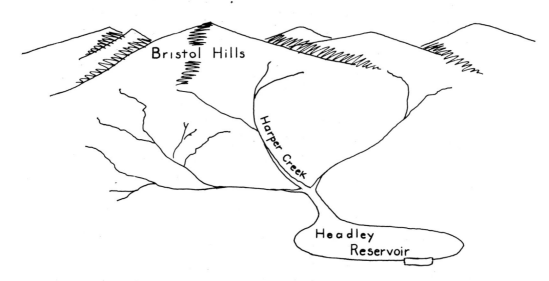

As you can see from the map, the top of the "roof" is the Bristol Hills. These hills rise to 1800 feet above sea level. Rain falls in the watershed. Raindrops become trickles, the trickles flow into rivulets, the rivulets into brooks, and the brooks drain into Harper Creek. Finally, the water of Harper Creek backs up behind the dam of Headley Reservoir.

To Discuss

1. Did Kathryn follow her outline?

2. How did she make her report more interesting than her outline?

3. What did she use to show clearly the location of the watershed?

146

Giving a Conclusion

A concluding statement is not always necessary. Usually, though, a brief summary of the main ideas will help your readers or listeners remember them.

How to Make a Report

Choose a limited subject.
Choose a good title.
Write a careful outline.
Plan an interesting introduction.
Explain every main topic in your outline, using the facts and ideas in the subtopics.
Refer to your notes or the references you have studied for interesting details that may not be in your outline.
Use maps, charts, and other helpful aids.
Conclude your report by restating the main ideas.

▶ **Practice: Planning the Parts of a Report**

Follow the guides above on how to plan a report. Choose a subject you have been studying. Write an outline, then plan the title, introduction, body of the report, and conclusion. Save your outline, as you may use it later.

TO MEMORIZE

America! America!
God shed His grace on thee,
And crown thy good with brotherhood
From sea to shining sea.

KATHERINE LEE BATES

Katherine Lee Bates was a teacher in Wellesley College when she wrote the familiar "America the Beautiful."

Have you ever thought, as you sang these words, that they are in reality a prayer? In your own words, tell what the poet asks for her country in the third line of this verse.

Expressing Yourself Well

One way to make a report interesting and clear is to choose words and expressions carefully and use them correctly.

Some Faults to Avoid

The three faults below can make interesting information seem very dull:

1. Too many sentences that begin with the same word.
2. Too many *I*'s.
3. Too many sentences joined by *and*'s.

To Discuss

Read the paragraphs below aloud. Talk over what could be done to make them more interesting.

1. The Library of Congress is located in Washington, D.C., and it has the largest collection of books in North America. It has the Declaration of Independence and the Consitution of the United States, and it is visited by people from all over the country.

2. The year before last I saw the Grand Canyon of the Yellowstone, in Yellowstone National Park. Last summer I saw the Grand Canyon of the Colorado, in Arizona. I found out that both canyons were formed by rivers.

► **Practice: Expressing Yourself Well**

Rewrite and improve each of the above paragraphs.

Review Practice: Possessive Nouns and Contractions

Write the sentences below, using apostrophes correctly. State the reason for each apostrophe.

1. Theyre in the childrens library.
2. Didnt he tell you the purpose of the firemens project?
3. Earl couldnt remember Mr. Streeters exact words.
4. He hasnt been the committees secretary very long.

Using Guiding Words and Phrases

Plan to use words and phrases that will help your reader to follow your ideas. Here are some examples: *first, second, in the first place, in addition, then, therefore*, and *finally*.

Read the following paragraphs from *The Incredible Journey*, by Sheila Burnford, and *Tinkerbelle*, by Robert Manry. Find the guiding words or phrases. Prepare to read them aloud.

1. Later on, when darkness fell, the young dog moved over and stretched out closely at his side and the cat stalked over to lie between his paws; and so, warmed and comforted by their closeness, the old dog slept, momentarily unconscious of his aching, tired body or his hunger. . . .

The following day the travelers came down from the hills to find themselves on the banks of a river running north and south.

2. Many small-boat voyagers had stated in their books that size has little or no bearing on a boat's seaworthiness, and . . . I was inclined to believe they were right. A small boat, first of all, is a great deal stronger, pound for pound, than a big ship. Secondly, a small boat, being light and buoyant, will recoil before waves and tend to ride over them, whereas a big ship will offer immense resistance.

▶ **Practice: Using Guiding Words and Phrases**

Read the sentences in the paragraphs below and think of a way to relate the thoughts. Then rewrite each paragraph, adding words that guide the reader from one point to another.

1. In its present state, our basement is untidy and dangerous. There are several things to be done. The stacks of old papers must be removed. The empty cartons must go. We must sweep the floor.

2. Bill and I had some difficulty moving that boulder. We tried to lift it. We struggled in vain. Bill found a board which we could use as a lever. With this device, we pried the rock loose.

Giving Credit to Sources of Information

If you have obtained a great deal of information from one source for your report, or if you use the ideas or exact words of another, it is only fair to name your source. To credit a source, name the person whose ideas or words you are using and tell where you found the information.

Notice how credit for information is given in the examples below. Answer the questions that follow.

1. Mrs. Emma Staver, who lived in England until five years ago, gave me these picture postcards of London.
2. Ralph Sutter made this point about the gold rush in "A Cabin on the Yukon." The article appeared in *Boys' Life*.

To Discuss

1. In the first sentence, how is credit for information given?

2. In the second selection, how is credit for information given? Notice that the title of the magazine article is placed in quotation marks. Notice that the name of the magazine is in italic type. Like the titles of books, the names of magazines are printed in italic, but are underlined in handwriting or typewriting.

Underline the names of books, magazines, and newspapers.

Place the titles of articles in books and magazines in quotation marks.

Using Direct and Indirect Quotations

When you repeat the exact words of another, you are making a *direct quotation*. In oral reports, simply tell your listeners that you are quoting another person. In written reports, put quotation marks around direct quotations.

When you refer to a person's ideas without using his exact words, you are using an *indirect quotation*. Do not put quotation marks around indirect quotations.

Notice how credit for information is given in this selection:

Did you know that bats have a kind of radar system that keeps them from bumping into things? I learned about this ability in *The Personality of Animals*, by Munro Fox. Mr. Fox explained that bats in flight make shrill squeaks that set up vibrations or waves in the air. When the waves strike an object, they bounce back. He said, "Bats emit supersonic sound waves, and the time taken for their echo to return to the bat's ear gives the distance away of the obstacle."

To Discuss

1. How is credit given in the above selection? Where did the writer find the information?
2. Find and read aloud a direct quotation.
3. Find and read aloud an indirect quotation.

Follow the rules below when you write direct quotations:

Place quotation marks around direct quotations.
Separate the quotation from the rest of the sentence by some mark of punctuation.
Begin a quotation with a capital letter.
Place a period that follows a quoted statement within the quotation marks.

► **Practice: Crediting Sources of Information**

Write the following sentences correctly:

1. In his lecture Dr. James White said my interest in plants started right in my own back yard.
2. The earthquake was the most disastrous in the country's history, according to an article in the times.
3. I found most of this information in an article by franklin folsom, which appeared in junior scholastic. The name of the article was lewis and clark.

Review Practice: Verbs

1. Read aloud the verb in each sentence below. Be prepared to tell whether it is a verb of action or a verb of being.

1. Betty overcame her fear of the dark.
2. Florence Nightingale was an English nurse.
3. The maple leaves were orange and red.
4. The rookie ball player rose rapidly to stardom.
5. A deep fog covered the city.

2. Write sentences for each of these action verbs:

screamed   darted   was lost   had been broken   slipped

152

Naming Sections of a Country

You have already learned to capitalize proper nouns. The italicized words below name a particular section of the country. They are proper nouns, too.

   1. What are the largest cities in the *East*?
   2. Many states in the *South* produce cotton.

Now read the third sentence:

   3. We say that the sun rises in the *east* and sets in the *west*.

The italicized words in that sentence name a direction. They do not name a particular place. Do not capitalize words that mean directions.

When a word such as **South, East,** or **Southwest** names a particular section of a country, begin it with a capital letter.
Words that indicate directions do not begin with a capital letter.

► **Practice: Using Capital Letters**

Write the sentences below, using capital letters correctly. Study each sentence. What words mean a section of the country? What words indicate a direction?

   1. New mexico is in the southwest.
   2. Turn north at jackson boulevard.
   3. Corn is the major crop in many states in the midwest.
   4. During our vacation in the south, we toured georgia.
   5. The trail goes west for two miles.
   6. Walk three blocks north to the library.
   7. The pioneers left the east in covered wagons.
   8. The sky toward the north was getting dark.

153

Composition: Preparing to Write a Report

A. Copy the following paragraph from a report. Use the necessary capital letters.

I live in a small city in the east, not far from Boston. Just one mile from my house the first pioneers left New England for the west. They traveled by covered wagon west to the Ohio River. There they built flatboats and floated south to found a new settlement on the river. Later, some of these pioneers settled the northwest.

B. Prepare the outline for a report on something of historical interest in or about your community, for example, the first settlers, the Indians who lived in the area, an old building, the first school.

Writing Paragraphs

In written reports, you develop the topics of your outline by writing good paragraphs about them. As you know, a paragraph is a group of sentences about a single idea or topic.

Planning a Paragraph

To make the main idea of a paragraph clear, a writer may use one sentence to state or hint at the topic. Usually, though not always, the *first sentence* is the *topic sentence.* You will find it helpful in writing good paragraphs to make your first sentence a topic sentence. Then write other sentences that develop the main idea.

In studying a paragraph to see whether it can be improved, ask yourself these questions:

1. Does the first sentence hint at the topic?
2. Does every sentence keep to the topic?
3. Does every sentence develop the topic?

Read the two paragraphs that follow. See if you can think of a way to improve each one.

Cumulus clouds are white and fluffy with rounded domes. Some of them are thousands of feet high. To really appreciate their size and shape, you should see them from an airplane, as I did last summer. I was flying to Montana to see my grandfather, and I stayed on his farm all summer. From above, these clouds looked like great rolling seas of white fog. We circled those that towered over our airplane. When we flew around a cumulus cloud, I could see that it looked like many clouds stacked together. I suppose that accounts for the name cumulus, which means accumulation in Latin.

Cirrus clouds look delicate and filmy. When you look at them, they seem filmy and you can see the sky through them. They are thin, feathery clouds. Clouds that are white and very thin are called cirrus clouds.

155

To Discuss

1. Refer to the three check questions as you check the content of each of the paragraphs on page 155. Which of the two paragraphs is better? Explain why.

2. How can the first paragraph be improved? What test of a good paragraph does it fail to meet?

3. What is wrong with the second paragraph? Suggest ways to improve it.

How to Write a Paragraph

Have your topic clearly in mind.
Write a first sentence that will suggest the topic.
See that every sentence keeps to the topic.
See that every sentence develops the topic.
Indent the first word of the paragraph.
Begin and end each sentence correctly.

Composition: Writing Paragraphs

A. Write a paragraph about cirrus clouds, using some of the details below.

Cirrus clouds are thin and delicate.
The word *cirrus* means "curl" in Latin.
They are the highest clouds, being formed
   at an altitude of nearly 20,000 feet.
They consist of crystals of ice.
They look like white feathers.

B. Write a paragraph on one of the topics below or on a topic of your choice. Follow the guides above.

A book you have read
A famous inventor or scientist
A place you have visited
A famous event
An animal (or plant)
A hurricane (or some kind of storm)

Sounds and Spelling

Silent Letters

Ever since you entered school and began learning to read, you have known that some letters in words are not pronounced. Probably your first encounter with this fact was with vowels. Your teacher may have helped you with this rhyme, "When two vowels go walking, the first does the talking."

This rule holds good for many words. In *boat, beat*, and *bait*, for example, the first vowel is heard, the second silent. It is not difficult, however, to find exceptions, like *great* or *aisle*, where the second vowel is heard and the first is silent. To be a good speller, one must be on the watch for both rules and exceptions.

Silent consonants are more numerous than you might think. It can be like a game to see how many different consonants in the alphabet are silent letters in one word or another. Here is a beginning list. Can you add other examples?

b	debt	*h*	rhyme	*p*	psalm
c	indict	*k*	know	*s*	island
d	edge	*l*	talk	*t*	listen
g	foreign	*n*	condemn	*w*	write

Spelling Checkup

1. Be ready to give the meaning, pronunciation, and spelling of all words listed on this page as examples. Some of the words you use often. Others may be less familiar to you.

2. Add these words to your spelling list:

often	answer	comb	scholar
ptomaine	Des Moines	sign	qualm
judgment	receipt	Wednesday	column

Proofreading and Revising Your Work

Form habits of neatness and accuracy in all written work. Once you are satisfied with the content, proofread your paper to see that it is written correctly, in good English. Use these questions as a check list:

1. Are words used correctly?
2. Are words spelled correctly?
3. Are the paragraphs indented?
4. Are capital letters and punctuation marks used correctly?
5. Is the general arrangement, including margins and the placement of the title, good?

After you have proofread your paper, copy it neatly in ink.

► **Practice: Proofreading Written Work**

1. Read each of the following selections from reports. Discuss the faults of each in class.

Yesterday we seen a movie about making flour. The movie began with a picture of a wheat field in harvest time. Machines were cutting. and sacking the wheat. The trucks carried beg loads of sacks to the mill where the wheet would be made into flour.

Pioneer Skeels

An early pioneer had to learn many trades to survive in the wilderness. A pioneer women she had to make cloth and she had to sew and a man he had to be a blacksmith and carpenter.

I learned something about life in the wilderness this summer when I visited a pioneer family's home. It had a spinning wheel and a loom for making cloth. There was a blacksmith shed outside for casting iron and making horseshoes. There was a rack for drying the split rails.

2. Write each selection above correctly.

On page 147 you were asked to choose a good subject for a report. Then you were to write an outline for the report, plan the title, introduction, body, and conclusion, and save your plans for later use. You then studied and practiced skills necessary in writing a report well, such as avoiding faults of expression, giving credit to sources of information, developing good paragraphs, and so on.

Now you are ready to prepare a written report on a topic of your choice. Use the plans you made earlier as the basis for the report, if you wish. Or you may select a new topic, outline it, and write the report.

Use the guides under "How to Make a Report" on page 147. Also, try your best to express yourself well, credit your sources of information correctly, and write good paragraphs.

After you have written your report, proofread your paper for errors, using the questions on page 159 as a check list. Read the report aloud; then copy it neatly in ink.

How Our Language Grew · • ● ●

A dictionary is a book in which the words of a language have been recorded. Notice the first four letters of the word. They came from a Latin word which means to speak words for others to write, remember, or obey. Here are some other words that have been built from *dict*:

> *Dictate* means to speak words for another to write.
> A *dictator* is one who speaks with absolute authority.
> *Dictation* is that which is spoken for another to write.
> A *dictaphone* is a machine that records the words that are spoken into its mouthpiece.

Look up these words in your dictionary: *diction, dictum, dictatorial.* Try to use them in sentences. You may find it interesting to study the history of words common to your own vocabulary.

160

Giving an Oral Report

An oral report is most interesting when the speaker does not read it from a paper or refer continually to his notes. Before you give an oral report, practice speaking from your outline until you can present your ideas clearly and directly to your audience.

Preparing to Speak from an Outline

Study your outline and decide what you are going to say about each major topic. If necessary, return to your notes for details that will add interest to the discussion. For example, some exact figures or a direct quotation might help you to develop a topic in an interesting way.

Write each major topic of your outline down on a file card, leaving space between topics for any details which you must report exactly, such as direct quotations. Be sure to write your facts down correctly.

Practicing the Report

After you have prepared note cards, practice your report, beginning with an interesting introduction. Then talk about each of the major ideas in the order you have outlined them. Finally, summarize the main ideas.

Practice your report aloud, until you can give it well. Refer only occasionally to your note cards for details.

Speaking Distinctly

As you practice delivering your report aloud, try to achieve these four goals:

1. Speak loudly enough to be heard.
2. Speak slowly enough to be understood.
3. Pronounce your words distinctly.
4. Speak with expression.

If possible, deliver your report aloud at home to a willing listener. Let him criticize your *volume, rate, articulation,* and *expression.*

► **Practice: Speaking Distinctly**

1. Practice pronouncing these words. Sound the italicized letters or syllables correctly.

mod*er*n	extr*a*	stren*g*th
*en*gine	fin*ally*	pic*t*ure
j*u*st	heigh*t*	sen*t*ence
wi*sh*	ha*ng*er	se*ver*al
six*th*	ri*nging*	in*tro*duce

2. Use the words above in sentences. Say sounds carefully.

3. Read these tongue twisters aloud, giving special attention to the final sound of the words:

1. In the bright moonlight, we caught sight of the night plane soaring at a great height.
2. Have you the strength to lift a box of that width and length?

162

Giving Your Oral Report

When you give your report, take your place confidently. Look straight at your audience. Wait until the members of the audience are settled in their seats and ready to give you their attention. Then begin. Follow these guides:

How to Give an Oral Report

Speak directly to your audience, referring to your notes for details.

Speak distinctly, loudly enough, and with expression.

Give an introduction that will capture the attention of your audience.

Discuss each major topic of your outline in order.

Keep to the topic.

Present enough facts and report them correctly.

Summarize the main ideas.

▶ Practice: Giving an Oral Report

1. Give an oral report on a topic you have studied. Follow the guides above.

2. Listen carefully to the reports your classmates give. After a report has been given, see if you remember the main points. Be ready to talk about the things you liked about a report. Suggest ways for improvement if you can.

Going Ahead ▶ ▶ ▶ ▶

Plan with four or five classmates to make a group report to the class on a community problem. Present your report in the form of a round-table discussion, with each member of the group reporting on a major part of the subject. Choose a chairman to introduce the subject and to conduct the discussion.

Work together as a committee in planning an interesting discussion. Agree on the main topics for discussion and on the order in which you will present them.

TRYOUT TIME

If you make a mistake on any test, take the Practice on page 165 with the same Roman numeral as the test.

Test I.   Expressing Yourself Well

Write the following paragraph, correcting its three faults:

I like the story about Paul Revere's ride and I am going to report on it and I hope you will like the story, too. He was a silversmith and he lived in Boston and he rode through the colony to warn the people that the British were going to attack by land. He was caught before he got to Concord, but two other riders went on to Concord.

Test II.   Writing Correctly

1. Write these titles of magazines correctly:

harper's magazine   seventeen   field and stream

2. Write titles of these articles correctly:

our tree house   let's keep our school clean

3. Write these sentences correctly:

1. Virgil said love conquers all.
2. We were in the northwest last month.

Test III.   Writing Paragraphs

Read the following paragraph and decide how it can be improved. Then copy the paragraph, making the improvements.

At noon we arrived at the famous Hawk's Nest in West Virginia. We stood high up and looked down on New River Gorge. it was a sheer drop of almost 585 feet down to the river. Once I saw the Grand Canyon of the Colorado. at the end of the Gorge, New River joins the Gauley River

Practice I. Expressing Yourself Well

1. List the three faults mentioned on page 148.

2. Correct these groups of sentences to form good paragraphs.

1. My dog is three years old. My dog can do tricks. My dog is learning a new trick now.
2. We are going to decorate the gym and we will use the school colors. The committee will bring plants from home and these will make the gym more attractive.
3. I should have written before, but I have been busy. I am studying hard, and I am taking trumpet lessons, too, which I like very much. I hope to play in the school band someday.

Practice II. Writing Correctly

1. Review the lesson on pages 150–53.

2. Write this paragraph correctly:

My brother gets the magazine science digest. Sometimes I find an article I like. This month I read one called big moon, here we come.

3. Write these sentences correctly:

1. The writer ralph waldo emerson said hitch your wagon to a star.
2. Emerson came from new england.

Practice III. Writing Paragraphs

1. Review the lesson on pages 155–56.

2. Check the paragraph in Test III with the guides on page 156. How can it be improved?

3. Write the paragraph again, making the improvements.

4. Write a paragraph of your own about a place you have visited recently. Follow the guides on page 156.

165

CHAPTER 8

Learning About Pronouns

You have been using words such as *I, he, she, we,* and *they* since you first learned to speak. These words are **pronouns.**

The Useful Pronoun

Read the two pairs of sentences below and note the changes in the second sentence of each pair.

1. *The mayor* gave *Jane* a book.
2. *He* gave *her* a book.

1. "Will *Jane* let *Mother* see the *book*?" *Mother* asked.
2. "Will *you* let *me* see *it*?" *she* asked.

In the first pair above, sentence 1 uses three nouns. Sentence 2 replaces two of them with pronouns. *He* stands for *the mayor; her* stands for *Jane.*

What pronouns replace the nouns in the second pair of sentences?

■ A **pronoun** is a word that is used in place of a noun.

► **Practice: Pronouns**

1. Read the following paragraph silently. Think of the correct pronoun to use in place of each italicized noun or noun and its signal. Then read the paragraph aloud.

Harry was never very good with *Harry's* skis. *Harry* didn't like to wax *the skis*; but when *Harry* did, *Harry* made *the skis* too slippery. Usually when *Harry* got *the skis* on, *Harry* found one ski traveling east and one west. The result? You guessed *the result*! A tumble.

167

2. Read each sentence below. The pronouns are set in italic type. Tell what noun each pronoun stands for.

1. A lioness was returning to *her* den.
2. *She* left *her* tracks on the sand.
3. The hunter saw *them* plainly.
4. *He* hastened along the river bank with *his* guide.

3. Substitute pronouns for the expressions in italics.

1. Are *Pete* and *Phil* playing ball today?
2. *Pete* may play this afternoon.
3. *My sister* likes ballgames.

Singular and Plural Pronouns

Just as nouns can be singular and plural, so can pronouns. Pronouns, however, do not form their plurals as nouns do. Pronouns have special singular and plural forms.

Here are the pronouns that are used to stand for the person or persons speaking or writing:

SINGULAR	PLURAL
I, me, my	we, us, our
mine, myself	ours, ourselves

Now look at the pronouns that are used to stand for the person or persons spoken or written to.

SINGULAR	PLURAL
you, your, yours	you, your, yours
yourself	yourselves

The pronouns listed below stand for other persons, places, or things.

SINGULAR	PLURAL
he, him, his, himself	they, them
she, her, hers, herself	their, theirs
it, its, itself	themselves

► **Practice: Singular and Plural Pronouns**

1. Study the italicized pronouns in this selection. Name the noun (or nouns) for which each pronoun stands.

In the mountains of Bohemia there lived long ago a miner with *his* wife and little daughter. *They* were happy in *their* little hut in the forest. But after a time both father and mother died, and the child was left alone in the world. *She* had no money and no relatives to take *her* in; but always there are kindly hearts among the poor, and a neighboring miner opened *his* house to little Hilda. *He* had six children of *his* own, and little bread and meat to spare; but *his* good wife said, "Though *we* have barely enough food for *our* children and *ourselves*, *we* will divide the little *we* have. This child will be *our* child and *our* own children will be *her* brothers and sisters."

2. On the board, write the headings *Singular* and *Plural*. List the pronouns from the paragraph above under the correct heading.

Old English J

Sounds and Spelling

The Letter J — an I with a Tail on It

The letter **J** begins as the **I** does but continues with a tail that hooks to the left. The small letters begin in the same way: *j, i.*

The early Roman alphabet did not contain the letter *j*, nor was it used until the last three or four centuries. Until then, the letter *i* represented sounds which we now spell with *i* or *j.*

The use of *j* probably began with those who wrote or copied manuscripts and who tended to make an initial *i* more ornate than the plain form used in the middle of a word. When it seemed wise to use separate letters for the vowel and consonant, the more ornate form was the natural choice for the consonant sound. Not many words used the letter *j* except at the beginning. Elsewhere in the word, that sound is usually spelled with **g**, as in *huge.*

In some countries, *j* represents a consonant **y** sound. The first name of the German composer Johann Sebastian Bach, for example, is pronounced "Yo'han," not "Jo'han." Also in the Swedish language, *j* is pronounced as **y.**

Spelling Checkup

1. Make a class list of words with a *j* sound spelled with **g.**

2. Spanish words use *j* for the sound of our **h.** Study the pronunciation of the two Spanish-named cities in California; then say their names. *San Jose* (San Ho zay'); *La Jolla* (La Hoi'a).

3. Prepare to pronounce and spell these words:

just	guest	justice	genius	jewel	John
jest	suggest	judge	jealous	Jerome	Juneau

170

Possessive Pronouns

Do you remember how nouns show possession? An apostrophe and *s* or simply an apostrophe is added to a noun, as in *mother's hat*, for example. Pronouns can show possession, too. However, unlike nouns, they never use an apostrophe and *s* or an apostrophe alone. Pronouns have special forms that show possession. We call these special forms **possessive pronouns.**

Turn back to the pronouns listed on page 168. Try to pick out the pronouns in the list which show possession. To guide you, think whether or not you could use the pronoun to show ownership. Compare your choices with these possessive pronouns:

my	our	your	his	its
mine	ours	yours	her	their
			hers	theirs

Saying Pronouns Correctly

Be on your guard whenever you pronounce the possessive pronouns listed below. Practice saying them aloud. Pronounce the italicized letters clearly and correctly.

ours   *ou*r   yours   his   hers   theirs

Writing Pronouns Correctly

Pay particular attention to the spelling of these possessive pronouns:

ours   yours   hers   its   theirs

Sometimes the contraction *it's* is mistaken for the possessive pronoun *its*. Study the difference between *it's* and *its* in these sentences:

It's a beautiful day. (*contraction for* it is)
The fish had injured *its* fins. (*possessive pronoun*)

171

Study the possessive pronoun *their* in this sentence:

The Scouts inspected *their* cabins.

Now study the italicized words in these sentences:

There was a grill for cooking.   (*introductory word*)
They're cooking supper.   (*contraction for* They are)

There and *they're* are not possessive pronouns. See how they differ in spelling from *their*.

► **Practice: Using Possessive Pronouns**

1. Use a possessive pronoun to complete each sentence below. Write the sentences. Be prepared to read your sentences aloud in class.

    1. "Tom, is this camera ___?___?"
    2. "It isn't __?__," Tom replied. "I forgot __?__ camera."
    3. "Mother let me borrow __?__," Frank said. "I'll take a picture of __?__ camp."
    4. Earl and Dan put up __?__ tents.
    5. Bill placed __?__ sleeping bag on the air mattress.
    6. In the evening, the boys built a fire and enjoyed __?__ warm glow.

2. Write the following sentences, using the correct expression in parentheses:

    1. The bear licked (its, it's) paw.
    2. (Its, It's) very cold this morning.
    3. I believe (its, it's) going to rain.
    4. The hikers are returning to (their, there, they're) camp.
    5. The wagon train continued on (its, it's) course.
    6. (Their, There, They're) house is built on a rock near the sea.
    7. The ancient castle stood before us in all (its, it's) splendor.
    8. (Their, There, They're) in the living room.

Review Practice: Sentences

1. Copy each sentence below. Underline the simple subject with one line and the verb with two lines.

1. Have you been to Europe?
2. Last·year I visited my relatives in Switzerland.
3. Their village is nestled in the mountains.
4. How beautiful it is!
5. Dairy farming is the main industry there.
6. In early summer the herdsmen drive the cattle to mountain pastures.
7. The cattle graze on the lower slopes for several weeks.
8. Then they are taken back down to the village.
9. What happens after their return?
10. The villagers have a big festival.

2. Write four sentences: a statement, a question, an exclamation, and a command. Be prepared to read your sentences aloud, naming the simple subject and verb in each one.

173

Pronouns as Subjects

Pronouns are used in sentences in the same way that nouns are. This means that they are often used as subjects. But pronouns have special subject forms. These forms are familiar to you. Read this list of pronoun subjects:

I	he	she	they	we

Because the subject pronouns *you* and *it* do not cause difficulty, they are omitted from the group of pronouns above. Read the following sentences. Note the subject pronouns.

1. *He* entered the room.
2. *She* saw the movie.
3. *They* sold newspapers.
4. *We* can form a new team.
5. *I* will help the committee.

Sometimes sentences have two subjects connected by the words *and* or *or*. Often one or both of these subjects are pronouns.

Another subject has been added to each of the sentences above. Read the new sentences aloud.

1. *Janet* and *he* entered the room.
2. *She* and *I* saw the movie.
3. *Bob* and *they* sold newspapers.
4. *You* and *we* can form a new team.
5. *Fred* or *I* will help the committee.

Notice that the subject form of a pronoun must be used whether there is one subject or more than one.

If you are confused about the correct pronoun to use in a sentence which has two subjects, use the pronoun alone as the subject. For example, in the sentence "Bill and (I, me) left early," try each pronoun alone. As you say "I left early," your ear will tell you that the correct pronoun is *I*. You would never say "Me left early."

174

Pronoun Subjects in Questions

If you remember how to find the subject in a question, you should have no difficulty in choosing the correct pronoun subject. Read the following sentences:

1. Will *Tom* and *he* make the report?
2. Can *Carl* and *they* explain their actions?

How can you know that *he* and *they* are correct? Turn the questions above into statements. This will help you tell whether the pronouns are used as subjects.

1. *Tom* and *he* will make the report.
2. *Carl* and *they* can explain their actions.

You have learned that *he* and *they* are the subject forms of pronouns. They are used correctly in the questions.

Always use the subject form of a pronoun when it is the subject of a sentence.

► **Practice: Using Subject Pronouns**

1. Read the sentences aloud. Use a subject pronoun in place of each of the blank spaces in the sentences.

1. My mother and __?__ enjoy shopping.
2. Are Harry and __?__ partners?
3. Marian and __?__ are sisters.
4. The class and __?__ are going on a hike.
5. When do Elsie and __?__ give our book reviews?

2. Read these sentences aloud. Use a subject pronoun in place of the persons mentioned in parentheses.

1. (Ronald) My brother and __?__ are good friends.
2. (Margaret) __?__ and her sister just left the room.
3. (Nora and I) You or __?__ can send the letters.
4. (Person speaking) Mike and __?__ read the book.
5. (Harriet and Janice) __?__ and Donna are there.

175

Review Practice: Verbs

1. Read the sentences below and name the verb in each one. Be prepared to tell whether it is a *verb of action* or a *verb of being*.

1. My favorite interest is skin diving.
2. Skin divers can explore conditions underseas.
3. Have you read any books by the great naturalist, William Beebe?
4. A naturalist is an authority on animals and plants.
5. I have just read about one of Beebe's expeditions to tropical seas.
6. The name of his ship was the *Arcturus*.
7. Every day, Beebe left the *Arcturus* in a flat-bottomed boat.
8. Through the windows in his helmet, the explorer studied undersea creatures.

2. In the sentences listed below, words or the contraction *n't* (or both) separate the parts of the verb. Write each sentence. Then underline the main verb and its helpers.

1. Should Barbara have waited for you?
2. John might never have found your note.
3. Have you eaten your breakfast?
4. Didn't you write a story about fishing?

Sentence Patterns: Word Order

The word *not* and words that tell *when* and *how* often come between the parts of a verb in a sentence.

The **N Vʰ** soon **V**   The visitor will soon leave.
N Vʰ not **V** the **N**   Rain should not stop the plans.
N Vʰ never **Vᵇᵉ** a **N**   Ted has never been a coward.

The order of words in most questions (interrogative sentences) is different from the normal word order of statements. The subject often comes between the parts of a verb.

Statement: $\overset{N}{\text{Felicia}}$ $\overset{V^h}{\text{will}}$ $\overset{V}{\text{win}}$ the $\overset{N}{\text{prize.}}$

Question: $\overset{V^h}{\text{Will}}$ $\overset{N}{\text{Felicia}}$ $\overset{V}{\text{win}}$ the $\overset{N}{\text{prize?}}$

● Copy the following sentences on your paper, leaving space between the sentences. Above each word, write the correct symbol for that word. Do not write symbols above the noun signals *a, an,* and *the.*

1. Lee has forgiven Paul.   3. The wheel will turn.
2. Vincent is an inventor.   4. A friend had helped Stan.

● Rewrite the statements above, turning each one into a question. Again, write the correct symbol above each word.

● Build sensible sentences, using the combinations of symbols listed below. You may choose helping verbs from the list or use any others you know. Vary your sentence ideas.

have	am	was	will	may have
has	is	were	shall	must
had	are	have been	will be	should have

1. **N Vʰ V**   6. The **N Vʰ** not **V**
2. **A N Vʰ V N**   7. **N Vʰ** always **V**
3. The **N Vʰ Vᵇᵉ N** 8. **Vʰ N V** the **N**
4. **N Vʰ** soon **V** 9. The **N Vʰ** not **V** the **N**
5. **Vʰ N V**   10. **N Vʰ Vʰ V** a **N**

Subject Pronouns After Verbs of Being

You have often been asked questions like "Who was here?" "Who was that?" The answers to these questions might be:

1. It wasn't *he.*
2. That was *she.*

Notice that the verbs in the sentences above are *verbs of being* and that the pronouns which follow the verbs are *subject pronouns.* Verbs of being help to tell who or what the subject *is.* Review these forms of the verb *be:*

| am | is | are | was | were |

When these verbs are followed by a pronoun, the pronoun and the subject mean the same person, as in these sentences:

1. The champion is *he.*
2. The winners are *they.*
3. Your mysterious callers were *we.*

In sentence 1 above, the pronoun *he* and the subject *champion* are the same person. In sentence 2, the pronoun *they* and the subject *winners* are the same persons. In sentence 3, the pronoun *we* and the subject *callers* are the same persons.

Sometimes both a noun and a pronoun follow a verb of being, as in these sentences:

4. The winners were Jonathan and *he.*
5. The prettiest girls in the class are Barbara and *she.*

In sentence 4 above, the subject *winners* and *Jonathan and he* are the same persons. In sentence 5, the subject *girls* and *Barbara and she* are the same persons.

Use the subject pronouns **I, she, he, we,** and **they** when they follow a verb of being and mean the same person or persons as the subject.

► **Practice: Using the Correct Pronoun**

1. Read each of the following sentences aloud. Supply the correct pronoun in place of the person or persons named in parentheses.

1. That was (the girl) in the blue coat.
2. It has always been (Jim) who was lucky.
3. The actors were Jim and (the speaker).
4. Wasn't it (two students) who spoke yesterday?

2. Write the following sentences, using the correct pronouns in parentheses:

1. Yes, it is (she, her).
2. The best tennis players in our class are Bill and (her, she).
3. The boy who made the touchdown was (he, him).
4. The losers were (they, them).
5. It was (she, her) who found the dog.

TO MEMORIZE

Requiem

Under the wide and starry sky,
Dig the grave and let me lie.
Glad did I live and gladly die,
    And I laid me down with a will.

This is the verse you grave for me:
Here he lies where he longed to be;
Home is the sailor, home from sea,
    And the hunter home from the hill.

ROBERT LOUIS STEVENSON

Robert Louis Stevenson, the English poet and story writer, chose to be buried in Samoa, where he lived the last years of his life. He wrote the above lines for the monument marking his grave. That might seem to be a somber thing to do, until one reads the lines. They express courage and happiness.

179

Pronouns After Action Verbs

Look at the following sentences:

1. *Tom* found the wallet.
2. Mother found *Tom.*

The noun *Tom* is used as the subject in sentence 1 above. In sentence 2 the noun *Tom* appears after an action verb. Did the noun *Tom* change from one sentence to the other?

Now let us use a pronoun in place of the noun *Tom.*

1. *He* found the wallet.
2. Mother found *him.*

Notice that the pronoun form changed in sentence 2. Unlike nouns, pronouns change their forms according to their use in a sentence. In sentence 2 the pronoun *him* follows an action verb. Because it receives the action of the verb, it is called the **object of the verb.** The pronoun *him* is an *object pronoun.* Study the forms of the object pronouns:

| me | us | him | her | them |

The pronouns *you* and *it* are also used as objects of verbs. However, they do not have different forms for subject and object, and we need not list them here.

Often an action verb has more than one object. An object pronoun must be used after an action verb whether there is one object or two, as in these sentences:

1. Lisa called *me.*
2. Lisa called Bob and *me.*
3. Frank invited *her.*
4. Frank invited the twins and *her.*

Always use the object forms of pronouns when they are the objects of action verbs.

▶ Practice: Using the Correct Pronoun

Read these sentences. Select the correct pronoun from the two in parentheses. Tell whether it is a subject or object pronoun and why you chose that form.

1. Jane and (I, me) are learning to ski.
2. Last week (she, her) and Mom stayed home.
3. Today the instructor showed Bob and (we, us) a new trick.
4. Bob and Harry saw Dad and (we, us) and waved.
5. (They, them) and Ted were on snowshoes.
6. Dad helped (we, us) and (they, them) with our gear.
7. The instructor taught Dad and (I, me) about waxing skis.
8. (He, him) and Jerry climbed the hill easily.
9. The ski lift brought Jane and (I, me) up the hill.
10. Shall Jane and (I, me) meet you later?

Composition: Writing a Short Narrative

A. Tell about an incident that happened to you or another person either in or out of school, for example, when you were engaged in some game or sport or on a trip. Make your opening sentence attract attention, and keep the reader's interest alive.

B. Describe an imaginary incident that might have occurred at a time and place which you have learned to know through reading or study. Help your readers to feel that the boy or girl you are telling about acted as one would who lived in that place or at that time.

Read the following sentences, using the correct form of the verb in parentheses:

1. (choose) · The boys have __?__ a mascot.
2. (do) She __?__ the cleaning yesterday.
3. (freeze) Mother __?__ some raspberries last week.
4. (grow) Haven't you __?__ taller this year?
5. (know) We haven't __?__ about the secret long.
6. (ride) Hasn't anyone __?__ in a helicopter?
7. (speak) The girls have __?__ to us about it.
8. (steal) Who has __?__ my pencils?
9. (freeze) Glaciers are snow that has __?__.
10. (ride) The horses had been __?__ too long.

How Our Language Grew · • • ●

Smog: Some words appeared in our language for the first time when two words were combined to make a new one. For example, someone said *smog* to refer to a combination of smoke and fog. The new word caught on, and now it is in our language and appears in our dictionaries.

Another word that originated in the same way is *brunch*. It refers to a late morning meal. What two words does it combine in one?

Pronouns After Prepositions

Words such as *to, in, for, at, by*, and *with* are called prepositions. Notice the prepositions in the following sentences:

1. I baked a birthday cake *for* Dad.
2. We keep our suits *in* lockers.
3. They took the keys *with* them.
4. Shall we go *without* her?
5. Don't throw that snowball *at* me!

Every preposition is followed by a noun or pronoun which is called the **object of the preposition.**

Pass the sandwiches to Sally.

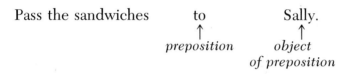

1. What is the preposition in sentence 1 above?
2. What is the object of the preposition in sentence 1?
3. Now name the prepositions and their objects in sentences 2, 3, 4, and 5.

Notice that when a pronoun is the object of a preposition, it is an object pronoun.

They took the keys with them.

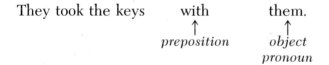

Sometimes a preposition is followed by more than one object, as shown in these sentences:

1. Did you speak to *Roger* and *her?*
2. We gave the presents to *Pauline* and *him.*
3. Don will go with *Jack* and *me.*

Always use object pronouns when the pronouns are objects of prepositions.

Do you remember the subject forms of pronouns and the object forms? Review them now before you do the practice exercises below.

SUBJECT PRONOUNS	OBJECT PRONOUNS
I	me
we	us
she	her
he	him
they	them

► **Practice: Using the Correct Pronoun**

1. Read aloud these sentences, using the correct pronoun for the person or persons referred to in parentheses:

1. The fire was discovered by Sally and (the speaker).
2. I wrote a letter of thanks to (my aunt).
3. We received these pamphlets from (the fire marshal).
4. The reporter wrote an article about (the astronauts).
5. The magazines are for (class members).
6. Jim gave these tickets to Ted and (the speakers).
7. Will you wait for Gene and (Gene's brother)?
8. Walk to the gate with Joan and (Joan's mother).

2. Write these sentences, using the correct pronouns in parentheses:

1. John threw the ball to (her, she).
2. The present is for Mother and (he, him).
3. Mother and (me, I) waited for (her, she).
4. The stranger looked at (they, them) and (I, me).
5. The posters were made by Robert and (he, him).
6. The music was enjoyed by (we, us).
7. Harry told (they, them) about (we, us).
8. Uncle John hid Don and (he, him) from (I, me).
9. (She, Her) and Ann played their flutes for (we, us).
10. (They, Them) and Uncle Bob took Mark and (I, me) to the circus.

Using Pronouns Correctly

Examine the expressions "we boys," "we girls," "us boys," and "us girls" as they are used in these sentences:

1. *We boys* are planning a science project. (*as subject of a sentence*)
2. The first dancers were *we girls*. (*after a verb of being*)
3. Mrs. Carter has invited *us boys* to brunch on Saturday. (*as object of an action verb*)
4. Your cousin can come with *us girls*. (*as object of a preposition*)

Use the expressions **we boys** and **we girls** when they are subjects or when they follow a verb of being.

Use the expressions **us boys** and **us girls** when they follow a verb of action or a preposition.

► **Practice: Using Pronouns Correctly**

Choose the correct pronoun given in parentheses.

1. (We, Us) boys are the best cooks.
2. The most graceful dancers are (we, us) girls.
3. Aunt Amy took (we, us) boys to the movies.
4. Dad took (we, us) girls to the skating rink.
5. The band marched by (we, us) girls.
6. Mother baked a cake for Dad and (we, us) boys.
7. (We, Us) boys usually play in the gym.
8. The visitors were (we, us) girls.
9. The message is for (we, us) students.
10. Did you see (we, us) swimmers yesterday?
11. Tell (we, us) fellows about your trip.
12. Miss Ray was standing near (we, us) girls.
13. (We, Us) committee members must meet soon.
14. The hardest workers here are (we, us) boys.
15. (We, Us) actors are having a rehearsal.

Sentence Patterns: Pronouns

Learn the new symbol below and review the others:

N = Noun   **V**^be^ = Verb of being (when it is part
N^p^ = Pronoun   of a predicate that tells what
V = Action verb   the subject *is* or *was*)
                V^h^ = Helping verb

Because pronouns are words that are used in place of nouns, they appear in sentences in the same places that nouns do.

Pattern 1: The books arrived.   They arrived.
            N   V   N^p   V

Pattern 2: Marie has fed the puppy.   She has fed him.
            N   V^h V   N   N^p V^h V   N^p

Pattern 3: The intruder was Mr. Carl.   The intruder was he.
            N   V^be N   N   V^be N^p

Remember that noun signals and helping verbs do not change the basic pattern of a sentence.

● Build sentences of your own, using the following symbols. Try to vary your sentence ideas.

1. **N V**
2. **N**^p **V**^h **V**
3. The **N V**^h **V N**^p
4. The **N V**^h **V**^be **N**^p
5. **N**^p **V**^h **V**^h **V** a **N**

6. **N V**^h **V N**^p
7. **N**^p **V**^h **V**^h **V N**^p
8. A **N V**^be the **N**
9. **N**^p **V**^h **V**^h **V**^be a **N**
10. The **N V**^h **V**^be **N**^p

Going Ahead ▶ ▶ ▶ ▶

A possessive pronoun also replaces a noun and its modifiers.

The cat chases *the cat's* tail.
She chases *her* tail (**N**^p **V N**^p **N**)

Write sentences following the symbols below. An **N**^p symbol before an **N** indicates a possessive pronoun.

1. **N**^p **V N**^p **N**
2. **N**^p **N V N**^p **N**

3. **N**^p **V**^h **V N**^p **N**
4. **N**^p **N V**^be the **N**

My Side of the Mountain

by Jean George
illustrated by the author
E. P. Dutton & Co., Inc.

Sam Gribley left New York City for the Catskill Mountains in May. He had with him a penknife, a ball of cord, an ax, forty dollars, and some flint and steel. He wore three sweaters and two pairs of trousers. With these provisions, Sam planned to live on the land for a year.

In one way, Sam was somewhat better equipped for survival than Robinson Crusoe had been. He had a few more of the basic survival tools. However, Sam discovered that tools are not very helpful if you don't know how to use them. He learned that lesson the first night, when, even with his flint and steel, he couldn't start a fire.

Sam knew very little about living in the woods — but what he lacked in skill and knowledge, he more than made up for in determination and courage. Drawing on these powerful assets, he learned what to do.

Sam tells his own story in *My Side of the Mountain* — how he burned out a room in the base of a tree, captured a falcon and trained it to hunt, learned to read the weather, and kept a record of his adventures.

If you have ever had a desire to try "roughing it" yourself, you won't want to miss Sam Gribley's great adventure.

187

TRYOUT TIME

If you make a mistake on any test, take the Practice on pages 189 with the same Roman numeral as the test.

Test I.   Singular and Plural Pronouns

Write these two headings on your paper: *Singular* and *Plural*.   List each of the pronouns in the following sentences under the correct heading.   Next to each pronoun, write the noun or nouns for which it stands.

1. Robert paid for the bike and rode it home.
2. The movie showed Mexico and its people.
3. Steve said, "My teacher told me about his trip."
4. The boys took their coats off and put them away.

Test II.   Possessive Pronouns

Answer these questions, using a possessive pronoun:

1. Do those books belong to you and Jay?   Yes, those books are __?__ .
2. Is this Janet's costume?   Yes, that costume is __?__ .

Test III.   Writing Pronouns Correctly

Write each sentence, using the correct form:

1. Is that (their, there, they're) lunchbox?
2. (Its, It's) cover is not on tight.
3. (Its, It's) a fine day for a picnic.
4. (Their, There, They're) planning to eat later.
5. Will (their, there, they're) bus be here at nine o'clock?

Test IV.   Pronoun Forms

Write these sentences, using the correct pronoun:

1. (We, Us) boys are listening to some jazz records.
2. Jerry found Renée and (he, him) near the pool.
3. Don and (I, me) left the game early.
4. Please send a letter to Tom and (she, her).

Practice I. Singular and Plural Pronouns

1. Review pages 168–69.

2. List the pronouns in the following conversation under the headings *Singular* and *Plural*. Beside each pronoun, write the noun or nouns for which it stands.

Rachel turned to Joe. "Did you know," she asked, "that raccoons make good pets? My brother found a raccoon in our garden and we tamed him."

"Don't raccoons bite and scratch?" he asked.

"Raccoons won't hurt you unless they are threatened," she replied. "I bought a leash and put it on ours and he didn't object."

Practice II. Possessive Pronouns

1. Review the lesson on pages 171–72.

2. Write a possessive pronoun for the words in parentheses.

1. The bracelet is (the girl's).
2. The problem is not mine; it is (the person's spoken to).
3. The prize is (Mark and Ned's).

Practice III. Writing Pronouns Correctly

1. Review the lesson on pages 171–72.

2. Write a sentence for each of these words: *their, them, they're, its, it's.*

Practice IV. Pronoun Forms

1. Review the lessons on pages 174–75, 178–79, 180–81, 183–84.

2. Write these sentences, using the correct pronouns.

1. Mother told Priscilla and (she, her) to come home.
2. The book was written by Les and (I, me).
3. (We, Us) girls will arrive ahead of the others.
4. Please wait for (us, we) boys.
5. The winner of the race was (she, her).

189

CHAPTER 9

Writing Letters

Almost as soon as man taught himself to write his language, he began to write letters. Letter writing is an ancient art. The pictures at the left show various ways that letters have been transported over the centuries.

Friendly Letters

Below is part of a friendly letter which was written by Mr. Henry Van Dyke to his young friend, Frankie. Read what Mr. Van Dyke says about writing interesting letters.

It is a long time since we have seen each other and I so fear that our friendship may grow cold through absence and silence. I think that we ought to exchange letters.

A letter is not so good as a talk, but it is better than nothing at all. The best way to write a letter is to do it almost as if you were talking.

I have made a little story of the things I have been doing and sent it to you on a separate sheet. Now I wish you to tell me what has happened to you. . . .

Tell me what was the happiest day that you have had since we went to the picnic together last June—do you remember? Tell me which book you like best of all that you have read and why you like it. Tell me whether you have made any new friends and why you have chosen them. Tell me whether any of your studies are too hard for you and what you are going to do about it. . . .

Write to me as simply as if we were sitting side by side on a log beside a little river.

To Discuss

1. Why do people write friendly letters? What reasons did Mr. Van Dyke give?

2. According to Mr. Van Dyke, what is the best way to write a friendly letter?

3. Read again the fourth paragraph of the letter. What are some of the things that the writer wants Frankie to tell him? Can you suggest other good topics to include in friendly letters?

How to Write Friendly Letters

Tell news about yourself.
Give interesting details.
Write about things which will interest your friend.
Ask about your friend's interests and activities.
Use friendly, natural language.

Using the Correct Form

Study the model letter on the next page. Notice how the parts are arranged, punctuated, and capitalized.

1. *The heading*: What information does it give? Why is each item of information important? What four rules for using capital letters are followed? What rules for using punctuation marks are followed?

2. *The greeting*: Notice that the greeting begins with a capital letter. What mark follows the greeting? Sometimes a space is left between the heading and the greeting.

3. *The body of the letter*: How many paragraphs are there in the letter? What is the topic of each paragraph? Explain the reasons for each capital letter and punctuation mark.

4. *The closing*: There are many closings that may be used in friendly letters. Among them are *Sincerely, Affectionately, With love, Cordially,* and *Yours truly.* What closing did Rod use? What rules for capital letters and punctuation did he follow?

192

5. *The signature*: The signature is placed directly under the closing.

6. Choose and be ready to read aloud parts of the letter which show that the writer followed each of the guides on page 192.

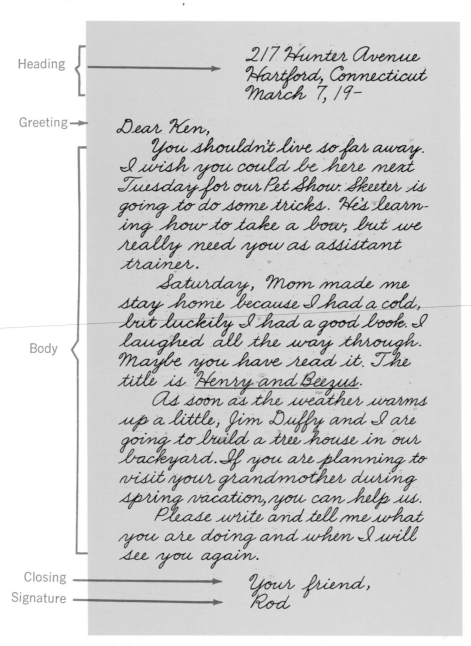

Heading

217 Hunter Avenue
Hartford, Connecticut
March 7, 19—

Greeting

Dear Ken,

Body

You shouldn't live so far away. I wish you could be here next Tuesday for our Pet Show. Skeeter is going to do some tricks. He's learning how to take a bow, but we really need you as assistant trainer.

Saturday, Mom made me stay home because I had a cold, but luckily I had a good book. I laughed all the way through. Maybe you have read it. The title is Henry and Beezus.

As soon as the weather warms up a little, Jim Duffy and I are going to build a tree house in our backyard. If you are planning to visit your grandmother during spring vacation, you can help us.

Please write and tell me what you are doing and when I will see you again.

Closing
Signature

Your friend,
Rod

► **Practice: Capitalization and Punctuation**

Show that you know how to write the parts of a friendly letter. Place the following parts correctly and neatly on your paper. Use capital letters and punctuation marks where needed.

1. Headings:

    1. 742 north elder street new york new york 10036 april 6 19___

    2. 643 northeast widener street portland oregon 97214 november 11 19___

2. Greetings, closings, and signatures:

    1. dear mrs albert   sincerely yours   helen
    2. dearest frannie   your cousin   john

The Appearance of a Letter

To send a letter that is easy to read is a courtesy. This means that your handwriting should be legible and neat. You should write on unlined paper, with even spaces left between uncrowded lines.

Always write letters in ink. A letter in pencil is hard to read and is likely to become smudged.

Place your letter on the page so that the margins make a frame for it. Keep the left-hand margin straight, but indent each paragraph. The right-hand margin should be as straight as possible, but it need not be rigidly so.

Composition: Writing a Friendly Letter

A. On a sheet of blank paper, write the heading and greeting of a letter you might write to (a) a friend your own age, (b) an aunt, (c) your teacher. Watch the capitalization and punctuation.

B. Write a letter to a real or imaginary friend. Use the correct form for all five parts of the letter. Plan your letter so that it can all be on one page for display.

194

Addressing an Envelope

Study the envelope which Rod prepared for his letter to Ken. There are two addresses on it. Notice the form in which they are written.

Return
Address {

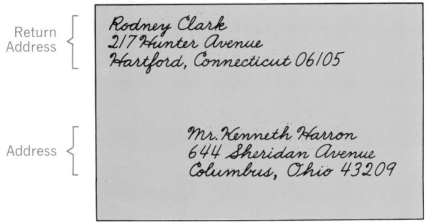

Rodney Clark
217 Hunter Avenue
Hartford, Connecticut 06105

Address {

Mr. Kenneth Harron
644 Sheridan Avenue
Columbus, Ohio 43209

Write the receiver's address a little below the middle of the envelope, and to the right of center, unless it is unusually long. If you do not have room to write city, state and ZIP Code on one line, write the state and ZIP Code directly under the city.

To Discuss

1. Why is the ZIP Code necessary? Is it set off by any punctuation mark?

2. Why is the *return address* important?

3. What rules for punctuation and capitalization are followed in *both addresses*? Notice that the names of cities and states are spelled out. Why is this helpful? Where is the ZIP Code for each address written?

▶ **Practice: Addressing Envelopes**

1. Study the model envelope. Then close your book. On paper, draw a rectangle the size of an envelope. As your teacher dictates them, write the two addresses correctly.

2. Prepare an envelope for the friendly letter which you wrote in exercise **B**, page 194.

Going Ahead ▸ ▸ ▸ ▸

Imagine that Mr. Van Dyke had written the letter on page 191 to you. Answer the letter, following the guides on page 192. Plan to read your letter to the class.

Write the first draft of your letter in pencil. Then read it over to see if you can improve any of the paragraphs. Make sure that its five parts are written correctly and in good form. Then copy the letter neatly in ink.

Review Practice: Correct Forms of Nouns

1. Write the plural form of each of these nouns:

mouse	library	holiday	tax
radio	gas	branch	life

2. Write each sentence, using the possessive form of the noun in parentheses:

1. The old (deer) antlers were huge.
2. We went to the primary (children) assembly.
3. (Monkeys) antics are always amusing.
4. The (actors) names were written on the board.
5. We all cheered our (team) success.

Review Practice: Pronouns

Complete each sentence, using the correct pronoun in parentheses.

1. (We, Us) __?__ boys were going to paint the fence.
2. (me, I) Only Rodney and __?__ were experienced painters.
3. (she, her) My sister's friends and __?__ wanted to paint, too.
4. (they, them) We thanked __?__ for their help.
5. (we, us) Later, Mother called __?__ boys and girls into the house.
6. (we, us) She had baked a cake for the girls and __?__ boys.

196

Sounds and Spelling

Consonant Sounds with No Single Letter of Their Own

In spelling you often use two letters for one sound. This combination is called a *digraph* (dī'graf). Vowel digraphs, like *ai* in *said,* are common. Name several others.

A few consonant digraphs, like those listed below, stand for sounds not otherwise represented in the alphabet.

Ch, as in *chocolate.* No single letter stands for the sound of *ch.* This digraph, then, is essential in spelling. Notice, however, that it may also stand for *k,* as in *chaos,* or for *sh,* as in *chef.*

Sh, as in *shepherd.* The sound of *sh* also has no single letter of its own. You will find in a later lesson that at least two words use *s* alone as a beginning *sh* sound.

Th, as in *thin* (a sound made only with breath) **and *then*** (made with voice). Look in the pronunciation key of your dictionary to see how these two sounds are marked. Some dictionaries show the voiced *th* with a bar through the letters. Say the words *breath* and *breathe.* Which *th* is voiced? Which is breath only? In spelling, a few words use the digraph *th* for a *t* sound, as in *Thomas.*

Zh. This digraph is used only in showing pronunciation, not in spelling. Look for it in your dictionary. It stands for a sound you hear in *pleasure, azure, garage.* In each of those words, which letter is sounded *zh?*

Spelling Checkup

1. Learn the sound and spelling of words shown in italics above.

2. Add these words to your spelling list: *Chicago, Cheyenne, schedule, composure, fisher, fissure.*

197

Using Words Correctly: <u>sit</u> and <u>set</u>

The verbs *sit* and *set* are easily confused. As you read the following sentences, think about the differences in their meaning:

1. *Sit* here, please. (to rest)
2. *Set* the plant on the windowsill. (to place)
3. *Set* your watch. (to put in a certain position, place, or condition)

Use a form of the verb **sit** when you mean "to rest."
Use **set** when you mean "to place" or "to put in order."

Before you can use a verb correctly, you must know its correct forms as well as its meaning. Study the correct forms of *sit* and *set* in the sentences that follow:

Sit

1. They *sit* in the last row. (*present*)
2. Howard *sat* on the porch. (*past*)
3. He has *sat* there for hours. (*past participle*)

Set

1. Please *set* the table. (*present*)
2. The men *set* the girders in place. (*past*)
3. They have *set* the chair on the porch. (*past participle*)

What is the past tense form of *sit*? What is the past participle form of *sit*?

What do you notice about the three forms of *set*? What are the three forms?

The three correct forms of *sit* and the three correct forms of *set* are as follows:

PRESENT	PAST	PAST PARTICIPLE
sit	sat	(have, has, or had) sat
set	set	(have, has, or had) set

► Practice: Using <u>sit</u> and <u>set</u>

Write the following sentences, using the correct form of *sit* or *set*.

1. Last year I (sat, set) near the window.
2. Now I (sit, set) near the door.
3. She always (sits, sets) the basket on that shelf.
4. Those mules have (sat, set) down again.
5. We have (sat, set) the flowers on the table.
6. The trapper (sat, set) a trap for the fox.

Review Practice: Punctuation

The sentences below require punctuation marks. Write them correctly.

1. I wish you were here Al.
2. My friend lives in St. Paul Minnesota.
3. George Washington was born on February 22 1732.
4. Dan would you like to go on a canoe trip?
5. I am very sorry Mary that you are ill.

TO MEMORIZE

Three Things

Three things there are that will never
    come back:
The arrow shot forth on its destined
    track;
The appointed hour that could not wait;
And the helpful word that was spoken
    too late.

Adapted from the Persian by LOUIS UNTERMEYER

The verse above is a kind of proverb, or wise saying. What three things does the author say "will never come back"? What does the second line mean to you? What is a *destined track*? What is an *appointed hour*?

199

Using Interjections

Certain words are used only to express feelings. They are not really a part of the sentence pattern. Such words are called *interjections*. Look up *interject* in a large dictionary to find the meanings of *inter* and *ject*. How do these meanings help to explain the word *interjection*?

Read each sentence below and find the interjection. Decide whether it expresses a strong feeling or a mild feeling. Notice the mark of punctuation that follows the interjection.

1. Whew! That was a close call.
2. Well, the joke was on me.
3. Oh, I'm sorry about that.
4. Whee! That was some toboggan ride.

Which sentences begin with strong interjections? mild?
What mark of punctuation follows a strong interjection? a mild interjection?

■ A word that is used to express a feeling is called an **interjection.**

Put an exclamation point after a strong interjection.
Place a comma after a mild interjection.

► **Practice: Using Interjections Correctly**

1. Write the sentences below correctly. Use the proper marks of punctuation after the interjections.

1. Hurrah Our team won.
2. Oh it is chilly outside.
3. Ah The boat seems to be tipping.
4. Help I'm slipping.
5. Well I'm sorry about that.
6. Alas I haven't done my homework yet.

2. Write six sentences using different interjections. Punctuate your sentences correctly.

200

Notes for Special Purposes

A sincere friend remembers to say *thank you, please, I am sorry,* or *congratulations.* When he cannot express these words of thoughtfulness in person, he writes a courtesy note.

Courtesy notes are a kind of friendly letter and are therefore written in the form of a friendly letter.

Review Practice: Correct Form for Friendly Letters

Study the note of congratulation below. Notice the placement of the parts, the punctuation, and the spelling. Then close your book and write the letter as your teacher dictates it.

Sandy, Idaho 82374
March 24, 19___

Dear John,

Mother just read me the part of Aunt Emma's letter about your robot man winning first prize at the state science fair. Congratulations! We are proud of you. When we come to visit you this summer, I hope you will show me how it works.

Your cousin,
Al

A Note of Appreciation

There are many occasions for writing a letter of appreciation or a thank-you note. If someone sends you a gift or does something for you, you will want to express your appreciation. It is courteous to write a note of thanks after visiting at the home of a friend or relative. This is sometimes called a bread-and-butter letter.

Read this note of appreciation. Be ready to discuss the questions that follow.

72 Oscar Street
Paula, California 95451
October 3, 19—

Dear Mrs. Stark,

Our class felt very lucky to have you visit us last Friday. The pictures of Mexico you showed helped us to feel better acquainted with the country and its people. We expecially liked your description of the fiesta and the wedding.

After we have studied more about Mexico, we plan to give a program for our parents. We will let you know when it will be. If you can come, Miss Thompson and our class will be very much pleased.

Yours sincerely,
Mary Stayton

To Discuss

1. Why did Mary write Mrs. Stark a note of thanks?
2. How did Mary show her class's appreciation?
3. Was the note written promptly? How can you tell?
4. Did Mary follow the correct form for all parts of a friendly letter? What rules for capital letters and punctuation did she follow?
5. Why did she use both her first and last names in the signature?
6. Prepare a list of suggestions to follow in writing courtesy notes, such as letters of thanks.

► **Practice: Writing a Note of Appreciation**

1. Pretend that Mr. Hill talked to your class about airplanes and that he used pictures and models to illustrate his talk. Write him a letter of thanks for the class. Include mention of some features of his talk that made it especially interesting.

2. Write a thank-you note for a gift, real or imaginary.

An Invitation

A good invitation is clear, interesting, and friendly in tone. It must contain all the necessary information.

Read this invitation. Discuss the questions that follow:

Conroy, Iowa 52220
April 12, 19—

Dear Joan,

Can you come next Saturday morning and stay with me until Sunday afternoon? Mother says your parents may be planning to attend the conference. If so, they could leave you here and call for you on their way home.

Right now the farm is a very busy place. We have six baby pigs that are as cute as they can be and about a dozen little fuzzy chickens.

If you can come, bring an extra sweater and boots or heavy shoes for outdoors. We can have fun indoors, too. I have a new game to show you.

With love,
Ruth

To Discuss

1. How did Ruth make her letter interesting?

2. What arrangements did Ruth suggest? Did she state them clearly?

3. What sentence shows that Ruth is a thoughtful person?

4. Is the invitation written correctly?

5. Should invitations be answered promptly? Why?

A. Write a letter inviting a friend to be your guest for a weekend, on a camping trip, or at a picnic. Follow the suggestions for writing courtesy notes which you have prepared. Read the invitation on page 203 again. Try to mention in your note some reasons why your friend would enjoy the affair that the invitation mentions.

B. Divide the class into writing teams, with team members numbered 1 and 2. Number 1 is to write to Number 2 a friendly letter expressing appreciation for a recent action of Number 2 in which he showed unusual courage or kindness or originality. Number 2 is to write to Number 1 thanking him for a gift he has just received from Number 1. Both writers may use their imagination to supply the facts. Have fun with this assignment. Read to the class some of the letters received.

How Our Language Grew • • ● ●

For thousands of years "going to the circus" has been a favorite pastime of human beings. In ancient Rome a *circus* was a kind of sports stadium, consisting of a race track with seats circling it. There the Romans watched chariot races and dangerous games in which gladiators fought each other and wild beasts.

The word *circus* is a Latin word which means "circle" or "ring." It has come into our language without change.

Look up the Latin term *Circus Maximus*. What did this mean to the people of Rome?

Using Words Correctly: <u>teach</u> and <u>learn</u>

The meanings of the verbs *teach* and *learn* are sometimes confused. The verb *teach* means "to show how" or "to give instruction." The verb *learn* means "to gain knowledge or skill." Study the ways in which these verbs are used in the sentences below:

1. Mr. Allan *teaches* us swimming.
2. He *taught* me the breast stroke.
3. Some of us *learn* the strokes more easily than others.
4. Have you *learned* how to tread water?

Use the verb **teach,** not **learn,** when you mean "to give instruction."

► **Practice: Using <u>teach</u> and <u>learn</u>**

1. Write the sentences below, using the correct verb in parentheses:

1. Will you (teach, learn) me how to drive a car?
2. Who (taught, learned) you that trick?
3. Terry is (teaching, learning) his dog some new tricks.
4. Mr. Jones (has taught, has learned) us the basic principles of first aid.
5. Carol and I (have taught, have learned) two new songs from the operetta.
6. Last summer Uncle Charles (taught, learned) Richard and me how to swim.

2. Use *teach* or *taught* or *learn* or *learned* in place of the blanks.

1. Have you __?__ Billy the song yet?
2. He __?__ his part very well.
3. She __?__ me how to cook.
4. The dictionary will help you __?__ to spell.
5. Will you __?__ me how to build a bookcase?

Business Letters

Business letters differ from friendly letters. In business letters, the message should be stated in a businesslike way. It should be clear and as brief as possible.

The business letter has six parts rather than five, as in a friendly letter. Study the form of the business letter on the next page.

To Discuss

1. *The heading*: What information does it give? What rules for capital letters and punctuation are followed? What is the ZIP Code? Why is it important?

2. *The inside address*: Whose address is it? Note the use of capital letters and punctuation. If a business letter is addressed to an individual, the person's name would come first in the *inside address*.

3. *The greeting*: Why is this greeting used? What other greetings may be used in business letters? What punctuation follows the greeting?

Place a colon after the greeting in a business letter.

---

4. *The body of the letter*: Is the request stated clearly and courteously? Is it brief and to the point? Are punctuation marks and capital letters used correctly? Why does the word *Northwest* have a capital letter?

5. *The closing*: What rules for capital letters and punctuation are followed? What other closing phrases may be used for business letters?

6. *The signature*: Whose signature is it? How is the signature placed in relation to the heading and closing? Why do you think Rex Allen wrote the letter?

7. Choose and be ready to read aloud parts of a letter which show the writer followed the suggestions on the next page that were called for in his letter.

206

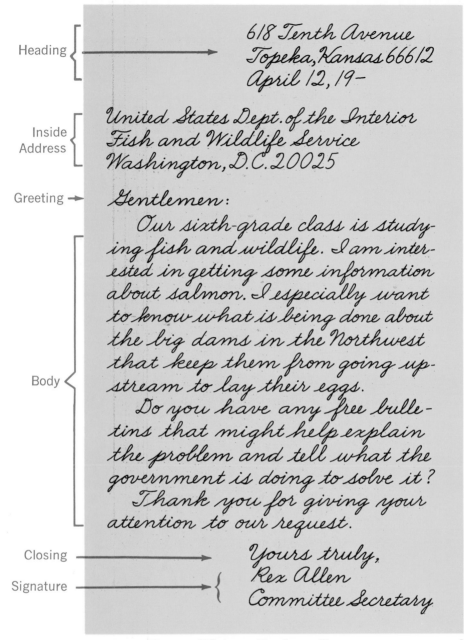

Heading

618 Tenth Avenue
Topeka, Kansas 66612
April 12, 19—

Inside Address

United States Dept. of the Interior
Fish and Wildlife Service
Washington, D.C. 20025

Greeting

Gentlemen:

Body

Our sixth-grade class is studying fish and wildlife. I am interested in getting some information about salmon. I especially want to know what is being done about the big dams in the Northwest that keep them from going upstream to lay their eggs.

Do you have any free bulletins that might help explain the problem and tell what the government is doing to solve it?

Thank you for giving your attention to our request.

Closing

Yours truly,

Signature

Rex Allen
Committee Secretary

How to Write a Business Letter

Explain exactly what you want.
Give all the information that your reader will need.
Be courteous.
Be brief and to the point.

A. Write the heading, inside address, greeting, closing, and signature for two business letters. Use the following information:

    1. A letter from you to mr r c davis
       the davis book store   816 foster avenue
       halsey oregon 97809

    2. A letter from you to the charleston public library
       circulation department   416 tenth avenue
       charleston nevada 89702

B. Write a business letter to order something you have seen advertised in a paper or magazine. Follow the guides on page 207. Use the correct form for business letters.

Addressing the Envelope for a Business Letter

On the envelope for a business letter, write the *receiver's address*, which is the inside address of the letter. Write also the *return address*. Follow the form you used in addressing an envelope for a friendly letter.

▶ **Practice: Preparing Business Envelopes**

1. Draw and address the envelope for the business letter you wrote for exercise **B** above.

2. Draw an envelope and address it correctly to your principal. Use your home address for the return address.

Review Practice: Capital Letters

1. Write the sentences below and at the top of the next page, using capital letters correctly:

    1. Where is the long island expressway?
    2. When are you leaving for the south?
    3. Our friends come from the middle west.
    4. We belong to the boy scouts of america.
    5. I study english in the morning.

6. My teacher is mr. harriman.
7. If a bus doesn't come soon, I'll write to the maysville transit system, inc.
8. We drove to the snow line on mt. hood.

2. Write these quotations, using the correct punctuation:

1. My brother belongs to the Appalachian Mountain Club Martin said.
2. What do the members of the club do asked Wally.
3. They go on long hikes through the woods and climb mountains Martin replied.
4. What fun they must have together Wally exclaimed.

Going Ahead ▶ ▶ ▶ ▶

Make a collection of business letters. Study each letter to see what is included in the inside address. What closing is used? Is any additional information given under the signature?

Notice, too, the contents of the letter. Is the message direct and clear?

Make a report on your findings, using some of the letters to illustrate your points.

TRYOUT TIME

If you make a mistake on any test, take the Practice on page 211 with the same Roman numeral as the test.

Test I.   Writing a Friendly Letter

Arrange and write these parts of a friendly letter correctly:

fairfield maine	dear theresa	with love
april 6 19__		edna

Test II.   Using sit and set

Write each sentence, using the correct verb form.

1. We (sat, set) near the back of the hall.
2. Please let me (set, sit) in a front seat.
3. Miss Hart has (sat, set) the model on display.
4. I will (set, sit) the table, Mother.

Test III.   Interjections

Begin each sentence below with an interjection. Put the correct mark of punctuation after the interjection.

1. __?__ I nearly missed the goal.
2. __?__ we do not have to leave yet.

Test IV.   Using teach and learn

Use a form of *teach* or *learn* correctly in each sentence:

1. Can you __?__ me to play tennis?
2. The mother will __?__ her cubs to find food.
3. The cubs will __?__ very quickly.
4. Who __?__ Jerry to play so well?

Test V.   Writing Business Letters

Write the heading, inside address, greeting, closing, and signature of a letter to the Girl Scouts of the U.S.A., 830 Third Avenue, New York, New York 10022.

Practice I.   Writing a Friendly Letter

1. Review the lesson on pages 191–93.   Correct any mistakes you made on Test I.

2. Write the following parts of a friendly letter correctly:

18 gaines avenue   your friend
larson montana   kim
september 8 19__

Practice II.   Using sit and set

1. Study again the lesson on page 198.

2. Write four sentences, using forms of *sit* and *set* correctly.

Practice III.   Interjections

1. Study the lesson on page 200.

2. Write sentences of your own, using these interjections: *ouch, help, oh, alas.*

Practice IV.   Using teach and learn

1. Review the lesson on page 205.

2. Write this paragraph, using *teach* and *learn* correctly:

Dad has promised to __?__ me to play chess.   It is a hard game to __?__ anyone.   Do you think he can __?__ me?   Danny said he __?__ to play last winter.

Practice V.   Writing Business Letters

1. Review the lesson on pages 206–08.

2. Correct any errors in form, punctuation, capitalization, and spelling in Test V.

3. Write the heading, inside address, greeting, closing, and signature of a letter to Reader's Digest, Pleasantville, New York 10570.

CHAPTER 10

Using Adjectives and Adverbs

Here are two paragraphs from *The Missing Violin*, by Jean Bothwell, a book about an American family living in India. Read them and see whether a clear, vivid picture comes to your mind.

The market was a fascinating place, like an enormous department store with dirt floor and open sides. There were strange fruits they had never heard of in the beautifully arranged displays — custard apples, huge loose-skinned oranges from Nagpur, and horrible-smelling jack fruit.

There were carpets and shirts and toys and cooking things, and one stall had nothing but bright-colored glass bracelets for girls and women to wear in rows on each arm. The owners of the stalls shouted at Mrs. Henderson to bring her guests to them. They sounded like the barkers in side shows at country fairs at home.

A good writer makes you see vividly the people, places, or things about which he is writing. He uses words that help you to see, hear, smell, and feel what he is describing. Two kinds of words that contribute to a writer's word picture are **adjectives** and **adverbs.** These two parts of speech help to make our language lively and colorful. An adjective or an adverb can change a dull statement to one that is so bright and new that it stands out on the page. Look at these two. Which one do you like better?

That monkey stole our lunch.

That mischievous, chattering monkey slyly stole our lunch.

The Adjective

Here are some of the words, italicized below, that helped you to see the Indian market in the paragraphs on page 212.

fascinating place   *strange* fruits
open sides   *huge loose-skinned* oranges

Each italicized word above changes or adds to the meaning of a noun. For example, a *"fascinating* place" presents a different picture from just "a place." Notice how the picture of *place* changes below:

horrible place   *ugly* place
familiar place   *empty* place
beautiful place   *crowded* place

Another word for *change* is **modify.** The words above that modify *place* are called **adjectives**.

In the two paragraphs quoted on page 212, find the adjectives that modify these nouns:

___?___ department store   ___?___ things
___?___ jack fruit   ___?___ glass bracelets

Show how a different adjective in each blank space above would leave an entirely different idea with the reader. Read the phrases aloud substituting other adjectives that could modify the nouns.

Change the meaning of each noun in the list below by substituting another modifier in place of the adjectives in italics.

musical voice   *strong* will   *false* friend

As you know, other parts of speech may be used like adjectives to modify nouns. Nouns and pronouns that show possession may be used like adjectives.

ADJECTIVES   POSSESSIVE NOUNS AND PRONOUNS

delicious fudge   *mother's* fudge
hot biscuits   *our* biscuits

▶ **Practice: Recognizing Adjectives**

Read the following description of Paul Bunyan from *Paul Bunyan and His Great Blue Ox*, by Wallace Wadsworth. Notice the adjectives. Be ready to answer the questions.

Paul Bunyan was of tremendous size and strength, the strongest man that ever swung an ax. He had curly black hair which his loving wife used to comb for him every morning with a great crosscut saw, after first parting it nicely with a broadax, and a big black beard that was as long as it was wide and as wide as it was long. He was rather proud of this beard, and took great care of it. Several times every day he would pull up a young pine tree by the roots and use its stiff branches in combing and brushing it smooth.

1. What adjective describes Paul Bunyan's size and strength?

2. Which two adjectives describe Paul's hair?

3. Which four adjectives describe Paul's beard?

4. The adjective *proud* describes how Paul felt about his beard. Does this adjective modify a noun or a pronoun? Does it precede or follow the word it modifies?

5. Which adjectives modify the following nouns?

___?___ man	___?___ times
___?___ morning	___?___ day
___?___ crosscut saw	___?___ pine tree
___?___ care	___?___ branches

214

Position of Adjectives

Did you notice that all the adjectives discussed on page 213 were placed directly before the nouns they modify? This is the most common position for adjectives, but you should learn to look elsewhere in the sentence for adjectives also.

1. Tom is a *musical* boy.
2. Tom, *musical* and *artistic*, leads the band.
3. Tom is *musical*.
4. He is *artistic*.

In sentence 4, notice that *artistic* modifies the pronoun *He*.

The adjectives in sentences 3 and 4 follow a verb of being. When you studied verbs of being, like *am, is, are, was,* and *were,* you learned that the predicate tells what the subject *is* or *is like*. The verb of being may be completed either by a noun or an adjective. Read this sentence: *Tom is a musician*. The words *musician* and *Tom* refer to the same person; *musician* is a noun, like *Tom*. Did the noun signal before the word also help you to know it was a noun? Try placing a noun signal before *musical* in the sentence *Tom is musical*. It is not a noun; it is an adjective that tells what Tom *is like*.

■ An **adjective** is a word that modifies a noun or a pronoun.

▶ **Practice: Using Adjectives in Different Positions**

Use adjectives in different positions as shown above by completing the following sentences. Choose interesting adjectives that make sense.

1. Hansel and Gretel lived near a __?__, __?__ forest.
2. Their parents were __?__.
3. They were also __?__.
4. The children, __?__ and __?__, were lost in the woods.
5. __?__ and __?__ was the forest.
6. Coming upon a __?__ house, they knocked, and a __?__ witch appeared.

Kinds of Adjectives

Some adjectives modify nouns by describing the nouns. They answer these questions: *What kind? What color? What size?*   *deep* forests   *red* barn   *long* hair

Adjectives that describe are called **descriptive adjectives.** Some adjectives do not describe. Notice these in italics:

forty-nine boys   *that* hat

The adjective *forty-nine* tells *how many.* The adjective *that* tells *which one.* These adjectives limit the meaning of a noun by telling *which one* or *how many.* They are called **limiting adjectives.**

These limiting adjectives tell *how many* or *which one*:

three players	*both* doors	*this* desk
several reasons	*some* teachers	*these* games
each child	*all* animals	*those* crayons
every boy	*few* people	*the* room

Notice the noun signal *the* in the list above. The noun signals *a, an,* and *the* are also limiting adjectives. They are sometimes called *articles.*

■ An **adjective** modifies a noun by telling *what kind, what color, what size, which one,* or *how many.*

216

► **Practice: Kinds of Adjectives**

1. Here is a list of adjectives with the nouns they modify. Name each adjective and tell whether it is *descriptive* or *limiting*. If it is descriptive, it will answer the questions: *What kind? What color? What size?* If it is limiting, it will answer the questions: *Which one? How many?*

1. each boy	6. small dogs	11. third choice
2. every girl	7. angry people	12. those men
3. tropical birds	8. true friend	13. blue wool
4. both teams	9. this toy	14. the friend
5. lazy cattle	10. these books	15. merry laughter

2. Copy each sentence below. Fill in each blank with an adjective that answers the question underneath the blank.

1. We saw a __?__ __?__ barn.
   What size? What color?
2. Herman bought __?__ __?__ notebooks.
   How many? What size?
3. __?__ __?__ dog won __?__ prizes.
   Which one? What kind? How many?
4. She wore a __?__ coat with a __?__ hat.
   What kind?   What color?

3. Write five sentences, using at least eight descriptive adjectives. Underline each adjective and draw an arrow from the adjective to the noun it modifies, like this:

The <u>little</u> girl wore a <u>blue</u> sweater.

Review Practice: Correct Word Forms

Write the sentence, using the correct word:

1. (Were, We're) leaving now.
2. (It's, Its) going to rain.
3. The wind blew in all (its, it's) fury.
4. (Your, you're) riddle was the best.
5. The fishermen launched (their, there) boats.
6. (There, their) goes the racer!

S | Sounds and Spelling

Success with <u>S</u>

The sound and spelling of *s* at the beginning of a word almost always match perfectly, but two words are exceptions. A story may help you to remember them. A man once said to a friend, "The word *sugar* is the only word in English that starts with *s* for the sound of *sh*." The friend replied, "Are you *sure*?"

Within a word or at the end of a word, the letter *s* may spell either an *s* or a *z* sound. Both sounds are in the word *business*. Which sound is spelled with *s*? which with *ss*? Can you pronounce these two words correctly: *lose* and *loose*? Remember the spelling by matching them with words of like spelling: *Whose* team will *lose*? The *goose* is *loose*.

List on the board in two columns eight or ten words in which *s* spells each sound, *s* and *z*. Choose words with *s* in the middle or at the end of the word.

A few words like *scissors* and *science* include a silent *c* following the initial *s*. Can you name others?

A few words use *s* in the middle to spell the sound *zh*, as in *television*. Can you name others?

If the final syllable of a word is pronounced "shun," it may be spelled *sion*, as in *permission*. But watch out! The same sound may be spelled *tion* or *cian* or *cion*, as in *perfection, musician, suspicion*.

Spelling Checkup

1. Learn to spell all words in italics on this page.
2. Add to your spelling lesson the words listed below:

possession	measure	physician	scenery
procession	duplication	extension	surely

Making Comparisons with Adjectives

Descriptive adjectives are often used to make comparisons. In the following sentences, the adjective *young* is used to compare the ages of Charles, Jack, and Bud:

1. Jack is *young*.
2. Bud is *younger* than Jack.
3. Charles is the *youngest* of the three brothers.

All three of the brothers are young, but they are not equally so. How was *young* changed in sentences 2 and 3?

You have just seen one way that an adjective shows comparison. Now examine these sentences. Notice that an adjective of more than one syllable may show comparison differently.

4. The first painting is *beautiful*.
5. The second painting is *more beautiful* than the first.
6. This painting is the *most beautiful* of all.

Did *beautiful* change its form?

The Three Degrees of Comparison

There are three *degrees of comparison*. They are called the **positive, comparative,** and **superlative degrees**. Study these examples:

POSITIVE	COMPARATIVE	SUPERLATIVE
large	larger	largest
difficult	more difficult	most difficult
difficult	less difficult	least difficult

■ The **positive degree** is the simple form of the adjective.

■ The **comparative degree** is the form used to compare *two* persons or things.

■ The **superlative degree** is the form used to compare *three* or *more* persons or things.

Rules for Making Comparisons

1. Most adjectives of one syllable form the comparative degree by adding *–er,* and the superlative by adding *–est:*

small, smaller, smallest   fine, finer, finest

2. Most two-syllable adjectives use **more** or **less, most** or **least:**

careless $\begin{cases} \text{more careless} \\ \text{less careless} \end{cases}$ $\begin{cases} \text{most careless} \\ \text{least careless} \end{cases}$

A few adjectives of two syllables add *–er* and *–est:*

happy, happier, happiest

3. Adjectives of three or more syllables use **more** or **less, most** or **least:**

wonderful $\begin{cases} \text{more wonderful} \\ \text{less wonderful} \end{cases}$ $\begin{cases} \text{most wonderful} \\ \text{least wonderful} \end{cases}$

Some Exceptions

Some adjectives, such as *good, bad,* and *little,* form the degrees of comparison in a different, or irregular, way:

a *good* circus   a *better* circus   the *best* circus
a *bad* view   a *worse* view   the *worst* view
a *little* trouble   *less* trouble   the *least* trouble

Comparing Adjectives Correctly

Use the comparative degree of an adjective when you compare two persons or things. Use the superlative degree when you compare three or more persons or things.

This road is *wider* than the old and the *widest* in the state.

Use only one form at a time in making comparisons.

RIGHT: The clowns were *funnier* this year.
WRONG: The clowns were "more funnier" this year.

RIGHT: This is the *hardest* problem in the book.
WRONG: This is the "most hardest" problem in the book.

Spelling of Comparative Forms

1. Some adjectives simply add *–er* or *–est* to the simple form, as *hard, harder, hardest; tall, taller, tallest.* If an adjective ends in *e,* it adds only *–r* or *–st: fine, finer, finest.*

2. Some adjectives double the last letter before adding *–er* or *–est: big, bigger, biggest; thin, thinner, thinnest.*

3. Adjectives that end in *y* preceded by a consonant change *y* to *i* before adding *–er* or *–est: lazy, lazier, laziest.*

▶ **Practice: Making Comparisons with Adjectives**

1. On the board, write the comparative and superlative forms of the words given below. If the dictionary does not give these forms, be ready to tell why.

| flat | funny | lean | gay |
| sad | wet | dry | lovely |

2. Read each sentence aloud, using the correct comparative or superlative form of the adjective in parentheses.

   1. (deep) The water is __?__ here than it is there.
   2. (green) We have the __?__ lawn on the avenue.
   3. (little) I had __?__ time to practice than Rex.
   4. (good) Jane is the __?__ cook of the two.
   5. (beautiful) Jack's painting is __?__ than mine.

3. Write four sentences, using adjectives to compare (1) two girls, (2) two boys, (3) two dogs, and (4) two sports. Use forms of these adjectives: *strong, lively, thoughtful, dangerous.*

4. Write three sentences comparing more than two persons or objects. Use forms of these adjectives: *good, distant, busy.*

Review Practice: Quotations

Write these quotations correctly:

   1. Those trucks made such a noise Mother complained.
   2. That's because they shift gears on the hill said Bill.
   3. Well Mother answered I wish they would stay away from our hill.

Using Negatives Correctly

Words that have a "no" meaning are called **negatives.**
Here are some examples: *no, not, never, none, nothing,* and
words ending in *n't.* Never use two or more of these words
in sentences such as those below. Only one negative is needed.

RIGHT: I *don't* know any of the answers.

RIGHT: I know *none* of the answers.

WRONG: I don't know none of the answers.

RIGHT: He *didn't* see anything.

RIGHT: He saw *nothing.*

WRONG: He didn't see nothing.

► **Practice: Using Negatives**

Read each sentence, using the correct form:

1. I didn't say (nothing, anything).
2. They haven't (any, none).
3. Weren't (any, none) of them at the party?
4. Haven't you (never, ever) been on a ship?
5. John hasn't eaten (any, no) lunch.
6. I don't have (no, any) time.

TO MEMORIZE

He drew a circle that shut me out—
Heretic, rebel, a thing to flout.
But love and I had the wit to win:
We drew a circle that took him in.

EDWIN MARKHAM

In the poem above, called "Outwitted," the poet suggests
one way to overcome unfriendliness and cruelty. Read the
lines and talk about their meaning. Have you ever felt left
out? Did you think of dealing with the situation as Markham
suggests?

How Our Language Grew •••●

Cab: The modern word *cab* is commonly used to refer to a taxicab or other vehicle for hire. The history of this word goes back to other lands and languages, as many of our words do. The English first used the word *cabriolet* to mean a light two-wheeled, horse-drawn carriage. They borrowed the word from the French *cabriole,* which meant "leap" or "caper." The French had previously borrowed from the Latin *capreolus,* which meant "wild goat."

Cabriolet was a long word for people who needed a carriage in a hurry. Little wonder that it was shortened to *cab.* If you ever see a taxicab leap down the street like a wild goat, you should remember the source of this word.

Using Adjectives Correctly

The words *this, that, these,* and *those* are often used as adjectives to answer the question *Which one?* They point out someone or something, as shown in these sentences:

1. *This* game requires four players.
2. Did you buy the game from *that* salesman?
3. *These* catalogs are useful.
4. *Those* books are in the library.

In the sentences above, which nouns do the italicized adjectives modify? Notice that these adjectives can do their own work; they do not need the words "here" and "there." "This *here* boat" is incorrect. Say "*This* boat."

Never join "here" and "there" to the words **this, that, these**, and **those**.

---

those and them

Once you learn the work that each part of speech does in a sentence, you can avoid many errors. The word *them,* you remember, is an object pronoun. It can never be used to modify a noun, as an adjective can.

In these sentences, *those* and *them* are used correctly. Read the sentences carefully.

1. *Those* paintings will be framed soon. (*Those* is an adjective.)
2. I have separated *them* from the others. (*Them* is an object pronoun. It takes the place of the noun *paintings*.)

Never use the pronoun **them** as an adjective to point out someone or something.

224

► **Practice: Using Adjectives Correctly**

1. Write four sentences, using *this, that, these,* and *those* as adjectives. Read your sentences aloud.

2. Write these sentences, using *those* or *them* in place of each blank.

1. Jack picked __?__ flowers today.
2. Shut __?__ windows.
3. __?__ model airplanes belong to __?__.
4. Did you take __?__ pictures?
5. We cannot solve __?__ problems for __?__.
6. Did you give all of __?__ cookies to __?__?

3. Write two sentences, using the word *them* correctly. Read your sentences aloud.

Going Ahead ▶ ▶ ▶ ▶

A committee of pupils who read many books can make recommendations for others who do not have titles in mind.

List your titles by topic or kind of book, as the chart below suggests, and add a line or two to tell what each book is about. Check your list with the librarian or your teacher. You may wish to read further in order to add new titles. If your list is approved, have it duplicated for everyone.

READERS' CHOICE

ADVENTURE STORIES	HISTORICAL FICTION

ANIMAL STORIES	POETRY

HUMOROUS STORIES	BIOGRAPHY

Proper Adjectives

Study the italicized words in the sentences below:

1. A *Dutch* fur trader discovered the lake.
2. Miss Norris showed us her collection of *Mexican* pottery.
3. Last summer we saw an *Indian* war dance.

Each of the italicized words above is an adjective that has been made from a proper noun. Such adjectives are called **proper adjectives.** Like proper nouns, proper adjectives are capitalized.

► **Practice: Writing Proper Adjectives**

Write these sentences correctly, capitalizing every proper adjective. Be prepared to read your sentences aloud, naming the proper adjectives.

1. Tamales and tacos are mexican dishes.
2. We stopped at the canadian border.
3. The violinist played hungarian music.
4. We are studying the english language.
5. My mother has a french cookbook.
6. Gold is a scotch game.
7. That swedish actress has talent.
8. An old roman wall surrounds the town.

The Adverb

Look at the italicized words in these sentences:

1. The elderly man spoke *slowly.*
2. Fred *soon* came to the window.
3. He looked *down.*
4. The boys *quickly* baited their hooks.
5. We *then* decided to leave.
6. Jack swung at the ball *wildly.*
7. We *never* go to the park.
8. Please play that record *again.*
9. Sue will *not* play with us.
10. Please speak *distinctly.*

In sentence 1, the verb is *spoke.* Which word tells *how* the man spoke? What is the verb in sentence 2? Which word tells *when* Fred came? What is the verb in sentence 3? Which word tells *where* he looked? In sentence 4, which word tells *how?*

Each word that you named is an *adverb*; it answered the question *How? When?* or *Where?* The adverbs in the sentences above modify (add to the meaning of) the verbs.

One adverb that modifies a verb but does not tell *how, when,* or *where* is the word *not.*

Do *not* eat that piece of cake.

In the sentence above, *not* modifies the verb *eat.*

Name the verbs in sentences 5 through 10 above; name the adverbs that modify them. Which question does each adverb answer: *How? When?* or *Where?*

The –ly Sign of an Adverb

Many adverbs end in *–ly: suddenly, happily, sadly, kindly.* Can you think of other adverbs that end in *–ly?*

Some adverbs do not have an *–ly* ending: *soon, often, too, up, down.* Can you think of others?

Special Adverbs

Most of the adverbs in our language answer the questions *How? When?* or *Where?* and modify verbs. There are a small number of adverbs, however, that act differently from the others.

Adverbs That Modify Adverbs

Examine these sentences:

1. Patricia works very carefully.
2. We arrived too late.

Find the adverb in sentence 1 that tells *how* Patricia works. Find the adverb in sentence 2 that tells *when* we arrived. Both *carefully* and *late* modify the verbs in the sentences, as most adverbs do. Now which word in sentence 1 tells *how carefully* Patricia works? Which word in sentence 2 tells *how late* we arrived? The words *very* and *too* are also adverbs. They answer the question *How much?* or *To what degree?* by modifying the adverbs *carefully* and *late*.

Adverbs That Modify Adjectives

In the sentences below, the two italicized adverbs modify adjectives. They answer the questions *How thoughtful?* and *How sad?*

1. Sue was *somewhat* thoughtful.
2. A *very* sad story was told.

Name the adjective in each of the sentences above.

■   An **adverb** is a word that modifies a verb, an adjective, or another adverb.

Write this list of adverbs in your notebook. As you discuss adverbs in class, keep adding to the list.

HOW?	WHEN?	WHERE?	HOW MUCH?
slowly	soon	down	very
quickly	then	here	too

228

► **Practice: Recognizing and Using Adverbs**

1. Read this paragraph from *Lad: A Dog*, by Albert Payson Terhune. Study the italicized adverbs. Be prepared to read aloud each italicized adverb, naming the word it modifies. Tell whether the adverb tells *where, how, when,* or *how much.*

There were other people at The Place—people to whom a dog must be courteous, as becomes a thoroughbred, and whose caresses he must accept. *Very often,* there were guests, too. And from puppyhood, Lad had been taught the sacredness of the Guest Law. *Civilly,* he would endure the pettings of these visiting outlanders. *Gravely* he would shake hands with them, on request. He would permit them to paw him or haul him *about,* if they were of the obnoxious, dog-mauling breed. But the moment politeness would permit, he *always* withdrew, *very quietly,* from their reach and, if possible, from their sight as well.

2. Use one or more adverbs to add to the meaning of each sentence below. Use an adverb that answers the question in parentheses. Then read the sentence aloud.

1. Mildred paints __?__. (How?)
2. The girls slept __?__ after their experience. (How?)
3. The skier glided __?__. (Where?)
4. The guests will arrive __?__. (When?)
5. The box is __?__ heavy. (To what degree?)
6. They visit us __?__ often. (To what degree?)

Review Practice: Correct Verb Forms

Write the following sentences, using the correct verbs:

1. He (set, sat) on the man's hat.
2. Who has (sat, set) the ink bottle on the table?
3. Mother (laid, lay) the blanket on the couch.
4. The treasure had (laid, lain) in a buried casket.
5. Who has (lain, laid) his coat on the barrel?
6. (Set, sit) the engine on the blocks.

Sentence Patterns:
Adjectives and Adverbs

Learn these two symbols:

> **Adj** = Adjective (including *a, an,* and *the*)
> **Adv** = Adverb

Note: From now on, the symbol **Adj** will stand for the noun signals *a, an,* and *the*, as well as for adjectives.

With an adjective you can now show the fourth sentence pattern. In such sentences an adjective comes after a verb of being and describes the subject:

Pattern 4:   **N V^{be} Adj**   Florence is beautiful.

You can now use the new symbols **Adj** and **Adv** to expand the sentence patterns you have learned:

> **Adj N Adv V Adj N**   White clouds almost hid the mountaintop.

● Number your paper from 1 to 3. Next to each numeral, write the letter (**a, b,** or **c**) of the sentence in the group which accurately follows the combination of symbols.

1. **N V^h V^{be} Adj N**
   (a) Pat had just called Frank.
   (b) Pat will be the president.
   (c) Pat called the new president.

2. **Adj N V^h V Adj N**
   (a) Two men discovered the gold mine.
   (b) The mine had been abandoned recently.
   (c) This stream may contain rich deposits.

3. **N^p V Adj N Adv**
   (a) He climbed the hill slowly.
   (b) Roger was soon very tired.
   (c) He saw a beautiful view.

● Build sentences from the following combinations of symbols. Avoid using the same words over and over.

1. **Adj N V**
2. **Adj Adj N V Adj N**
3. **Adj N V Adv**
4. **N V^h Adv V**
5. **N V^h V Adv**

6. **N^p V^{be} Adj**
7. **Adj Adj N V Adv**
8. **N V^h V^{be} Adj Adj N**
9. **Adj N V^h V Adj Adj N**
10. **Adj N V^h V^h V Adv**

Composition: Adverbs

English sentence patterns allow adverbs more freedom to move around than other classes (groups) of words. Most adverbs can be placed in any of these positions:

Angrily he left the party.
He *angrily* left the party.
He left the party *angrily*.

A. Study the picture below. Then, using adverbs in different positions, write four sentences that tell what is pictured.

B. Write an account of an action that you recently observed.

Making Comparisons with Adverbs

Adverbs are used to compare actions as to *time* or *manner* in sentences such as those below:

time: late, later, latest

1. Ted walked into the meeting *late*.
2. Did he arrive *later* than Harold?
3. Of all the members, Ted arrived *latest*.

manner: gracefully, more gracefully, most gracefully

4. Swans swim *gracefully*.
5. Do swans swim *more gracefully* than seagulls?
6. Of all water birds, swans swim *most gracefully*.

Like adjectives, adverbs have three degrees of comparison:

POSITIVE	COMPARATIVE	SUPERLATIVE
soon	sooner	soonest
late	later	latest
loudly	more ⎱ loudly less ⎰	most ⎱ loudly least ⎰
carefully	more ⎱ carefully less ⎰	most ⎱ carefully least ⎰

1. Adverbs of one syllable usually add *–er* and *–est* to make the comparative and superlative forms:

fast, faster, fastest

232

2. Most two-syllable adverbs use **more** or **less, most** or **least:**

$$\text{calmly} \quad \left.\begin{array}{l}\text{more}\\\text{less}\end{array}\right\} \text{calmly} \qquad \left.\begin{array}{l}\text{most}\\\text{least}\end{array}\right\} \text{calmly}$$

A few two-syllable adverbs add *–er* or *–est*:

early, earlier, earliest

3. All three-syllable adverbs use **more** or **less, most** or **least:**

$$\text{quietly} \quad \left.\begin{array}{l}\text{more}\\\text{less}\end{array}\right\} \text{quietly} \qquad \left.\begin{array}{l}\text{most}\\\text{least}\end{array}\right\} \text{quietly}$$

4. A few adverbs form the comparative and superlative forms in irregular ways:

well	better	best
far	farther	farthest
little	less	least
much	more	most

5. There are some adverbs that cannot be used in making comparisons. These include: *not, never, here, there, now, again, down, up.*

▶ **Practice: Making Comparisons with Adverbs**

1. Read each sentence aloud, using the correct comparative form of the adverb in parentheses.

1. (well) Jack draws well, but Larry draws __?__ than Jack.
2. (soon) Of the three girls Miriam finished __?__.
3. (loudly) Of all the actors, Harold speaks __?__.
4. (rapidly) My plant has grown __?__ than yours.
5. (early) The train arrived __?__ today than yesterday.
6. (quickly) Emma worked __?__ than Grace.
7. (far) We have hiked __?__ today than yesterday.
8. (well) Of the three boys, Harold draws __?__.

2. Write six sentences. Make three a comparison of two and three a comparison of more than two persons. Use these adverbs: *well, calmly, far.*

Using good and well

The word *good* is always an adjective. You may never use it to modify a verb.

1. I made a *good* grade. (adjective)
2. This pie is *good*. (adjective)

Well may be either an adjective or an adverb.

3. Jack is *well*. (adjective)
4. Jim speaks *well*. (adverb)

Which noun does the adjective *good* describe in the first sentence? in the second sentence?

In sentence 3, *well* is an adjective meaning "in good health." Which noun does it describe?

In sentence 4, *well* is an adverb because it modifies the verb *speaks*. It tells *how* the action was performed.

Use the adjective **good** to describe or modify a noun. Use the adjective **well** to describe health or appearance. Use the adverb **well** to express how an action was performed.

► **Practice: Using good and well**

Read these sentences aloud, using the correct word in parentheses. Tell whether the word is used as an adjective or an adverb.

1. Harry played (good, well) in every inning.
2. This cake is (well, good).
3. My little sister reads (well, good).
4. Doesn't Nancy skate (well, good)?
5. I can't do this (good, well).
6. The doctor said that you are now (good, well).
7. Nancy read the poem (well, good).
8. Is your dog (good, well) after getting his shots?

Now read the sentences aloud.

Sentence Patterns:
Adjectives and Adverbs

With the exception of the adjective in a Pattern 4 sentence, adjectives and adverbs do not change the basic pattern.

   Adj   Adj   N   Adv   V
1. Tall majestic trees suddenly toppled.

   Adj   Adj Adj   N   Adv   V   Adj N
2. Those two heavy storms soon destroyed the crops.

   Adj   N V^{be} Adv   N
3. Both storms were surely tornados.

   Adj   N V^{be} Adv   Adj
4. The villagers were very courageous.

Now examine the sentence parts that make up the basic sentence patterns of the sentences above:

Pattern 1: **N V** (Noun — Verb) Trees toppled.

Pattern 2: **N V N** (Noun — Action verb — Noun)
                Storms destroyed crops.

Pattern 3: **N V^{be} N** (Noun — Verb of being — Noun)
                Storms were tornados.

Pattern 4: **N V^{be} Adj** (Noun — Verb of being — Adjective)
                Villagers were courageous.

● Copy the following sentences, leaving space between them. Above each word, write its symbol. Then, identify the pattern of each sentence by writing *1, 2, 3,* or *4.*

    1. The lazy crocodiles moved slowly.
    2. Patrick is a good artist.
    3. He quickly sketched some drawings.
    4. This small picture is very beautiful.

● Build interesting sentences, following these symbols:

1. **Adj Adj N V^h V Adv**   5. **Adj Adj N V^{be} Adj N**
2. **Adj N V^h Adv V N^p**   6. **N^p V^{be} Adv Adj**
3. **Adj Adj N V^{be} N**   7. **N V^h Adv V Adj N**
4. **Adj Adj N V^h V N**   8. **Adj N V^{be} Adj Adj N**

Snow Dog
by Jim Kjelgaard
illustrated by Jacob Landau
Holiday House

The third puppy of Queen's litter was different from the others. There was more of the Husky strain in him. His ears were more pointed than those of his brothers; his chest was wider and deeper. His legs were straight and strong, foretelling unusual power.

Snow Dog is the story of this puppy. It tells how he learned to outwit the strong ones, such as the black wolf who had killed his mother. It tells how he grew to be a strong, beautiful dog that could outfight and outwit any creature — that is, until he encountered the steel trap and a man.

If you like to read about the struggles of animals and human beings in the wilderness, you will enjoy this stirring adventure story.

TRYOUT TIME

If you make a mistake on any of these tests, do the Practice on pages 239–40 with the same Roman numeral as the test.

Test I. Adjectives

Make a list of the adjectives in the following sentences. Next to each adjective, write the noun it modifies. (Do not include *a, an,* and *the.*)

1. Have you seen that ancient vase in the side window of the shop?
2. The vase is blue with a pattern of small white doves on it.
3. Mrs. Barton is a pleasant old lady.
4. She feeds the few birds that stay here in the cold winter.
5. Yesterday several Girl Scouts saw four grosbeaks.

Test II. Making Comparisons with Adjectives

Write the sentences below. Change the adjectives in parentheses to the comparative or superlative degree, as required.

1. (cautious) John is the __?__ of the three children.
2. (fast) The __?__ runner in the class is Donald.
3. (easy) This problem is the __?__ one of the two.
4. (friendly) Mr. Black is the __?__ teacher in our entire school.
5. (humorous) He told the __?__ story of all.
6. (bad) That problem is __?__ than this one.

Test III. Proper Adjectives

List the names below on your paper. Opposite each, write a proper adjective made from it.

Mexico	Canada
Japan	Spain
America	France

Test IV. The Adverb

Copy these sentences. Underline the adverbs in each sentence.

1. Ralph keeps his stamp collection carefully.
2. He never loses any stamps.
3. He pastes each stamp slowly and neatly in place.
4. Ralph often buys new stamps.
5. He corresponds regularly and eagerly with other stamp collectors.
6. Stamp collectors exchange their stamps occasionally.

Test V.   Making Comparisons with Adverbs

Write the sentences below. In place of each blank, write the correct form of the adverb in parentheses.

1. (early) Sally arrived __?__ than I.
2. (loudly) Of all the roosters, that one crows __?__.
3. (fast) Jim can swim __?__ than Susan.
4. (gently) This valuable vase must be handled __?__ than that one.
5. (well) Of all the club members, Alice did __?__ with her report.

Test VI.   Using Words Correctly

Write these sentences, using the correct word from the parentheses in place of the blank:

1. (good, well) Drake plays the trumpet __?__.
2. (Those, Them) __?__ gym shoes are mine.
3. (those, them) Can you lift __?__ weights?
4. (good, well) Jimmy played __?__ this afternoon.
5. (anyone, no one) They can't expect __?__ today.
6. (never, ever) She hadn't __?__ been there before.
7. (good, well) You arranged that display __?__.
8. (those, them) Please hand all of __?__ bundles to me.

238

✔ IF YOU NEED MORE PRACTICE ✔

Practice I.   Adjectives

1. Review the lessons on pages 212–14 and 216.

2. List the adjectives in the following sentences.   Next to each one, write the noun it modifies:

1. Several persons saw the huge kite sail into the gray clouds.
2. This garage is small and cannot hold two cars.
3. The bright golden color of the jewels shone in the dim light.
4. A small black kitten walked into the dark theater.

Practice II.   Making Comparisons with Adjectives

1. Review the lesson on pages 219–21.

2. List the following words on your paper.   Opposite each, write the comparative and superlative forms.

1. slow
2. funny
3. beautiful
4. important
5. good
6. bad

Practice III.   Proper Adjectives

1. Review the lesson on page 226.

2. Write these sentences.   Use proper adjectives.

1. I saw some __?__ Mounted Police on television.
2. Many __?__ animals live in the jungle.

Practice IV.   The Adverb

1. Study the lessons on pages 227–29 again.

2. Write these sentences.   Underline the adverbs.

1. Yesterday Jane found a small stone.
2. She had never seen one like it.
3. Jane took the stone to her teacher immediately.
4. Her teacher examined the stone carefully.

Practice V.   Making Comparisons with Adverbs

1. Review the lesson on pages 232–33.   Read the rules and be sure you understand why you made errors on your test.

2. Write these sentences.   Use an adverb in each.

1. Sally did __?__ in her test than I.
2. Dick did __?__ than Sally.
3. Eva sings sweetly, but Lois sings __?__ of all.
4. Charles speaks clearly, but Ben speaks __?__ than he.
5. That car runs the __?__ of all those in the race.
6. Next time, do your work more __?__.

Practice VI.   Using Words Correctly

1. Review the lessons on pages 222 and 224 and the lesson on page 234.

2. Write these sentences, using the correct word in each one:

1. (those, them)   Peg made __?__ cookies.
2. (those, them)   What did she put in __?__?
3. (good, well)   I cannot dance __?__.
4. (good, well)   Can you see __?__ from the top balcony?
5. (those, them)   Watch out for __?__ ropes.
6. (good, well)   I don't feel __?__, Doctor.
7. (anything, nothing)   Can't you do __?__ to help?
8. (any, none)   Don't you know __?__ of the answers?

3. Write four sentences, using these words as adjectives: *this, that, these,* and *those.*

CHAPTER 11

Writing for Fun

You often write to share an experience or to express your personal ideas and feelings. Much of the pleasure you find in this kind of writing comes from making your experiences and moods seem real to others. It is fun to help your readers see what you have seen and to put them in the same mood you remember or imagine. The suggestions in this chapter will help you to develop skill in this kind of writing. Then you can write with satisfaction and pleasure.

Making an Experience Seem Real

A good writer makes us sense what is happening. Often the setting of the place where events are about to occur is made very real. This gives the reader a feeling of taking part in whatever experiences the writer wishes to share with him.

Read the selection below, which is from *The Cheerful Heart*, by Elizabeth Janet Gray, and see how this writer makes you feel a part of the scene that she is describing in this paragraph. Be prepared to answer the questions on page 242.

The rainy season came early. Every day when they woke up they knew that the sky would be gray, the air cool and damp, and the rain falling steadily. Sometimes it was a fine mist; sometimes it slanted in white lines through the air; sometimes it poured straight down as if a huge faucet had been turned on. At night they heard it pattering on the roof or lashing against the shutters.

To Discuss

1. Notice the details. What does the author tell us about the rainy season? Find an interesting detail and read it aloud.

2. Notice the order in which the details are presented. What part of a rainy day did the author describe first? last?

3. What three things did "they" expect to find every morning of the rainy season? Which words appeal to the sense of sight? the sense of touch?

4. Read the sentence that brings out the differences or contrasts in the rainfall from time to time. Does this kind of comparison make the description seem more lifelike?

5. Notice that the author compares pouring rain to an open faucet. Do you see the resemblance? Does this comparison make the scene more vivid?

Composition: Using Details

A. Write your answers to questions **2** and **3** above.

B. Write a paragraph, making one of the following situations seem real. Use specific details and words that appeal to the senses.

A lazy, sunny day at the beach
A windstorm at a camp in the woods
A traffic jam
Waiting for a thunderstorm to end
A hot day on a city street
Signs of spring where you live

Appealing to the Sense of Sight

Many words and expressions can be used to help the reader "see" the scene being described. In Elizabeth Enright's *The Saturdays*, the Melendy children have a playroom, which they call their office. Read the description of it below. Notice how the author shows you its outstanding characteristics.

The floor was covered with scarred red linoleum that didn't matter, and the yellow walls were encrusted with hundreds of indispensable objects: bookcases bursting with books, pictures both by the Melendy children and less important grown-up artists, dusty Indian war bonnets . . . In one corner of the room stood an old upright piano that always looked offended, for some reason, and whose rack was littered with music all patched and held together with Scotch tape.

To Discuss

1. What does the adjective *indispensable* mean? (Use your dictionary to check the meaning.)

2. What indispensable objects did the office contain?

3. What is *scarred* linoleum? Can you picture a wall *encrusted* with objects?

4. Did the children have many books? Read the words that give the answer.

5. How could a piano look "offended"?

6. In the selection, find and read some vivid word pictures.

Composition: Telling How Something Looks

A. In order to help your readers know just how something looks to you, you must sharpen your own skills of observation. Look around the classroom. Then, without looking again, list as many things that you saw as you can remember.

B. Write a paragraph in class describing a room you know so well that you can see its details accurately when you close your eyes. Make your description vivid.

Appealing to Other Senses

The senses of hearing, smell, taste, and touch, as well as the sense of sight, can also be appealed to by skillful writers to add vividness to a scene. Read the description of a barn from *Charlotte's Web*, by E. B. White. Notice how the author appeals to your sense of smell by telling about the things to be found in the old barn.

The barn was very large. It was very old. It smelled of hay and it smelled of manure. It smelled of the perspiration of tired horses and the wonderful sweet breath of patient cows. It often had a sort of peaceful smell — as though nothing bad could happen ever again in the world. It smelled of grain and of harness dressing and of axle grease and of rubber boots and of new rope. And whenever the cat was given a fish-head to eat, the barn would smell of fish. But mostly it smelled of hay, for there was always hay in the great loft overhead. And there was always hay being pitched down to the cows and the horses and the sheep.

To Discuss

1. What did the barn smell of mainly? How does the author make this detail stand out?

2. Notice the *nouns* that appeal to your sense of smell. Give an example and read it aloud. What words help you to see things in the barn as the author tells of the smells in the barn? What is a "peaceful smell"?

3. Suppose the author had wanted to appeal to your sense of hearing. What sound might one hear in a barn? What words might he have used?

4. Can you think of words to describe how some of the objects in a barn feel to the touch — for example, hay, rope, harnesses, milk pails?

5. Does the author tell how he felt about the barn in any way? If so, read what he says that makes you think that he liked or did not like the barn.

► **Practice: Appealing to the Senses**

Before you can describe anything, you must have a sharp picture of it in your own mind. How closely do you observe the shapes, colors, sounds, odors, flavors, and textures of things? Think of a room in your home — the kitchen, for example. How many of the following details can you recall?

1. *Appearance.* What is its shape? What are the colors of the walls? What are the furnishings? How does the kitchen look at different times of the day?

2. *Sounds.* What are the sounds that come from the kitchen?

3. *Textures.* How do the appliances in the kitchen feel to the touch — for example, the top of the stove, the sink, or the water tap? Are they cold, hard, soft, warm, smooth, rough?

4. *Smells.* What are some of the aromas in the kitchen? Describe the odor of soapsuds. What foods have pleasing aromas? How would you describe the smell of something burning?

Composition: Appealing to the Senses

A. Write in good sentences answers to one of the three groups of questions above.

B. Write a paragraph description of a place that has made a strong impression on you. It may be a garage, a bakery, a schoolroom, a cafeteria, or something else. Include sentences that refer to sounds as well as sights, and, if appropriate, to smells and textures.

Write in your notebook, for your own information only, the impression you tried to give your readers.

Divide the class in groups of four and pass the compositions around the small circle. Let each reader sign on the back and write the word that best tells his impression of the place you described. When your paper comes back to you, tell whether your readers received the impression you tried to give.

Speaking Distinctly

1. Read aloud the questions below. Say the italicized letters correctly.

1. Don't you want to eat now?
2. Didn't you bring your raincoat?
3. What time does the library open?
4. Wouldn't you like a sixth-grade club?
5. What are the facts that you learned?
6. As soon as the sun comes up, will you call me?

2. Read aloud the sentences below. Say the italicized letters correctly.

1. Ada lived in Canada.
2. Dictionaries have guide words.
3. The principal speaker is the president of our organization.
4. Yesterday the car needed oil and water in the radiator.
5. Bananas grow where there is a hot, moist climate.

3. Study each word below. Think of the sound that the italicized letters spell. Say each word correctly.

million	roofs
twenty	fists

Going Ahead ◗ ◗ ◗ ◗

Find descriptive passages in books you have read and prepare to read them as examples for the class to hear.

Practice aloud with someone listening as you read. Ask your listener if every word was clearly understood. Do you drop your voice at the end of a sentence or a thought? Do you pause when necessary for the best effect? Do you have a pleasant variation in tone of voice?

Introduce your selection to the class by naming the author and title. Tell your audience the kind of description they may expect and let them tell you the senses to which the author appealed.

Write each sentence, using the correct word:

1. You dramatized that conversation (good, well).
2. I can do that (easy, easily) enough.
3. Isn't there (no, any) room for my suitcase?
4. I never gave Jane (nothing, anything).
5. Ronald sang (good, well).
6. We landed (safe, safely).
7. Who left (this, this here) book?
8. Do you own (those, them) boots?

How Our Language Grew • • • ●

In the Middle Ages a young craftsman had to pass a special test before the master craftsmen of his trade would admit him to their guild or association. He had to produce a masterpiece that he had created. A young weaver might offer a fine tapestry as proof of his ability; a potter, a bowl; and a metal worker, a medal. If the masters agreed that the work was a masterpiece, the young man was admitted to their ranks. What does the word *masterpiece* mean today?

247

Improving Your Word Choice

Synonyms are words that have the same, or nearly the same, meaning. The words *bathe* and *wash* might be synonyms, for example. Synonyms help to give variety to conversation. They also can be used to make meanings more specific and expressions more vivid.

Using a Variety of Words

Using the same word over and over is dull. Do you notice too much repetition of a word in the following sentences?

> A *little* old lady lives in that *little* white cottage. She has a parakeet which can ring a *little* silver bell.

When you notice an overworked word such as *little* in your writing, get variety by using synonyms. For example:

> A *little* old lady lives in that *small* white cottage. She has a parakeet which can ring a *tiny* silver bell.

To Discuss

1. Decide on synonyms for the following words: *clean, good, pretty, go, big*. List them on the board.

2. Look up the words in a large dictionary and check the synonyms. Discuss the differences in meaning.

► **Practice: Using a Variety of Words**

1. Rewrite each of the following quotations, using a different word for *said* each time:

1. The girl *said,* "I don't know that boy."
2. Bob *said,* "Look out for that car!"
3. Mary *said,* "Let's not let Edith hear us."
4. The boy *said,* "Have you seen my dog?"

2. Write two or more words you could use instead of each of the following words to put variety into your writing:

came   nice   thing   liked   walked

Using Vivid and Specific Words

The following sentence contains a verb so general in meaning that it leaves very little impression.

The boy *went* on to school.

More specific and interesting verbs can be used instead of *went*. Say the sentence substituting each of these words: *skipped, sauntered, swaggered, dashed.* On the board list other specific words that could be used.

The next sentence contains an adjective that is not specific enough to create a vivid picture.

A *big* man came to our room.

More exact and interesting adjectives give the readers a better clue to your idea. Say the sentence substituting each of these words: *tall, fat, important.* On the board list interesting words that suggest a *small* man.

To Discuss

1. Did the words substituted for the verb *went* in the sentences above change the picture you had of the boy going to school?

2. Did the words substituted for *big* change the picture you had of the man?

3. Why are the words suggested as substitutes for the general words more effective?

► Practice: Using Vivid and Specific Words

Rewrite the sentences below, substituting a more definite or vivid word for the verb or adjective in italics:

1. The half-starved cat *ate* the ground beef.
2. The frightened deer *ran* into the woods.
3. Ellen *talked* gaily with the other girls.
4. Jerry had an *interesting* adventure.
5. A *poor* old woman asked me for directions.
6. Mrs. Davis makes *good* ice cream.

Composition: Using Vivid and Specific Words

A. Write sentences using these words: *shrill, rare, brilliant, tottered, pathetic.*

B. Select a pair of contrasting scenes to describe, using one paragraph for each. Choose one of these pairs or think of topics for yourself.

1. A wild animal free in its natural setting and one that is caged in a zoo
2. A country scene in summer and in winter
3. A city street on a busy week day and the same street on a Sunday afternoon
4. The kitchen in your house on a schoolday morning and at midnight

Going Ahead ▶ ▶ ▶ ▶

Make a bridge of words from *bad* to *good*. First find as many words as you can that suggest some degree of badness. Arrange them in order from those meaning most to least bad. Then continue the bridge by finding and arranging words that suggest goodness, from the least to the best. You may wish to arrange them on the page to look like an arched bridge, like this:

Using Words Correctly: <u>could</u> <u>have</u>

Study the sentence below. One word is used incorrectly. What word is it?

> Bill could of warned us.

In the sentence, *of* is used incorrectly. It is used as a verb, but it is not a verb. Perhaps the writer was thinking of *could've*, which is a contraction for *could have*. The sentences below are correct:

> Bill *could have warned* us.
> Bill *could've warned* us.

Now study the verbs and their contractions in the sentences below.

> Lois *should have gone* home.
> Lois *should've gone* home.
>
> Al *would have played* ball.
> Al *would've played* ball.

Notice that *should've* is a contraction for *should have*, not *should of*. *Would've* is a contraction for *would have*, not *would of*.

Read aloud the following sentences, pronouncing each word distinctly:

1. Robert could have told us.
2. Would Jane have gone with you?
3. I should have been there.
4. Couldn't he have left the door open?
5. They would not have known that.
6. We shouldn't have been late.
7. The boy could not have been kinder.
8. Wouldn't Ruth have enjoyed the show?

► **Practice: Using Words Correctly**

Write sentences using *couldn't have, wouldn't have.*

Phi
Greek letter

Sounds and Spelling

Some Consonant Sounds Spelled More Than One Way

C, K, and CK. In ancient Latin there was little use for **k** because **c** was used to spell the same sound. In French, however, **c** is often used to spell the "soft," or **s**, sound. Since English has borrowed words from Latin, French, and many other languages, it has had to fit varied sounds and spelling to its own system of writing.

In English, therefore, **c** is often used to spell both the hard and soft sounds, as in *circus* and *concert*. Before **e** or **i**, however, the letter **k** is used instead of **c** to spell the hard sound, as in *keg* and *keep*. Can you name other words in which **c** and **k** are used to spell the hard sound?

F, PH, and GH. In the Greek alphabet, the symbol Φ stands for *phi* (fī), which corresponds to the sound of **f** in English. In spelling words borrowed directly from Greek, we use the letters **ph** in place of **f**, as in *phone*.

If the Romans had used the Greek *phi* instead of **f** in their alphabet, we might be spelling such words as *fuss* and *feathers* like this: *phuss* and *pheathers*. One other way to spell the **f** sound in English is **gh**, as in *enough*.

Spelling Checkup

1. Just for fun, write this sentence with **ph** instead of **f**: Fifty-five fine fiddlers followed the fleet.

2. Think of two or three other words that spell the sound **f** as in *enough*.

3. List five words with **c** pronounced **s**; five with **c** pronounced **k**; five with **ck** pronounced **k**.

252

Writing Conversation

In your stories, plan to let the characters talk. Let them say things that reveal their basic traits, just as people do in real life.

Rules for Writing Conversation

Study this written conversation from *A Lemon and a Star,* by E. C. Spykman. Notice that the quotations are divided.

"Hi," said Hubert breathlessly, "want to help?"

"Sure," said Jane, looking at Theodore warily. "What is it?"

"It's a fox," said Hubert. "I caught him. We've got to get the trap off his paw."

To Discuss

1. Find a paragraph in the selection above in which the second part of the divided quotation is the beginning of a new sentence. How are capital letters and punctuation used?

2. Read the paragraph in which the second part of the quotation is not the beginning of a sentence. How are capital letters and punctuation marks used?

When the second part of a divided quotation is not the beginning of a sentence, begin it with a small letter.

3. Below are other rules for writing conversations. Find an example of each rule in the above model.

1. Begin a new paragraph for each speaker.
2. Enclose each quotation in quotation marks.
3. Separate the quotation from the rest of the sentence by some mark of punctuation.
4. Capitalize the first word in a quotation.
5. Put the punctuation mark that ends the quotation within the quotation marks.

Other Uses for Commas in Conversation

Conversation often includes words that refer directly to the person spoken to, or words of *direct address.* The name in direct address may be a proper noun or a common noun.

    1. "Where are you going, my pretty maid?"
    2. "I'm going milking, sir," she said.
    3. "How are you, John?" he asked.
    4. "Listen, my friend, I cannot do that!" Bill exclaimed.

Name the words of direct address in the sentences above.

Use commas to separate words of direct address from the rest of the sentence.

Words such as *yes, no,* and *well* may appear at the beginning of a quotation or a sentence. Study these examples:

"Yes, I hope so," she said.
"Well, he won't do that," Bill informed me.

What mark of punctuation follows words such as *yes, no,* or *well* when they appear at the beginning of a sentence?

Use commas to separate introductory words, such as **yes, no,** and **well** from the rest of the sentence.

▶ **Practice: Writing Conversation**

1. Turn again to the model conversation on page 253. Study the spelling, punctuation, and form. Then close your book and write the conversation as your teacher dictates it.

2. Rewrite the following sentences, using capital letters and punctuation marks correctly:

    1. Isn't Tim's birthday on April Fool's Day Eddie asked.
    2. Yes Mother answered I must bake a cake for him.
    3. Let's have an April Fool's birthday cake Mother Ellen suggested.
    4. That's a good idea agreed Mother.

Composition: Writing Conversation

A. The following conversation is from *Alice's Adventures in Wonderland* by Lewis Carroll. Write it correctly.

Take off your hat the King said to the Hatter. It isn't mine said the Hatter. Stolen the King exclaimed, turning to the jury, who instantly made a memorandum of the fact. I keep them to sell, the Hatter added as an explanation. I've none of my own. I'm a Hatter.

B. Write an imaginary conversation between two characters who have different traits. What they say should reveal their traits. Choose one of these situations or use one of your own:

1. A dog scolds a turtle for being so slow
2. A peacock brags about his beauty to a monkey
3. A talkative person asks a quiet person to tell him about his vacation
4. A sales clerk tries to please a shopper who cannot make up her mind

TO MEMORIZE

This above all: to thine own self be true,
And it must follow, as the night the day,
Thou canst not then be false to any man.

WILLIAM SHAKESPEARE

This quotation is from William Shakespeare's *Hamlet*. It gives the final words of Polonius as he offers some advice to his son Laertes, who is leaving home. Read them and think about the meaning.

255

Using Words Correctly: say, says, said

When you talk or write about something that has already happened, use the past tense of the verb. Study the correct use of *say* and *said* in the sentences below.

"Did you *say* when to expect Tom?" asked Earl.

"I *said* next Thursday," John answered. "Tom *said* he'd like to see the boat your uncle built."

"It's a masterpiece," *said* Earl.

"I *say* it is, too," John agreed.

▶ **Practice: Using say, says, and said**

In each sentence, decide which verb form in parentheses is correct. Read the sentence, using the correct verb form.

1. As soon as he arrived, he (says, said), "I'm hungry."
2. Then I (says, said), "We'll have dinner soon."
3. Last week Bill (says, said) that he caught three trout.
4. Yesterday, she (says, said) one thing, but now she (says, said) something quite different.
5. This book (says, said) that wild animals rarely attack unless provoked.
6. I (say, says) that we must be firm.

Review Practice: Adjectives and Adverbs

In each sentence, use the correct form of the adjective or the adverb in parentheses. Consult your dictionary when in doubt.

1. (old) John is the __?__ of the two brothers.
2. (early) The sun set __?__ today than yesterday.
3. (well) James skates __?__ than I.
4. (lively) The yellow kitten is the __?__ of the three.
5. (beautiful) Which of the two trees is the __?__?
6. (bad) Of the two of us, I had the __?__ luck.
7. (good) Her grades are __?__ than mine.
8. (quiet) The children are playing more __?__ today.

256

Writing Stories

All good stories capture and hold the reader's interest. They keep him wondering what is going to happen next.

Planning a Story

A story's power to keep the reader in suspense has something to do with the order in which it is put together or told. In most stories, you will find this development:

1. *The opening of the story* sets the stage for what is going to happen. It usually gives the time of action and tells *who* the characters are, *where* they are, and *what* they are doing.

2. From the beginning there is a strong *chain of events.* In other words, one incident leads to another.

3. The action leads to an unexpected problem or difficulty for one or more of the characters. This is the *turning point,* or *crisis,* of the story.

4. Something interesting happens to the characters as a result of the difficult situation. For example, they may show unusual courage, strength, or cleverness. Someone may find a friend or learn a lesson. What happens as a result of the crisis provides the climax of the story.

5. The *ending* follows soon after the climax.

Here are some situations that could be the subjects of interesting stories.

1. Two characters set out to find a treasure which they believe is buried in a cave. When they approach the cave, they see a strange creature sitting on a box.
2. Two characters are hiking along a marked trail in the woods. They leave the trail to wade in a creek. When they return, they have lost their way.
3. Two characters are caught in a sudden downpour. The only shelter within miles is a house which one of them believes is haunted.
4. Two characters are sunbathing on a raft. Suddenly one notices that they have drifted out into the water.
5. Two characters are riding horses. One falls off and sprains his ankle.
6. A young lady suddenly discovers, as the train on which she is riding travels speedily past her home station, that she is on an express train headed fifty miles north before it is due to stop.

To Discuss

Discuss each of the situations above and think how you might develop an adventure story from it. Use these questions and suggestions to help you plan the *characters, setting,* and *chain of events*:

1. Think of two characters with contrasting traits.
2. How will you set the stage or describe the scene of action?
3. How important is the time of action?
4. What will be the outcome of the story? Will the characters learn a lesson? Will they do something clever or brave? Will something funny happen?
5. Plan a chain of events for one of the situations above, working together in class.

A. Read situation 1 at the top of page 258 again. Study the picture on page 259. Write a short story about it. Think about what the strange creature did. Maybe he was somebody in disguise. Did he disappear or speak to the man? Decide upon some such ending to your story.

B. Write a story about some experience you have had. The questions below may help you think of one:

1. Have you ever been frightened, lost, or in danger?
2. Has a dog or horse ever been a help or trouble to you?
3. Have you tried something difficult and finally succeeded?
4. What is the hardest work you have ever done?
5. Have you ever had an amusing or a frightening experience while baby-sitting?

Sharing Your Stories

Half the fun of writing a story comes from sharing it with others, letting others read it, or reading it to them. Before you give your story to others to read, proofread your paper carefully. Correct errors in spelling, capitalization, and punctuation. Check to see that you have used words correctly. Then copy your story neatly in ink.

Reading Stories Aloud

If you are going to read your story to the class, practice beforehand at home. Here are some goals to aim for as you practice:

1. Read slowly enough to be understood.
2. Pronounce words distinctly and correctly.
3. Adjust your rate of speech to fit the mood of the story.
4. Emphasize important words.
5. Let your voice show the mood of the story.
6. Show through your voice your own interest in the story.

If you have written several stories, prepare your own book of stories. Ask two or three people to read the stories and select those which they believe are the best. Then prepare the manuscripts carefully and place them in an attractive cover with an interesting title.

A committee can prepare a class booklet with the best work from each pupil. Arrange the selections, write a table of contents and a foreword, and bind them attractively.

Review Practice: Choosing the Correct Verb

1. Write each of the sentences below, using the correct verb in parentheses:

1. Who has (set, sat) the pitcher on the table?
2. He (lay, laid) down on the soft feather mattress.
3. The old man (set, sat) on the porch during the afternoon.
4. (Let, Leave) us sing folk songs.
5. How long has the old dog (laid, lain) in the ditch?
6. (Sit, Set) the tools on the bench.
7. How long have you (set, sat) on that bench?
8. The policeman will (leave, let) us cross now.

2. Write each sentence below, using the correct form of the verb in parentheses:

1. (ride)   He has __?__ on the chair lift at the ski resort.
2. (break)   Yesterday John __?__ the record for the jump.
3. (break)   I have __?__ my ski.
4. (drink)   Martha has __?__ the hot chocolate.
5. (teach)   Who __?__ you that step?
6. (learn)   Have you __?__ your lesson?
7. (teach)   Were you __?__ by Mr. James?
8. (drink)   I __?__ some orange juice this morning.
9. (ride)   I have never __?__ a pony.
10. (drink)   Bob __?__ all the lemonade.

261

TRYOUT TIME

If you make a mistake on a test, take the Practice on pages 264–65 with the same Roman numeral as the test.

Test I. Improving Your Word Choice

The italicized word in each sentence below is often over-worked. Replace it with the most vivid word in parentheses.

1. (spotless, tidy) After she had swept, dusted, and scrubbed, the room was *clean*.
2. (advised, shouted) "Stop the presses!" the city editor *said*.
3. (swaggered, walked) The conceited young man *went* down the street.
4. (dashed, ran) The frightened girls *came* out of the old deserted house.
5. (gulped, sipped) The thirsty hikers *drank* the water.
6. (beautiful, breath-taking) We had a *nice* view of the Grand Canyon of the Colorado.
7. (mammoth, huge) The gorilla is a *big* creature.
8. (amusing, hilarious) Beth told a *funny* story.

Test II. Using the Correct Expression

Write the sentences below, using the correct expression:

1. John might (of, have) swept the steps.
2. You could (of, have) gone to the show.
3. Why shouldn't you (of, have) been angry?
4. Mary couldn't (of, have) finished her work.

Test III. Writing Conversation

Write the conversation below correctly:

When is your cousin from Chicago coming I asked Tom. He wrote that he would arrive on Thursday said Tom. Then tomorrow I said you will have to meet him at the station.

Test IV.   Using the Comma

Copy the following sentences, using commas where they are needed:

1. "Have you bathed the dog yet Harry?" Mother asked.
2. "Yes he is lily white Mother," Harry replied.
3. Well Jimmy's little brother isn't even seven yet.
4. We put on our skit Jack before the class.

Test V.   Using say, says, and said

Write each of the following sentences, using the correct verb in parentheses:

1. Yesterday Bert (says, said) that the fish were not biting.
2. Look! the sign ahead (says, said) "Detour."
3. "I told Mr. Smith about our problem," (says, said) Mark.
4. The next day, Mother (says, said) we could go.
5. I (say, says) you are mistaken.

Test VI.   Writing Stories

Complete each statement below, using the correct group of words:

1. The opening of a story usually (a) gives a preview of what is going to happen, (b) gives the time and place of action and introduces the characters.
2. A strong chain of events is one in which (a) one incident leads to another, (b) something fantastic is always happening.
3. One way to make characters seem real is to have them (a) doing things all the time, (b) say and do things that reveal their traits.
4. In most stories the characters get involved in (a) funny situations, (b) a situation they had not expected.
5. The purpose of the climax is usually (a) to show what happens to the characters as a result of the unexpected development, (b) to shock the reader.

✔ IF YOU NEED MORE PRACTICE ✔

Practice I.   Improving Your Word Choice

1. Review the lesson on pages 248–49.

2. Write two or more synonyms you could use for each of the italicized words below.   Put variety into your writing.

an *interesting* story	a *difficult* thing
a *poor* road	an *old* car

3. Suggest a synonym for each italicized verb below.

  . 1. He *works* from sun-up to sundown.
    2. Let us *rest* for a moment.
    3. The man *said,* "Do you know where the library is?"

Practice II.   Using the Correct Expression

1. Study the lesson on page 251.

2. Write four sentences using *could have, wouldn't have, should have, couldn't have.*

3. Read your sentences aloud.   Be sure to pronounce every word distinctly.

Practice III.   Writing Conversation

1. Review the lesson on page 253.

2. Write this conversation correctly:

My home said Tom is the white one on the hill.   Is that a swimming pool at the back asked Jim.   No Tom replied.   Mother has a rose garden there.   Yesterday he added someone said that her roses are the prettiest in the county.

Practice IV.   Using the Comma

1. Review the lesson on page 254.

2. Write these sentences, using commas correctly:

    1. Well I cannot decide.
    2. Yes I remember the picnic Frank.

Practice V.   Using say, says, and said

1. Review the lesson on page 256.
2. Write three sentences using *say, says,* and *said* correctly.

Practice VI.   Writing Stories

1. Try to decide why you made a mistake in Test VI.
2. Read again the lesson on page 257.
3. Write the answers to these questions:

    1. What three goals should you try to achieve in the opening part of the story?
    2. How do the individuals you meet reveal their traits? Is it possible for characters in a story to reveal theirs in the same way?
    3. What is a chain of events?   (Think of the meaning of the word *chain.*)
    4. Would a strong chain of events alone make a good story?   Why is an *unexpected event* important?

CHAPTER 12

Prepositions and Conjunctions

So far this year, you have seen some of the differences among five parts of speech — how they differ from one another in their forms, in their positions in a sentence, and in their use.

Prepositions and conjunctions add two more parts of speech to your list. These are words that do not change form, are limited in number, and serve a useful purpose of their own.

The Preposition

Look at this list of frequently used words. Notice how familiar they are.

about	behind	down	inside	over
across	below	during	into	to
among	beside	for	near	under
around	between	from	of	up
at	by	in	on	with

When the words above are used with nouns and pronouns, they are called prepositions. Read the following sentences aloud, filling the blanks with prepositions.

1. The book __?__ the desk is not mine.
2. The plane flew __?__ the airport.

A preposition is followed by a noun or pronoun, which is called the object of the preposition. In sentence 1 above, the noun *desk* follows the preposition you chose; for example, *in* the desk, *on* the desk, *behind* the desk. The noun *desk* is the *object of the preposition*. Complete sentence 2 above and tell the preposition and the object of the preposition.

Study the following sentences:

1. The rehearsal will be held at my house.
2. Play the record for Flo and me.
3. Can you swim across the lake?
4. The money inside the envelope is yours.

In sentence 1 above, which word is the preposition? Which word is the object of the preposition?

In sentence 2, which word is the preposition? A preposition may be followed by more than one object. Name the objects of the preposition in this sentence.

Now name the prepositions and their objects in sentences 3 and 4.

► **Practice: Recognizing and Using Prepositions**

1. Read the sentences below and name the prepositions and their objects. Tell whether the object or objects are *nouns* or *pronouns.*

1. The three doctors in Pinocchio's room left.
2. The fairy put her hand on his forehead.
3. "You are burning with fever," she said.
4. She put white powder into a glass.
5. She handed it to Pinocchio.
6. "This drink is good for you," the fairy said.
7. Pinocchio looked at the glass.
8. "I don't like the taste of medicine," he complained to the fairy.
9. "Do not think about the taste," the fairy advised.
10. "In a very short time, you will be feeling better," she added.

2. Write sentences of your own, using the following prepositions. Underline the noun or pronoun used as the object of the preposition.

with	around	during	under
across	below	near	for

267

Prepositional Phrases

Read these sentences:

1. The junk in this basement is a fire hazard.
2. Did you see the picture of the Chinese junk?
3. Our neighbors have just returned from a junket to the West Indies.
4. The note from the sailor was found in a bottle.

A preposition and its object or objects form a unit called a **prepositional phrase.** In sentence 1 above, the word group *in this basement* is a prepositional phrase. Notice that the object of a preposition sometimes has modifiers. These modifiers are part of the prepositional phrase.

What are the prepositional phrases in sentences 2, 3, and 4? There are two phrases in sentence 3 and in sentence 4. Name the preposition that starts each phrase. Name the object of each preposition.

How Prepositions Show Relationship

It is easy to recognize prepositional phrases because they always begin with a preposition and end with an object of the preposition. The preposition connects its object or objects to another word in the sentence.

Read these prepositional phrases:

The mosquito flew . . .

under the table.	*near* the table.
over the table.	*to* the table.
beside the table.	*behind* the table.
around the table.	*across* the table.

Each preposition above connects the noun *table* to the verb *flew.* Notice how each phrase adds to the meaning of the verb. The phrase modifies the verb in the same way that an adverb does.

Now look at these examples. Each prepositional phrase adds to the meaning of the noun *dog*. It modifies a noun in the same way that an adjective does.

$$\text{The dog} \dots \begin{cases} near \text{ the kennel} \\ in \text{ the kennel} \\ behind \text{ the kennel} \\ inside \text{ the kennel} \end{cases} \text{has been sold.}$$

■ A preposition and its object or objects form a **prepositional phrase.**

► **Practice: Recognizing and Using Prepositional Phrases**

1. Find and read aloud the prepositional phrases in the sentences below. Name the word which each phrase modifies.

1. Mark ran around the block.
2. The elm beside the house is very old.
3. The groceries were left on the doorstep.
4. We parked our car near yours.
5. The stranger walked behind the speaker.

2. Rewrite the following sentences. Add a prepositional phrase to modify the italicized noun in each one. Use a different preposition in each sentence.

1. The *girl* ran away.
2. The *chest* was empty.
3. The *road* was bumpy.
4. We explored the *cave.*

3. Rewrite these sentences, adding a prepositional phrase to modify the italicized verb in each sentence. Use different prepositions.

1. He *ran* swiftly.
2. He *left.*
3. The lamp *flickered.*
4. Everybody *jumped.*

Preposition or Adverb?

Some words can be used as a preposition in one sentence but as an adverb in another. Read these sentences:

1. He stood *near* the umpire.
2. I was standing *near*.

To test whether a word is a preposition or not, look for the object of the preposition.

Near is a preposition in sentence 1 above. How do you know? Look at sentence 2 above. Does *near* have an object? What question does it answer about the verb? *Near* is an adverb in this sentence.

► **Practice: Preposition or Adverb**

1. Read the pairs of sentences below. Tell whether the italicized word in each sentence is used as a *preposition* or as an *adverb*.

1. He fell *off* the springboard.
2. Did James fall *off*?

3. We were playing *inside*.
4. *Inside* the fence stood an old man.

5. Jerry bounded *up* the stairs.
6. He looked *up* and saw his brother.

7. Agnes remained *behind*.
8. She sat *behind* the desk.

9. Who lives *near* the library?
10. The lost dog came *near*.

2. Write two sentences for each word listed below. In one sentence, use the word as a *preposition*. In the other use it as an *adverb*.

behind   down   above   about   near

Sentence Patterns: Prepositions

Review all the symbols you have studied so far this year. Notice the new symbol below, **P** for *preposition*.

N = Noun	**V**h = Helping verb
Np = Pronoun	**Adj** = Adjective
V = Action	(including *a, an,*
Vbe = Verb of being (when it is	and *the*)
part of a predicate that tells	**Adv** = Adverb
what the subject *is* or *is like*)	**P** = Preposition

You can now expand the sentences you are writing by adding prepositional phrases. Here are some examples:

P N to school
P Np for you
P Adj N with the paintbrush

1. **N V P N** Roger rushed to school.
2. **Adj N V P N**p The members voted for you.
3. **Adj N P Adj N V**be **Adj** The boy with the paintbrush is messy.

● Build sentences of your own, following the symbols below:

1. **Adj N P Adj N V**be **Adj**
2. **N V P Adj N**
3. **N V P Adj Adj N**
4. **Adj N P Adj Adj N V**be **Adj**
5. **N V Adj N P Adj N**
6. **N**p **V P Adj N**
7. **Adj N P N**p **V**be **Adj N**
8. **Adj N V**h **V P Adj Adj N**
9. **Adj N P Adj N V**h **V Adj N**
10. **Adj N P Adj Adj N V P N**p

● Review the basic patterns you have studied. Copy the following sentences. Underline those words in each sentence which make up the basic sentence pattern. Then identify the pattern as **NV**, **NVN**, **NV**be **N**, or **NV**be **Adj**.

1. The postman always delivers our mail early.
2. Those two people are my best friends.
3. This good weather may soon change.
4. Paula has been unhappy.

Using the Correct Preposition

There are a few prepositions which can cause confusion if you do not know their meanings. Study the meanings of the six prepositions listed below.

at and to

Use *at* when you mean someone or something *already there*:

> Pauline is *at* your house.
> The boys are *at* the clubhouse.

Use *to* when you mean *going toward*. *To* shows movement:

> We went *to* the stadium.
> The boys are going *to* the clubhouse.

among and between

Use *among* to refer to *more than two* persons, places, or things.

> We divided the flowers *among* all the guests.
> I sat *among* the members of our baseball team.

Use *between* to refer to *only two* persons, places, or things.

> We divided the flowers *between* Betty and Grace.
> I sat *between* the two girls.

in and into

Use *in* when you mean something or someone *within* or *already inside*. You may say:

> They were *in* the garage.
> The chicken is *in* the coop.

Use *into* to show movement *from* the outside *to* the inside, as:

> I walked *into* the museum.
> Put the hamster *into* the cage.

► **Practice: Using the Correct Preposition**

Read aloud the following sentences, using the correct preposition in parentheses:

1. Divide the apple (among, between) Michael and Kent.
2. The cook divided the beans (among, between) the three cowboys.
3. They drove the cattle (in, into) the corral.
4. Set the chair (among, between) Tim and Pat.
5. Anthony stayed (at, to) home last week.
6. He is back (at, to) school now.
7. Larry dived (in, into) the pool.
8. The sugar is (in, into) the cupboard.
9. The red hat stood out (among, between) all the others.
10. Mary is (at, to) the dance.

Review Practice: Pronouns

1. Write four sentences, using *we girls, we boys, us girls,* and *us boys.*

2. Write sentences using pronouns as the objects of these prepositions: *in, with, around, for, to.*

3. Write each sentence below, using a possessive pronoun in place of the blank. Do not use the same pronoun twice.

1. Which cap is __?__ ?
2. That pencil is __?__ .
3. Is this drawing __?__ ?
4. Victory was __?__ .

4. Read your sentences aloud several times so that your ear will become accustomed to hearing the correct pronoun.

Going Ahead ▶ ▶ ▶ ▶

Do you have some favorite poems? Borrow from the library a variety of poetry books for your room. Find a poem or lines from a longer poem that you can memorize.

Organize a poetry period. Have a program chairman who can arrange the order in which the poems will be given and introduce each person in turn. Before presenting your poem, practice reading it aloud with an expressive voice.

Review Practice: Using Words Correctly

Write each sentence, using the correct form:

1. (That there, That) play was good.
2. Where is your uncle (staying, staying at)?
3. (Mr. Lewis, Mr. Lewis he) took us on a field trip.
4. Take the flowers (off of, off) the table.
5. These shoes fit (well, good).
6. Yesterday I (lay, laid) on the beach too long.
7. He has (set, sat) the jar on the shelf.
8. Will you (teach, learn) me to skate?
9. (Let, Leave) us play in your yard.
10. Gerald stepped (off, off of) the scales.

Composition: Writing a Summary

A. When you have finished studying any topic in one of your school subjects, writing a summary will help you to remember the most important points you learned. For example, write a summary of a topic recently completed in science. Explain briefly the important steps of an experiment: (1) what you wanted to find out, (2) the materials you worked with, (3) how you set up the experiment, and (4) what you found out.

B. Write on the board a number of topics you have studied in social studies. Limit the topics so that a summary of one need not be very long. Choose one and include in your summary the question you studied, important facts you learned, and ideas you consider important.

274

The Conjunction

In sentences, you very often need to connect words or groups of words that are equal in importance.

Connecting Words

Look at the following examples:

1. Jimmy *and* Robbie are on the same team.
2. He should glue *or* nail the parts together.
3. He gave orders quietly *but* firmly.
4. She *and* I joined the others.

The italicized words above are connecting words and are called **conjunctions.** Look at the word on the left of the conjunction *and* in sentence 1. Then look at the word on the right of the conjunction. Notice that *and* connects two subjects. Name them. What part of speech are they?

In sentence 2, which words are connected by the conjunction *or*? What part of speech are they?

In sentence 3, which words are connected by the conjunction *but*? What part of speech are they?

In sentence 4, name the conjunction. Which words does it connect? What part of speech are they?

Connecting Word Groups

You have just seen how conjunctions can connect single words that are equal in importance. Read these sentences:

1. The car rolled off the road *and* into a ditch.
2. Boys on the committee *or* with special passes need not wait.
3. In the street *and* on the sidewalk are broken crates of oranges.

The conjunctions *and* and *or* connect two prepositional phrases in the sentences above. Name the two phrases in sentence 1. Name the two phrases in sentence 2. Name the two phrases in sentence 3.

Connecting Sentences

Conjunctions frequently join two sentences that are related to each other in thought:

1. Janet left a few minutes ago. Lynn is still home.
2. Janet left a few minutes ago, *but* Lynn is still home.

3. Bernard took these photographs. I pasted them into the album.
4. Bernard took these photographs, *and* I pasted them into the album.

5. We may go to the movies. We may come back here.
6. We may go to the movies, *or* we may come back here.

Notice the comma before each conjunction in sentences 2, 4, and 6 above. If you read the sentences aloud, you will notice that you pause slightly before the conjunction. The comma indicates this pause and makes the long sentence easier to read. A comma is not needed when the sentence is very short, as in the sentence below:

You can but I can't.

Use a comma before a conjunction that connects two sentences, unless the sentences are very short.

▶ **Practice: Recognizing and Using Conjunctions**

1. Name the conjunction in each sentence below. Then tell whether the conjunction joins single words, prepositional phrases, or two sentences.

1. Why hasn't John studied or prepared his lesson?
2. The wood was ready, but we had no matches.
3. We walked over the hills and through the valley.
4. The deer ran swiftly and gracefully.
5. Tom passed the ballots, and I collected them.

276

2. Combine each pair of sentences below by connecting the sentences with the conjunction given in parentheses. Write the new sentence correctly.

(and)   1. The windows are boarded up.
         The place is deserted.
(but)   2. The sun was shining.
         The wind was cold.
(or)   3. Bob may fly to Dallas.
         He may take the train.
(but)   4. The game was very close.
         We finally won.
(and)   5. Stewart mowed the lawn.
         Warner swept the garage.

How Our Language Grew ・ ● ●

Astronomy—astrology: The scientific study of the stars is called *astronomy*. The word originated from the Greek word for "star." Before the scientific age, *astrology*, now looked upon as a false, or pseudo, science, was considered a way of foretelling the future. Persons born when the sun, moon, and stars were in a favorable position were considered lucky. Those who suffered many misfortunes were thought to be born under an evil star.

You can find the Greek root, *astron*, in a number of English words. The word *disaster*, meaning "misfortune" or "calamity," suggests astrology; a synonym for *disastrous* is *ill-starred*.

Can you guess why a certain flower was named *aster*? What are the two roots of the word *astronaut*? What is an *asterisk*? If you cannot answer all these questions, look for the origins of the words in a college dictionary.

Review Practice: Punctuation

Copy and punctuate these sentences correctly:

1. The coach shouted watch the ball
2. I'd like to go with you May said
3. I think Ted warned we'll be late

Compound Subjects

You know that conjunctions connect words that are equal in importance. These equal parts are subjects:

1. The cider *and* doughnuts are delicious.
2. June *and* July are my favorite months.

The subjects in the sentences above are called **compound subjects.** Name the compound subject in sentence 1. Name the compound subject in sentence 2.

Now study these examples of compound subjects:

3. Ted, Barry, *or* I will be at the door.
4. Hats, coats, *and* sweaters are in a pile on the bed.

Look at sentences 3 and 4. Name the compound subject in each sentence. What mark of punctuation do you see? When you join three or more items in a compound subject, use commas to separate the items from one another.

■ Two or more subjects (nouns or pronouns) joined by a conjunction form a **compound subject.**

▶ **Practice: Compound Subjects**

1. Name the compound subject in each sentence below:

1. Father and Mother entered the room.
2. Books, records, or games are welcome gifts.
3. Bill Andrews, Mike Harris, and John Fox are here.
4. Tulips and jonquils could be used to decorate the stage for the spring festival.

2. In each of the sentences below more than two items are joined by a conjunction. Copy the sentences. Decide where commas are needed and punctuate the sentences correctly.

1. Poems jingles or jokes are acceptable.
2. Thursday Friday and Saturday are our holidays.
3. Jane Miss Jones or I will be there to meet you.
4. Did Mary Ted and Shirley paint that mural?

Compound Predicates

Sometimes verbs also may be joined by a conjunction, as in these sentences:

1. The old fence sagged *and* tilted.
2. The wind stirred the grass *and* bent the birches.
3. You can follow the fence *or* find a path in the woods.
4. In the woods a deer stood, listened, *and* dashed away.

The verbs in the sentences above are called **compound predicates.** Name the compound predicate in each sentence. Can you explain why there are commas in sentence 4?

■　Two or more verbs joined by a conjunction form a **compound predicate.**

▶ **Practice: Compound Predicates**

1. Name the compound predicate in each of the following sentences:

1. Father washed and waxed the car.
2. The campers fished or hunted during the day.
3. We sang songs, told stories, and played games.
4. We sewed, mended, or knitted during the afternoon.

2. Write five sentences, using compound predicates. Write at least two sentences in which more than two items are joined by conjunctions.

Punctuating Words in a Series

Three or more items joined by a conjunction form a *series.* Study the following sentences:

1. *News stories, poems,* and *anecdotes* make up our school newspaper.
2. We dusted *chairs, tables, desks,* and *books.*
3. Howie ran *from the house, through the yard,* and *into the street.*

Notice the commas in the sentences above. They separate the items in a series.

Use a comma to separate words or phrases in a series joined by a conjunction.

▶ **Practice: Punctuating Words in a Series**

1. Write each sentence and punctuate it correctly:

1. Jerry ran up the stairs down the hall and into the room.
2. The campers ate hot dogs beans and potato salad.
3. Please buy me a pair of orange yellow or tan socks.
4. The alarm was sharp loud and long.
5. You he or I must go.

2. Write four sentences of your own, joining in a series each group of items below. Use the correct punctuation.

1	3
apples	glue
pears	tape
plums	ruler

2	4
under the chair	Larry
behind the door	Lester
near the sofa	the twins

Say *he* and *we*. Which consonant sound used breath only? Which keeps the lips close together? Now say *when*. Can you hear the combination of *w* and *h*? Which sound do you hear in *who*?

In Old English, certain words that you know well were spelled *hwaet, hwanne, hwāer,* and *hwȳ.* Notice the first two letters. Now listen to the modern pronunciation of *what, when, where,* and *why.* You may think the old spelling, *hw,* was good.

The change from *hw* to *wh* began before printing was invented. Perhaps some weary, scribbling monks turned these letters around. When books were written by hand, mistakes must have been frequent. Or possibly during the Middle Ages, when the change occurred, it seemed more natural to write *wh* to match *ch, sh,* and *th.*

The digraph *ng,* as in *long,* represents a different sound from the *n* in *lawn.* Listen to the word endings when you say the phrase *comin' and goin'.* Now say the same words, taking care to pronounce them with the *ng* sound, *coming and going.*

The letters *n* and *g* do not always combine for a single sound. Words like *change,* with a soft *g,* sound the *n* and *g* separately. Remember that words with soft *g* are spelled with an *e, i,* or *y* after the *g,* as *range, change, dingy.*

Spelling Checkup

Make a spelling list as follows: four words using the digraph *ng;* four using *n* and *g* with a soft *g;* four with combined sounds of *w* and *h;* and two with *wh* pronounced as *h.*

281

Subject and Verb Agreement

A verb must agree with its subject in number. A singular subject names one person, place, or thing. A plural subject names more than one.

Study the sentences below. Notice the number of persons, places, or things named in each compound subject.

1. Athens and Babylon have left their mark.
2. Communications, lighting, and heating were affected.
3. Bill and she don't have a dog.

Which conjunction connects the compound subject in the sentences above? Are the subjects singular or plural? Are the verbs singular or plural?

A compound subject connected by the conjunction **and** is plural and must be used with a plural verb.

Now study these sentences, in which the compound subjects are connected by the conjunction *or*.

1. The boys or girls have the ball.
2. Peppers, chilies, or onions have been added.
3. A boy or a girl has the ball.
4. A lion, a leopard, or a tiger has left some tracks.

Read aloud the nouns in the compound subjects of sentences 1 and 2 above. Notice that each item named is *plural*. Therefore, the verb must be *plural*.

Read aloud the compound subjects in sentences 3 and 4. Notice that each of the items connected by *or* is singular. The conjunction *or* means *"one* or the *other."* Therefore, the subject is singular and must have a singular verb.

When each noun or pronoun in a compound subject connected by **or** is singular, use a singular verb.

► **Practice: Subject-Verb Agreement**

1. Read aloud the following sentences, using the correct form of the verb in parentheses:

1. Sarah or Cathy (is, are) going to help me.
2. Mary and she (doesn't, don't) like to sing.
3. The dinosaurs, mastodons, and other prehistoric beasts (have, has) disappeared.
4. Chipmunks, rock chucks, or squirrels (have, has) been here.
5. Horses, donkeys, and mules (was, were) the main beasts of burden.

2. Write these sentences, using the correct form of the verb in parentheses:

1. Mary and I (was, were) invited.
2. Bill and he (don't, doesn't) take the bus now.
3. The story and its author (have, has) been discussed.
4. The kitten or the puppy (have, has) my slippers.
5. A wire, a string, and a piece of tape (is, are) needed.
6. The newspaper, magazine, or book (have, has) the information.

TO MEMORIZE

Loveliest of trees, the cherry now
Is hung with bloom along the bough
And stands about the woodland ride
Wearing white for Eastertide.

A. E. HOUSMAN

Housman wrote these lines when a young man. He is determined not to lose a moment of this spring's beauty:

> About the woodlands I will go
> To see the cherry hung with snow.

Find the poem under the title "Loveliest of Trees." If you like it, memorize all three stanzas.

Sentence Patterns

● List all of the symbols you have studied this year. Next to each one, write what the symbol stands for.

● Write the symbols which represent each basic pattern you have studied. Then write two sentences to illustrate each pattern.

● Copy the following sentences, leaving space between them. Above each word, write its symbol. Then, after each sentence, write *Pattern 1, 2, 3, or 4.*

1. The mangy dog had wanted a bone.
2. Goats scattered quickly into the hills.
3. A few children were unhappy.
4. Paula has been a good friend of yours.

● Use the following symbols to build sentences. In some of the groups, there are conjunctions which have been written out for you.

Example: N and N V P Adj N
          Bob and Mary went to the store.

1. Adj N Vh Adv V
2. N Vh V Adj N P Adj N
3. Vh N V Adj N
4. Adj Adj N V P Adj N
5. Adj N P Adj Adj N V Adv
6. N and N Vbe P Adj N
7. N and N Vh V P Np
8. Vh Adj Adj N V P Adj N
9. N and Np Vh Adv V P Adj N
10. N or Adj N V P Adj Adj N
11. N V Adj N and N V Adj N
12. N V P Adj N and Np V Np

● Now make up an exercise of your own. First write three sentences. On a separate sheet of paper, write the symbols that stand for each word. Exchange papers with a classmate. Write sentences of your own following his symbols just as he will do with your set of symbols.

Onion John

by Joseph Krumgold
illustrated by Symeon Shimin
Thomas Y. Crowell Company

No one else in Serenity was at all like Onion John. He lived in a shack he built for himself and went about his work contentedly, eating onions and exploring the dump yard for his needs as others might a supermarket. Most people could not understand his strange mixture of language.

Andy caught on to the language. He and his friends liked Onion John's good nature and found his superstitions and magic fascinating. Perhaps the real magic, however, was that Andy's interest spread like ripples in water, until the townspeople decided to build a house for John—the kind of house that *they* would like.

They found it hard to realize that John might prefer his old possessions and his own way of doing things. It was Andy and his father who discovered that a grown-up must live his own life in his own way to find real happiness. One can't expect others to fit a pattern cut out for himself.

Strangely enough, this discovery applied to Andy too. In this year of growing up, he learned how to face his future. The book is as much a story of Andy as of Onion John. It is a book you will enjoy discussing.

TRYOUT TIME

If you make a mistake on a test, take the Practice on pages 288 or 289 with the same Roman numeral as the test.

Test I. Recognizing Prepositions

List the prepositions in these sentences:

1. Into the house and up the stairs dashed Tom.
2. After school, the Bird Watchers will meet under the elm tree.
3. The balloon soared over the trees.
4. Please leave your muddy boots on the rack outside.
5. David and Paul took the elevator to the fourth floor, but they walked down.

Test II. Prepositional Phrases

Copy each sentence below. Underline each prepositional phrase.

1. The house around the corner is being painted.
2. We will leave the house after lunch.
3. The girl in the blue coat dropped her glove.
4. The car was splattered with mud.
5. The two swimmers dived under the boat.
6. Those boys are members of my class.

Test III. Using Words Correctly

Write the following sentences, using the correct word:

1. Were you (at, to) home yesterday?
2. Divide the work (among, between) Jake and me.
3. Hazel jumped (in, into) the pool.
4. The ball was lost (among, between) the geraniums.
5. The guest speaker sat (among, between) the principal and the chairman of the committee.
6. We sensed the strong feeling of excitement and good will (among, between) the holiday shoppers.

Test IV. Conjunctions, Words in a Series

Write each sentence and punctuate it correctly:

1. Copper silver and gold were mined in the state.
2. The kittens rolled tumbled and leaped.
3. The children can dance play or sing.
4. The boy studied patiently carefully and well.
5. The old horse trotted down the street through the intersection and into the parking lot.

Test V. Writing Sentences Correctly

Make a single sentence of each pair of sentences below, using the conjunction in parentheses. Punctuate each sentence correctly.

1. (but) Richard had the book yesterday.
   He lost it on his way home from school.
2. (and) Jane washed the windows.
   Sara made curtains for them.
3. (or) I can deliver the ice cream now.
   Robert can bring it home with him later.
4. (but) We stopped at the gas station.
   It was closed for remodeling.

Test VI. Subject and Verb Agreement

Write each sentence below, using the correct form of the verb:

1. Dan and I (has, have) new sweaters.
2. (Don't, Doesn't) the deer or the elk come to this watering hole now?
3. Tom and Bob (doesn't, don't) play on the basketball team this year.
4. The eagles, coyotes, and wildcats (is, are) disappearing from the country.
5. The dog or the cat (has, have) eaten the scraps.
6. Mary and she (hasn't, haven't) arrived yet.

✔ IF YOU NEED MORE PRACTICE ✔

Practice I.   Recognizing Prepositions

1. Review the lesson on pages 266–67.

2. List the prepositions in these sentences:

1. Look behind the barn for the clue to the buried treasure.
2. At the third lap, the racer on the red bicycle fell behind.
3. The water trickled down the side of the house and splashed into little puddles.
4. The light on the porch just went off.
5. We walked up the street.

Practice II.   Prepositional Phrases

1. Study again the lesson on pages 268–69.

2. Copy each sentence below.   Underline each prepositional phrase.

1. The trip to the city was slow.
2. My raincoat was covered with mud.
3. I want the seat by the window.
4. Warren usually calls in the evening.

3. Write two sentences, using prepositional phrases to modify a noun.

4. Write two sentences, using prepositional phrases to modify a verb.

Practice III.   Using Words Correctly

1. Review the lesson on page 272.

2. Write the following sentences, using the correct preposition in parentheses:

1. We walked (among, between) the people.
2. Go (in, into) the house.
3. Jack drew a line (among, between) the two teams.
4. Art stayed (at, to) his aunt's house.

Practice IV.   Conjunctions, Words in a Series

1. Review the lessons on pages 275–80.
2. Write five sentences using *or, and,* or *but* to connect the following:

> two subjects   two adjectives
> two verbs   two prepositional phrases

3. Write these sentences correctly:

1. The school's colors are gray blue and yellow.
2. Earthquakes occur when the earth's crust cracks slips or folds.
3. There were moose elk and deer in the forest.
4. The tortoise moved slowly steadily and surely.
5. We looked under the table behind the stove and inside the cupboard.

Practice V.   Writing Sentences Correctly

1. Review the lesson on page 276.
2. Write these sentences correctly:

1. Ted washed the car and Henry cleaned out the garage.
2. Mary will sing a folk song or her sister will play the harmonica.
3. Jim picked a quart of berries but Al picked only a pint.

Practice VI.   Subject and Verb Agreement

1. Study the lesson on pages 282–83.
2. Read the sentences below.   Decide whether the subject is singular or plural.   Write each sentence, using the correct form of the verb.

1. The poem and story (is, are) original.
2. Bill or Dennis (has, have) the key.
3. The twins and their sister (was, were) here.
4. The roses or carnations (is, are) my choice.
5. (Doesn't, Don't) Betty and Nan live there now?

CHAPTER 13

Sharing Stories

Long before most people knew how to read, people told stories to one another. Sometimes they acted them out, made up songs about them, or painted pictures of favorite scenes and characters. Stories that were told by one generation to the next over the centuries are known as folk literature. Common forms include myths, fables, fairy tales, ballads, and legends.

Myths

The gods and goddesses of Greek and Roman mythology had powers that man could never possess, but their actions and desires were often like those of mortals, and their faults sometimes led them into trouble. The stories of these gods and goddesses are called myths.

According to ancient storytellers, Mercury, son of Jupiter, was a fun-loving, quick-witted youth, a great storyteller, and an athlete. Because of his grace and speed, Jupiter chose him to be messenger to the gods.

Pictures of Mercury are easy to identify because he wore wings on his sandals and on his cap. The magic wand he carried was decorated with two golden snakes intertwined and a pair of tiny wings at the top. The wand was a gift from Apollo.

How Mercury Played a Trick on Apollo

On the very day of his birth, Mercury began to develop godlike powers, growing swiftly in strength and cunning. He left his crib and walked into the hills to see the world. In a meadow he saw a herd of beautiful cattle that belonged to Apollo, his brother.

291

Apollo was nowhere near, for as sun god he was busy driving the chariot of the sun across the sky. The small child thought it would be fun to lead the cattle away and hide them. The difficulty was that, in the soft earth, his own footprints and the cattle's would give him away. As he pondered on this problem, a solution came to him. Under his feet he tied small bundles of twigs. As for the cattle, he decided to make them back away to their hiding place so that the direction of the footprints would lead toward their home meadow rather than away.

At the end of the day, when Apollo found his cattle gone, he was angry and perplexed. He saw only the strange marks of the sticks and the tracks of the herd leading to their own pasture. Then a stranger, in chatting, told him about seeing a mere baby making the cattle back down the hill and into a secluded valley.

This clue was enough for Apollo. Soon he found the herd grazing in the hidden meadow and realized that his new brother Mercury was the culprit. He felt that punishment for such a trick must surely follow and that Jupiter, their father, should be the judge.

Jupiter agreed. Then Apollo set down two requirements: first, that Mercury promise never again to play such a trick on his brother; and second, that Mercury give him the lyre which he had that morning cut out from a tortoise shell. Mercury found the promise of better behavior was easy to make, but the loss of his lyre was difficult to bear. Realizing that the punishment was severe for one so young and pleased that Mercury complied willingly, Apollo gave him the magic wand.

To Discuss

1. What parts of the story show that Mercury was superhuman? What parts show that he had human traits too?

2. Have you seen the name Mercury in modern advertising? Why did the advertisers want to link their product with Mercury?

Telling a Mythical Story

Two kinds of people are needed for a story to be told successfully, good storytellers and good listeners. Both are important.

Plan to read some myths about gods and goddesses or heroes in books your teacher or the librarian will recommend. Select an interesting one to tell the class. Good stories can be found about these subjects:

Narcissus	The Wooden Horse	Pandora's Box
Hercules	Pegasus	Prometheus
Ceres	Daedalus	Pygmalion

Follow these steps in preparing to tell a story:

1. Read the selection until you know it well. Notice how the story opens. Think of the steps of the story.

2. Learn to pronounce all the names correctly. If you cannot find them in your dictionary, look in a large dictionary.

3. Notice the interesting words and expressions and plan to use some of them when you tell the story.

4. Practice telling the story aloud to a member of your family or a friend.

5. Be a courteous, intelligent listener as others tell their stories. What attitudes will this require on your part?

Now you are ready to tell your story. Here are some guides to follow. Add others you may think of to add to the list.

How to Tell a Story

Wait until you have the attention of your listeners.
Give the title and the name of the author (when known).
Speak distinctly and loudly enough to be understood.
Speak with expression.
Present the incidents in the correct order. Keep the final outcome until the end.
Use vivid verbs, adjectives, and adverbs.
Begin your sentences in different ways.

▶ **Practice: Telling and Listening to Stories**

Tell the story you selected to your class. Follow the guides above.

How Our Language Grew · · ● ●

Salary: The word *sal* or *salarium,* in Latin, meant "salt." At one time, Roman officers and soldiers received a regular allowance of salt. Later they were given money to buy their own salt. This part of their wages was called *salt money.* As the word worked its way into Old French and then into the English word *salary,* it carried the idea of regular pay, but the original reference to salt was forgotten. The saying, "That man is worth his salt" means he is a good worker and worth his salary.

Going Ahead ▶ ▶ ▶ ▶

The word *mercury* has come into our language to name several different things. List as many as you can. Sometimes the word is spelled with a capital letter. What does that word refer to? Consult your dictionary for help.

Actors have always put on a false face to play certain roles. In ancient times they wore masks. Masking is still the practice for certain kinds of dramatization in Japan and other countries. Find out all you can about the word *mask.*

294

Using Words Correctly: _is_ and _are_

You have learned when to use different forms of the verb _be_. The subject and verb in a sentence must agree in number. Read the sentences below. Name the subject and tell whether it is singular or plural. Notice the form of the verb that is used.

Bill _is_ on the roof.   I _was_ in the kitchen.
The toys _are_ in the box.   You _were_ home.

In sentences that begin with _There is_ or _Once there was_, the subject follows the predicate or part of the predicate. Study each sentence below, noticing the subject and predicate. Name the subject and tell whether it is singular or plural.

Once there _was_ a beautiful goddess named Venus.
There _were_ many thunderbolts hurled by Jupiter.
Once there _were_ two beautiful lemon trees at the bottom
of a hill.

In any sentence that you write or speak, make sure that the subject and the verb agree in number.

▶ **Practice: Using _is_ and _are_**

Write each sentence correctly, using the correct verb or contraction in parentheses.

1. (Is, Are) there legends from many countries?
2. Once there (was, were) an old mill on that lot.
3. There (is, are) gods and goddesses in the myths.
4. Once there (was, were) apples, oranges, and pears growing in that orchard.
5. (Wasn't, Weren't) there a prince in the story?
6. There once (was, were) coyotes and lions in the hills.
7. (Was, Were) there talking animals in the stories?
8. (Isn't, Aren't) there any books of fables in the public library?
9. Those kinds of cakes (is, are) very good.
10. There (wasn't, weren't) any records to play.

295

Fables

Fables are very short stories that point out human faults or weaknesses. Usually a fable suggests a way to improve human conduct. It teaches a moral lesson.

Some of the most famous fables were first told around 2,600 years ago by a Greek slave named Aesop. At first, these fables were passed from one generation to another by word of mouth. Then about 200 years after Aesop's death, they were written down. Today you can read many versions of Aesop's fables.

In Aesop's fables, animal characters show the same weaknesses and faults that human beings have. The fable below is from *The Fables of Aesop*, by Willis L. Parker. What human qualities do the animals in this fable have?

Jupiter and the Animals

Jupiter one day, being in great good humor, called upon all living things to come before him, and if, looking at themselves and at one another, there was in the appearance of any one of them anything which could be improved, they were to speak of it without fear.

"Come, Master Ape," said he, "you shall speak first. Look around you, and then say, are you satisfied with your good looks?"

"I should think so," answered the Ape, "and have I not reason? If I were like my brother, the Bear, now, I might have something to say."

"Nay," growled the Bear, "I don't see that there's much to find fault with in me; but if you could manage to lengthen the tail and trim the ears of our friend, the Elephant, that might be an improvement."

The Elephant in his turn said that he had always considered the Whale a great deal too big to be comely. The Ant thought the Mite so small as to be beneath notice. Jupiter became angry to witness so much conceit and sent them all about their business.

296

To Discuss

The lesson of a fable may often be expressed in the form of a proverb or wise saying. Decide which of the proverbs below best expresses the moral in the fable about Jupiter:

Don't count your chickens before they are hatched.
Birds of a feather flock together.
He can see another's faults who will not see his own.

Review Practice: Punctuation

1. Write these sentences correctly, using commas as needed:

1. One of Aesop's fables is about a wolf a fox and an ape.
2. Fables tell about animals but point out human faults.
3. No Dan is not going with Jim.
4. Can you imagine Harry how we felt?

2. Write the following fable correctly. Remember the rules for writing conversation.

One day the mice held a council to decide how to guard against their enemy, the cat. A young mouse solemnly delivered his advice. Someone he said should fasten a bell to the cat's collar. Then every step he takes will cause a tinkling. In this way we will all be warned when the cat is near. Almost everyone applauded upon hearing such a new and excellent idea. Then up rose an old gray mouse, whose age and wisdom everyone respected. My young friend he said has an admirable idea. One difficulty must be overcome, however, before it can be put to work. We must find among us someone who is willing to place the bell on the cat. Not I said one and then another. As yet no mouse has volunteered to bell the cat.

3. The sentences below contain interjections. Write them, using capital letters and punctuation marks as needed.

1. Whew this is a hot day.
2. Help the fish is getting away.
3. Oh he tells such funny stories.

Write these sentences, using the correct form of the verb in parentheses:

1. Hal or Jim (have, has) my catcher's mitt.
2. (Doesn't, Don't) Mary and her sister look alike?
3. The shrews and the crows (was, were) the first to arrive at the council of animals.
4. (Wasn't, Weren't) Lucile or Cathy at the meeting?
5. (Has, Have) Father or Mother been here?
6. (Doesn't, Don't) Edith want to go with us?
7. (Hasn't, Haven't) you anything else to do?
8. We (were, was) both glad when the game was over.

Composition: Writing a Fable

A. Choose a proverb that points out a human weakness. Some proverbs from which you may choose are listed below. Write a paragraph telling about something that might have occurred to which your chosen proverb applies.

> Actions speak louder than words.
> Look before you leap.
> Don't cry over spilled milk.
> A bird in the hand is worth two in the bush.
> A stitch in time saves nine.
> Too many cooks spoil the broth.

B. Choose an incident, using animals instead of persons, that illustrates a human weakness to which a proverb might apply. Use conversation to bring out the attitudes and traits of the characters. Write the conversation correctly. Keep your fable brief.

At the end of the fable, write the proverb you chose. Read your fable to the class. See whether your classmates can tell what proverb your fable illustrates.

298

Legends

When you tell someone about an adventure, you may exaggerate some of the events to make a more exciting story. If your friend then repeats the story, the events may become further exaggerated.

Legends are the stories that people have told about their favorite heroes. Some of them are based on events that really happened, but in the retelling they have gone beyond truth.

The complete story of one legendary figure may include many episodes, or adventures. For example, here are some famous episodes in the story of King Arthur:

> How Arthur becomes King
> How Arthur wins the sword Excalibur
> Sir Lancelot and Elaine
> How Sir Galahad searches for the Holy Grail

Reading an Episode Aloud

As you read legendary tales, look for incidents that others may enjoy hearing. If a story is short enough, the class might like to hear you read it.

In oral reading, the first step is to understand the meaning yourself. Then use your voice to convey the meaning to others.

How to Use Your Voice in Reading Aloud

Separate your words from one another just enough for listeners to hear each word distinctly.

Pause after reading the title or at the end of a paragraph to show that you are beginning a new part.

End a statement with a drop in voice tone; end a question requiring a Yes or No response with a rising tone.

Stress words and phrases to show emphasis.

Use natural ups and downs of intonation to excite interest and relieve vocal monotony.

► **Practice: Sharing Legends**

1. Select an incident from a legend to read to the class. Follow the guides on page 299 in preparing to read it aloud; or tell it in your own words, using the guides on page 294.

2. Listen carefully to the stories. You may hear several versions of the same tale. Decide which you like best and why.

3. After you have heard a number of legends, plan to discuss the characters of the legendary heroes.

Review Practice:
Using Prepositions and Conjunctions

1. Write sentences using the following prepositional phrases:

toward the ball	on the roof
after the storm	above the clouds
from England	within an hour

2. Write two sentences for each word below. In one use the word as a preposition. In the other, use it as an adverb.

inside	up	above
near	off	about

3. Write three sentences, using conjunctions as follows:

1. Use *or* to connect two subjects.
2. Use *but* to connect two verbs.
3. Use *and* to connect two prepositional phrases.

Going Ahead ▸ ▸ ▸ ▸

If you like to draw, sketch scenes from episodes or descriptions in books. Here are two possible projects to carry out:

1. Plan a mural with several pupils who have read the same stories. You might draw different episodes or incidents in chalk on the board or on colored paper.

2. If you draw easily and rapidly, give a chalk talk, sketching the scenes and events as you tell a story.

Dramatizing a Story

After you have read and heard a number of tales, fables, and legends, choose several to *act out,* or *dramatize.* Choose stories with plenty of action and opportunities for good speaking parts, or *dialogue.*

Planning the Acts or Scenes

Divide the story into acts or scenes, according to the parts or main events of the story. Then write a description of what is going to happen in each act.

Read the following descriptions of the scenes and acts for a play based on the adventures of Aladdin:

Aladdin and His Wonderful Lamp

ACT I. The *discovery of the magic lamp*

SCENE 1. Tricked by an evil magician, Aladdin becomes the astonished possessor of a magic lamp and ring. He discovers to his delight that his pockets are full of priceless jewels.

SCENE 2. By chance Aladdin discovers the Genie, who keeps Aladdin and his mother from starvation.

ACT II. *The rise of Aladdin*

SCENE 1. Aladdin appears before the Sultan and asks for the hand of the Sultan's daughter in marriage. The Sultan grants his request.

SCENE 2. Aladdin uses the magic lamp and the Genie to build a lovely palace, which is suited to the tastes of the beautiful Princess.

ACT III. *Aladdin's encounter with the wicked magician*

SCENE 1. During Aladdin's absence, the evil magician tricks the Princess and gains the lamp.

SCENE 2. Aladdin saves the Princess and himself.

Aladdin had many adventures. Find and read a version of them. See if you would plan different acts.

Planning the Characters

Choose a literary or historical episode and plan the dramatization. What characters will you need to include?

List the characters you will need for each act. Plan to have as many speaking parts as possible. For example, for the second act described on page 301, you might have members of the court speaking to one another. You may wish to review the story to see how the author showed the nature of each character through action and talk.

The examples below may refer to some part of history you have recently studied, or to a book you have read. If not, they may suggest something else with which you are familiar.

Historical source: A dramatic period in the history of a country you are studying.

Literary source: Robin Hood and his adventures in the forest.

When you have decided upon the episode for each scene, list the characters and their traits on the board. Make sure that they have contrasting traits which will show both in action and in words. Let pupils show how they would dramatize the traits you have listed by their way of walking and talking.

Planning the Action and Dialogue

When the action for each scene has been carefully plotted, let volunteers show how they would act out a small part of one scene. Part of the fun in acting out a story in class is in seeing different groups of actors put on the same play. The class should be divided into groups so that everyone will have a chance to participate. After one group has presented part of a scene, another group may try.

While one group is acting a scene, other members of the class will be the audience. When you are a member of the audience, watch and listen carefully.

Preparing a Formal Play

Most of your plays will be put on without scenery, costumes, or much rehearsal. You will not need to write out
the dialogue and memorize the lines.

However, sometimes you may wish to put on a favorite
play before an audience other than your own class. When
you do this, proceed as you would for an informal classroom
dramatization. After several groups of actors have presented
the same scenes, choose the best dialogue.

When you put on a formal play, plan to have each member
of the class contribute. Some of you will participate as actors.
Others may serve on committees to prepare scenery, collect
the furnishings for the stage, or plan the costumes.

▶ **Practice: Acting Out Stories**

Agree on several stories that would be suitable for classroom dramatization. Then participate in planning and acting out plays. Follow the suggestions you have just read.

Review Practice: Choosing the Correct Word

1. Write each sentence, choosing the correct verb in parentheses:

1. I (says, said) that I had made my own mask.
2. This morning Andy (says, said) he had chosen a costume.
3. This invitation (says, said) "Choose your own costume."
4. Yesterday Bill (says, said) that he would masquerade as a pirate.

2. Write these sentences, using the correct expression in parentheses:

1. Jane (should have, should of) been with us.
2. Could you (have, of) left your purse on the bus?
3. The play (could not have, could not of) been better.
4. Wouldn't Bill (have, of) been funny in that role?

3. Write each sentence, using the correct preposition:

1. There was an agreement (among, between) the members of the class.
2. Divide the questions (among, between) the five members of the panel.
3. Come (in, into) the house.
4. Were you (at, to) the meeting last night?

TO MEMORIZE

He prayeth best, who loveth best
All things both great and small;
For the dear God, who loveth us,
He made and loveth all.

SAMUEL T. COLERIDGE

The quotation above is taken from a long story poem called *The Rime of the Ancient Mariner*. The poem is written in the form of a ballad.

304

Runic letter

Sounds and Spelling

The Letters U, V, W, and Y

The letter *v* in the alphabet was originally another way of writing the letter *u*. As late as 1800, some people still used *u* for the initial consonant sound in *vase*, for example. At the same time, *u* was also being used as a vowel. The letter *v* was added to the alphabet as a separate consonant letter to clear up this confusion.

In the early days of English history, another alphabet, which we now call the Old English Alphabet, was used by priests and magicians who knew how to write. The letters of this alphabet, called *runes*, may still be seen carved in the stones of ancient ruins. One of these runes was used to spell the consonant sound that begins *wade*. There was no letter in the Roman alphabet corresponding to this rune, so a letter was invented. It consisted of *v v* put together: *w*. As *u* and *v* at that time were merely two forms of the same letter, the new letter was called *double u*.

Another Old English rune was a single letter, called a *thorn*, that stood for the *th* sound in *the*. It was shaped a little like the Roman letter *y*.

It was natural enough for early printers in England to use the letter *y* for a thorn as a short cut for the digraph *th* when they spelled the word *the*. This explains why shop signs such as "Ye Olde Antique Shoppe" first spelled *Y*^{e} for *The*.

Spelling Checkup

Make a spelling list of fifteen words that you may need in writing. Include three words with each of these consonant sounds: *v,* *w,* and *y;* and three for each of these vowel sounds: *u* and *y*. Learn the spelling of your words.

305

Fiction

In most present-day short stories and fiction the characters do not kill dragons; their experiences are more nearly like those of real people. Yet, like legendary heroes, they may set out to do great deeds, and they often prove to be stout-hearted in the face of danger or hardship.

Examine some books of fiction in your library. Then choose one to read. After you finish it, plan to tell your friends about it. Point out the outstanding features. The following questions may help you think of some:

1. Who are the main characters?
2. Where and when did they live?
3. What is the story about? What dangers, hardships, or problems did the characters face?
4. What traits did the characters reveal? Which characters do you admire most? Why?
5. Is there some interesting detail or incident which you might describe without spoiling the story?

Holding a Book Chat

Here are some suggestions to follow when you participate in a book chat with four or five classmates:

Show the book to your audience. You may also wish to show an interesting illustration. Pass the book around the class.

Give the name of the book and author. Write the names on the board. Present any interesting facts you know about the author, and name other books he has written.

Describe the outstanding features of the book. Tell who the main characters are and give the time and place of the story. Describe the heroes. Explain what danger, hardship, or difficulty they tried to face. You may be able to tell some incident that brings out the nature of the adventure. However, do not spoil the story by telling too much.

After the book chat, display the book in an interesting way.

Plan with several classmates to hold a book chat.

Writing a Book Opinion

Write book opinions on cards, which can be filed. At the top of the card, write a heading that tells the subject of the book; then cards on books of the same subject can be arranged together in the file.

Read this opinion. Notice the information given and the form.

Pioneer Adventures

Courageous Comrades was written by Fredrika Shumway Smith. The setting is Milwaukee, Wisconsin, in the year 1836. The story tells how two pioneer boys and the son of an Indian chief became good friends and how together they did a remarkable thing.

The pictures help to make the story interesting. The map inside the front cover shows the Indian village, the trading post, the sawmills, and a cluster of stores. I like pioneer stories, and this is one of my favorites.

Joan Davis

To Discuss

1. Tell what Joan included in writing her opinion of the book. What does the title of her paper tell us?

2. What information did Joan give in her opinion?

How to Write a Book Opinion

Write a heading that tells the subject of the book.
Give the name of the book and its author.
Tell when and where the story takes place.
Tell what or whom the book is about.
Mention an interesting detail about the book.
Give your reason for enjoying it.

Composition: Writing a Book Opinion

A. Write an opinion of a book you have read.

B. Write a character sketch of a book character. Do this from memory without using the book.

TRYOUT TIME

If you make a mistake on a test, take the Practice on page 309 having the same Roman numeral as the test.

Test I.   Stories of the Past and Present

Number your paper from 1–3.   After each numeral, write the letter of the words which best complete the sentence.

1. The purpose of a fable is (a) to tell an exciting story, (b) to point out a human weakness, (c) to explain the forces of nature.
2. Many legends are (a) biographies, (b) stories about heroes who once lived, (c) nonfiction.
3. The characters in modern fiction resemble the heroes in (a) myths, (b) legends, (c) real life.

Test II.   is and are

Write the following sentences.   Use the correct form.

1. There (was, were) potatoes in this sack.
2. There (is, are) two boys at the door.
3. (Wasn't, Weren't) there seven robins on the lawn?
4. Once there (was, were) two giants and a dolphin.

Test III.   Writing Book Opinions

Read the following book opinion for a class file.   Decide on a good subject heading for it.   Then write the opinion correctly, supplying the heading and your own signature.

Dragon prows westward was written by william h bunce.   It is a story of how eric crossed the atlantic ocean in a viking ship.   He landed on the shores of north america, which the vikings called vineland.   Then, eric was captured by the indians.

I enjoy reading about the adventures of the early explorers.   and this is one of the most exciting stories I have read.

✔ IF YOU NEED MORE PRACTICE ✔

Practice I.   Stories of the Past and Present

1. Depending on the question or questions you missed, turn to the discussion of fables, page 296, legends, page 299, or fiction, page 306.

2. Number your paper from 1–4.   After each numeral, write the letter of the words which best complete the sentence.

> 1. Aesop was (a) a character in Greek folk tales, (b) a writer of modern fiction, (c) a great author of fables.
> 2. An example of a legendary figure is (a) Robin Hood, (b) Aesop, (c) Master Ape.
> 3. An example of an episode is (a) the story about Sir Galahad's quest for the Holy Grail, (b) the complete legend of Robin Hood, (c) any fable.
> 4. A major part of a play is called an (a) episode, (b) an act, (c) a chapter.

Practice II.   is and are

1. Turn to the lesson on page 295 and study it carefully.

2. Write the following sentences, using the correct verb or contraction in parentheses:

> 1. There (is, are) the planes on the runway.
> 2. There once (was, were) several theaters in the town.
> 3. (Wasn't, Weren't) there some letters for you?
> 4. (Isn't, Aren't) there more pickles in the refrigerator?

Practice III.   Writing Book Opinions

1. Review the suggestions for writing book opinions on page 307.   What special features might a particular book have?

2. If you are writing a book opinion for the class file, why is it a good idea to supply a subject heading for your opinion?

3. Correct any mistakes you made on Test III, page 308.

4. Write a book opinion for the class file.

CHAPTER 14

Enjoying Poetry

Have you ever wondered what magic some poems possess that makes you remember them so well? Is it the picture they create, or their musical rhythm and rhyme, or their new ideas, or their words that intrigue you?

Poems that hold magic for you call forth your own imagination and make you more aware of life.

Pictures and Imagination in Poems

A beautiful spring day is a temptation to almost anyone to put work away and go off somewhere. Read the following poem and see how the poet creates the picture of such a day.

I Meant to Do My Work Today

I meant to do my work today,
But a brown bird sang in the apple tree
And a butterfly flitted across the field,
And all the leaves were calling me.

And the wind went sighing over the land,
Tossing the grasses to and fro,
And a rainbow held out its shining hand—
So what could I do but laugh and go?

RICHARD LE GALLIENNE

To Discuss

1. Which words give sound and motion to the poet's picture of the brown bird and the butterfly?

2. Which words make you hear the wind and see it pass by? Which line makes something in nature seem to be human?

3. What sights and sounds would tempt you away from work?

310

Discovering the Magic of Poetry

Here is a poem about swift things. Read it to yourself, taking time to enjoy the word pictures.

Swift Things Are Beautiful

Swift things are beautiful:
Swallows and deer,
And lightning that falls
Bright-veined and clear,
Rivers and meteors,
Wind in the wheat,
The strong-withered horse,
The runner's sure feet.

ELIZABETH COATSWORTH

To Discuss

1. Find some nouns in "Swift Things Are Beautiful" that paint pictures of swift things.

2. How is lightning described?

3. How does the poet help you see the wind?

4. Listen as the poem is read. Notice how the rhythm and the sounds of words help you catch the feeling, or mood.

▶ **Practice: Understanding Poetry**

1. The poem below is a very famous one from the Old Testament. Read it, noticing how the poet shows us one sign of spring after another, leading us finally to one bird song—the song of the turtledove.

> For, lo, the winter is past,
> The rain is over and gone;
> The flowers appear on the earth;
> The time of the singing of birds
>   Is come,
> And the voice of the turtle
>   Is heard in our land.
>
> SONG OF SOLOMON, 2:11–12

2. What signs of spring are mentioned in the poem?

3. Does this poem have a rhythm?

4. Think how you could help a reader picture the coming of autumn. Think of words and expressions that appeal to the senses. Think of signs that show fall is coming.

5. How could you help a reader picture the things listed below? Think of words and expressions that appeal to the senses. Think of comparisons that might help.

> The color and shape of the new moon
> Stars on a clear night
> An exciting athletic event
> A busy, noisy street
> A department store during a big sale
> A thunderstorm

Review Practice: Adjectives and Adverbs

Head two columns Adjectives, Adverbs. Think of colorful words that could be used in sentences about the six topics listed in **5** above. List the words in the proper columns on your paper. Then write sentences using the words in your list.

312

Discovering the Mood of a Poem

Think again of the dreamy feeling you got as you listened to the poem "I Meant to Do My Work Today" on page 310. In this poem the poet created a mood suitable to his feelings about a soft summer day.

Listen as the following poem is read, and sense its mood.

Windy Nights

Whenever the moon and stars are set,
   Whenever the wind is high,
All night long in the dark and wet,
   A man goes riding by.
Late in the night when the fires are out,
Why does he gallop and gallop about?

Whenever the trees are crying aloud,
   And ships are tossed at sea,
By, on the highway, low and loud,
   By at the gallop goes he.
By at the gallop he goes, and then
By he comes back at the gallop again.

ROBERT LOUIS STEVENSON

To Discuss

1. Would you describe the mood of "Windy Nights" as peaceful? joyous? restless?

2. Is the rhythm of the poem like the gallop of a horseman? Does the rhythm help create a mood?

Discovering the Meaning of a Poem

The poem below tells about a frightened young colt on a wintry evening. The colt belonged to a breed of horses common in New England—the Morgan breed.

The poem is like a moving picture. Read it carefully to let each picture register.

The Runaway

Once when the snow of the year was beginning to fall,
We stopped by a mountain pasture to say, "Whose colt?"
A little Morgan had one forefoot on the wall,
The other curled at his breast. He dipped his head
And snorted to us. And then he had to bolt.
We heard the miniature thunder where he fled
And we saw him, or thought we saw him, dim and gray,
Like a shadow against the curtain of falling flakes.
"I think the little fellow's afraid of the snow.
He isn't winter-broken. It isn't play
With the little fellow at all. He's running away.
I doubt if even his mother could tell him, 'Sakes,
It's only weather!' He'd think she didn't know!
Where is his mother? He can't be out alone."
And now he comes again with a clatter of stone
And mounts the wall again with whited eyes
And all his tail that isn't hair up straight.
He shudders his coat as if to throw off flies.
"Whoever it is that leaves him out so late,
When other creatures have gone to stall and bin,
Ought to be told to come and take him in."

ROBERT FROST

314

To Discuss

1. Why do you think the poet called the poem "The Run-away"?

2. The first five lines of the poem set the stage. Where is the setting? What time of year is it? How do you know the poet wasn't alone? Why did the passers-by stop? Read the lines that show us the little Morgan, as the poet first saw him.

3. What does the word *bolt* mean? Why did the colt bolt?

4. Notice how the poet helped us hear the bolting. What is "miniature thunder"?

5. There are other comparisons that help to make the scenes vivid. Read the lines that tell what the colt looked like after he bolted.

6. How did the poet feel about what he saw? What does *winter-broken* mean? Why did he think the colt was a run-away? Did he think that the colt's mother might be able to show the little animal that his fears were groundless?

Finding Humor in a Poem

Some poetry is written to be humorous. Even though its purpose is not serious, the poet may paint word pictures with great skill or tell a story skillfully in verse. Read the following humorous account of the tragic fall of a local hero.

Casey at the Bat

It looked extremely rocky for the Mudville nine that day;
The score stood two to four, with but one inning left to play.
So, when Cooney died at second, and Burrows did the same,
A pallor wreathed the features of the patrons of the game.

A straggling few got up to go, leaving there the rest,
With that hope which springs eternal within the human breast.
For they thought: "If only Casey could get a whack at that,"
They'd put even money now, with Casey at the bat.

But Flynn preceded Casey, and likewise so did Blake,
And the former was a pudd'n, and the latter was a fake.
So on that stricken multitude a deathlike silence sat;
For there seemed but little chance of Casey's getting to the bat.

But Flynn let drive a single, to the wonderment of all.
And the much-despised Blakey "tore the cover off the ball."
And when the dust had lifted, and they saw what had occurred,
There was Blakey safe at second, and Flynn a-huggin' third.

Then from the gladdened multitude went up a joyous yell—
It rumbled in the mountaintops, it rattled in the dell;
It struck upon the hillside and rebounded on the flat;
For Casey, mighty Casey, was advancing to the bat.

There was ease in Casey's manner as he stepped into his place,
There was pride in Casey's bearing and a smile on Casey's
    face;
And when, responding to the cheers, he lightly doffed his hat,
No stranger in the crowd could doubt 'twas Casey at the bat.

Ten thousand eyes were on him as he rubbed his hands with
    dirt,
Five thousand tongues applauded when he wiped them on his
    shirt;
Then when the writhing pitcher ground the ball into his hip,
Defiance glanced in Casey's eye, a sneer curled Casey's lip.

And now the leather-covered sphere came hurtling through
    the air,
And Casey stood a-watching it in haughty grandeur there.
Close by the sturdy batsman the ball unheeded sped;
"That ain't my style," said Casey.   "Strike one," the umpire
    said.

From the benches, black with people, there went up a muffled
    roar,
Like the beating of the storm waves on the stern and distant
    shore.
"Kill him! kill the umpire!" shouted someone in the stand;
And it's likely they'd have killed him had not Casey raised his
    hand.

With a smile of Christian charity great Casey's visage shone;
He stilled the rising tumult, he bade the game go on;
He signaled to the pitcher, and once more the spheroid flew;
But Casey still ignored it, and the umpire said, "Strike two."

"Fraud!" cried the maddened thousands, and the echo answered
    "Fraud!"
But one scornful look from Casey and the audience was awed;
They saw his face grow stern and cold, they saw his muscles
    strain,
And they knew that Casey wouldn't let the ball go by again.

The sneer is gone from Casey's lips, his teeth are clenched in
    hate,
He pounds with cruel vengeance his bat upon the plate;
And now the pitcher holds the ball, and now he lets it go,
And now the air is shattered by the force of Casey's blow.

Oh, somewhere in this favored land the sun is shining bright,
The band is playing somewhere, and somewhere hearts are
    light;
And somewhere men are laughing, and somewhere children
    shout,
But there is no joy in Mudville — mighty Casey has struck out.

ERNEST LAWRENCE THAYER

To Discuss

1. Talk over the meanings of special baseball words and expressions such as *rocky, died at second, single, spheroid.* Then listen as your teacher reads the poem.

2. Do you think the poet really believes a baseball game is as important as he makes it sound?

3. Casey is a proud man. Do you think he was showing off when he let two good pitches go by him? How does this build up the climax — the downfall of a proud man?

4. According to the poet, is the crowd on Casey's side when he lets two pitches go by? How do you know?

5. In the last stanza, what situations are contrasted and what words does the poet use to make the contrast sharp?

6. What makes this a humorous poem as well as a good story?

TO MEMORIZE

There is no frigate like a book
To take us lands away,
Nor any coursers like a page
Of prancing poetry.

EMILY DICKINSON

The word *frigate* might suggest to some readers a swift sailing vessel roaming the seas far from home. What does it suggest to you? How does your idea about this word add to the meaning of the poem?

If you were to paint coursers, what would you have your horses doing? In what way would "a page of prancing poetry" make you think of coursers?

Reading Poetry Aloud

To appreciate a poem fully, you should hear it read aloud and read it aloud yourself. This is the best way to enjoy the music of its rhythms and rhymes.

In reading a poem aloud, the meaning and the mood are the most important things to bring out. By emphasizing the meaning and mood, you can avoid sing-song reading without losing the beat of the rhythm built into the poem. Here are some suggestions for reading a poem aloud:

How to Read a Poem Aloud

Read the poem silently to determine its meaning and mood.

Learn the meaning and pronunciation of unfamiliar words.

Practice reading the poem aloud, saying each word distinctly.

Group the words to make the meaning clear.

Bring out the musical qualities of rhythm and rhyme, but avoid a sing-song rhythm.

By the tones of your voice, indicate the poet's mood.

► **Practice: Reading Poetry Aloud**

1. Study the following stanza from "The Bells," in preparation for reading it aloud. Follow the guides on page 320.

The Bells

Hear the sledges with the bells,
  Silver bells!
What a world of merriment their melody foretells!
 How they tinkle, tinkle, tinkle,
  In the icy air of night!
 While the stars, that oversprinkle
 All the heavens, seem to twinkle
  With a crystalline delight;
 Keeping time, time, time,
 In a sort of runic rhyme,
To the tintinnabulation that so musically wells
 From the bells, bells, bells, bells,
  Bells, bells, bells—
 From the jingling and the tinkling of the bells.

EDGAR ALLAN POE

2. Practice pronouncing the words *crystalline, runic,* and *tintinnabulation* after you have learned what they mean. Which word compares the rhythm of bells to the rhythm of ancient poetry written in alphabetical symbols called *runes*? Which word that means the ringing of bells sounds like the ringing of bells when you say it? Which word means *transparent* or *crystal-like*? What does the repetition of the word "bells" for two lines suggest to you?

3. Read the stanza to yourself until you feel the rhythm. It has a powerful, regular beat. Do not let the powerful rhythm cause you to read in a sing-song way. Tap out the rhythm with your finger as you read silently.

4. Now read the poem aloud. Even though you do not read in a sing-song, try to make your voice suggest the rhythm and music of the bells.

Choral Speaking

Some poems, like some songs, are good selections for a choir of voices. They may have parts in them for solos, duets, trios, quartets, or an entire choir.

You can have a verse choir in your own classroom with a little planning, study, and practice. Your first step will be to find and study a suitable poem.

Reading a Poem in Chorus

A narrative poem, if not too long, is often a good choice for choral reading. Since the musical qualities of rhythm and rhyme are effective in a choral arrangement, poems with a marked rhythm and interesting rhyme are good.

In reading a poem, just as in singing a song, a choral group may want some lines read as solos or by small groups and others by the whole choir. The group may want to assign some lines for boys to read and others for girls. Or, one section of the room may read a few lines and another section respond with the lines that follow.

On the next page are stanzas from a rollicking poem about a pirate. Read the poem carefully so that you understand it fully. Then plan a choral reading of it with your classmates. Discuss the questions that follow.

To Discuss

1. What does each stanza have to say about the pirate? Did you notice that there are lines that tell of his wickedness? Did you notice the lines that describe his dashing ways? Read aloud the lines that describe his conscience. Which lines paint his picture?

2. Talk over ways you could divide this poem into speaking parts.

3. Decide how the lines should be spoken to bring out their feeling.

4. What words must be pronounced with particular care? Practice saying those words together.

The Pirate Don Durk of Dowdee

Ho, for the Pirate Don Durk of Dowdee!
He was as wicked as wicked could be,
But oh, he was perfectly gorgeous to see!
The Pirate Don Durk of Dowdee.

His conscience, of course, was as black as a bat,
But he had a floppety plume on his hat,
And when he went walking it jiggled — like that!
The plume of the Pirate Dowdee. . . .

Oh, he had a cutlass that swung at his thigh,
And he had a parrot called Pepperkin Pye,
And a zigzaggy scar at the end of his eye,
Had Pirate Don Durk of Dowdee. . . .

His conscience, of course, it was crook'd like a squash,
But both of his boots made a slickery slosh,
And he went through the world with a wonderful swash,
Did Pirate Don Durk of Dowdee. . . .

It's true he was wicked as wicked could be,
His sins they outnumbered a hundred and three,
But oh, he was perfectly gorgeous to see,
The Pirate Don Durk of Dowdee.

MILDRED PLEW MEIGS

How to Plan for a Verse Choir

Find a suitable poem which you all enjoy.

Read and discuss the poem until you understand it fully.

Know the meaning and pronunciation of every word.

Study the pattern of rhythm and rhyme. Notice other musical qualities of the poem—for example, the repetition of consonant sounds or the use of words to imitate sounds.

Talk over some ways in which you might divide the poem to bring out its meaning. Some of the lines or stanzas should be spoken by the entire group. Some might be spoken by single voices.

Decide the manner in which each part should be said to bring out the meaning and feeling expressed by the poet.

Practice any difficult words or expressions.

▶ **Practice: Choral Speaking**

1. Read the poem "The Pirate Don Durk of Dowdee" in chorus.

2. Several of the poems in this chapter would make excellent selections for choral reading. Look back and find some that have lines that could be spoken by one or two persons and lines that could be spoken in chorus. Choose one and prepare to read it, following the suggestions above.

Review Practice: Capitalization

Write these sentences, using capital letters correctly:

1. We bought some mexican pottery in the shop.
2. The bill of rights guarantees fundamental rights to every american.
3. We saw the chinese paintings at the museum of fine arts in boston.
4. The pioneers hewed down forests beyond the allegheny mountains and all the way to the great plains.
5. We boarded the ferryboat for a visit to the statue of liberty in new york harbor.

324

Sounds and Spelling

Seven Consonant Sounds with Varied Spellings

You have learned that certain consonant sounds can be spelled in more than one way, even though our alphabet contains a letter for each of those sounds. We can begin by reviewing some and then study a few more.

Tell which letter or letters in each word spell these sounds:

1. The *f* sound in *fun*: phonograph, laugh, fat
2. The *k* sound in *keep*: kid, back, cap, coquette, chorus
3. The *s* sound in *sit*: son, cell, toss, science
4. The *t* sound in *till*: top, tacked, Thames
5. The *w* sound in *wet*: we, quit, suede
6. The *y* sound in *yet*: young, union
7. The *z* sound in *zoo*: zone, hose, xylophone

In respelling to show pronunciation, most dictionaries use the single letters *f, k, s, t, w, y,* and *z* to respell all the consonant sounds illustrated above.

Spelling Checkup

1. Each word below is incomplete, with a blank to be filled with the correct spelling of the sound shown in parentheses. Rewrite the words correctly.

1. blo_?_(k)	5. on_?_(y)on	9. lo_?_(z)e
2. (T)_?_ompson	6. (z)_?_ylophone	10. con_?_(k)er
3. (k)_?_art	7. pers_?_(w)ade	11. (f)_?_oto
4. gra_?_(f)	8. (k)_?_aracter	12. q(w)_?_eer

2. List some other words in which the sounds represented by *f, k, s, t, w, y,* and *z* are spelled in other ways.

325

Finding Patterns of Rhythm and Rhyme

You have found that poetry has a kind of music in it. As you studied poems and especially if you tried writing one of your own, you discovered the importance of rhythm and rhyme. Did you notice that both of these qualities appear in a variety of patterns? And did you discover that the sounds of words may be poetic in other ways besides rhyming?

Patterns of Rhythm

Rhythm occurs in our language because of the changing stress or accent we place on syllables of words. In the poems in this chapter, the poets chose words whose syllables are accented to fit a definite pattern. A regular pattern of rhythm is called *meter*. Read the following line aloud and show the meter by softly clapping for each syllable:

But oh'/ he was wick'/ed as wick'/ed could be'/

The groups of syllables above, separated by slanting lines, are called *feet*. Each poetic *foot* except one has two light stresses followed by a heavy one. Which foot is the exception? Study other lines from "The Pirate Don Durk of Dowdee" to see whether the meter is the same all the way through.

Read this line from "Casey at the Bat." Clap to the meter:

There was ease'/ in Ca'/sey's man'/ner as'/ he stepped'/ into'/ his place'/

How Our Language Grew · · ● ●

Meter: The word *meter* comes from a Greek word meaning "measure." In poetry and music, *meter* refers to the measure of rhythm. What measure does it refer to in these words: *speedometer, altimeter, thermometer, barometer?* Use your dictionary if necessary.

Can you tell why the system of weights and measures used by scientists is called the *metric system?*

326

Rhyming Words

It is not only the rhythm of the lines but the sound of them that makes poetry musical. In many poems there is a repetition of sound at the ends of the lines which makes music. As you know, this device is called *rhyme.*

Words rhyme when their accented vowel sounds and any sounds that follow are identical, as in these words:

na'tion   sta'tion

What is the accented vowel sound in *nation?* in *station?* Notice that the sounds are identical. What sound comes after the accented vowel? These sounds, too, are identical.

For *true rhyme,* the consonant sounds before the accented vowel sounds should differ. What consonant sound do you hear before the accented vowel in *nation?* in *station?* Are *nation* and *station* examples of true rhyme?

Notice that syllables can rhyme though spelling differs. Which of these words rhyme: main, reign, same, plane, aim? Even when syllables are spelled the same, they do not rhyme unless the sound is the same. Which of these words rhyme: dove, move, rove, shove, love, prove? Only the sound, not the spelling, matters in rhyme.

To Discuss

1. Apply the above explanation of rhyme to the words below and see which words rhyme and which do not:

most boast	like sight	port court
seeming teaming	high dry	meat meet
dancing singing	turn return	neighbor labor

2. In which of the words listed above are the accented vowel sounds different? Do these words rhyme?

3. In which words are the sounds that follow the accented vowel sounds different?

4. Are the words *meat* and *meet* examples of true rhyme?

Patterns of Rhyme

It is not only the rhyme but the pattern of rhyme in some poems that helps make them musical. Poems differ in their patterns of rhyme, just as they differ in their patterns of rhythm.

The simplest pattern of rhyme is the one in which all the lines rhyme. Here is a *couplet*, or two rhyming lines:

> Maud Muller on a summer's day
> Raked the meadow sweet with hay.
> JOHN GREENLEAF WHITTIER

It is common to show the pattern of rhyme by using letters of the alphabet. Lines that rhyme have the same letters. Thus the pattern of rhyme for the couplet above would be *aa*. If the poem were four lines long and every line rhymed, the pattern would be *aaaa*. These patterns of rhyme are frequently used: *abab, aabb, abcb, ababcc*.

Look back and decide which pattern the poets used in these poems:

1. "Casey at the Bat," page 316
2. "I Meant to Do My Work Today" (second stanza), page 310
3. "Windy Nights," page 313
4. "Swift Things Are Beautiful," page 311

Other Musical Characteristics

In some poems several words in a line begin with the same consonant sound. Notice these examples:

1. He had a *p*arrot called *P*epper*k*in *P*ye
2. *B*oth of his *b*oots made a *s*lishery *s*losh

Find other examples in "The Pirate Don Durk of Dowdee."

Still another way to make poems musical is to choose words whose sounds imitate sounds mentioned. Poe does this in "The Bells" with words like *jingling* and *tinkling*. Can you think of others he uses?

► **Practice: Other Music Makers**

1. Here are pairs of rhyming words from poems in this chapter. Try to think of at least two more words to add to each group:

land	hand	night	delight	then	again
straight	late	occurred	third	time	rhyme
bat	that	sped	said	three	see

2. Write a couplet, or two lines of poetry that rhyme. Choose your own rhymes.

3. Write a line of verse in which you use several words that begin with the same consonants.

4. Think of at least one word that would imitate the sound of each of the following:

telephone	rain falling on the roof	fire
drums	an airplane taking off	a bee

━━ Composition: Writing a Poem

A. Look at the following suggestions for the first lines of a poem, and think of others. List them on the board.

1. What is crimson?
2. I know someone who has spring fever.
3. Down beats the rain on the windowpane.

B. Write a poem. Decide what mood you want to express and include details that express that mood. Use one of the lines suggested in part **A,** above, as a beginning, or make up one of your own.

Writing Limericks

A limerick is a five-line stanza written for fun. There is humor in what it says, and its rhythm and rhyme add to the fun. Read this limerick and notice its pattern of rhyme and rhythm.

> There was an old man of Tarentum
> Who gnashed his false teeth till he bent 'em;
> And when asked for the cost
> Of what he had lost,
> Said, "I really can't tell, for I rent 'em."

To Discuss

1. What is the pattern of rhyme? All limericks have this same pattern of rhyme.

2. As your teacher reads the limerick, tap out the rhythm on your desk.

3. Usually, it is the last line that gives the real point of humor or the surprise ending. See if you can suggest a last line for this limerick:

> There once was a fat girl named Mabel
> Who gobbled much food at the table.
> She'd clean up her platter,
> Grow fatter and fatter,
> ? ? ? ? ? ? ?

Composition: Writing Rhymes for Fun

A. Read some limericks and other nonsense verse. Then together in class, write an original limerick.

B. Write your own limerick or nonsense verse.

Going Ahead ▶ ▶ ▶ ▶

Plan to make a booklet of your favorite poems about a subject of your choice. When you copy a poem in your notebook, write the author's name and the book or magazine in which you found it. If it is long, you may copy only a stanza or two.

TRYOUT TIME

If you make a mistake on a test, take the Practice on page 333 having the same Roman numeral as the test.

Test I. Discovering the Meaning and Mood of a Poem

Read the following verse from "Snow-Bound," by John Greenleaf Whittier. Try to visualize each word picture. Answer the questions below.

> Unwarmed by any sunset light
> The gray day darkened into night,
> A night made hoary with the swarm
> And whirl-dance of the blinding storm,
> As zigzag, wavering to and fro,
> Crossed and recrossed the winged snow:
> And ere the early bedtime came,
> The white drift piled the window frame,
> And through the glass the clothesline posts
> Looked in like tall and sheeted ghosts.

1. Write the line that helps you to sense the cold.
2. What made the night hoary? Try to figure out the meaning of the word *hoary* from its context. Have you ever heard the word used to describe a frost or perhaps the hair of an older person? Give a synonym for *hoary.*
3. What word does the poet use to help us see how the swarm of snowflakes looked?
4. How deep was the snow before the early bedtime?
5. Write the words that help us to picture the posts of the clothesline.
6. What is the mood of the poem? Do you think the poet had a feeling of joy? regret? excitement? slight uneasiness, that is, a sense of being threatened?
7. Does the rhythm help create the mood? Is it a gay, dancing rhythm? a somber, rather stately rhythm? a dreamy rhythm?

Test II. Music in Poetry

1. Read the verse below from "Sweet and Low," by Alfred, Lord Tennyson. Notice particularly its musical qualities. Then write four statements about these qualities by completing the sentences below.

Sweet and Low

Sweet and low, sweet and low,
   Wind of the western sea,
Low, low, breathe and blow,
   Wind of the western sea!
   Over the rolling waters go,
   Come from the dying moon, and blow,
   Blow him again to me;
While my little one, while my pretty one sleeps.

1. The rhythm of the verse is most like that of a (a) lullaby, (b) march, (c) rollicking ballad.

2. The pattern of rhyme in the poem is (a) aabbccdd, (b) abababab, (c) ababaabc.

3. In the poem a word that sounds like the wind is repeated several times; it is the word (a) sweet, (b) low, (c) blow.

4. The words *breathe* and *blow* are music-makers because they (a) both rhyme, (b) both describe the wind, (c) both begin with consonant sounds.

2. Copy the words in the left-hand column. After each, list any of the twenty words on the right that are exact rhymes.

1. height
2. seat
3. flowed
4. weather
5. surprise

high, eye, whether, floated, meet, light, wise, together, piece, supple, thief, sighs, bright, complete, road, towed, ties, showed, feet, bite

Practice I. Discovering the Meaning and Mood of a Poem

1. If you missed a question in Test I, try to figure out why. Did you read the poem too rapidly?

2. Read the following lines from Edwin Markham's "How the Great Guest Came" and answer the questions below:

> Tall was the cobbler and gray and thin
> And a full moon shone where the hair had been.

1. What kind of work did the man do?
2. Was the man old or young? Tell how you know.
3. What does the second line mean? Explain by expressing the same thought in your own words.

Practice II. Music in Poetry

1. Review the lesson on pages 326–28.

2. Read the following lines, also taken from "How the Great Guest Came," by Edwin Markham. Then follow the instructions below the lines.

> Doubled all day on his busy bench,
> Hard at his cobbling for master and hench,
> He pounded away at a brisk rat-tat,
> Shearing and shaping with pull and pat,
> Hide well hammered and pegs sent home,
> Till the shoe was fit for the Prince of Rome.

1. List the pairs of words that rhyme.
2. Which pairs of words have a musical effect because of their repetition of consonant sounds?
3. Write the word which imitates a sound which the poet is describing.
4. Write letters to show the rhyme pattern.
5. What words describe how the cobbler looked?
6. What line tells you he did a good job?

CONTENTS

The Sentence
The Paragraph
The Letter

The Noun
The Verb
The Pronoun
The Adjective
The Adverb
Adjectives and Adverbs in Comparisons
The Preposition
The Conjunction
The Interjection

Capitalization
Punctuation

Usage

The Sentence

A **sentence** begins with a capital letter and ends with a mark of punctuation. There are four kinds of sentences:

1. A **statement** is a sentence that tells something.
   Statement: We are flying to Chicago.

A statement is also called a **declarative sentence.**

2. A **question** is a sentence that asks something.
   Question: May we board Flight 607?

A question is also called an **interrogative sentence.**

3. A **command** or **request** is a sentence that gives an order or tells someone what to do.
   Command: Hurry through Gate 22.

A command or request is also called an **imperative sentence.**

4. An **exclamation** expresses a strong feeling.
   Exclamation: Your plane is about to take off!

An exclamation is also called an **exclamatory sentence.**

▶ **Practice**

1. Write the numerals 1–5 down the side of your paper. Write *S* after the numeral of each sentence.

   1. The tunnel has been closed for two weeks.
   2. About fossils.
   3. The mountains in North Carolina.
   4. We climbed the apple tree.
   5. Leave now.

2. Write a statement, a question, a command or request, and an exclamation.

335

Subject and Predicate

The **subject** of a sentence names what the sentence is about. The **predicate** tells something about the subject.

In the sentence below, a vertical line separates the *complete subject* from the *complete predicate*.

The man in the plaid jacket | walked rapidly.

The main word in the complete subject is called the **simple subject.** In the sentence above, it is the noun *man*. The other words in the complete subject are modifiers of the simple subject.

The key word in the complete predicate is called the **simple predicate.** It is always a verb. In the sentence above the verb is *walked*. The other word in the complete predicate, *rapidly*, is a modifier of the verb.

► **Practice**

1. Write each sentence below. Draw a vertical line between the complete subject and the complete predicate.

2. Draw a single line under the simple subject and a double line under the verb.

1. The woman with the yellow umbrella is my mother.
2. The thirsty boys gulped the water.
3. Actors must speak with expression.
4. The tired children slept soundly.

The Paragraph

A **paragraph** is a group of sentences about a single idea or topic. The first line of a paragraph is indented.

To write a good paragraph, follow these suggestions:

1. Decide on the main topic.
2. Make your first sentence state or hint at the topic.
3. Write other sentences that develop the topic.
4. Follow the correct paragraph form.

► **Practice**

1. Read this paragraph. Answer the questions below.

Thomas Jefferson was a man of many talents. He was a great statesman, and he had many other talents. Besides being a great statesman, he was an inventor. One of his inventions was a wall clock that told both the time and the day of the week. A town in our state is named after him.

2. What is the topic sentence?
3. Which sentence does not keep to the topic?
4. Which sentence fails to develop the topic?

The Letter

Both friendly letters and business letters have these five parts: a *heading*, a *greeting*, a *body*, a *closing*, and a *signature*. In addition, a business letter has an *inside address*.

Read the business letter below. Name its *six* parts.

Sperry, Colorado 80610
April 11, 19—

Mr. R. A. Wallace
Editor of the *Silver Creek News*
122 Main Street
Silver Creek, Colorado 80607

Dear Mr. Wallace:

I am looking forward to the interview next Friday at 3:30 P.M. It is very kind of you to let me see the presses. Thank you for everything.

Yours truly,
Dan Riley

► **Practice**

Study the letter above carefully. Then, close your books and write the letter as your teacher dictates it.

The Noun

The words below are all nouns. What does each noun name?

president	James Monroe	freedom	honesty
leader	Mulberry Street	Ohio	Nigeria
ocean	path	health	lizard

A noun that names a particular person, place, or thing is a **proper noun.** In the list of nouns above, *James Monroe, Mulberry Street, Ohio,* and *Nigeria* are *proper nouns.* The other nouns in the list are **common nouns.**

Proper nouns begin with capital letters. If a proper noun consists of more than one word, each important word begins with a capital letter, for example, *Museum of Fine Arts.*

► **Practice**

1. Write a proper noun for each of these common nouns:

mountain	street	continent	historic event
leader	ocean	country	building

2. Write common nouns for ten things you see around you.

Singular and Plural Nouns

A noun that names one is said to be **singular.**
A noun that names more than one is said to be **plural.**
Nouns form their plurals in the following ways:

1. Most nouns form their plurals by adding **s,** as:

table tables   chair chairs

2. Nouns that end in **s, sh, ch, x,** and **z** form their plurals by adding **es,** as:

bus buses	wish wishes	fox foxes
guess guesses	torch torches	waltz waltzes

338

3. Noun ending in **y** following a consonant change **y** to **i** and add **es,** as: baby bab*ies*   fly fl*ies*

Nouns ending in **y** following a vowel add **s,** as:

convoy convoy*s*   journey journey*s*   day day*s*

4. Some nouns ending in **o** add **s,** as:

piano piano*s*   dynamo dynamo*s*   banjo banjo*s*

Other nouns ending in **o** add **es,** as:

echo echo*es*   cargo cargo*es*   tomato tomato*es*

5. Most nouns ending.in **f** or **fe** change **f** to **v** and add **es,** as: half hal*ves*   knife kni*ves*   wharf whar*ves*

A few nouns do not follow the above rule but add **s:**

chief chief*s*   roof roof*s*

6. Some nouns form their plurals irregularly, as:

child child*ren*   ox ox*en*

7. Some nouns form their plurals by changing a vowel or vowels within the words, as: woman wom*en*

8. Some nouns have the same form for both the singular and the plural, as: Portuguese   deer   sheep

► **Practice**

Write the plural form of each noun listed below. Use your dictionary if necessary.

sister	tax	mosquito	life
play	hero	solo	mouse
candy	potato	leaf	tooth
dwarf	march	country	torpedo
turkey	radio	moose	family

Possessive Forms of Nouns

A noun changes its form to show possession. Here are some rules to follow in forming possessive nouns:

1. Form the possessive of a singular noun by adding an apostrophe and **s ('s),** as: dog's ears   baby's toy

2. Add only an apostrophe to plural nouns ending in **s.**

dogs' ears   babies' toys

3. Form the possessive of a plural noun that does not end in **s** by adding an apostrophe and **s,** as:

firemen's hose   children's voices

► **Practice**

1. Write the possessive form of each of these singular nouns: *man, Jane, calf,* and *country.*

2. Write the possessive form of each of these plural nouns: *women, boys, animals,* and *foxes.*

The Verb

Every sentence contains a verb.

Some verbs express *action.* The verbs in the sentences below express action that can be seen or heard:

The cowboy *branded* the calf.
The bacon *sizzled* in the pan.

Other verbs express action of the mind, which cannot be seen or heard, as:

Jack *thought* about the problem on his way home.

Some verbs do not express action. They are usually found in predicates that tell what or where the subject *is* or what the subject is *like.* They are called *verbs of being*:

The rose *is* bright yellow.   *Are* you ready?

340

► **Practice**

Find the verb in each sentence below. Tell whether it is an *action verb* or a *verb of being*.

1. Harry toasted the marshmallows.
2. The bacon was crisp.
3. The dry twigs crackled in the fire.
4. The lemonade is in the cooler.

Helping Verbs

A verb may include more than one word, as in *may have been chosen.* In that example, *chosen* is the *main verb*; the verbs *may have been* are *helping verbs.*

► **Practice**

Copy each sentence below. Draw one line under the main verb and two lines under the helping verb.

1. The carpenter has been sawing wood.
2. Mary may leave tomorrow.
3. Have these books been read?
4. Has your cousin ever visited the cave?
5. Who is always complaining about the work?

How Verbs Express Time

A verb may express present, past, or future time by changing its form or by using a helping verb. The time which a verb expresses is called **tense**. Study these tenses:

I often *hike* through the woods. (*present tense*)
John *hikes* every Saturday. (*present tense*)
We *hiked* three miles last week. (*past tense*)
Will you *hike* with us next Saturday? (*future tense*)

► **Practice**

Give sentences, using the present, past, and future tenses of the verbs *work* and *climb.*

The Pronoun

A **pronoun** is a word that is used in place of a noun. Like nouns, pronouns may be singular, plural, or possessive in form.

Subject pronouns		Object pronouns	
SINGULAR	PLURAL	SINGULAR	PLURAL
I	we	me	us
you	you	you	you
he, she	they	him, her	them
it	they	it	them

Possessive pronouns

SINGULAR	PLURAL
my, mine	our, ours
your, yours	your, yours
his, hers	their, theirs
its	their, theirs

Subject pronouns are used in place of noun subjects or in place of nouns after verbs of being.

Object pronouns are used after a verb of action or after a preposition.

Possessive pronouns are used in place of possessive nouns.

► **Practice**

1. Write each sentence, using any correct pronoun.

1. The boys thought the ball was __?__.
2. This letter is for Jim and __?__.
3. You and __?__ are on the same committee.
4. Did you see Robert and __?__?
5. Jane gave __?__ share of the cake to Tom.
6. This book is __?__.

2. Write sentences using these possessive pronouns correctly: *its, yours, theirs.*

The Adjective

An **adjective** is a word that modifies a noun. **Descriptive adjectives** tell *what kind*, and **limiting adjectives** tell *how many* or *which one*:

Descriptive:	*red* flannel	*short* post
Limiting:	*those* horses	*seven* cards

► **Practice**

Copy each sentence below. Draw an arrow from each adjective to the word it modifies.

1. The hungry girls ate two hamburgers.
2. Two boys were riding the old gray mare.
3. Those girls in front are waving crimson pennants.
4. The dilapidated old car chugged along the dusty road.

The Adverb

An **adverb** is a word that modifies a verb, adjective, or another adverb. It usually answers the questions *how, when, where, how much,* or *to what degree.* Notice the use of the adverbs in the sentences below:

The schooner drifted *slowly* from its course.

A *perfectly* reasonable explanation was given.

The boat docks *very soon.*

It is *almost here.*

► **Practice**

Find the verb in each sentence below. Then write or read the sentence, using an adverb that modifies the verb.

1. The deer leaped __?__ over the log.
2. The campers __?__ made a fire.
3. The trout snapped __?__ at the bait.
4. The angry man knocked __?__ on the door.

343

Adjectives and Adverbs in Comparisons

Adjectives and adverbs may compare persons or objects:

Adjective Forms

POSITIVE	COMPARATIVE	SUPERLATIVE
slow	slower	slowest
useful	more, less useful	most, least useful
good	better	best

Adverb Forms

soon	sooner	soonest
distinctly	more, less distinctly	most, least distinctly
well	better	best

The **positive degree** is the simple form of the adjective or adverb. The **comparative degree** is used to compare two persons, objects, or actions. The **superlative degree** is used to compare three or more.

The Comparative and Superlative Degrees

1. Most adjectives and adverbs of one syllable add **er** to form the comparative degree and **est** to form the superlative degree, as:

(*adj.*)   tall — taller — tallest
(*adv.*)   near — nearer — nearest

2. A few adjectives and adverbs of two syllables add **er** and **est,** as:

(*adj.*)   pleasant — pleasanter — pleasantest
(*adv.*)   often — oftener — oftenest

3. Most two-syllable adjectives and adverbs use **more** or **less** and **most** or **least,** as:

(*adj.*)   active — more (less) active — most (least) active
(*adv.*)   slowly — more (less) slowly — most (least) slowly

4. Adjectives and adverbs of more than two syllables use **more** or **less** and **most** or **least,** as:

> (*adj.*) popular — more (less) popular — most (least) popular
>
> (*adv.*) quietly — more (less) quietly — most (least) quietly

5. Some adjectives and adverbs form the degrees of comparison in irregular ways.

► **Practice**

1. In each sentence, use the correct adjective form:

1. (old)   Which is the ___?___ of the two houses?
2. (small)   This apple is ___?___ than that one.
3. (active)   Tom is ___?___ than Bill in the club.
4. (beautiful)   This is the ___?___ rose in the garden.

2. In each sentence, use the correct adverb form:

1. (fast)   Fred runs ___?___ than Al.
2. (clearly)   Carol speaks ___?___ than Patricia.
3. (well)   Of all the performers, who dances ___?___?
4. (promptly)   Richard came ___?___ of all.

The Preposition

A **preposition** is followed by a noun or pronoun, which is called the object of the preposition, as:

> *for* Bill   *over* the steep hill

Each of the word groups above is a prepositional phrase.

A *prepositional phrase* consists of a preposition, its object, and any modifiers of the object.

► **Practice**

Make up sentences, using six different prepositions.

The Conjunction

The **conjunction** is a word that is used to join words, phrases, or sentences. The conjunctions *and, but,* and *or* are common.

▶ **Practice**

1. In each sentence, name the conjunction and tell what words, phrases, or sentences it connects:

1. The deer dashed into the bushes and out of sight.
2. Tom or Dick will be there.
3. Divide the cake between Al and Walt.
4. Helen must hurry, or I will be late.
5. The horses pranced, trotted, and galloped.
6. I called for Dennis, but he had left.

2. Write three sentences, using the conjunctions *and, or,* and *but* to connect words or phrases. Use a different conjunction in each sentence.

The Interjection

An **interjection** is a word that is used to express a feeling. A *strong* interjection at the beginning of a sentence is followed by an exclamation point. Notice the strong interjection at the beginning of this sentence:

Ouch! That water is hot.

A *mild* interjection at the beginning of a sentence is followed by a comma, as in this example:

Oh, I left my pen home.

▶ **Practice**

Write five sentences, using these words as interjections: *hurrah, ha, help, well, bah.* Begin at least one of your sentences with a mild interjection.

Capitalization

Capital Letters for Beginnings

1. Capitalize the first word in a sentence.

2. Capitalize the first word in the second part of a divided quotation if it begins a sentence.

"Those are dark clouds," Tony observed. "Father believes it's going to rain."

3. Capitalize the first word in the greeting and closing of a letter.

My dear Aunt Emily,   Very truly yours,

4. Capitalize the first word of each topic of an outline.

    I. Educational
       A. News broadcasts
       B. Science shows

Capital Letters for Proper Nouns

5. Capitalize the names of particular persons, including their titles and initials.

Cynthia A. Edwards   Uncle Walter

6. Capitalize the names of cities, towns, counties, states, and countries.

Denver, Colorado   Los Angeles County

7. Capitalize the names of geographical areas.

Mount Everest   Gulf of Mexico   the Southeast

8. Capitalize the names of streets, bridges, monuments, natural wonders, and buildings.

Statue of Liberty   Museum of Modern Art

9. Capitalize the names of particular documents and historical events, as: Bill of Rights, War of 1812.

10. Capitalize the names of peoples of a country.

Spanish   French   Americans

11. Capitalize the names of institutions, businesses, organizations, and departments of government.

Jones Pharmacy   Department of Labor   Photo Club

12. Capitalize the names of days, months, holidays, and special events, as: Library Week.

13. Capitalize the names of ships, aircraft, and trains.

Queen Mary   Spirit of St. Louis   Zephyr

14. Capitalize the names of races and religions.

Indian   Negro   Buddhism

15. Capitalize abbreviations for proper nouns.

St. Louis   Wed.   U.S.A.

16. Capitalize proper adjectives, as: American flag, British sailors.

17. Capitalize the pronoun I.

18. Capitalize the first word and all important words in titles, as: The Pyramids of Egypt.

► **Practice**

1. Write the sentences, using capital letters correctly:
   1. alice giggled, "whatever is a unicorn?"
   2. "here is a picture of one," replied her friend. "a unicorn is a mythical beast."
   3. On st. patrick's day, a group of students from the parkdale school visited the museum of natural history.

Punctuation

The Apostrophe

1. Use an apostrophe in a contraction: hadn't

2. Use an apostrophe in nouns that show possession.

horse's bridle   cowboys' saddles   children's toys

The Colon

3. Place a colon after the greeting of a business letter.

Gentlemen: Dear Sir: Dear Mr. Green:

4. Place a colon between the numerals that represent the hour and the minutes: 4:16 P.M.   9:30 A.M.

The Comma

5. Use a comma in dates to separate the day from the year and the weekday from the month.

November 11, 1918   Thursday, January 1, 1970

6. Use a comma to separate city and state or country.

Dallas, Texas   London, England

7. Use a comma after a greeting in a friendly letter.

Dear Sam,   My dear Mrs. Hill,

8. Use a comma after the closing of a letter.

Yours truly,   Your friend,

9. Use a comma between last and first names when listing last names first.   Smith, Mary   White, Edward

10. Use a comma or commas to separate names in direct address from the rest of the sentence.

I saw you, Tom, at the grocery store.

349

11. Use a comma after mild interjections and words such as **yes** and **no** at the beginning of a sentence.

Yes, this is a surprise.

12. Use commas to separate words and phrases in a series.

The children raced, jumped, and tumbled.

13. Use a comma to set off a quoted sentence.

They shouted, "Over the fence is out!"

14. Use commas to separate any words that interrupt a quoted sentence.

"I hope," said the spider, "that you will come into my parlor."

15. Use a comma before a conjunction that joins two sentences.

Martha bought the stationery, but she left it home.

16. Use a comma to make the meaning of a sentence clear.

After painting, Sam cleaned the brushes.

► **Practice**

1. Write the contractions for each expression below:

will not	they are	I have
are not	we are	it is

2. Write these sentences, using commas correctly:

1. "I believe" Fred said "that you are wrong."
2. We hurried to the station but the train had left.
3. Dennis help me or I will drop the box.
4. No I haven't made any plans.

The Exclamation Point

17. Place an exclamation point at the end of a sentence that is an exclamation: That house is on fire!

18. Place an exclamation point after a strong interjection at the beginning of a sentence.

Hurrah!   We won the game.

The Hyphen

19. Use the hyphen to divide words correctly between syllables at the end of a line: re-construct

20. Use the hyphen in writing compound words and number words: make-believe   thirty-three

The Period

21. Place a period after statements and requests or commands.

Mother has baked an apple pie.
Open the window, Tom.

22. Place a period after an abbreviation or an initial.

Dr. Richard B. Lowe   812 A.D.

23. Place a period after numerals and letters of an outline.

I. The many uses of steel
  A. In the automobile industry
  B. In construction
  C. In the manufacture of containers

The Question Mark

24. Place a question mark at the end of a question.

Where are you going?

Quotation Marks

25. Place quotation marks around direct quotations.

"You've done a good job," said Uncle Bill, "but don't forget to clean the paintbrushes."

26. Place quotation marks around the title of a story, poem, article, or chapter in a book.

Have you read "The Runaway," by Robert Frost?

Underlining

27. When writing or typing, underline the titles of books, magazines, and newspapers.

► **Practice**

1. The sentences below require some punctuation marks or an underline. Write each sentence correctly.

1. Did you read that story in the Morning Chronicle?
2. Have you read Casey at the Bat?
3. Tom shouted Look out for that curb Roy.
4. Oh That was a close call, Roy sighed wasn't it?
5. Was our conversation that interesting asked Tom.

2. Write the following divided quotation correctly:

If you listen carefully Ruth whispered youll hear it.

3. In the following sentences there are errors in capitalization and punctuation. Write the sentences correctly.

1. We traveled three hundred miles. Along the Blue Ridge Parkway.
2. We will have baked beans, they are easy to prepare.
3. Do you see the little junco under the pine tree it's looking for crumbs.

Usage

a or an

Use **a** before a word that begins with a consonant sound.

Use **an** before a word that begins with a vowel sound.

▶ **Practice**

Write each sentence, choosing the correct word or words:

1. We waited (a, an) hour for (a, an) taxi.
2. Bring (a, an) raincoat and (a, an) umbrella.

Adjective or Adverb

Use an adjective to modify a noun and an adverb to modify a verb, as:

> John's room is *neat*. (*adjective*)
> John paints *neatly*. (*adverb*)

▶ **Practice**

Write sentences, using these words correctly: *easy, easily; quiet, quietly; patient, patiently.*

among and between

Use **among** when you refer to more than two.
Use **between** when you refer to only two.

▶ **Practice**

Write these sentences, using the correct words:

1. Distribute the horns (among, between) the guests.
2. Divide the work (among, between) you and me.
3. We walked (among, between) the two rows of trees.

any or no

Study the correct use of *any* and *no* in the sentences below:

We have *no* paper.   We haven't *any* paper.

Use **any** with words that have a "no" meaning such as **not, none, never,** or contractions that end in **n't.**

► **Practice**

1. Write each sentence, using the correct word:

    1. We never had (any, no) trouble.
    2. I don't have (any, no) polish.
    3. Haven't the boys (no, any) means of transportation?

2. Write two sentences using *no* correctly.

at and to

Use **at** when you mean "already there."
Use **to** when you mean "going toward."

The boys are *at* camp.   They went *to* the park.

► **Practice**

Write four sentences using *at* and *to* correctly.

begin, eat, give, and write

Turn to page 359 and study the correct forms of these verbs: *begin, eat, give,* and *write.*

► **Practice**

Write each sentence, using the correct form of the verb:

    1. Has the game (began, begun)?
    2. The pastry had been (ate, eaten).
    3. He (began, begun) his homework.
    4. They have (given, gave) the magazines away.
    5. Have you (wrote, written) the announcement?

blow, come, and draw

Turn to page 359 and study the correct forms of these verbs: *blow, come,* and *draw.*

► **Practice**

Write sentences, using each of the following verbs correctly: *blew, came, drew, had blown, have come, has drawn.*

could have

The word *of* is a preposition and may not be used as a helping verb. Do not use *of* when you should use *have.*

► **Practice**

1. Read aloud each sentence below, supplying the correct helping verb:

1. Wouldn't Mary __?__ called before this hour?
2. Frank could __?__ won the race.

2. Write or give six sentences of your own, using *could have, couldn't have, should have, shouldn't have, would have, wouldn't have.*

doesn't and don't

Use **doesn't** when the subject of a sentence is a singular noun or when it is the pronoun **she, he,** or **it.**

Use **don't** with any plural subject and when the subject is **I** or **you.**

► **Practice**

Write these sentences, using the correct words:

1. It (don't, doesn't) cost much.
2. She (don't, doesn't) shop there often.
3. Why (doesn't, don't) Jane ask the librarian for help?
4. Carol and she (doesn't, don't) live here now.

fly, grow, know, take, throw

Turn to page 359 and study the correct forms of these verbs: *fly, grow, know, take,* and *throw.*

► **Practice**

1. Write each sentence, using the correct verb:

    1. Where have they (took, taken) my scissors?
    2. Yesterday the junk was (thrown, threw) out.
    3. Has your elm tree (grew, grown)?
    4. The oriole has (flew, flown) away.
    5. He had (knew, known) about the short cut.

2. Write five sentences, using these verbs correctly: *flew, knew, grew, took,* and *has thrown.*

good and well

The word *good* is an adjective. It may be used to modify a noun, as in each of these sentences:

This is a *good* sketch.   That painting is *good.*

Never use *good* as an adverb.
The word *well* may be used either as an adjective or adverb:

Mother is *well.* (*adjective*)   Ed swims *well.* (*adverb*)

► **Practice**

1. Write or read these sentences. Use *good* or *well,* whichever is correct.

    1. This is a __?__ photograph.
    2. Does he play tennis __?__?
    3. The cake was very __?__.
    4. Larry swims __?__ now.

2. Write two sentences, using *well* correctly. Use it as an adjective in one sentence and as an adverb in the other.

356

hear and here

The words *hear* and *here* sound alike but differ in meaning and spelling.

The word *hear* is a verb which means "to gather sounds."

The word *here* is an adverb which means "this place."

▶ **Practice**

Write sentences, using *hear* and *here* correctly.

himself and themselves

Think of the sounds which the italicized letters in these words should be given: hi*m*self and the*m*selves.

▶ **Practice**

Read these sentences aloud, saying *himself* and *themselves* correctly:

> Donald hurt himself.
> The girls are enjoying themselves.

in and into

Use **in** when you mean "within or inside." Use **into** when you mean "movement from the outside to the inside."

> The salt is *in* the cupboard.
> We drove *into* the parking lot.

▶ **Practice**

1. Write these sentences, using *in* or *into* correctly:

   1. The horses went (in, into) the barn.
   2. The cowboys drove the steers (in, into) the corral.
   3. Jim dashed (in, into) the room.
   4. Were the maps put (in, into) the drawer?

2. Write two sentences, using *in* and *into* correctly.

357

Irregular Verbs

Some verbs in our language do not form their past tense in the regular way, that is, by adding *d* or *ed* to the present tense. They are called **irregular verbs.**

In the list of verbs on the next page, you will find the three principal parts of irregular verbs you have studied this year and in previous years.

▶ **Practice**

1. Write each sentence, using the correct form of the verb in parentheses:

1. Have we (broke, broken) the window?
2. Don had (chose, chosen) the beagle.
3. Bette (drank, drunk) the lemonade.
4. Has the bell (rang, rung)?
5. The boys (sang, sung) a rousing chorus.
6. Where have the boys (went, gone)?
7. Last summer we (saw, seen) Niagara Falls.
8. The acrobats (did, done) the stunt again.
9. They have (rode, ridden) bicycles on the high wire.
10. We have (ate, eaten) here many times.
11. A helicopter has often (flew, flown) over our house.
12. Betsy has (went, gone) swimming.
13. Our dog likes to (lie, lay) on that rug.
14. He has (lay, lain) there all evening.
15. School had (began, begun) when I arrived.
16. Please (lay, lie) those knives down.

2. Write eight sentences, using the past and the past participle of each of these verbs: *freeze, ride, speak, know,* and *steal.*

3. Be prepared to read your sentences aloud to the class. Did the class find any errors?

358

IRREGULAR VERBS

PRESENT	PAST	PAST PARTICIPLE
begin	began	(has, have, had) begun
blow	blew	(has, have, had) blown
break	broke	(has, have, had) broken
bring	brought	(has, have, had) brought
choose	chose	(has, have, had) chosen
come	came	(has, have, had) come
do	did	(has, have, had) done
draw	drew	(has, have, had) drawn
drink	drank	(has, have, had) drunk
eat	ate	(has, have, had) eaten
fly	flew	(has, have, had) flown
freeze	froze	(has, have, had) frozen
give	gave	(has, have, had) given
go	went	(has, have, had) gone
grow	grew	(has, have, had) grown
know	knew	(has, have, had) known
lay	laid	(has, have, had) laid
leave	left	(has, have, had) left
let	let	(has, have, had) let
lie	lay	(has, have, had) lain
ride	rode	(has, have, had) ridden
ring	rang	(has, have, had) rung
run	ran	(has, have, had) run
say	said	(has, have, had) said
see	saw	(has, have, had) seen
set	set	(has, have, had) set
sing	sang	(has, have, had) sung
sit	sat	(has, have, had) sat
speak	spoke	(has, have, had) spoken
steal	stole	(has, have, had) stolen
take	took	(has, have, had) taken
teach	taught	(has, have, had) taught
throw	threw	(has, have, had) thrown
write	wrote	(has, have, had) written

is and are

Use **is, isn't, am not, was,** and **wasn't** with subjects that name only one.

Use **are, aren't, were,** and **weren't** with plural subjects.

▶ **Practice**

Write each sentence, using the correct verb:

1. (Is, Are) the poplar trees still there?
2. The coach and I (was, were) pleased with the score.
3. The postman and the milkman (was, were) late today.
4. (Isn't, Aren't) Tom and Amy here?

its and it's

Notice the differences between *its* and *it's*:

The ring had lost *its* luster.   (*a possessive pronoun*)
Yes, *it's* a beautiful moon.   (*a contraction for* it is)

▶ **Practice**

Write two sentences using *its* and *it's*.

lay and lie

Use a form of the verb **lay** when you mean "to put or place something."

Use a form of the verb **lie** when you mean "to rest or recline."

Refer to the table on page 359 to review the principal parts.

▶ **Practice**

Write these sentences, using the correct verbs:

1. A long road (lies, lays) ahead of us.
2. The swimmers (lay, laid) on the beach.
3. Have you (lain, laid) the extra blanket on the bed?
4. Walter had (lain, laid) in the hammock.

learn and teach

Use a form of the verb **learn** when you mean "to gain knowledge or skill." Use the verb **teach** when you mean "to give instruction."

This year Kevin *learned* to play the recorder.
His neighbor, Mr. Jones, *taught* him.

► **Practice**

Write four sentences, using these verbs correctly: *learned, taught, have learned,* and *has taught.*

leave and let

Use a form of the verb **leave** when you mean "to go away from" or "to go away." Use **let** to mean "allow."

The bus for St. Louis *left* a few minutes ago.
My brother *let* us borrow his camera.

► **Practice**

1. Write or read aloud these sentences, using a form of *let* or *leave,* whichever is correct:

1. __?__ us go this way.
2. Bill __?__ us look at his costume.
3. Has he __?__ George read his story?

2. Write two sentences. In one, use a form of the verb *let.* In the other, use a form of the verb *leave.*

Regular Verbs

Verbs that form their past tense by adding the ending *ed* or *d* are called **regular verbs.** Study these examples:

PRESENT	PAST	PAST PARTICIPLE
hear	heard	(has, have, had) heard
learn	learned	(has, have, had) learned

say or said

Use **say** or **says** when you speak of present time.
Use **said** when you speak of the past.

The sign ahead *says*, "Fresh Raspberries for Sale."
Yesterday, Mr. Roberts *said*, "Good work, Paul."

► **Practice**

Write four sentences, using these verbs correctly: *says, said, have said, say.*

set and sit

Use **set** when you mean "to place" or "to put in order."
Use a form of the verb **sit** when you mean "to rest."

► **Practice**

Write or read aloud each sentence, using the correct verb:

1. The hunter has (set, sat) a trap.
2. We (set, sat) on the lawn.
3. (Set, Sit) the boxes on the porch.
4. Have you (set, sat) in the new chair yet?

their, there, and they're

Study the different meanings of the italicized homonyms:

The twins have *their* new bicycles.   (*possessive pronoun*)
They live *there.*   (*adverb, telling where*)
Look, *they're* coming.   (*contraction for* they are)

► **Practice**

Write each sentence, using the correct expression:

1. In a moment (their, there, they're) leaving.
2. My friends are already (their, there, they're).
3. The birds have left (their, there, they're) nest.

there with Forms of is

In sentences that begin with **There is, There are, Once there was,** or **Once there were,** the subject and the verb are in inverted order. If the subject is singular, use **is** or **was;** if plural, use **are** or **were.**

► **Practice**

Write each sentence, using the correct verb:

1. Once there (was, were) two mules and a fox.
2. There (is, are) mice in the house.
3. Once there (was, were) deposits of iron ore here.
4. There (was, were) three meadowlarks on the fence.

this, that, these, those

The words *this* and *that* modify singular nouns:

this tie   *that* shirt

The words *these* and *those* may modify plural nouns:

these raspberries   *those* bushes

► **Practice**

Write four sentences, using the following adjectives correctly: *this, that, these, those.*

those and them

Them is an object pronoun. It may be used after an action verb or as an object of a preposition but not as an adjective to modify a noun. Use *those,* not *them,* to point out things or persons.

► **Practice**

Write the sentences below, using *those* or *them* correctly:

1. ___?___ pencils are mine.
2. I put the flowers in water after I had picked ___?___.

Unnecessary Words

Do not use an unnecessary pronoun after the noun subject of a sentence.

> *Correct:*   The girls wore masks.
> *Incorrect:*   The girls they wore masks.

▶ **Practice**

Read each sentence below. Notice that the meaning of each one is clear without the crossed-out word.

> Where is he staying ~~at~~?
> Jack dived off ~~of~~ the boat.

Write these sentences, using the correct expression:

1. (Tom, Tom he) is an excellent carpenter.
2. (The dog, The dog it) buried the bone.
3. The cat jumped (off, off of) the roof.
4. Do you know where John (is, is at)?

we or us with Nouns

Use the expressions **we boys** and **we girls** when they are subjects or when they follow a verb of being.

Use the expressions **us boys** and **us girls** when they follow a verb of action or a preposition.

▶ **Practice**

Write each sentence, using the correct pronoun:

1. Mr. Daniels and (we, us) boys are going.
2. The writers are (we, us) girls.
3. Dr. Andrews talked to (we, us) students.
4. Mother helped (we, us) children with our costumes.

MAKING SURE

Use these exercises after Chapter One.

I. Discussions

1. Review pages 12–13 and 16–17.

2. Read the following sentences. Then decide if they are *true* or *false*.

1. A summary at the end of a discussion is useful.
2. Facts are not necessary.
3. Guesses should not be expressed.
4. Questions may not be asked.

II. let and leave

1. Review the lesson on page 18.

2. Rewrite each sentence. Use *let* or *leave* to fill the blank.

1. _____ your purse in your desk.
2. You may _____ the secretary hold it.
3. Jean had to _____ school in the middle of a class.
4. Will the doctor _____ her come back on Monday?
5. Yes, because he _____ her get up today.
6. Perhaps she can _____ early if she feels ill again.
7. Should one of us _____ with her?

III. Good Usage

1. Review the lesson on page 19.

2. Rewrite these sentences, choosing the correct words from those in parentheses.

1. Lift the cat (off, off of) the desk.
2. I don't know where my pencil (is, is at).
3. Please take this caterpillar (off of, off) my arm.
4. You can brush it (off, off of) my sleeve with a leaf.
5. Where (at are, are) the birds?
6. I know where they (are, are at).
7. One just flew (off, off of) that branch.

Use these exercises after Chapter Two.

I. Sentences

1. Review pages 23–24.
2. Read these word groups. Then copy them. Add words to those groups of words which are not sentences to make them sentences. Punctuate all the sentences correctly.

1. My mule Sal
2. She can pull a canal-boat
3. One day, she pulled so hard that the boat went sailing on dry land
4. When she puts her mind to it
5. De Witt Clinton would have admired Sal
6. From the Erie Canal
7. Do you know the song about Sal
8. What a marvelous mule she is

II. Subject and Predicate

1. Review pages 25–26.
2. Copy each sentence below. Draw a vertical line between the complete subject and the complete predicate.

1. A moonwinder is a whittled wooden toy.
2. The mountain men of North Carolina make it.
3. It has a string on it.
4. The string "winds the moon."
5. Moonwinders cost very little.
6. They are quite easy to make.
7. Children enjoy them so much.
8. Many adults like them too.
9. Some people prefer flipper-dingers.
10. These are more difficult to use.
11. A little wooden ball has to hook onto a circle.

III. Finding Simple Subjects and Verbs

1. Review pages 29, 32, and 36.

2. Copy each sentence. Underline the simple subject with one line and the verb with two lines.

1. The scent of water refreshed me.
2. Across the water I saw berry trees.
3. Through the branches flew tiny birds.
4. The birds were brown with bright eyes.
5. Their gay chirping sounded cheerful.
6. The spray from the water soaked into the grass.
7. A few berries lay among the blades.
8. Who ate the fallen berries?

IV. Inverted Order

1. Review page 36.

2. Write a sentence using the phrase "down in the valley." Then rewrite your sentence, inverting the order of the subject and predicate.

V. Writing Sentences Correctly

1. Review pages 45–46.

2. Rewrite correctly the following sentences:

1. My coat needs to be cleaned, will you take it to the cleaner?
2. That's the one around the corner. With Dorkin's Dry-Cleaning on the front.
3. Sy Goldberg has been the owner. For ten years.

3. Write a complete sentence for each of the following fragments:

1. on the darkest night
2. by the light of the moon
3. with garlic and tomatoes

Use these exercises after Chapter Three.

I. Prefixes and Suffixes

1. Review pages 61–64.
2. Match the words below with the prefixes and suffixes to make new words. You should make at least eight words.

re	un	ness	ful
play	kind	cap	light	do

3. Copy these sentences. Add a prefix or suffix to the incomplete word to make the word you need.

1. Kitty was _____happy about the mistake.
2. Dan _____nounced the Spanish word correct_____.
3. Wally Wonderful was _____human.
4. Wild boars can be danger_____.
5. It would be frighten_____ to meet one.

II. Finding Entries in a Dictionary

1. Review pages 68–69.
2. Alphabetize:

1. hairy, handsome, hasten, haste, hank
2. sunder, Sunday, sundry, sundew, sundown
3. gorge, gorgon, gorgeous, gorget, gorgerin
4. trust, talk, tumble, teach, thimble

3. The guide words on a page are *fall-fanfare*. Write the words from the list below that you would find on the page.

fallacy	fallow	fail	fallfish
fanfaronade	family	fancy	falcon
fallible	fanner	fantastic	fame

370

4. Answer the following questions. Write *true* or *false*.

1. A primary accent shows more stress than a secondary accent.
2. Only one meaning is given for each word in the dictionary.
3. A word may be spelled more than one way.

III. Finding Word Meanings

1. Review page 73.

2. Read each of the following sentences. Then write the meaning of each word in italics. Do not use a dictionary.

1. Amy joined the *Feline* Friends' Club after she bought her fourth cat.
2. Marion's *culinary* ability was praised by everyone who tasted her good meals.
3. *Pedestrians* must be careful when they cross streets full of fast cars.
4. This *pugilist* was the heavyweight boxing champion for three years in a row.
5. John's *epidermis* felt hot and painful after a long day at the sunny beach.
6. The *belligerents* reached an agreement with the help of a United Nations advisor.

3. Match each word in column 1 with a word in column 2 that would help you to know its meaning.

1.	2.
a. braggadocio	h. name
b. miraculous	i. character
c. cyclical	j. brag
d. gelatin	k. miracle
e. characteristics	l. person
f. nomenclature	m. bicycle
g. personification	n. jelly

Use these exercises after Chapter Four.

I. Common and Proper Nouns

1. Review pages 86–87.

2. For each common noun below, give a proper noun.

1. street
2. lake
3. country
4. organization
5. building

3. For each proper noun below, give a common noun.

1. Korean War
2. Ohio
3. Congress
4. Italian
5. Beth B. Bird

4. Rewrite these sentences, beginning each proper noun with a capital letter:

1. joan is flying to paris.
2. She will visit the louvre museum.
3. Perhaps she will ride up the eiffel tower.
4. How fortunate that she speaks french as well as she does english!
5. Many americans stay at the ritz hotel.

5. Rewrite the following sentences. Be sure each common noun begins with a small letter and each proper noun with a capital one.

1. Dina wrote a Report about the american revolution for her history Class.
2. In the report She mentioned Betsy ross, mary McCauley, and Molly Stark.
3. she also wrote about important Battles.
4. The Battle of yorktown was one of Them.

II. Singular and Plural Nouns

1. Review pages 88–89.
2. Write the plurals for these nouns:

   1. country
   2. sheep
   3. watch
   4. handkerchief
   5. man
   6. pear
   7. tree
   8. tomato
   9. wife
   10. foot
   11. cow
   12. typewriter

3. Write singulars for these nouns:

   1. axes
   2. moose
   3. oxen
   4. children
   5. heroes
   6. fish

4. On your paper, write the answers which complete the following statements:

   1. Nouns that end in **s, sh,** soft **ch,** and **x** form their plurals by adding _____.
   2. A noun whose plural has an irregular ending is _____.
   3. If you do not know how to form the plural of a noun, use your _____.
   4. A noun with the same singular and plural forms is _____.
   5. Some nouns ending in **o** add _____ to form the plural.
   6. Nouns ending in **y** following a consonant change **y** to _____ and add _____ to form the plural.
   7. The dictionary shows only the singular form of a noun if the plural is formed by adding _____ or _____.
   8. Three nouns whose plurals end in **en** are _____.

III. How Nouns Show Possession

1. Review page 91.
2. Rewrite these sentences. Replace the nouns in parentheses with possessive nouns.

   1. (Peg) puppy is adorable.
   2. It played with the (cat) toy.
   3. The (Ladies) Auxiliary meets on Thursdays.
   4. That (men) store had a sale.
   5. The (children) party was a great success.
   6. Where is (Al) car parked?
   7. Our (nephews) model planes won prizes.

3. Rewrite the sentences below. Put in apostrophes and possessive endings where they are needed.

   1. Johns Pizza Parlor sells Sicilian pizzas.
   2. On Tuesdays, the Middlebury Men Bowling Association meets there.
   3. Harry Hotel is known for its indoor swimming pool and ice rink.
   4. The pools water is kept at seventy degrees.
   5. The caretaker job is interesting but difficult.

4. Write the singular and plural possessive of each of the nouns below.

   1. establishment
   2. plantain
   3. teacher
   4. ribbon
   5. dog
   6. mystery
   7. church

Use these exercises after Chapter Five.

I. Correct Verb Forms

1. Review page 103.

2. Rewrite the sentences below, using the correct form of the verb in parentheses.

1. Who (break) the window?
2. The kitten (drink) the milk greedily.
3. Your phone (ring) while you were out.
4. Last night, the judges (choose) Sonia as Queen of Beauty.
5. Two years ago he (sing) with the Dessoff Choirs.

3. Rewrite the sentences below, using the correct form of the verb in parentheses.

1. Elena has (choose) to go to Mexico.
2. Have you (ring) Mrs. Lum's bell?
3. Billy has (drink) three quarts of cranberry juice.
4. Has he (break) the cranberry juice drinking record?
5. Mrs. Machado has (sing) in several operas.

II. Writing a Bibliography

1. Review page 111.

2. Read the bibliography entry below. Then answer the questions which follow it.

Kalnay, Francis, *It Happened in Chichipica.*
New York: Harcourt Brace Jovanovich, Inc., 1971.

1. Who wrote the book?
2. Where was it published?
3. What other information could appear in the entry?

3. List the following books in alphabetical order by the authors' last names. Use the correct form for a bibliography.

1. golden cities, golden ships, by glen dines
2. the blind colt, by glen rounds
3. hans brinker, by mary dodge
4. the buffalo soldiers in the indian wars, by fairfax downey
5. yvette, by leon harris
6. secret of the emerald star, by phyllis whitney

III. Outlining

1. Review pages 114–15.
2. Use the following jumbled items to make an outline. Remember to supply the title and to list items correctly by indenting and using numerals and letters.

> trees, tomatoes, roses, corn
> plants, oak, vegetables, flowers
> maple, sunflowers

3. Write a short outline for one of the following topics. Use correct outline form.

> Caring for a Pet
> Cleaning a Car
> Why I Like My Sister (or Brother)
> How to Raise Corn
> Postage Stamps
> Making Model Cars

4. Write the following items in correct outline form.

pea soup	dessert
sandwich	lunch
turkey salad	tuna
soup	chicken soup
cookies	fruit

Use these exercises after Chapter Six.

I. Recognizing Verbs

1. Review pages 119–20.

2. Copy the following words. Then underline each one which is a verb.

door	eat
write	staircase
enjoy	frighten
three	choose

3. Copy the following phrases. Underline the main verb in each.

1. would never go
2. will run
3. can watch television
4. did know it

II. Verbs of Action or Being

1. Review pages 120–21.

2. Write these two headings on your paper: *Action Verbs* and *Verbs of Being.* Write the verb in each of the following sentences under the proper heading.

1. The air seemed unusually clear.
2. We saw the rising sun.
3. It glowed like a fresh orange.
4. Then it became a bright, pale yellow.
5. It was the color of a lemon drop.

3. Copy these sentences. Fill each blank with a verb of being.

1. The county fair _____ last week.
2. We _____ all there.
3. Everyone _____ to be having a good time.
4. Johnny _____ so excited he started hiccuping.
5. Excitement always _____ to affect him that way.
6. _____ you able to win a prize?

4. Write three sentences using action verbs. Write three sentences using verbs of being. Underline the verb in each sentence.

III. Verbs in Contractions

1. Review pages 126–27.
2. Find the verb in each of these sentences:

   1. Couldn't Sancha come to the movie?
   2. I've been here since nine o'clock.
   3. She'll never catch the first showing.
   4. That's too bad.
   5. Didn't she hear about the coming attractions?

3. Make contractions from these words:

you have	it is
should not	you are
they will	were not

IV. Principal Parts of Verbs

1. Review pages 129–30.
2. Copy these sentences. Use the form of the verb called for in parentheses.

   1. (start, *past*) The rain _____ early this morning.
   2. (expect, *past part.*) We _____ _____ it last night.
   3. (pour, *past part.*) It _____ _____ for three hours.
   4. (stop, *past*) In Tucson, it _____ soon.
   5. (predict, *past part.*) The announcer _____ _____ snow.
   6. (rake, *past*) Yesterday Emilio _____ the leaves.
   7. (want, *past part.*) He _____ _____ to make a bonfire.
   8. (burn, *past*) Last year's fire _____ out quickly.
   9. (turn, *past*) Who _____ off the light?
  10. (switch, *past part.*) They _____ _____ off the generator.

3. Write the principal parts of the following verbs:

1. jump
2. mail
3. carve
4. perform
5. tickle

V. Irregular Verbs

1. Review pages 130–31.

2. Write the past tense of these verbs:

1. steal	5. eat
2. ring	6. come
3. begin	7. write
4. fly	8. take

3. Rewrite each sentence. Use the past tense form of the verb in parentheses.

1. The wind (blow) till it knocked the chimney down.
2. It (leave) me breathless.
3. It (put) snowy frosting on the houses.
4. Then it (slide) away on ice skates.

4. Write the past participle of these verbs:

1. sing	5. blow
2. freeze	6. leave
3. draw	7. drink
4. catch	8. let

5. Rewrite each sentence. Use the past participle of each verb in parentheses.

1. Who (make) dinner?
2. The roast (fall) on the floor.
3. The cat and the dog (eat) part of it.
4. Mom and Dad (go) to a restaurant.

6. Write the correct form of the verb in parentheses.

1. (speak) Have you _____ to Mr. Gutierrez about that?
2. (go) Sheila _____ to Scotland.
3. (do) Have you _____ the whole assignment?
4. (lay) They have _____ the foundation for the new apartment house.
5. (lie) The reports have _____ on her desk for a week.
6. (leave) Mr. Benkovitz, you _____ your umbrella here.
7. (give) My parents _____ me a necklace for my birthday.
8. (shake) The wind has _____ the apples off the tree.

7. On your paper, complete these sentences:

1. The third principal part of a verb _____ needs a helping verb.
2. Verbs which do not add **d** or **ed** to form their past tense are called _____.
3. The second principal part of a verb _____ needs a helping verb.

8. Match each verb in column 1 with a verb from column 2 which has similar principal parts.

1.	**2.**
(a) fly	(d) bring
(b) ring	(e) break
(c) fight	(f) sing
(d) speak	(g) blow

9. On your paper, write each irregular verb from this list:

1. catch	3. hoe	5. buy	7. read
2. snatch	4. go	6. swim	8. twist

Use these exercises after Chapter Seven.

I. Expressing Yourself Well

1. Review page 148.
2. Tell what fault is shown in each paragraph:

   1. I went to the store. I bought some beans. I bought some rice. I looked for tomatoes too. I didn't see any.
   2. My cat is called Mouse and she is gray and white and has long whiskers too. She likes catnip and chocolate-covered mints and she also enjoys cheese.
   3. Mrs. Jamison makes sweet potato pie. Mrs. Jamison grows the potatoes herself. Mrs. Jamison has a large vegetable garden. Mrs. Jamison gardens every day.

3. Correct these groups of sentences to form good paragraphs.

   1. We are going to Lone Wolf Mountain and we are going to have a picnic there. Afterwards, Luisa and Ray will take us rowing and that will be fun.
   2. Greta comes from Delft in Holland and she has been in America for only six weeks and she speaks English quite well. She began to learn it in Holland. She has an accent yet. She will soon lose it.
   3. I have always wanted to go to Holland. I have heard so much about the tulips there. I love tulips. I like lilies too. I prefer tulips.
   4. Will you take me to the zoo? Show me the African Plains there and I would like to see the new building just for baby animals and their mothers. Let me ride a camel. Let me feed a seal too.
   5. Baby cats are called kittens. Baby foxes are called kits. Baby lynxes are called kittens.

II. Writing Correctly

1. Review pages 150–53.
2. Rewrite these paragraphs correctly:

   1. Norma knits beautifully. She buys all her patterns from the magazine woman's day. She was just looking at an article called swedish sweaters: knitting news.
   2. Trolls and elves are described in some detail by j. tolkien in his book the hobbit. The story tells of Bilbo Baggins' adventures in the east.
   3. The old guide book said, ride five miles north and three miles west. You'll be at the highest point in nevada, the best state in the west.
   4. William Shakespeare was an englishman who wrote many plays. Some of his plays are so famous that they appear in theaters from new england to new zealand.
   5. Many animals are in danger of extinction. One such animal is discussed in an article in the latest issue of natural history magazine. The article is entitled The search for the tasmanian tiger.
   6. Many people like the climate in the southwest. Uncle Howard, who had lived in the east for years, is now very happy in northern arizona.

III. Writing Paragraphs

1. Review pages 155–56.
2. Write a paragraph about one of these topics:

   The Street Where I Live   Monday
   My Favorite Color   Naming a Puppy

Use these exercises after Chapter Eight.

I. Singular and Plural Pronouns

1. Review pages 168–69.

2. List the pronouns used in the conversation below under the headings *Singular* and *Plural*. Beside each pronoun, write the noun or nouns for which it stands.

> Tina turned her head so she could look at the
> hen. "Have you laid any eggs for Juan and me?"
> she laughed. "Mama wants them for our
> breakfast. We are so hungry."
>
> Tina's brother Juan came out of their house.
> "Hurry, Tina," he called. "Papa wants to see you
> before he goes to work. His friends are waiting.
> Bring the eggs with you."

II. Possessive Pronouns

1. Review the lesson on pages 171–72.

2. Copy the sentences below. Underline each possessive pronoun.

    1. It's a lovely day for their picnic.
    2. Where is her woolly scarf?
    3. It's not in its usual place.
    4. He must have lent it to his little brother.
    5. Who has my car keys?
    6. Their car is over there beside yours.
    7. If it's not ours, it must be yours.

3. Write a different possessive pronoun for each blank:

    1. Is that _____?
    2. No, it's _____.
    3. Joe said it was _____.
    4. Well, it's certainly not _____.
    5. It's _____!

4. Read the following rhymes. Choose the correct possessive pronoun for each blank.

> Two dogs were fighting in the street.
> "This bone is mine and so is _____ meat!"
> "Leave it alone! You're out of line."
> "I saw it first. You know it's _____."
> A smart cat licked her paws and furs,
> Then grabbed the bone. Now it was _____.
> A butcher said to the dogs outdoors,
> "The bone is hers. It once was _____."
> A policeman said to the dogs, "Gee whiz,
> The butcher's sorry it isn't _____!"
> The dogs soon settled their affairs.
> They shared the next bone. It was _____.
> Then they barked for several hours,
> "Not mine! Not yours! The bone is _____."

III. Writing Pronouns Correctly

1. Review the lesson on pages 171–72.

2. Write a sentence for each of these words: *there's, theirs, their*. Which two words are possessive pronouns? Which one is a contraction?

3. Write a sentence using *its* correctly. Write a sentence using *it's* correctly.

IV. Pronoun Forms

1. Review the lessons on pages 174–75, 178–79, 180–81, and 183–84.

2. Rewrite these sentences. Choose the correct pronouns from the ones in parentheses.

1. May (we, us) go to the movies?
2. (She, Her) and Carol want to go Saturday.
3. The picture features (he, him) and Wayne Marvel.
4. Buy some popcorn for Jody and (I, me.)
5. Would you buy some for (we, us) too?

Use these exercises after Chapter Nine.

I. Writing a Friendly Letter

1. Review pages 191–93.
2. Tell whether the following sentences are *true* or *false.*

1. A friendly letter should be all about you and not say anything about your friend.
2. You should use the same language in a friendly letter that you use most of the time.
3. You should write general statements and leave out interesting details.

3. Write the following parts of a friendly letter correctly:

1. 339 hermosa street
   waco texas
   december 4 19_____
2. albany, new york
   may 15, 19_____
   425 shaker road
3. your friend
   nancy

II. Using sit and set

1. Review the lesson on page 198.
2. What is the past tense form of *sit?* of *set?* Write one sentence for *sat* and *set.*
3. Choose the correct verb from the parentheses to complete the sentences below.

1. He had (sat, set) in the dentist's chair for an hour.
2. If I have to (sit, set) here much longer, I'll scream.
3. Doctor, you (sat, set) my appointment for six o'clock.
4. If you'll (sit, set) still for ten minutes, I'll be finished.

III. Interjections

1. Review page 200.
2. Complete the following sentences, using interjections and correct punctuation.

    1. _____ A giant octopus has grabbed my leg.
    2. _____ perhaps I can help you later.
    3. _____ that would be nice.
    4. _____ It's going to bite me.

IV. Using **teach** and **learn**

1. Review page 205.
2. Rewrite these sentences, using forms of *teach* and *learn*.

    1. Who _____ you to crochet?
    2. I _____ it from my mother.
    3. Would you _____ me how to do it?
    4. Yes, you'll _____ it quickly.

V. Business Letters

1. Review pages 206–08.
2. Write the heading, inside address, greeting, closing, and signature of a letter to:

> Spanish National Tourist Office, 180 N. Michigan Avenue, Chicago, Illinois, 60601

3. Look through a magazine or mail-order catalogue and order something you want from the company that makes it.
4. List these letter parts in order on your paper.

signature	body
greeting	closing
heading	inside address

Use these exercises after Chapter Ten.

I. Adjectives

1. Review pages 212–14 and 216.
2. Write two adjectives to describe each of these:

   1. The color of a streak of lightning.
   2. The sound of a baby's cry.
   3. The way your hair feels.

3. Rewrite the following paragraph. Choose adjectives to fit the blanks.

> An octopus lived in a _____, _____ cave. This octopus was very _____ and _____. He was so _____ that he could eat _____ fish at a time. He ate _____ fish. His favorite meal was _____ fish with _____ clams.

II. Making Comparisons with Adjectives

1. Review the lesson on pages 219–21.
2. Rewrite these sentences. Use the comparative or superlative form of the adjective in parentheses.

   1. Her mother cooks (well) than she does.
   2. They're (greasy) than any of the others.
   3. Is this the most (effective) way to do it?
   4. No, but it's probably the (easy).
   5. She is the more (intelligent) of the sisters.

III. Proper Adjectives

1. Review page 226.
2. Write four sentences of your own using proper adjectives correctly.
3. Change each of these proper nouns in parentheses into proper adjectives. Write the completed phrases.

   1. (Venezuela) bolivars   3. (Alaska) oil
   2. (Jamaica) fishermen   4. (China) pandas

IV. The Adverb

1. Review the lessons on pages 227–29.
2. Read these sentences. Then write all the adverbs from them on your paper.

1. The gray cat ran quickly.
2. Suddenly she saw a little ball.
3. Soon she had snatched it.
4. Then she batted it and bounced it.
5. She had never had a red ball.
6. She pushed the ball up and down and around.
7. Sometimes it would slip from her.
8. She would soon recover it.

V. Making Comparisons with Adverbs

1. Review pages 232–33.
2. Rewrite these sentences. Choose an adverb for each blank.

1. Charlie has always played _____ than I.
2. Harry plays more _____ than he.
3. Of the three boys, Mike plays most _____.

VI. Using Words Correctly

1. Review the lessons on pages 222, 224, and 234.
2. Copy these sentences. Choose a word from those in parentheses to make each sentence correct.

1. How (good, well) do you know him?
2. He works in one of (them, those) factories.
3. Doesn't he know (anything, nothing) about cars?
4. He's not familiar with (any, none) of the latest models.

388

Use these exercises after Chapter Eleven.

I. Improving Your Word Choice

1. Review the lesson on pages 248–49.

2. Match each adjective in column 1 with its synonym from column 2. Then use each word from column 2 in a sentence.

1.	2.
a. nice	e. careworn
b. unhappy	f. sluggish
c. fast	g. friendly
d. slow	h. swift

3. Match each verb in column 1 with its synonym from column 2. Then use each word from column 2 in a sentence.

1.	2.
a. cry	e. modernize
b. joke	f. blubber
c. renew	g. liberate
d. free	h. jest

II. Using the Correct Expression

1. Review the lesson on page 251.

2. Read the sentences below. Rewrite any which are incorrect.

1. Miriam should have come by now.
2. Could she of missed the bus?
3. I think she would've called in that case.
4. Wouldent she have gotten a lift from Mr. Akers?
5. She couldn't of taken the wrong bus.
6. Shouldn't Jack of offered to bring her?

III. Writing Conversation

1. Review the lesson on page 253.
2. Rewrite this conversation correctly.

This horse said the tall cowboy must be the fastest animal in the world   Do you really think so asked the dude or are you just fooling   This horse is so fast retorted the cowboy that he makes a hurricane seem slow

IV. Using the Comma

1. Review the lesson on page 254.
2. Rewrite these sentences. Use commas correctly.

1. "See here young man that's my coat you have."
2. "I'm sorry sir. I didn't realize it."
3. "Well we all make mistakes."

V. Using <u>say</u>, <u>says</u>, and <u>said</u>

1. Review the lesson on page 256.
2. Rewrite these sentences. Fill each blank with the correct form of the verb.

1. Last night June _____ she was going to Rita's.
2. Did she _____ what time she'd be home?
3. This note _____ she'll be back at midnight.

VI. Writing Stories

1. Review the lesson on page 257.
2. On your paper, write the word or words that make each sentence below correct.

1. When one incident leads to another, they form _____.
2. After the _____, there is nothing left.
3. The _____ of the story is usually the most interesting part.
4. An unexpected problem can be the _____ of the story.

Use these exercises after Chapter Twelve.

I. Recognizing Prepositions

1. Review the lesson on pages 266–67.
2. On your paper, write all the prepositions from the following sentences.
    1. Run around the reservoir three times.
    2. During the concert, the audience was absolutely silent.
    3. Go over Pine Hill, through Bridal Vale, across the brook, and up the dale.
    4. Do it with a pen in your best handwriting.

II. Prepositional Phrases

1. Review the lesson on pages 268–69.
2. Read these sentences. Copy each prepositional phrase. Write the word it modifies next to it.

    1. This card has been left inside the book.
    2. Was the book on the counter?
    3. No, it lay in the bin.
    4. That bin beside the door is always full.

III. Using Words Correctly

1. Review the lesson on page 272.
2. Rewrite the following sentences. Choose the correct preposition from the ones in parentheses.

    1. Is Pablo (at, to) home now?
    2. No, he's (in, into) school.
    3. He's coming to our clubhouse (among, between) the two oaks.
    4. Don't get (in, into) trouble by staying too late.
    5. We'll just go up (at, to) the old barn and back.
    6. Here are some cookies to share (among, between) all of you.

IV. Conjunctions, Words in a Series

1. Review pages 275–80.
2. Combine each set of sentences. Use conjunctions and commas where they are needed.

1. Brian went to the stadium. Dick went to the stadium.
2. You may visit Aunt Louise. You may not stay till Monday.
3. Amati was a violinmaker. Stradivarius was a violinmaker. Guarneri was a violinmaker.
4. Irene may eat spinach and have dessert. Irene may leave her spinach and go without dessert.

V. Writing Sentences Correctly

1. Review the lesson on page 277.
2. Write these sentences correctly.

1. Jaime plays the guitar and his brother plays the drums.
2. Cats are smart but pigs are said to be smarter.
3. Was the number 85709 or was it 85907?
4. My friend likes *Captains Courageous* but I prefer *Kim.*

VI. Subject and Verb Agreement

1. Review pages 282–83.
2. Rewrite each sentence below. Choose the correct form of the verb from those in parentheses.

1. (Haven't, Hasn't) they gone to Hawaii?
2. Yes, they (was, were) going to see their son.
3. I'm sure he (are, is) awaiting them eagerly.
4. Peg and George always (takes, take) so many pictures.
5. (Is, Are) Nikon or Kodak the camera they use?

Use these exercises after Chapter Thirteen.

I. Stories of the Past and Present

1. Review pages 296, 299, and 306.

2. Number your paper from 1–5. For each question below, write the word that best completes the sentence.

1. An _____ is part of a legend.
2. A fable is often based upon one _____.
3. Do you prefer factual books or works of_____?

II. is and are

1. Review the lesson on page 295.

2. Copy the following sentences. Fill each blank with *is* or *are*.

1. That truck _____ making a lot of noise.
2. _____ there a policeman nearby?
3. There _____ ordinances against making loud noises.
4. Who _____ the driver of the truck?
5. _____ you the owners of the truck?
6. Yes, but who _____ you?

III. Writing Book Opinions

1. Review page 307.

2. Read the following book opinion. Write down what information was left out.

A Brave Rescue

The Rescuers is a very exciting story. It tells about three mice who help a poor young poet escape from a guarded castle.

I liked the story because the mice have such different backgrounds and characters. Each one makes a different contribution to the rescue.

Use these exercises after Chapter Fourteen.

I. Discovering the Meaning and Mood of a Poem

1. Review pages 310–19.

2. Sometimes you can guess what the mood of a poem will be by reading the title. Read the titles below. On your paper, write *humorous* or *serious* for each poem title.

1. "The Mock Turtle's Song," by Lewis Carroll
2. "Hymn to the Night," by Henry Wadsworth Longfellow

II. Music in Poetry

1. Review pages 326–28.

2. Match each word from column 1 with a rhyming word from column 2.

1.	2.
a. grieve	i. try
b. go	j. ate
c. high	k. through
d. cast	l. know
e. weight	m. reign
f. new	n. leave
g. might	o. kite
h. train	p. past

3. Which phrases below have a musical effect because of their repetition of consonant sounds?

1. soft and silky
2. soft and warm
3. laugh and joke
4. hail and bait
5. wet and wild
6. the light of love
7. at dawn and dusk

INDEX

INDEX

Numerals in heavy black type indicate the teaching pages.

stole, stolen, **130**, 131, 141, 143, 182, 338, **359**

this, that, these, those, **224**, 225, 363

"this here," "that there," **224**–25, 247, 274, **363**

those, them, **224**–25, 238, 240, 247, 274, **363**

threw, thrown, 35, 135, 139, 141, **356, 359**

took, taken, 35, 135, 139, **356, 359**

we, us, **185**, 188, 189, 196, 273, **364**

went, gone, 139, 141, **358, 359**

wrote, written, 80, 131, 135, 139, **354, 359**

See also Pronouns, as objects after action verbs, as objects of prepositions, possessives, *and* as subjects

Verbs:
of action, **90**, **120–21**, **122**, 138, 140, 152, 176, **230, 235, 271, 284, 340–41**

agreement of subjects and, **129**, **282**–83, 287, 289, 295, 308, 309, **363**

of being, **120–21**, **122**, 138, 140, 152, 176, 177, 186, **230, 235, 271, 284, 340–41**

choice of, 134, 135

correct forms of. *See* Usage, correct

defined, **119**

finding or naming, 32, **36**–37, **38**–39, 42, 50, 52, **90**, 120, 121, 123, 124, 126, 127, 134, 135, 138, 140, 152, 173, 176, 279, **336, 341**

helping, **123, 124, 125, 128, 129, 130–31**, 132, 135, 139, 141, 176, **177, 341, 358, 359**

irregular, **130–31**, 139, 141, **358**–59

with *not,* 123

objects of, **180**, 181

principal parts of, **129**, 130, 131, 132, 139, 141, **358, 359**

in questions, **38**–39

tenses of, **128–29, 130, 131, 341**

Vocabulary enrichment. *See* Description; Dictionary; How Our Language Grew; Poetry; Words

Voice. *See* Speech

Words:
building, **62**

choice of, **248**, 262, 264

dividing, **72–73**

keeping a list of new, **60**

meanings of, discovering, **73–75**, 77, 78, 243

origins of. *See* How Our Language Grew

overworked, **248**, 262, 264

parts of, **61**, 62, **63–64**

in a series, **280**, 287, 289

unnecessary, **19**, 21, 274

vivid and specific, **212–13**, 214, **216**, 229, 231, **241**, 242, 243–45, 246, 248, 249–50, 255, 262, 264

Writing, creative. *See* Composition; Description; Letters; Paragraph; Poetry; Sentences; Stories

Writing systems, facts about, 10

ZIP Code, 195, **206, 207**